AFTER THE CANAL DUKE

JAMES LOCH

AFTER
THE CANAL DUKE

A Study of the Industrial Estates
administered by the
Trustees of the Third Duke of Bridgewater
in the Age of Railway Building
1825–1872

BY

F. C. MATHER

OXFORD
AT THE CLARENDON PRESS
1970

Oxford University Press, Ely House, London W. 1

GLASGOW NEW YORK TORONTO MELBOURNE WELLINGTON
CAPE TOWN SALISBURY IBADAN NAIROBI DAR ES SALAAM LUSAKA ADDIS ABABA
BOMBAY CALCUTTA MADRAS KARACHI LAHORE DACCA
KUALA LUMPUR SINGAPORE HONG KONG TOKYO

PRINTED IN GREAT BRITAIN
AT THE UNIVERSITY PRESS, OXFORD
BY VIVIAN RIDLER
PRINTER TO THE UNIVERSITY

TO MY WIFE

PREFACE

To study the history of England during the nineteenth century is to become aware that a large element of continuity accompanied the great economic, social, and constitutional changes of the period. As Dr. Kitson Clark has observed: 'Survivals are in fact to be found round every Victorian corner.' Old institutions, manners, and techniques lingered when the conditions which created them declined, and were often adapted to accord with progress rather than displaced by it. This is a book about adaptation. It is concerned to show firstly how an economic unit in which industrial ownership appeared as a function of landholding, as it sometimes did during the eighteenth century, managed to survive into the later years of the nineteenth, when the finance and management of industry had become more specific and highly developed; secondly how the principal asset of the concern, a transport undertaking characteristic of an early and relatively immature industrial system, succeeded in holding its own in an age when the technology of transport was much more advanced. The two themes are interwoven in the story of the Duke of Bridgewater's Trustees.

My thanks are due especially to His Grace the Duke of Sutherland for placing at my disposal over a lengthy period a vast quantity of manuscript material from his family archives, on which this study is principally based. I am also in the debt of Mr. A. Hayman, manager of the Bridgewater Department of the Manchester Ship Canal Company, for permission to consult the records deposited in his office, and of his staff for their kind hospitality during my researches there in the winter of 1960–1. There, in the cordiality with which I was received, I sensed the authentic spirit of 'The Duke's', surviving in a branch of the great company which had long ago absorbed the handiwork of the renowned eighteenth-century Duke of Bridgewater and conscious still of the glories of its past. The following have rendered to me valuable assistance in locating source material—Dr. W. H. Chaloner, Reader in Modern Economic History in the University of Manchester,

Mr. P. I. King and Mr. F. Stitt, Chief Archivists of Northamptonshire and Staffordshire respectively, Dr. W. C. R. Hicks, Mr. John Bryon, formerly librarian of the Eccles Borough Library, and the staffs of the Lancashire, Cheshire, and Hertfordshire Record Offices, of the British Transport Historical Records at Royal Oak, of the Manchester City Reference Library, and of the House of Lords Record Office. Mr. F. Mullineux allowed me to draw freely upon his immense knowledge of the history of mining in the Worsley district. Others who have answered questions and supplied information are Her Grace the Duchess of Sutherland, Professor A. Aspinall, Mr. D. J. Hodgkins, Mr. C. H. Shaw (librarian of Harrow School), Mr. T. S. Wragg (librarian to the Duke of Devonshire), and Mr. R. P. Fereday. To Dr. Chaloner and the late Professor Redford I owe the earliest direction of my studies in this field. To Professor T. S. Willan I am also indebted for advice. Mr. Charles Hadfield read the manuscript and made many valuable suggestions.

My wife has helped me more than I can say, not only by undertaking the laborious task of typing the manuscript and preparing the maps and index, but also by her constant encouragement and by useful criticism based upon her knowledge of the history of ports and shipping during the nineteenth century.

I am indebted to the University of Manchester for an Advanced Graduate Research Scholarship in Arts, which enabled me to begin work on this project, and to the University of Southampton for two sabbatical terms, during which I was able to give it my undivided attention. Professor J. S. Bromley, Emeritus Professor Harry Rothwell, and other colleagues and students of the History Department of Southampton University have contributed indirectly to the making of this book by their interest and by the stimulus which their fellowship has provided during many years. Them also I must thank, whilst reserving to myself the responsibility for the imperfections which the work retains.

F. C. MATHER

CONTENTS

MAPS AND ILLUSTRATIONS   *page* xi

ABBREVIATIONS   xiii

INTRODUCTION   xv

I.   Before the Storm   1

II. The Break-through of the Railways   27

III. The Rival Springs to Life   44

IV. New Foes to Face   63

V.   The Struggle for Mastery   83

VI. New Brooms Sweep Clean   98

VII. The Years of Equipoise (1837–1844). I   121

VIII. The Years of Equipoise (1837–1844). II   152

IX. The Bridgewater Trustees and the Railway
     Mania (1845–1847)   176

X.   The Heat of Battle (1849–1851)   195

XI. The Quest of a New Ally (1851–1855)   226

XII. Reform and Reappraisal   257

XIII. The Age of Improvement (1857–1872)   279

XIV. Progress and Paternalism in the Worsley
     Mines   305

XV. The End of an Era   334

XVI. Retrospect   343

APPENDIXES

A. *Income of the Bridgewater Trust, 1806–1871*   *page* 357

B. *Quantity of Traffic Conveyed on the Bridgewater Canal, 1803–c. 1885*   362

C. *Coal Production: Bridgewater Collieries*   364

D. *Officers of the Bridgewater Trust*   366

BIBLIOGRAPHY   367

INDEX   375

CORRIGENDA

Page 30, line 3 from bottom. *For* both the *read* both of

Page 54, line 6 from bottom. *For* canal and river, *read* canal and river, and

Page 117, line 1. *For* to reduce, notably his debts, the mortgage *read* to reduce his debts, notably the mortgage

Page 165, line 1. *For* Old Quays, were *read* Old Quay were

MAPS AND ILLUSTRATIONS

James Loch *Frontispiece*
(*By courtesy of the National Portrait Gallery, London*)

Section of the Liverpool Docks, *c.* 1860 *page* 18

Runcorn, *c.* 1860 19

Worsley New Hall, built 1840–6 to the design of
Edward Blore, with the Duke of Bridgewater's
Canal *facing page* 118
(*By courtesy of the Radio Times Hulton Picture Library*)

Principal Rail and Canal Connections in Manchester
c. 1850 *page* 143

Canal Connections of the Great Western and Shrewsbury Railways in the Midlands and North,
December 1850 230

The Duke's Canal at Runcorn, showing Bridgewater
House and the entrance to the docks and to the
Runcorn and Weston Canal, 1955 *facing page* 282
(*By courtesy of the Radio Times Hulton Picture Library*)

Collieries and Canal and Rail Connections in the
Worsley District, *c.* 1870 *page* 313

Railways and Canals of the Manchester and Liverpool
District to *c.* 1870 *at end*

ABBREVIATIONS

A.H.C.	Ashridge House Collection
B.P.P.	Bound Parliamentary Papers
B.T.H.R	British Transport Historical Records
B.T.P. (Mertoun)	Bridgewater Trust Papers at Mertoun
C.R.O.	County Record Office
E. & C.C.C.	Ellesmere and Chester Canal Company
E.B.C.	Ellesmere Brackley Collection
E.L.R.	East Lancashire Railway
G.J.R.	Grand Junction Railway
G.W.R.	Great Western Railway
J.H.C.	*Journal of the House of Commons*
J.H.L.	*Journal of the House of Lords*
L. & M.R.	Liverpool and Manchester Railway
L. & N.W.R.	London and North Western Railway
L. & Y.R.	Lancashire and Yorkshire Railway
L.E.P.	Loch–Egerton Papers
M. & B.R.	Manchester and Birmingham Railway
M. & I.N.C.	Mersey and Irwell Navigation Company
M. & L.R.	Manchester and Leeds Railway
M.B. & B.C.	Manchester, Bolton, and Bury Canal
M.S. & L.R.	Manchester, Sheffield, and Lincolnshire Railway
M.S.C.C.	Manchester Ship Canal Company
M.S.J. & A.R.	Manchester, South Junction, and Altrincham Railway
N.S.	New Series
N.S.R.	North Staffordshire Railway
Old Quay	Mersey and Irwell Navigation
O.W. & W.R.	Oxford, Worcester, and Wolverhampton Railway
S.A. & M.R.	Sheffield, Ashton-under-Lyne, and Manchester Railway
S.E.P.	Sutherland Estate Papers, Chief Agents' Correspondence
W. & S.R.	Warrington and Stockport Railway

INTRODUCTION

In the early and middle years of the nineteenth century Great Britain was unquestionably the foremost industrial power; she was also a land in which an aristocracy rooted in the soil retained and even added to its wealth, and together with the gentry largely controlled the machinery of government. Many reasons underlay this paradox. One, of noteworthy importance, was that a number of great proprietors had come to terms with industrial progress by participating in it. They were encouraged to do so both by the law governing the inheritance of land, which compelled younger sons to seek a livelihood outside the family estates, and by the resources of coal, copper, lime, and building stone which abounded on many of their properties. Ever since the sixteenth century, if not earlier, landlords had been exploiting the mineral deposits under their estates. Such activity had led them in due course into constructing docks and canals to connect their supplies with a market, and this in its turn into promoting waterways for general commercial purposes. During the eighteenth century the Duke of Rutland had a smelting house at Rowsley, the Marquess of Rockingham showed a personal interest in the operation of collieries and of kilns for lime, brick, and tiles, whilst the Earl of Egremont was a chief mover in promoting the Arun Navigation, the Wey and Arun Junction, and the Portsmouth and Arundel Canals.[1] For the English nobleman of that period, moreover, participation in industry was more than an exercise in profit-making. It could be also a social duty, in that the early canal ventures of the years 1755–75, less certain of success than those of a later date, sometimes needed the support of a local magnate to encourage others to invest in them, to enable them to raise loans, and generally to protect their interests.

This book is concerned with a great industrial estate which was created in these conditions. Its founder was Francis

[1] G. E. Mingay, *English Landed Society in the Eighteenth Century*, pp. 194–5, 199.

Egerton, third Duke of Bridgewater (1736–1803), the most
notable English aristocrat to link his fortunes with the industrial revolution. The story of how it was built up has been
often told, and can be read in its most up-to-date and re-
liable form in Frank Mullineux's *The Duke of Bridgewater's
Canal* (Eccles and District History Society, 1959), in V. I.
Tomlinson's 'Salford Activities Connected with the Bridgewater Canal' (*Transactions of the Lancashire and Cheshire
Antiquarian Society*, lxvi (1956)), in parts of W. H. Chaloner's
'Charles Roe of Macclesfield, 1715–81' (ibid. lxii (1950–1)), and
in Hugh Malet's *The Canal Duke*. Here it may be briefly
summarized. The young Duke of Bridgewater, on assuming
the control of his estates from his guardian in 1757, sought to
exploit the resources of coal under his Lancashire properties
in response to the mid eighteenth-century 'fuel famine'.
Owing to the parlous state of the roads in that neighbourhood, the first priority was to create an effective communication by water between Worsley and the nearby towns of
Manchester and Salford. Already a group of Manchester
merchants had taken the initiative by promoting an Act of
Parliament in 1737 to render Worsley Brook navigable down
to the River Irwell. The Act, however, was not implemented,
and it was left to the Duke to realise these aspirations with the
aid of borrowed capital and of his two skilful engineers, John
Gilbert and James Brindley.

His plans were unfolded in three main stages. The first was
for the much needed coal canal from Worsley. Originally
intending to go direct to Salford by a line which avoided
entanglement with the River Irwell, he changed his mind
whilst the work was in progress and adopted a more circuitous
route to Manchester by way of Longford Bridge near Stretford. This stretch was completed between 1759 and *c.* 1765.
A possible reason for the change of plan was that the Duke
did not intend to rest content with being a mere carrier of
coals, but already aspired to compete with the Mersey and
Irwell Navigation Company for the traffic in goods between
Manchester and Liverpool. With this object more immediately
in view, he then threw out a longer arm of canal from
Stretford across the northern portion of the Cheshire plain
to Runcorn on the upper Mersey estuary. Cleverly he

manœuvred the Trent and Mersey Canal promoters into allowing him to cut the last six miles of their line to the Mersey and to adopt that section as his own route from Preston Brook to Runcorn. This gave him command of a vast industrial traffic to and from the Midlands, which might otherwise have been appropriated by the Weaver Trustees, had the latter forestalled him in effecting a junction with the Trent and Mersey. The Cheshire branch was authorized in 1762 and finished as far as Runcorn in 1776. All that remained of the Duke of Bridgewater's canal-building activities was to make an extension at the Worsley end as far as Leigh, with a view to linking Manchester with the Leeds and Liverpool Canal, a waterway which, when it was completed, would give access to vast new industrial areas round Bradford, Blackburn, and Wigan as well as to the Lancaster Canal. The Duke cut his Leigh branch in the years 1797–1800,[1] but did not live to see the junction made with the Leeds and Liverpool. Not until 1821 did the proprietors of the latter complete the cut of six miles' length which was to link their own main line at Wigan with the Bridgewater Canal at Leigh.

The making of the Canal involved the Duke in a number of ancillary enterprises of a commercial character. Some were engineering wonders, like the system of underground canals at Worsley which carried the boats almost to the coal face, or the canal basin at Castlefield in Manchester, where the expeditious unloading of coal barges, by means of a crane worked by a water wheel, impressed Arthur Young in 1768–9.[2] Francis also had his own small dock at Liverpool with adjacent quays and timber yard, and a dock at Runcorn, opened in 1791, to bring sea-going traffic on to the Canal. In the mortar for docks magnesium lime was a valuable ingredient, and the Duke's agents developed lime-burning on a considerable scale at Worsley. The local Sutton stone quarried on Chat Moss was used for the purpose, as were also, by the early nineteenth

---

[1] Payments on Account of the Leigh Canal, 1795–1801, E.B.C., Northamptonshire, C.R.O. The payments for the work of construction began in 1797 and ended in 1800.

[2] A. Young, *A Six Months' Tour through the North of England* (1st edn., 1770), cited in H. Clegg, 'The Third Duke of Bridgewater's Canal Works in Manchester', *Transactions of the Lancashire and Cheshire Antiquarian Society*, lxv (1955).

century, large quantities of Peak Forest limestone which were brought up by canal.[1] At Worsley, also, the Duke established a boat-building and works yard alongside the Canal, thus becoming the employer of a host of boat-builders, sailmakers, riggers, carpenters, and blacksmiths. He entered extensively into the business of carrying by water, which was in those days normally separate from that of navigation owner. His own craft were almost exclusively carriers for the public between Liverpool and Manchester, using the Duke's Canal and the river estuary. They even conveyed coal and a small quantity of other merchandise along neighbouring waterways.

On the Duke of Bridgewater's death in March 1803 the industrial properties, together with the estates in Lancashire and Brackley in Northamptonshire, were separated from the other ducal domains in Shropshire and Hertfordshire and placed in trust for the benefit of the Duke's nephew, George Granville Leveson-Gower, Marquess of Stafford, later to be first Duke of Sutherland, a wealthy nobleman with lands in Shropshire, Staffordshire, and the Sutherlandshire Highlands. By the terms of the will, a formidable document running in the printed version to sixty-six pages, the income was to be paid to Lord Stafford during his lifetime, and was then to go to the Marquess's second son, Francis, on condition that he adopted the name and style of Egerton, and in due course to the latter's own heirs and successors. Control, however, was vested in a body of three Trustees, of whom one was to be Superintendent with almost despotic powers of management. This arrangement was to last for the lives of all the peers of the United Kingdom, and of certain relatives of the Duke of Bridgewater alive at the time of his death, and for a further twenty years. In this way the Trustees of the third Duke of Bridgewater were launched as a business house. With a continually changing personnel, they traded in this corporate name for exactly a hundred years, though colloquially they were better known as 'the Duke's', as if the deceased Duke of Bridgewater still

---

[1] In 1806 the Bridgewater Trustees burnt 147,384 measures of lime; 3,100 measures of this were from Sutton stone burnt at Worsley. The remainder was from Peak Forest stone burnt at Worsley and Castle Quay. Bridgewater Trust, General Accounts, 1790–1810, Lancs. C.R.O.

directed personally the properties which his genius had called into being.

The century after 1803 was one of rapid economic growth and revolutionary technical and economic change. The internal transport sector, in particular, was radically transformed by the coming of the railways, which challenged established navigational interests such as those of the Bridgewater Trust. It is said that the Duke sensed the danger afar off, remarking to a nobleman who congratulated him upon the success of his Canal: 'Yes, we shall do well enough if we can steer clear of those demmed tramroads.' In the following pages the first full-length account is given of how his appointed successors confronted the threat when it emerged. This is more than an episode in the history of canals, for it shows how the proprietors of one of Britain's most important waterways, with greater resourcefulness than has hitherto been attributed to canal owners, sought to turn docks and steamboats and even the railways themselves to their own account in a not altogether ineffective struggle to survive. Professor Jack Simmons rightly argues that 'the history of railways ought properly to be read as part of the history of transport as a whole'.[1] The same is emphatically true of canals. Even transport history as a whole is a limit insufficiently wide, for the role of the Duke of Bridgewater's Canal in the struggle between waterways and railways cannot be wholly understood, unless account is taken of the fact that the men who controlled its destinies also had a stake in coal-mining, and possessed the closest connections with a landed aristocracy which was itself under challenge for social and political, as well as economic, reasons.

Though the horizons to be kept in view must be broad, the study is itself undertaken in depth. It is based upon a large quantity of unpublished manuscript material, chiefly letters. These, because they were mostly written between business intimates and not for propagandist or diplomatic reasons, afford an unusually frank insight into the motives behind decision-making within the firm. The chronological limits have been set at 1825–72, mainly because it was in those years, more than any others, that the Duke's Trustees grappled with the effects of the nineteenth-century revolution in internal

[1] *The Railways of Britain*, p. 233.

transport. A further reason is that it would be impossible to write the history of the industrial possessions bequeathed by the third Duke of Bridgewater as a single story after 1872, when the canals were sold to a limited company, and only the collieries and the landed estates remained in trust. In the first chapter, however, a brief attempt is made to bridge the gap between the well-known events of the Canal Duke's lifetime and the beginning of the railway era. Events after 1872 have also been briefly touched upon towards the end, where some treatment of them was considered necessary to round off the theme.

CHAPTER I

Before the Storm

BY the standards of early nineteenth-century England the Bridgewater Trust was, in every respect, a great concern. When Lord Francis Egerton gained control of it in 1837, he boasted of the influence which it gave him 'over the immediate destinies of between three and four thousand people, not to mention mules and horses'.[1] It is not clear from the context whether he was referring to all the employees or merely to those in the immediate neighbourhood of Worsley, or whether he included the wives and families of workpeople in the calculation. Other evidence shows, however, that the collieries alone found employment for just over 1,200—men, women, and boys[2]—and Worsley Yard for more than 200.[3] When allowance is made for the crews of the 73 rigged flats, 13 narrow or fly boats, 76 lighters and packet boats, 187 M boats and 33 T boats then owned by the carrying department,[4] as well as for dock workers, lime burners, farm labourers, office clerks, and others, it seems improbable that the working force directly employed by the Trustees fell far short of 3,000. Few businesses in the 1830s could command the services of so many. There were ironworks in South Wales with 5,000 workers, but these were exceptional. The average cotton mill in Manchester had only 400 early in the decade.[5] Even by themselves, the Bridgewater collieries must have been amongst

[1] *Personal Reminiscences of the Duke of Wellington by Francis, the First Earl of Ellesmere, edited with a Memoir of Lord Ellesmere by his Daughter Alice,* p. 47.

[2] A statement for Sept. 1842 gives 610 men, 133 girls, and 476 boys. F. Smith to J. Loch, 21 Sept. 1842, L.E.P.

[3] There is a list of 207 in F. Smith to J. Loch, 1 Nov. 1837, ibid.

[4] Bridgewater Trust, General Abstract of Accounts, 1837 (statement of Capital, 23 Dec. 1837), Lancs. C.R.O.

[5] S. Pollard, *The Genesis of Modern Management,* pp. 96, 114.

the largest in the country. With an annual sale of 134,000 tons of coal in 1803, and 273,000 tons in 1837, they bore comparison even with the mines of Tyneside, where the average output was only 60,000 to 70,000 tons per colliery in 1830, though some establishments were a good deal larger.[1]

The Trust, however, was not merely a business. At Worsley it was an estate, consisting of about 6,000 acres situated in the manors of Worsley, Middle Hulton, and Bedford.[2] Agriculturally speaking the land was poor, the soil being generally of a strong clayey loam which was both difficult and expensive to drain. Large tracts of it remained as marsh, waste, and swamp, like the notorious Chat Moss, and less than a twentieth was under the plough. But, as Wheeler pointed out in 1836, the spirit of improvement was not absent from the region in the twenty years after Waterloo.[3] Encouraged by the rising Manchester market, dairy farming was practised, especially in the low-lying southern portions around Worsley. Though much of their land was let out in tenancies, the Trustees participated in the improvements by planting trees and by running the demesne farms which they retained in their own hands. These were used both for breeding the Canal horses and for fattening cattle, which were bought as a speculation from the Scottish Highlands and elsewhere and then sold. The farm stock in 1829 consisted of 313 horses, 25 mules, 703 sheep, and 156 horned cattle.[4] With the estate, moreover, went two eligible residences, an old half-timbered manor house, and a new hall built by the Canal Duke. Here the Trust Superintendent could live the life of a country gentleman, shooting game, holding parties, and dispensing justice on the magisterial bench. The letters of R. H. Bradshaw, first holder of the office, give a glimpse of him 'justicing for seven hours' and 'lecturing' the lads and lasses of Worsley who came

[1] Bridgewater Trust General Accounts, 1790–1810, and General Abstract of Accounts, 1837, Lancs. C.R.O. Cf. J. H. Clapham, *The Early Railway Age, 1820–1850* p. 186.

[2] Statement of Lands belonging to the late Duke of Bridgewater in Lancashire, 27 July 1803, A.H.C., Herts. C.R.O.

[3] James Wheeler, *Manchester: Its Political, Social and Commercial History*, pp. 433, 444–7.

[4] Bridgewater Trust, General Abstract of Accounts, 1829 (Statement of Capital, Dec. 1829), Lancs. C.R.O.

before him on affiliation orders, 'on their frailties, or accidents (as they term it)'.[1]

If the estates lent social prestige, it was above all the Canal which conferred economic importance. By reason of its own geographical position and of its connections with other waterways, it was to serve, in the early nineteenth century, as one of the principal arteries of the Industrial Revolution in Britain. Already in 1803 it carried a weight of 334,495 tons of goods, an average of 6,432 tons per week. By 1836 the figure had almost trebled, rising to 968,795 tons.[2] The pattern of trade was varied and the contribution to the nation's economic growth manysided. Coal was, and remained, the largest single commodity to be carried, accounting for a quarter to a third of the total tonnage in the year of the Duke of Bridgewater's death. In 1836 more than a fifth of the coal brought into Manchester by all available means passed down the Duke's Canal to Castlefield or to the Rochdale Canal beyond.[3] Even in 1803, however, the coal trade was smaller than the traffic in general merchandise exchanged with the Trent and Mersey (or Grand Trunk) Canal at Preston Brook. This was in full, ebullient growth about that time. By 1810 it had risen to 237,000 tons, more than a half of the whole tonnage of the Canal. About 100,000 tons of this was Liverpool traffic, which used the Duke's Canal for less than six miles, between Runcorn and Preston Brook, but was also freighted along the Mersey estuary for more than twice that distance in the Duke's flats, and was dependent upon facilities provided by the Trustees, at one or the other of those two places, for trans-shipment into the narrow boats which operated on the Trent and Mersey Canal. The composition of this trade was briefly sketched in *Gore's Liverpool Directory* for 1805, under the heading, 'Inland Navigation from Liverpool':[4] 'The Duke of Bridgewater's Canal . . . takes clay and flints to the Potteries, groceries and

[1] R. H. Bradshaw to James Loch, 18 Sept. 1828, S.E.P., Staffs. C.R.O.

[2] These and other figures for the Canal trade given in the ensuing pages are cited, unless otherwise stated, from the Bridgewater Trust General Accounts, 1790–1810 and from the annual General Abstracts of Accounts for the years 1829–37 (incl.) at the Lancashire C.R.O. Most of them are given to the nearest thousand tons.

[3] *Royal Commission on Coal*, vol. iii, Committee E, Appendix, p. 77, 1871 [C. 435 ii] XVIII.

[4] Appendix, p. 98.

West Indian produce to every part of the island, and returns
loaded with the products and manufactories of almost all the
countries to the South of the Humber, Mersey, etc. (earthenware, etc.).' The Canal route through Preston Brook was used
by many Midland industries, carrying iron from South
Staffordshire, hardwares from Birmingham, even some salt
from the Cheshire saltfield, though most of this went down
the Weaver. It was of particular importance, however, as the
advertisement implies, to the economy of the North Staffordshire Potteries, which it served, both by carrying into the
interior the potters' raw materials—China clay and stone,
brought round to the Mersey by sea from the coasts of Devon,
Dorset, and Cornwall, and flints from Gravesend and Newhaven—and by conveying the manufactured earthenware to
port at Liverpool.

The third main component of the Canal trade, the interchange of goods between Liverpool and Manchester, was at
first smaller than either of the two already mentioned—
60,000 tons in 1803 (79,000 if the item entered as 'country
goods' is included). It increased greatly, however, in the
quarter of a century after Waterloo, when the British cotton
industry, taking advantage of the new techniques in weaving
and of improvements in machine spinning, moved into its
phase of maximum growth. The composition of this traffic was
at first extremely varied. A list of rates, simultaneously
advertised by the Duke's and the Mersey and Irwell Navigation Company in 1810,[1] specified charges for raw cotton and
raw wool, linen, flax, hemp, bale goods, timber of all kinds,
bricks, dyewoods, grain, flour and meal, tea, sugar, tobacco,
and coffee, to say nothing of rice, dry and wet, clog soles, and
feathers. Forty-one years later, however, eighty per cent of
the up trade from Liverpool by the two waterways was constituted by three main categories of goods—raw cotton;
timber; and grain, meal, and flour.[2] Once Liverpool had
displaced London as the leading port of importation for raw
cotton, which it did in the 1790s,[3] the Duke's Canal became

---

[1] *Manchester Mercury*, 4 Sept. 1810.
[2] 'Return of Goods Carried by Water between Liverpool and Manchester,
Year Ending 31 December 1851', enclosed in F. Smith to J. Loch, 8 Apr. 1852
L.E.P.
[3] M. M. Edwards, *The Growth of the British Cotton Trade, 1780–1815*, p. 110.

one of two main feeders of raw material to the industries of
Lancashire. In the years 1840–2 (incl.), the weight of raw
cotton carried annually along it from Liverpool to Manchester
averaged about 55,000 tons[1]—about a quarter of the total
consumed by all the factories of Great Britain.[2]

A down traffic in manufactured goods from Manchester to
Liverpool built up much more slowly than the reverse trade.
The amount entered as 'to Liverpool' was only 3,900 tons
in the accounts for 1803. Nevertheless, from this early date
the Duke's had a part to play in the distribution of Manchester
wares to other great centres—to London and to the large
concentrations of internal purchasing power in Nottinghamshire and Derbyshire and in Staffordshire, Warwickshire,
Worcestershire, Leicestershire, and Northamptonshire. From
the early 1790s onwards, independent carriers operating from
Castlefield were conveying goods by the Bridgewater and
Grand Trunk Canals to Shardlow on the Trent, and thence by
wagon overland to London; also to Coventry, Birmingham,
Stourport, Lichfield, Leicester, and Warwick.[3] At Shardlow,
half a century later, Manchester packs were being exchanged
for cargoes of malt, flour, and grain, from the eastern counties,
which were brought back to Manchester via Preston Brook.[4]
This was only part, moreover, of the role of the Bridgewater
Canal in the provisioning of Manchester. There was also, in the
early 1840s, a thriving traffic in potatoes from the agricultural
districts at the western end of the navigation. Cheese was
conveyed to Manchester from the southern portions of Cheshire
by the Grand Trunk and the Duke's until the Manchester and
Birmingham railway cut into the traffic, and a special milk boat
known as the Moore boat plied along the Duke's as late as 1845.[5]

---

[1] Quantities of 47,272 tons, 51,054 tons, and 54,956 tons for the first forty-
eight weeks of the years 1840, 1841, and 1842 respectively. Comparative statement enclosed in F. Smith to J. Loch, 20 Dec. 1842, L.E.P.

[2] The total national consumption of raw cotton was 528, 437, and 474 million
lb. in 1840, 1841, and 1842 respectively. A. D. Gayer, W. W. Rostow, and A. J.
Schwartz, *The Growth and Fluctuation of the British Economy, 1790–1850*,
vol. i, p. 294.

[3] See the lists of carriers in the Manchester Directories for 1794, 1797, 1800,
1802, 1804, and 1808–9; also H. Clegg, op. cit.

[4] Mitchell to F. Smith, 2 Nov. 1841, L.E.P.

[5] There are many references to the market goods trade in L.E.P. See
especially F. Smith to J. Loch, 16 Oct. 1841, 9 Jan. 1845, and 12 Nov. 1846.

The dispositions which were made, on the death of the third Duke of Bridgewater, for the custody of this vast industrial empire were strangely inadequate to the needs which required to be fulfilled. As we have seen, the ownership was vested in three Trustees. Two of these, Sir Archibald Macdonald, Lord Chief Baron of the Exchequer, and Edward Venables Vernon-Harcourt, Bishop of Carlisle and later Archbishop of York, who had each married one of the Duke's nieces, were dummy trustees. The real direction of the concern was entrusted to their colleague, Robert Haldane Bradshaw, who was to receive a salary of £2,000 per year, and was to have the mansions at Worsley and Runcorn to his own use and the power to nominate his successor. The Duke's will confined the beneficiaries of the Trust, the Marquess of Stafford and his descendants, to the role of mere *rentiers*, divorcing financial interest from control. This arrangement did not work satisfactorily, and proved the source of many of the later difficulties of the Trust. It discouraged investment, fomented quarrels, and hindered the formulation of a coherent policy towards outsiders. As will be shown, the history of the concern during the first half of the nineteenth century is, in one of its aspects, the story of a bid to reverse it. The reasons why the Canal Duke, a man of undoubted enterprise and ability, should have saddled posterity with so anomalous a plan are not clear. It is possible that the will was simply master-minded by Bradshaw, who had so much to gain from it, but James Sothern, whose family had a prominent connection with the estates going well back into the eighteenth century, advanced a different theory. He claimed in 1836 that the late Duke

in bestowing his great and princely bounty on the Sutherland family did so in the most qualified and restricted manner, his object being to with-hold as long as possible all controul or interference of that family over the property, as from its anomalous nature he felt convinced any such controul or interference would wholly paralyse and destroy the great objects he had in view.[1]

Perhaps it was the Sutherland investment in other waterways, such as the Grand Trunk, the interests of which were not wholly harmonized with those of the Duke's, or the family's

---

[1] *Manchester Guardian*, 27 Feb. 1836.

stake in other coal mines, such as those of Shropshire, which aroused the suspicions of the dying Duke. We are left to guess.

For some twenty years, however, after the Duke's death, the problems of the Trust were masked by intense prosperity. In the sixteen years 1806–21, the profits of the Lancashire and Cheshire estates fluctuated about a mean of some £66,000 per annum, and then surged forward in the boom of the middle twenties to £100,743 in 1823 and to £119,497 in 1824.[1] The Canal was the principal profit maker, and although some exaggerated notions of its yield, based upon an uncritical acceptance of the writings of the early railway promoters like Joseph Sandars, have gained currency, it can hardly be denied that the enterprise was exceedingly lucrative. Sandars misled in stating that the 'nett income of the Duke's Canal has, for the last twenty years, averaged nearly £100,000',[2] and the historian Jackman still more so in suggesting that in 1826 the waterways between Liverpool and Manchester were making more than 100 per cent profit.[3] Nevertheless, the Bridgewater navigation did generate a profit ranging from £23,000 to £80,000 per annum in the years 1806–26, and the average was about £45,000.[4] On a capital outlay of perhaps £355,000 at the time of the Duke's death,[5] this represented 13 per cent per annum for the average, and 23 per cent for 1824, the best year of the series.

Historians of transport have generally perceived something sinister and unhealthy in this prosperity. They have treated it as a consequence of the intrusion into the affairs of the Trust

---

[1] See below, Appendix A.

[2] J. Sandars, *A Letter on the Subject of the Projected Railroad between Liverpool and Manchester . . . with an Exposure of the Exorbitant and Unjust Charges of the Water Carriers*, 3rd edn. (1825), p. 21.

[3] W. T. Jackman, *The Development of Transportation in Modern England*, p. 520.

[4] See below, Appendix A.

[5] This sum is reached by adding to the accumulated debt for making the navigation, which stood at its highest point of £346,806 in January 1786 (volume entitled 'General State of His Grace the Duke of Bridgewater's Navigation', etc.', E.B.C.), the £7,784 expended on the construction of the Leigh branch of the Canal between 1796 and 1801 (Payments on Account of the Leigh Canal, 1795–1801, E.B.C.). Though a mere approximation, it is preferable to Jackman's figure of £200,000–£220,000, which left out of account all extensions of the Canal and all ancillary dock construction after 1776.

of a sordid, grasping commercialism, which had been absent
during the Duke's lifetime and was to sow the seeds of the
future embarrassments of the Canal. With this new spirit is
associated pre-eminently the name of Robert Haldane
Bradshaw, who ruled the Trust estates as Superintendent for
thirty years after the Duke's death. Bradshaw has been
harshly treated by the historians. He has been described as
'a virtuoso in the art of profit manipulation, an example of
great capacity and untiring industry chained to purely
materialistic aims',[1] and as 'the epitome of a newer type of
business man, the type indirectly responsible for some of the
least attractive aspects of modern industrialism'.[2] This
picture in some ways misleads. An exact portrait, while it
would not flatter, would find place for more sympathetic lines.

Bradshaw was a man of the old social order rather than the
new. He came late into the world of canals and coalmines,
which men like John Gilbert and James Brindley had created
at Worsley. He was born in 1759, the eldest son of Thomas
Bradshaw, an eighteenth-century political adventurer of
somewhat unsavoury reputation, who rose to be Secretary
of the Treasury through the influence of the Duke of Grafton.
Thomas ran into debt through extravagance, however, and
died in the prime of life, by his own hand, it was rumoured,
leaving for the upkeep of his family the income from a
hereditary sinecure office of which he held only the reversion.
Robert's uncle, James Bradshaw, was chief supercargo in the
service of the East India Company at Canton, and he himself
had the right of voting in elections at India House. Of his
early career nothing is known. It was probably an uphill
struggle, for his father's will could not be proved.[3] The 1808
edition of Wilson's *Biographical Index to the Present House of
Commons* states, however, that he was educated at Harrow,[4]

---

[1] B. Falk, *The Bridgewater Millions*, p. 128.

[2] H. Malet, *The Canal Duke*, p. 173.

[3] The principal sources for these details of Bradshaw's birth and family
connections are: L. B. Namier and J. Brooke, *The House of Commons, 1754–
1790*, vol. ii, pp. 110–11; Burke's *Landed Gentry* (1952), p. 248; H. B. Morse,
The Chronicles of the East India Company Trading to China, vol. ii, p. 61;
Memoirs of William Hickey, ed. A. Spencer, vol. i, p. 319; the Will of Thomas
Bradshaw in the Probate Records of the Prerogative Court of Canterbury,
1774.

[4] The School records do not confirm this.

and a much later account, preserved at Mertoun, mentions a report that he had himself been in the public service before entering that of the Duke of Bridgewater.[1] By 1800 he had become agent to the Duke, with responsibilities similar to those previously discharged by Thomas Gilbert, the chief legal agent for all the ducal estates.[2] These, however, did not require him to desert London, and he lived first in Cleveland Court, almost on the doorstep of Bridgewater House, where the Duke was in the habit of wintering, and later at an address in Berners Street, off Oxford Street. Even after he became Superintendent he was slow to take up permanent residence at Worsley,[3] and when he eventually did so, it was not without wistful glances back at the life he had left. He wrote to a London correspondent in 1814:

> You add not a word of news. It is charity to enlighten us country gem'men now and then with a little information from Head Quarters, and especially here, as a relief from the continual scolding and squabbling with refractory clerks and rascally flatmen, with which I am so agreeably amused.[4]

His correspondence does not support the view that he was, by nature, unhealthily preoccupied with profit-making. That for the earlier years of his superintendentship contains much semi-humorous comment on the politics of the time, for he was M.P. for the Trustees' pocket borough of Brackley from 1802 until its disfranchisement by the Great Reform Act. He confessed a fondness for shooting, and planned to visit Paris, after it had fallen to the allies in 1814, for the purpose of seeing the art treasures at the Louvre 'before honesty may induce the

---

[1] A short account of the various Trust Superintendents by the late Mr. Strachan Holme, formerly Librarian to the Earl of Ellesmere. I owe this reference to Her Grace the Duchess of Sutherland.

[2] See the correspondence arising from the claim of Henry Tomkinson against the Duke of Bridgewater for repayment of his late father's legal expenses, Nov. 1800–May 1801. R. H. Bradshaw was acting for the Duke, and was described as 'His Grace's agent' in a submission for a legal opinion bearing the date 10 Dec. 1800 (A.H.C.).

[3] He wrote to William Sergeant from Berners Street on 10 June 1806, stating that he hoped to be in Worsley by the next meeting of the Bolton and Bury Canal Company. In a lease dated 24 June 1809, however, he was still described as of Berners Street. These documents are in the B.T.P. (Mertoun, Roxburghshire), Files 129 and 130. Evidence of his domicile before 1803 is to be found in the Tomkinson Correspondence, A.H.C.

[4] R. H. Bradshaw to Wrottesley, 2 July 1814, B.T.P. (Mertoun), File 131.

return of a part at least of the stolen goods deposited there'.[1]
He even professed to have a social conscience, for he wrote to
his co-M.P. Wrottesley in December 1816, expressing admiration for the 'most exemplary' conduct of the labouring classes
in the Worsley district, 'under such privations and distress as in
many instances . . . would scarcely be believed'. He added that
he was doing all he could 'to keep things quiet and jogging on',
employing numbers 'even at the risk of ruining Lord Stafford'
and giving nearly half his time 'to hearing their grievances as a
magistrate and applying relief where absolutely necessary'.[2]

From about 1813 onwards, however, his letters were full of
complaints of overwork and lack of sufficient assistance at the
managerial level. These do not lack credibility, for the Duke
of Bridgewater's will had concentrated an excessive responsibility for decision-making in the hands of one man. Doubtless
he made his burden heavier than it need have been by an
inability to delegate,[3] always the mark of a second-rate mind,
for he at least had Benjamin Sothern, a veteran of the Duke's
day, as his Principal Agent at Worsley down to 1826, and was
eventually able to associate his son Captain James Bradshaw,
a retired naval officer, with him in the management, in the
capacity of a deputy. Even so, he was unable to escape from
the routine which kept him tied to his house day after day
from morning until night. Even on Christmas Day he had
'people to see and plague' him 'all the evening'.[4] The strain
of these labours, acting upon a naturally assertive personality,
slowly turned him into the crabby eccentric he became by the
time that his Canal faced the really serious challenge of railway
building. But it was never the love of profit-making alone that
drove him to expend himself, for he had a genuinely senti-
mental attachment to the property. In an interview with John
Moss the railway promoter in October 1828 he claimed that
'the old duke had made him promise twenty-six years ago to
attend to the interests of the Canal, from which day, he, Mr.
B., had not once dined out'.[5]

[1] R. H. Bradshaw to Wrottesley, 25 July 1814, B.T.P. (Mertoun), File 131.
[2] R. H. Bradshaw to Wrottesley, 5 Dec. 1816, ibid., File 132.
[3] His son and deputy referred in 1833 to his insistence on doing 'all the business'. J. Bradshaw to J. Loch, 20 Apr. 1833, S.E.P.
[4] R. H. Bradshaw to J. Loch, 25 Dec. 1824, ibid.
[5] Memorandum enclosed in J. Moss to J. Loch, 22 Oct. 1828, ibid.

It would be idle, however, to conceal his faults. Intensely conservative, he was never at ease in the world of the 1820s. Even in his letters to James Loch, who was known to belong to the opposing camp, he sneered at 'the march of intellect' and 'the age of reason' and proudly proclaimed himself 'one of the old school'.[1] 'He is not fond of any change even though good would result from it,' observed a man who knew him well, in 1833.[2] His temper, which was always uncertain, deteriorated with age and with the paralytic stroke which laid him low in November 1831.[3] 'Were he interfered with in his plans, without his consent,' continued the above-mentioned observer, 'I think it might have a serious effect upon his health and temper, and become a very awkward person to manage either to his family or friends.'[4]

In the outside world he had the reputation of being a formidable bargainer. John Moss, himself an expert in commercial negotiation, observed in 1828:

I must confess that I go to him with more reluctance than I usually visit a gentleman, because I hear from all quarters that he is not content to have a fair share of the contract, but that those who deal with him must prepare to concede more than he has a right to demand, that even those who are notorious for the zeal with which they protect their own interests, always find, after an arrangement with Mr. Bradshaw, that they have nothing to boast of.[5]

It would be easy, however, to over-estimate the irrational element in Bradshaw's character. There are grounds for thinking that he sometimes used apparent intransigence as a bargaining counter to drive his opponents to a compromise. He observed in 1813, commenting upon the attitude which should be adopted by the allies towards the falling Napoleon: 'I have always found it the best way, when I am obliged to live upon terms with a great rascal, to take the first opportunity of thrashing him unmercifully and then (as a friend) to come to a clear understanding with him upon all points.'[6]

---

[1] R. H. Bradshaw to J. Loch, 12 July 1828, ibid.
[2] G. Winter to J. Loch, 27 Aug. 1833, ibid.
[3] J. Bradshaw to J. Loch, 17 Nov. 1831, ibid.
[4] G. Winter to J. Loch, 27 Aug. 1833, ibid.
[5] J. Moss to J. Loch, 30 Sept. 1828, ibid.
[6] R. H. Bradshaw to Wrottesley, 12 Dec. 1813, B.T.P. (Mertoun), File 131.

He was to put this policy into practice on more than one occasion when confronting the railway promoters, whose plans threatened the prosperity of his Canal. Those of his opponents who grasped his strategy stood up to him and often gained a point. Those who tried to circumvent him did so at their peril.

Such failings as we have noted hitherto can be readily excused on grounds of overwork, temperament, or advancing years. In the writings of historians, however, Bradshaw's reputation has been tarnished by two specific indictments of a more serious character. The first is that he entered into monopolistic agreements, as a result of which the trade between Manchester and Liverpool was oppressed by heavy charges. The second is that his parsimony caused him to neglect essential expenditure upon the Canal, to the detriment of the service which was offered to the public. In both respects his policies are believed to have profited the Trust in the short run, whilst damaging it in the long, by driving the exasperated merchants of Liverpool to press for the construction of a railway.

The burden of the first charge is that, by an agreement made with the Mersey and Irwell Navigation Company in 1810, the rates of freight between Liverpool and Manchester were raised to 'nearly three times those of 1795', and that they were maintained at this high level until there was a possibility of putting down a railway between these two places. W. T. Jackman, who made these assertions, basing them largely upon the allegations of the highly polemical Sandars, implied that the prosperity of the Canal under Bradshaw's management stemmed from these monopolistic practices.[1] Further investigation suggests, however, that both the extent and the importance of such arrangements have been exaggerated. In September 1810 the Bridgewater Trustees and the Mersey and Irwell Navigation Company, indeed, issued simultaneous notices in the press, announcing amended rates of freight. A comparison of these rates with figures collected for the late eighteenth century hardly bears out the generalization that there had been an almost threefold increase since the 1790s. The freight of raw cotton, as disclosed in Scholes's

[1] Op. cit., pp. 519–21.

Directory of Manchester for 1794 and 1797, was 10s. 6d. per ton; in 1810 it was 20s. 0d. It is impossible to be so precise in comparing other items, as Scholes makes only one further entry, the undiscriminating one of 'goods', and one cannot be absolutely certain what is included in this. The figure which he quotes for it, viz. 7s. 2d. per ton, has to be compared with the following rates for 1810: 20s. 0d. for bale goods, 18s. 4d. for tobacco and coffee, 16s. 8d. for flour, ale, sugar, butter, potatoes, and sundries, 15s. 0d. for grain, and 13s. 4d. for timber, iron, clay, dyewoods, bricks, and slates.[1] It seems probable, therefore, that the near threefold increase occurred only in respect of bale goods. For most other commodities it was nearer twofold.

A rise such as this was admittedly larger than the increase in the general cost of living during the intervening period.[2] Nevertheless, there had been a sharp rise in transport costs in the years before the high freights of 1810 were announced, and this would have warranted some adjustment of charges in an upward direction. In consequence of the demands of the navy and the interruption of supplies from the Baltic, the price of timber, from which canal boats were constructed, had increased by some 300 per cent since 1795,[3] and owing to the deficiency of the crop, there was an abnormal rise in that of the hay which was used to sustain the Canal horses, in 1810.[4] The main point, however, which has generally escaped attention is that the arrangement of 1810 was not destined to endure. The view that the contracting parties were able to maintain freight charges until the construction of the Liverpool and Manchester railway was seriously threatened is discredited by the minute books of the Mersey and Irwell Navigation Company, which record a sequence of reductions beginning in 1812. During that year the Mersey and Irwell Company reduced the freight of timber from 13s. 4d. to

---

[1] *Manchester Mercury*, 4 Sept. 1810.

[2] The Silberling 'Index of Wholesale Commodity Prices' shows an increase of about 40 per cent between 1795 and 1810; the Gayer, Rostow, and Schwartz 'Index of Wholesale Prices of Domestic and Imported Commodities', one of about 33 per cent (Gayer, Rostow, and Schwartz, op. cit., vol. i, pp. 468 and 524).

[3] T. Tooke and W. Newmarch, *A History of Prices*, vol. ii, p. 417.

[4] Ibid. i. 295.

C

10*s.* 0*d.* per ton, that of cotton and linens from 20*s.* 0*d.* to
18*s.* 4*d.* In 1816 they lowered grain freights from 18*s.* 4*d.* to
13*s.* 4*d.*, whilst the Bridgewater Trustees took the initiative in
reducing bark by 3*s.* 4*d.* per ton. Two years later the Trustees
and a firm of water carriers known as the Grocers' Company
brought the freight of soda down from 16*s.* 8*d.* to 13*s.* 4*d.*, the
Mersey Company following. Although there is evidence to
suggest collusion between the latter, commonly called the Old
Quay Company, and the Duke's Trustees in the reductions
made in 1812, from 1816 onwards the two concerns appear to
have acted quite independently of each other. The M. and I.
Committee reduced the freight of bark in January 1816,
because the Trustees had carried at that rate for some time
past. Lingard, the Old Quay agent, had only established the
fact by examining freight notes issued by the Trustees.[1] It is
difficult to resist the conclusion that the alliance between the
two navigations, which seems in any case to have been little
more than an agreement to communicate proposed changes
of rate, was for all practical purposes defunct before the first
survey for the Liverpool and Manchester railway was carried
out in 1821. The threat of a railroad did no more than complete
the disorganization of the rates of carriage between the two
towns, a process already well in course.

Basically, the reason for the failure of this early attempt to
establish a rate-fixing 'conference' was that, contrary to what
has often been supposed, neither the conditions of monopoly
nor the serious determination to create them existed in the
sphere of waterways', twixt Liverpool and Manchester during
the first quarter of the nineteenth century. The spirit of
competition was too keen and vigorous to admit of anything
but a temporary truce between contending parties, and the
only effect of raising freight charges was to draw fresh capital
into the industry to bring them down again. The intrusion in
this case was by firms of independent carriers, which were set
up *ad hoc* to ply upon the existing waterways. In the Duke of
Bridgewater's time establishments of this kind had been
principally confined to the traffic originating or ending on
other waterways; they now entered the Liverpool and Man-

[1] M. & I.N.C. Order Books, 1810–20 and 1821–8, M.S.C.C., Bridgewater
Department.

chester trade. Within a year or two of the announcement of the increases in 1810, advertisements from carriers operating between those two towns began to appear in the Manchester commercial directories. In 1813 it was Marsden's, Hartley & Co., advertising fly boats to London and Liverpool; in 1815 the Manchester Grocers' Company, E. and I. Thompson, and J. Cogswell. There is evidence that the Grocers' Company was formed in 1811 specifically to combat the rate-fixing compact of the Bridgewater Trust and the Old Quay Company.[1] The private trade on the Duke's Canal grew rapidly during Bradshaw's superintendentship. In 1824 it exceeded in weight for the first time the traffic conveyed by the Trustees' carrying department.[2]

Bradshaw can claim no particular credit for initiating these developments. They could scarcely have taken place, however, if he had resolutely opposed them, for he could have denied to the newcomers essential facilities such as warehousing at Castlefield. In fact, however, the Manchester Grocers' Company was allowed to take possession of a warehouse there in the year of its inception,[3] and Bradshaw gave every evidence of having leagued himself afterwards with the Company to overturn the structure of rates which he had previously agreed with the Mersey and Irwell Navigation Committee. On four occasions between April 1818 and October 1822 the minutes of the latter record decisions to reduce freight charges to a level already adopted by the Duke's Trustees and the Grocers' Company.[4] He seems to have realized that more profit was to be made from tonnage traffic, where only the maintenance of the track was involved, than from freights, where boats had to be supplied, horsed, and manned, for his son and deputy once observed to James Loch that there was a loss on freight.[5]

---

[1] V. I. Tomlinson, 'Early Warehouses on Manchester Waterways', *Transactions of the Lancashire and Cheshire Antiquarian Society*, lxxi (1961).

[2] Bridgewater Trust General Accounts, 1790–1810 and 1811–30. This conclusion is reached by examining the annual navigation accounts. The items listed as coal and limestone and as both 'freight and tonnage' have been included in the carrying trade. Those described as 'tonnage, porterage, wharfage, and warehouseroom' have been computed as tonnage traffic.

[3] H. Clegg, op. cit.

[4] M. & I.N.C. Order Books, 1810–20 and 1821–8: entries for 1 Apr. 1818, 2 May 1821, 6 Feb. 1822, and 2 Oct. 1822.

[5] J. Loch's Memorandum of an Interview, 5 Mar. 1837, E.B.C.

It was from the work of the private carriers, expanding with the growth of industry and trade, not from swollen freight charges engineered by monopolistic agreement, that the bulk of Bradshaw's extensive profits accrued. Of the increase in the average annual gross receipts from the navigation from the quinquennium 1803–7 to that of 1821–5, which was of the order of £53,000, £34,000, or nearly two-thirds, came from tonnage traffic.[1] The year of maximum profit on the navigation was not 1810 or 1811, when the arrangement with the Old Quay Company stood unimpaired, but 1824, when freight charges had been drastically lowered.[2]

Under Bradshaw's lead the Trustees neither intended nor achieved overall monopoly. Their outlook was much more empirical. They seldom hesitated, it is true, to act in restraint of particular acts of competition likely to prove detrimental to their waterway, whenever they had the power to do so. In this respect, however, their behaviour scarcely differed from that of the Duke of Bridgewater before them, and was part of the general commercial morality of the time. The Duke had bought up land in Salford to frustrate plans for creating in the area a canal centre to rival Castlefield; his devisees disposed of that land for building purposes, but inserted clauses preventing the purchasers from letting it for wharves and landing places useful to the Mersey and Irwell Navigation Company. The Duke cast the full weight of his parliamentary influence against the proposals for linking Macclesfield, Stockport, and Manchester to the River Weaver by canal in 1766;[3] Bradshaw boasted in 1821 that likewise he had 'knocked up' a scheme for building a bridge at Runcorn by which the Canal's Preston Brook traffic was threatened with abstraction.[4] Given sufficient *locus standi*, he would also have opposed the Sheffield and Tinsley Canal Bill in 1815, for he believed that the intended waterway was 'part of a plan . . . of forming a grand eastern communication with Yorkshire and which if

---

[1] Bridgewater Trust General Accounts, 1790–1810 and 1811–30. See above, p. 15, n. 2, for the mode of deducing freight and tonnage figures from the annual navigation accounts.

[2] See below, Appendix A.

[3] V. I. Tomlinson, 'Salford Activities Connected with the Bridgewater Canal', *Transactions of the Lancashire and Cheshire Antiquarian Society*, lxvi (1956).   [4] R. H. Bradshaw to J. Loch, 25 Dec. 1821, S.E.P.

carried into effect would play the very D . . .l with us and the Trent and Mersey'.[1] If, unlike Bradshaw, the Canal Duke would never contemplate an agreement with the Old Quay Company to fix prices, he was at least moving in the closing years of his life towards a closer co-operation with that concern, which was founded upon the conviction that there would be trade enough for both waterways.[2] From this it was not too great a step to the agreeing of rates of carriage.

The second outstanding allegation against Bradshaw, that his avarice reduced the efficiency of the Canal by denying it necessary improvements, also contains a large element of unfairness. There can be little doubt, it is true, that the service upon the waterway, immediately before the coming of the railways, was marred by delays and inefficiencies, and that the condition of the property was, by and large, worse than it had been at the time of the third Duke of Bridgewater's death. Contemporary complaints made much of these defects. In the winter of 1824–5 a timber consignment for Manchester had to wait four months upon the wharf at Liverpool, and, even at the end of that period, most of it had not been shipped.[3] In some instances goods were said to have taken longer in their passage from Liverpool to Manchester than in crossing the Atlantic to Liverpool.[4] But these were surely isolated cases. Moreover, responsibility for delays must be apportioned.

To a certain extent, the difficulties stemmed from natural disadvantages inherent in the canal system generally and in the water route from Liverpool to Manchester in particular. Most inland navigations were subject to stoppage by frost or drought, and one which utilized a river estuary for more than a third of its route incurred the additional disadvantage that the sail-propelled flats operating upon the tideway could be held up by adverse winds.[4] Moreover, in the upper portion of the estuary, round about Runcorn, the configuration of the river and the operation of the tides presented special problems. Just below Runcorn the Mersey narrowed sharply and entered upon a circuitous course, intersected by sandbanks and by marshland projecting from the banks. The navigable

[1] R. H. Bradshaw to Wrottesley, 16 Feb. 1815, B.T.P. (Mertoun), File 132.
[2] Malet, op. cit., p. 151.   [3] Ibid., p. 174.
[4] Jackman, op. cit., p. 519.

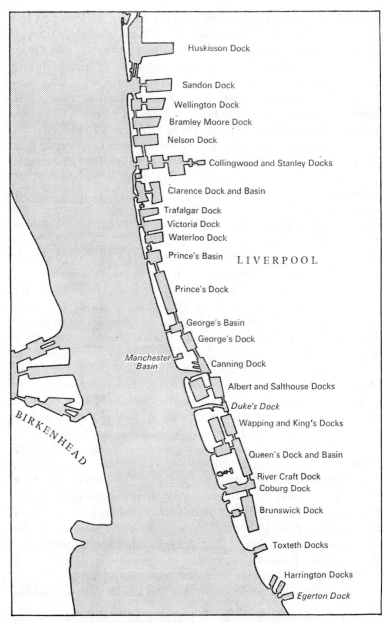

Map 1. Section of the Liverpool Docks, *c.* 1860

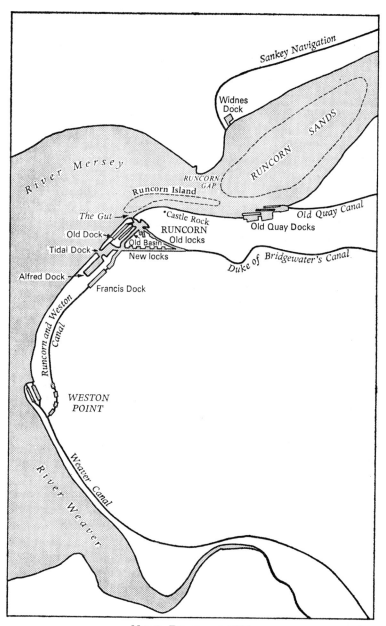

Map 2. Runcorn, *c.* 1860

channel was apt to change sides with disconcerting consequences for the flatmen. Shortly after 1800 its course lay along
the Lancashire shore from a point near the Decoy (almost
opposite Weston Point), where it crossed from the Cheshire
side, to Runcorn Gap. Vessels coming up the tideway to the
Duke of Bridgewater's locks were then obliged to go more than
a mile round, approaching their destination from the north along
the edge of Runcorn Island. This route was also hazardous,
as the Lancashire coast was studded with rocks, such as the
Medstone and Hosiers Rocks. Thirty years later the channel
had gone over to the Cheshire bank, which was much more
convenient to the trade of the Bridgewater Canal, but the
grounds of many complaints must have been laid before it
did so. There was the further difficulty that the ebbing tide
tended to deposit mud and other alluvial matter on the edge
of the marshes above the Duke's Locks, thus causing the entrance to the locks to silt up. To obviate this the Duke cut a
narrow channel through these marshes in 1773, separating
what was to become Runcorn Island from the mainland. He
equipped this 'gut' with gates at either end so that it might
act as an accumulator for tidal waters, which could be released
when the tide was ebbing, to scour and carry away the mud.
Despite this contrivance, the deep near the Duke's Locks was
in a bad state when Bradshaw took over. Samuel Meacock, who
was the agent employed by the Trustees at Runcorn, afterwards
testified in a legal action that, about the year 1807, six feet of
tidal water was necessary to enable boats to get over the sill.
Seventy vessels were neaped on the banks opposite the pier
head 'on account of the channel being recked up'. Bradshaw
can scarcely be blamed for these contingencies which occurred
so early in his superintendentship, and, as Meacock made
clear, steps were taken by him to correct them. The deposited
mud was scoured away by means of a gutter which was cut
into the mud from the bottom of the locks to the deep. He
seems also to have taken action to prevent further mischief,
placing bar stones along the edge of Runcorn Island at the
lower water mark in order to preserve the deep along the
adjoining channel and to prevent the formation of sand banks.[1]

---

[1] These particulars of the difficulties besetting navigation in the Upper
Mersey estuary, and of the steps taken to rectify them, are based on 'the

Many of the faults from which the navigation suffered arose, however, from want of adequate outlay on repairs and improvements. Even the impediments to water traffic from winds in the Mersey estuary could have been overcome to some extent by running steamboats between Liverpool and Runcorn. From the closing years of the Napoleonic Wars steamers began to ply on a number of English rivers, including the Thames, the Mersey, the Ouse, and the Humber. The earliest, however, were mainly packets. Steam tugs capable of drawing flats made little headway before the railways came. On the Yorkshire Ouse they appeared between 1826 and 1828.[1] Even so the Trustees lagged somewhat. A remark made by Captain Bradshaw to James Loch in 1833 suggests that it was not until the end of Robert Bradshaw's trusteeship, when railway competition had become an actuality, that the Duke's resorted to 'the adoption of steam on the River'.[2]

Further evidence of insufficient expenditure came from the overcrowded warehouses and docks and the state of advanced dilapidation into which some of the principal canal works and ancillary installations had fallen by the middle and later 1820s. The great flight of locks at Runcorn, which had been completed in 1773, was wearing out. The Duke's Dock at Liverpool had deteriorated so much that by 1828 the gates had to be tied up with rope. Several portions of the dock wall had become ruinous, and the whole structure was too small to furnish the accommodation needed for the increasing trade. For want of sufficient space, flats arriving by the half tide were kept waiting for so long outside the entrance that they could not be unloaded and loaded in time to leave by half-tide on the day of arrival. Hence a whole tide was wasted on each trip, and more flats had to be employed in the trade than would otherwise have been necessary to maintain a given volume of business. Moreover, the dock was so constructed as to prove injurious to the navigation of the stretch of river

Brief Indictment and Case for the Defendants in the Case of the King against James Sothern Esq. and Others at the Liverpool Spring Assizes, March 30th 1836', and 'the Brief Proofs for the Defendants' in the same action, B.T.P. (Mertoun).

[1] Jackman, op. cit., p. 455; Baron F. Duckham, *The Yorkshire Ouse: the History of a River Navigation*, pp. 84–5.

[2] J. Bradshaw to J. Loch, 22 June 1833, S.E.P.

adjacent to it. Begun in the third Duke of Bridgewater's time as a building slip on the muddy shore of the river, it was added to, piecemeal, and came to present to the estuary an irregular frontage, which contrasted sharply with the even line of the docks built at a later stage on either side of it. Hence the tide, sweeping along the straight wall of these more recent installations, turned into an eddy opposite the Duke's Dock, and created a shoal which impeded shipping.[1] Two new warehouses were urgently needed, one at Liverpool and the other at Manchester,[2] and others would soon be required at Manchester, Preston Brook, and Broadheath.[3]

To say that the concern was starved of capital is not tantamount to ascribing the defect to Bradshaw's avarice. Much of the explanation lies in the inadequate provisions of the third Duke of Bridgewater's will. By that eccentric testament, the Superintendent was obliged to pay over to the Marquess of Stafford, with some specified amendments the annual net profit of the Trust. There is evidence too that he was sometimes called upon to make considerable exertions to ensure that this payment reached a certain level. In September 1825 the Marquess, anxious to lend Lord Reay £100,000 on his estate in Sutherlandshire, put out a feeler through his agent James Loch to discover how much he was likely to get from the Bridgewater Trustees that year.[4] Two years later Bradshaw wrote to Loch: 'I have contrived by means of the sweepings of the till, squeezing both debtors and creditors a little, and running our bankers harder than I like, to scrape together another £10,000 which you will find at Messrs. Drummonds and Co. to Lord Stafford's credit.'[5] This heavy annual drain may, therefore, have been at the expense even of the ordinary day-to-day maintenance of the Canal.

Certainly there was no proper provision for investment in the further development of the concern. It is true that the Duke's will established an improvement fund of £50,000 for extending the Canal and building wharves and warehouses. This was to be defrayed originally from the Duke of Bridge-

---

[1] J. Loch to Lord F. L. Gower, 17 Sept. 1828, S.E.P.

[2] R. H. Bradshaw to J. Loch, 6 Dec. 1828 ; J. Bradshaw to J. Loch, 13 Dec. 1828, ibid.　　　　　　　　　　[3] J. Bradshaw to J. Loch, 27 Feb. 1833, ibid.

[4] J. Loch to R. H. Bradshaw, 25 Sept. 1825, ibid.

[5] R. H. Bradshaw to J. Loch, 22 Dec. 1827, ibid.

water's personal estate as bequeathed at his death, and Bradshaw was empowered to replace any outlays from the account during the two subsequent decades by withholding up to £4,000 per annum from the profit due to the Marquess of Stafford. He could not, however, spend more than £10,000 per year, or £50,000 in all, on the construction of new canals, and there was no provision at all for replenishing the improvement fund once the initial twenty years had elapsed.[1]

Bradshaw at first made good use of the limited powers he possessed for ploughing back profits into the concern. Every year from 1805 to 1810 he held back £4,000 from the sum paid over to the Marquess of Stafford and invested it, together with the original £50,000, in exchequer bills. During the same period he expended £36,000 on improvements. Most of this went on the extension of the Duke's Dock in Liverpool, but there were also outlays on warehouses and offices at Preston Brook and Castle Quay, and in 1809 £2,450 was used for the purchase of an estate at Farnworth, near Bolton, which was probably needed for the coal underlying it. Within seven years of the Duke's death the amount in the improvement fund had been reduced by almost a quarter.[2] After 1810 the rate of outlay must have slackened, for according to James Loch the fund still contained £40,000 'reduced Consols' in the later 1820s.[3] Perhaps Bradshaw may be blamed a little, therefore, for not investing more of it in the Canal and ancillary works, but it can scarcely be denied that the Duke of Bridgewater's will placed him in a financial straitjacket. He was not even allowed to add the interest on the exchequer bills to the stock. This had to be paid each year to the life tenant along with the rest of the income from the Trust. Moreover, the capital remaining in the fund after 1825 was wholly inadequate to the task which then faced the Trustees of bringing their property into line with current needs. On the lowest estimate the expenditure required over the years 1826–33 was £129,000: £44,000 on warehouses, £35,000 on new locks at Runcorn, and

---

[1] *Will of the Duke of Bridgewater* (printed, London, 1836).

[2] Bridgewater Trust General Accounts, 1790–1810. This information is drawn from the annual accounts for the £50,000 Fund and for 'Purchases and Improvements Other than Annual and Ordinary Repairs'.

[3] J. Loch to Lord F. L. Gower, 17 Sept. 1828, S.E.P.

£50,000 on Duke's Dock, Liverpool[1]. Bradshaw, who was by that
time, at least, much alive to the need for fresh investment in
the Canal works, talked in terms of £150,000 as being required
for 'improvements and conveniences' in December 1824.[2] Nor
could the gap between means and requirements easily be met
by borrowing. The law interposed an obstacle. Properties held
in trust could not be mortgaged without specific authorization in the will of the person establishing the trust or by Act of
Parliament, for in the event of a need for foreclosure there
would be legal difficulties about alienating any portion of
the estates in question. In the Duke of Bridgewater's will,
authority to mortgage was granted only as a means of covering
an annual loss.

The only way in which the financial difficulties of the Trust
could have been cut through was by close co-operation
between the Trustees and the tenant for life. With the support
of the Marquess of Stafford, the former could go to Parliament
for an estate bill, authorizing them to borrow upon mortgage,
with some prospect of success. Alternatively, the beneficiary
of the Trust might himself advance the capital for carrying
out the much needed improvements of the Canal works.
Unfortunately, the Duke of Bridgewater's will had placed
obstacles in the way of such co-operation. By depriving the
life tenant of any say in the management of the Trust, it
diminished *pro tanto* that nobleman's awareness of the needs
of the concern, and also his confidence in investing capital
in it. Moreover, the Marquess of Stafford's enthusiasm for
the long-term improvement of the Canal cannot have been
enhanced by the provision that, upon his death, the income
from the estates would pass to a branch of his family which
no longer bore his name. The law of primogeniture and the
practice of making strict settlements reflected, and encouraged
in the minds of the English aristocracy, a habit of looking
principally to the interests of the eldest son and heir to the
family title.

It is impossible to be certain how close in practice were the
links between Lord Stafford and Robert Haldane Bradshaw,
the undisputed master of the Trust. Certain business connec-

[1] J. Bradshaw to J. Loch, 13 Dec. 1828 and 27 Feb. 1833, S.E.P.
[2] R. H. Bradshaw to J. Loch, 30 Dec. 1824, ibid.

tions existed between them. Bradshaw assisted the Marquess to market the kelp which was produced on the family's Highland estates. This was sold at Liverpool by John Owen, the Trustees' agent there, and the bills of exchange drawn on London, which were received in payment for it, were discounted by the Trustees' bankers. The Marquess's agent had merely to draw the cash in London from Messrs. Praed & Co. of Fleet Street.[1] At first, however, relations were distant. They were cordial rather than intimate, more like the dealings of two friendly businesses than the internal transactions of a single concern. From 1816 onwards they became closer. Bradshaw was invited to visit Lord Stafford in June of that year,[2] and arrangements were made for a return visit to Worsley by Lord Francis Leveson-Gower and James Loch in July.[3] Two years later, Loch, who was the Marquess's agent, was going over the Trust accounts with Bradshaw.[4] Probably the latter's willingness to permit an external interference in the affairs committed to his charge was itself a sign that the problems of management were intensifying and that the Superintendent needed help. The negotiations with the Leeds and Liverpool Canal Company in 1818 for a junction between their waterway and the Leigh branch of the Duke's proved especially difficult. James Loch lent a hand in them and was approached by Bradshaw to support the Bill which the two navigational concerns eventually agreed to promote with all the interest and assistance he could give.[5] The Bill was strenuously opposed, as Bradshaw expected that it would be, by the Manchester, Bolton, and Bury Canal Company and by many coal-owners, merchants, and landowners who felt themselves threatened by it.[6]

It was still a far cry from such limited co-operation to concerted action by the two authorities to cure the waterway of its defects, and, whilst the high profits of the Bradshaw era

[1] R. H. Bradshaw to J. Loch, 29 Aug., 1 Sept., and 31 Oct. 1818, 26 Nov. 1820, ibid.

[2] R. H. Bradshaw to Lord Stafford, 10 June 1816, ibid.

[3] R. H. Bradshaw to J. Loch, 16 July 1816, ibid.

[4] R. H. Bradshaw to J. Loch, 1 Mar. 1818, ibid.

[5] R. H. Bradshaw to J. Loch, 20 Dec. 1818, ibid.

[6] *J.H.C.* lxxiv (1818–19), 334, 337, 382, 422, 442, 446. The opposition came mainly from Leeds, Wigan, Burnley, Bolton, and Bury.

continued unmenaced, the need for drastic action was obscured. In 1821, however, a cloud appeared upon the horizon, at first no bigger than a man's hand, but destined to grow within the next four years until it threatened to blot out the sunlight of prosperity. As it increased, Bradshaw and Loch from their differing viewpoints were obliged to devote some intensive study to the measures they would adopt to protect from ruin the enterprise in which both were interested. The answers which they produced differed considerably, but the differences left some scope for increased collaboration. The twelve years after 1825, when the foundations of the British railway system were being laid, were years of confusion for the Canal, when contemporaries must often have wondered where the Duke's stood in relation to the new force. Out of them came, however, a greater responsibility on the part of the life tenant for the welfare of the navigation, and, in the end, a closing of the gap between financial interest and control.

CHAPTER II

The Break-through of the Railways

DURING the early 1820s dissatisfaction with the canals rose sharply in England, especially in the business communities of great towns and cities like Birmingham, Manchester, and Liverpool. Behind it lay the frustrations resulting from the failure of the waterways, cut mainly in the second half of the eighteenth century, to keep pace with the rapid growth of internal trade which occurred in the early years of the nineteenth. With the industrialization of north-western England and the northern Midlands, timber, foodstuffs, and industrial raw materials poured in through the port of Liverpool in increasing quantities, causing bottlenecks in the system whereby they were conveyed inland. Between 1800 and 1823 the quantity of cotton wool imported in packages grew more than sixfold.[1] Over roughly the same period there was an almost ninefold increase in the importation of Irish wheat and flour into Great Britain, and the intake of oats and oatmeal from the sister isle more than quadrupled.[2] These were trades in which Liverpool, by virtue of her geographical situation, dealt extensively. It is not surprising, therefore, that among the earliest petitions for a bill to construct a railway between Liverpool and Manchester were those from the Dublin corn trade, the Chamber of Commerce of Waterford, the merchants of Cork, and the chambers and associations of Liverpool merchants trading with Brazil, the U.S.A., and the Far East,[3] or that Joseph Sandars, whose fortunes were linked to the grain

---

[1] H. Smithers, *Liverpool, its Commerce, Statistics, and Institutions*, table facing p. 146.

[2] The comparison is between the averages for 1799–1806 and for 1820–7. See *Account of the Quantity of Wheat and of Wheat Meal and Wheat Flour in Quarters and Bushels Imported from Ireland into Great Britain, 1799–1806 and 1820–27*, 1826–7 (123) XVI; B.P.P.

[3] *J.H.C.* lxxx (1825–6), 121, 130.

trade in Liverpool, should have been the foremost protagonist of that scheme.

An important subsidiary factor was the sharp fall occurring in the price of this kind of merchandise, as well as of some manufactured articles, in the years after Waterloo. Raw cotton decreased in value by more than 50 per cent between 1818 and 1822.[1] Wheat prices reached their lowest point since 1798 in the closing months of 1821,[2] those of hardware manufactures produced in the Birmingham area fell by something in the region of 17–20 per cent in the years 1818–24.[3] These reductions no doubt attracted unfavourable attention to the canal charges, even though, in some instances, these were falling too.

What made the discontent especially dangerous to the canals was the fact that the possibility now existed of supplying an alternative outlet for the trade. Until very recently the navigation owners had rested secure in the knowledge that, because they controlled the water supplies of the districts through which their properties passed, they could easily frustrate attempts to construct competing lines of canal. Now, however, as a result of years of careful experimentation with improved rails and superior modes of traction, it had become practicable to build railways which would no longer be mere feeders to canals but might in some cases be employed as substitutes for them. Technologically speaking, railways were still immature. Viewed simply as one form of transport against another, they possessed at the most only marginal advantages over the waterways. For example, the locomotives employed in the collieries at Killingworth and Hetton in Northumberland at the end of 1824 moved at speeds of $3\frac{1}{2}$ or 4 miles per hour, and drew loads of only 48–64 tons. The maximum speed envisaged was 8 miles per hour,[4] and it was by no means certain that these 'travelling engines' would displace horses on the lines that were being planned. Nevertheless, however primitive, railroads did furnish the means of intensifying competition in the transport world, and were appreciably

---

[1] Gayer, Rostow, and Schwartz, op. cit., i. 154, 197.

[2] Ibid., p. 156, n. 4.

[3] A. Briggs, 'Thomas Attwood and the Economic Background of the Birmingham Political Union', *Cambridge Historical Journal*, ix (1947–9).

[4] J. Loch to Lord Gower, 1 Jan. 1825, S.E.P.

less dependent than canals upon favourable weather conditions for their successful running.

Impelled by these considerations, the leading merchants of Liverpool first became seriously interested in constructing a railway to link their city with Manchester in July 1822. The line was to pass through Newton-le-Willows, and the use of steam carriages was contemplated from the outset.[1] William James, a disciple of George Stephenson, completed a survey of the route at the beginning of October, but lack of experience and difficulty in drawing up plans, coupled perhaps with opposition from neighbouring landowners, prevented the Liverpool Committee from making any further progress until late in 1824.[2] A prospectus was then issued on 29 October, and a bill was introduced into Parliament in the February of the following year.[3] By that time the clamour for railways had become widespread and the businessmen of Birmingham had brought forward their own plan for a line joining their town to the port of Liverpool. It was to pass through Wolverhampton and Nantwich, and branches were to be constructed to bring Dudley and Stourbridge in the Black Country, the Staffordshire Potteries, and the collieries and ironworks of Shropshire into the system. A meeting to explain and advertise the scheme was held in Birmingham in September 1824, good local support was evinced, and a company was formed to co-operate with one working from the Liverpool end in constructing the line.[4]

Together these two projects constituted the greatest threat that the Duke of Bridgewater's Canal had had to face since its opening in the later eighteenth century. At the same moment the Trustees found both their east–west trade and the lucrative traffic with the Midlands and south which they exchanged at Preston Brook menaced by competition. If ever a canal had reasons for opposing railways this was such an occasion. Historians of transport have usually assumed that navigation

---

[1] *The Times*, 29 July and 23 Sept. 1822.

[2] H. Pollins, 'The Finances of the Liverpool and Manchester Railway', *Economic History Review*, 2nd ser., v (1952–3).

[3] H. Booth, *An Account of the Liverpool and Manchester Railway*, pp. 11–12; G. S. Veitch, *The Struggle for the Liverpool and Manchester Railway*, p. 45.

[4] C. Gill and A. Briggs, *History of Birmingham*, vol. i, p. 284; Jackman, op. cit., p. 538.

D

owners, actuated by a narrow concern for their immediate economic interests, unreservedly obstructed railroad development with every resource at their command. The opposition of the Bridgewater Trustees to the Liverpool and Manchester line has been cited as a particularly apt example.[1] In reality the position was more complex. The outward façade of resistance concealed important differences of opinion among those principally interested in the Canal as to how far it was proper or practicable merely to oppose railways, and even in the quarters where hostility was at its greatest there was a willingness ultimately to compromise with the enemy that has not been generally recognized by the historian.

The most liberal position was that adopted by James Loch, Principal Agent of the Marquess of Stafford. His background and past experience go far to explain his attitude. Born in 1780, the son of an impecunious Scottish landed proprietor who was shortly afterwards obliged to sell the family estate at Drylaw, Loch sought a living for himself by practising at the Bar, in the department of law which was concerned with conveyancing, and by estate management. His early experience of the latter was gained upon the lands of his uncle, William Adam of Blair Adam, but in 1812 he became Principal Agent to the Marquess of Stafford. This appointment entailed responsibilities of the highest magnitude. The Marquess was, in Greville's phrase, 'a leviathan of wealth'.[2] His properties included, as well as a life interest in the Bridgewater Canal and coal-mines, more than 800,000 acres of the Scottish Highlands, where Loch superintended for him the notorious Sutherland clearances between 1811 and 1820, and a considerable acreage of farmland and mineral wealth round Lilleshall and Donnington in Shropshire and Trentham in Staffordshire.[3] In addition to assuming responsibility for these, Loch took over the management of the estates of the Earl of Carlisle and of the trust estates both the Earl Dudley and of Viscount Keith. If, however, his situation cast him for the role of defender of great vested interests, his upbringing was such as

---

[1] See Jackman, op. cit., pp. 522–3.

[2] C. C. F. Greville, *Journals of the Reigns of King George IV and King William IV*, vol. iii, p. 19.

[3] J. Loch, *An Account of the Improvements on the Estates of the Marquess of Stafford*, pp. 15, 171.

to ensure that he would interpret those rights liberally, at least according to the standards of liberality prevailing at the time. Educated in the University of Edinburgh, he acquired a sympathy with scientific and technological improvement which led him to become a Fellow of the Geological, Statistical, and Zoological Society, a member of the Committee of the Society for the Diffusion of Useful Knowledge, and one of the founders of London University. Politically, too, his affiliations were liberal. Like his employer, the Marquess of Stafford, he was a Whig in party allegiance, and he built up strong friendships with those Whigs who were most in tune with the rising public opinion of the middle classes outside the House of Commons, notably with Henry Brougham. With Brougham, Francis Horner, and Francis Jeffery, he shared membership of the Speculative Society, which flourished at Edinburgh at the end of the eighteenth century, and he was a contributor to the *Edinburgh Review*.[1]

For a man of his outlook it was not easy to oppose outright the projects for railroad construction which were advanced in 1824, even though those plans struck at the heart of the interests which he was commissioned to protect. There was the strong evidence of public demand. There were the irresistible arguments of the railway pamphleteers, Joseph Sandars of Liverpool and Joseph Parkes of Birmingham, who attacked the canals in the name of freedom of trade against monopoly. Pleading for a line of communication by rail between Birmingham and Liverpool in 1825, Parkes invoked the 'luminous works' of Turgot, Adam Smith, Bentham, Say, Ricardo, Mill, McCulloch, and Torrens, to prove 'that there is no exception to the great principle of free trade'.[2] Loch could hardly be indifferent to these arguments, when he had himself delivered, in 1804, in a review of a book by a certain Dr. Tennant, a forthright attack on the East India Company's monopoly based on the principles enumerated in 'The Wealth of Nations'.[3] Moreover, his friends were deeply committed to the

---

[1] These biographical details of James Loch are drawn from *Brougham and His Early Friends: Letters to James Loch, 1798–1809*, collected and arranged by R. H. M. Buddle Atkinson and G. A. Jackson; and from Gordon Loch, *The Family of Loch*, pp. 243–9.

[2] J. K. Buckley, *Joseph Parkes of Birmingham*, pp. 28, 30.

[3] *Edinburgh Review*, 5th ser., iv (Apr.–July 1804), pp. 303–29. For proof of

railway. Brougham's younger brother, William, and Loch's own kinsman, Adam, were counsel for the first Liverpool and Manchester Bill in 1825, and Brougham, himself, lent the measure his support.[1] 'I find all my friends railway mad', Loch wrote to Bradshaw in December 1824.[2]

Not only conviction and affinity but a prudent concern for the interests which he had to defend offered inducements to a compromise. The tone of the agitation as it was conducted in Liverpool and Birmingham was exceedingly virulent, and threatened to snatch from the canals their last shred of reputation. Strongly worded denunciations of 'the most arbitrary exactions' and 'exorbitant charges of the water carriers' figured prominently in the first prospectus of the Liverpool and Manchester Railway.[3] Nor was it only the good name of the canals as such that was at stake. Owing to the interest in canals possessed by noblemen like the Marquess of Stafford, Lord Harrowby, and Lord Clive, and to the opposition to railways encountered from those like Lord Derby and Lord Sefton, whose estates would be bisected by the proposed lines, an element of class feeling had been imported into the struggle. On 26 December 1824 James Abercromby, auditor of the Duke of Devonshire's estates, advised Loch to oppose 'with as little appearance of violence as possible'. He added by way of explanation:

I think that in the situation in which you stand, you can scarcely fail to see that the conflict between canals and railways is also a conflict between two classes of society, and that the middling (and lower orders probably) will take part with the merchants and manufacturers who are opposed to the grandees. Lord Gower speaks very simply and truly when he says to Mr. Spooner, can you wonder that Lord Francis should oppose railways? But, there, I ask you, is it wonderful if Mr. Spooner should walk away saying to himself, 'Well, after all, when self is concerned, there is no difference between a marquis [*sic*] and a merchant'? It may be, too, that this feeling is quickened by a recollection of the thousand, unguarded things which have been uttered against merchants and

the authorship of this article see Buddle Atkinson and Jackson, op. cit. ii. 143–6.

[1] Veitch, op. cit., pp. 46–51.
[2] J. Loch to R. H. Bradshaw, 26 Dec. 1824, S.E.P.
[3] Booth, op. cit., pp. 11–12.

manufacturers. Why should there be any run against Baring, as not being entitled to be interested to an amount of his supposed interests, if these doctrines are to be acted upon by a large body of the aristocracy in perhaps the only question, corn excepted, where they, according to their own reasoning, think they have an especial and peculiar interest.[1]

Abercromby's impressions are confirmed, as he claimed they were, by the language of Sandars's pamphlet in support of the Liverpool and Manchester line, which referred to the charges levied on the Bridgewater Canal as the exactions of 'His Grace', as though the third Duke of Bridgewater was still alive. The writer added:

It may be very pleasant for noblemen to exclude from the precincts of their domains the industrious classes of society. They may derive a morning's entertainment from visiting a manufacturing or sea port town, as they would from a view on the Lakes, or from inspecting a community of bees in a glass hive; but these feelings and these times, are fast wearing away. . . . Where the general good is concerned, society knows nothing of privileged classes.[2]

For a variety of reasons, therefore, Loch had become convinced, several days before the end of December 1824, that there was a general demand for additional means of transport which must be met in some way or other. Accordingly he began to prepare the minds of Bradshaw and Lord Stafford's family for concession. For the moment he hesitated between two solutions. One was the plan of the Birmingham Canal Company to placate the demand for a railway between Birmingham and Liverpool by providing a shorter and less heavily locked canal route than the existing one via the Staffordshire and Worcestershire, Grand Trunk, and Bridgewater canals. This would involve making a new cut, to be known as the Birmingham and Liverpool Junction Canal, from

---

[1] J(ames) A(bercromby) to James Loch, 26 Dec. 1824. This letter, wrongly ascribed to James Nasmyth from a misreading of the initials with which it is signed, appears in a file of 'Fourteen Letters from James Nasmyth to James and George Loch, 1824–60' at the Library of the Patent Office. 'Spooner' is presumably Richard Spooner the Birmingham banker, a partner of Thomas Attwood. Attwood, Spooner & Co. were treasurers for the revived Liverpool and Birmingham Railway project in 1830. See Gill and Briggs, op. cit. i. 284.

[2] J. Sandars, *A Letter on the Subject of the Projected Railroad between Liverpool and Manchester* . . ., 3rd edn.

Autherley near Wolverhampton on the Staffordshire and Worcestershire to Nantwich, which was already connected with Ellesmere Port on the Mersey estuary by the Ellesmere and Chester Canal. The promoters proposed to buy off expected opposition from the Duke's Trustees, the Grand Trunk, and the Staffordshire and Worcestershire companies by reserving shares in the new undertaking for the two companies and the Stafford family. Propounding the scheme to James Loch in a personal encounter on 26 December, Thomas Telford, engineering adviser to the Birmingham Canal Company, also mentioned that his old employers, the Ellesmere and Chester Canal Company, were about to approach the Trustees and the Grand Trunk Company for permission to construct a branch from Wardle Green, a few miles North of Nantwich, to the Trent and Mersey Canal near Middlewich. Such consent was necessary owing to a clause in the Chester Canal Act of 1777 which forbade the carrying of a Middlewich branch of the canal within a hundred yards of the Grand Trunk. The Canal Duke and the proprietors of the Trunk had strenuously opposed the making of this branch, on the grounds that the canal trade from Birmingham to Liverpool might be syphoned off the Trent and Mersey Canal at Middlewich and diverted to Chester by the Chester Canal. Now, however, the Ellesmere people were striving to persuade the Trustees that, if it was cut, they would gain a traffic in grain from Chester and Shropshire to Manchester which would be handed to them through the junction at Middlewich.[1]

Loch was by no means convinced that the proposal of the Birmingham Canal Company provided a satisfactory solution for the dilemma of the canals. Using the contacts in Northumberland which his position as agent to the Earl of Carlisle afforded him, he turned his attention in the opening days of 1825 to exploring honestly and conscientiously the capacity of the steam locomotives which were in use in the collieries of Killingworth and Hetton. The information which he gleaned from the Morpeth agent strengthened his suspicions that in the last resort it might prove impossible to deflect the public from railways by any extension of the canal system that might be conceived. This was not merely

[1] J. Loch to R. H. Bradshaw, 26 Dec. 1824, S.E.P.

because of the technical superiority of the locomotive, which was still in doubt, but also because, as he told Lord Gower, whereas the proposed new canal was to be 'executed by the existing monopolists for the purpose of continuing the advantage they now enjoy', the railway was 'supported by a new set of adventurers whose interest it must be to carry as cheap as possible'.[1]

Nevertheless, the issue of the struggle for supremacy between water and rail was sufficiently uncertain to make it worth while to give the Birmingham and Liverpool Junction Canal project a trial, and Loch, realizing this, submitted Telford's proposals to Robert Haldane Bradshaw, who was the recognized authority in matters affecting the Duke's Canal. Bradshaw's response was not encouraging. He poohpoohed the idea of Lord Stafford's investing in the Junction Canal, suggesting that the Marquess might more profitably lay out the £150,000 which Telford said he required in some much needed improvements on the Bridgewater Canal. A close perusal of his letter prompts the conclusion that deep in his mind Bradshaw too perceived the need to come to terms with the proposal, and that he was merely manoeuvring for a position of strength from which to bargain.[2] This is confirmed by subsequent events, for at a meeting in Telford's house on 17 June 1825 he assented to the Birmingham and Liverpool cut on condition that the Middlewich branch of the Ellesmere and Chester Canal was made as well. Accordingly Lord Stafford bought 200 shares in the former, which was constructed between 1827 and 1835. Bradshaw believed that the Trustees would be compensated for any loss of Birmingham trade by gaining the carriage to Manchester of the produce of the whole of North Wales and Shropshire.[3] As events transpired, they were to be largely cheated of the fruits of this arrangement by the short-sightedness of the Grand Trunk Canal Company which, in the supposed interest of the trade passing the whole length of its line, obstructed all

---

[1] J. Loch to Lord Gower, 1 Jan. 1825, ibid.

[2] R. H. Bradshaw to J. Loch, 30 Dec. 1824, ibid.

[3] J. Loch to A. Macdonald, 18 June 1825; R. H. Bradshaw to J. Loch, 14 Nov. 1825; J. Loch to Eyre Lee, 7 July 1825, ibid. For the dates of construction of the Birmingham and Liverpool Junction Canal see L. T. C. Rolt, *Thomas Telford*, xi, *passim*.

attempts to feed into it at Middlewich. At first, in November 1825, the company refused permission altogether for the junction at Middlewich to be made.[1] When, on the authority of an Act of Parliament passed two years later, the Middlewich branch was actually constructed, being opened in 1833, the Grand Trunk blocked the egress from it at Middlewich with a heavy bar toll.[2]

In another respect the Trustees, in common with the generality of canal proprietors between Birmingham and Liverpool, had greater cause for rejoicing. The Birmingham and Liverpool railway project which they had been endeavouring to avert failed to materialize. In August 1826 its promoters abandoned it for the time being in favour of a shorter line between Birmingham and Wolverhampton. Frustrated by the opposition of vested interests, and by the failure of the Liverpool men to support it keenly enough, the main proposal slumbered for another three years, to be revived only towards the end of 1829.[3]

The same was not true of the twin railway project, that for a line between Liverpool and Manchester, which was being doggedly pushed by a group of Liverpool merchants against stalwart opposition. Unlike the Birmingham line, this was not countered by any proposals for extending the canal network. A few minor initiatives were taken towards improving the efficiency of carriage on the Bridgewater Canal. Bradshaw let it be known that he was ready to let or sell land at Manchester for the building of warehouses with a view to encouraging new carrying firms to settle on the navigation, but the response was disappointing.[4] He also discussed with Loch and the Marquess of Stafford the possibility of introducing a new method of propulsion, William Burk's 'artificial fish's tail'. The tone of his letter to Loch suggested willingness to try the experiment but no tremendous sense of urgency.[5] The main response of the Trustees to the threat to their trade between Liverpool and Manchester was that of obstruction.

[1] J. Loch to Eyre Lee, 17 Nov. 1825, S.E.P.
[2] See below, p. 127; for date of opening of the Middlewich branch see Hadfield, *The Canals of the West Midlands*, p. 181.
[3] Jackman, op. cit., pp. 538–40.
[4] J. Bradshaw to J. Loch, 13 Oct. 1825, S.E.P.
[5] R. H. Bradshaw to J. Loch, 2 July 1825, ibid.

Bradshaw displayed an unqualified hostility towards the railway as towards almost every innovation. He had none of Loch's scruples as to opposing the public demand. Less able than Loch to see, or at least to sympathize with, his opponent's point of view, he pressed the advantage of the Duke's Canal as he himself conceived it, with single-minded enthusiasm. As is well known, he placed every obstacle in the way of the railway surveyors as they went to work in the autumn of 1824. He forbade them to come upon his lands, and fired guns in his grounds at night to prevent them from advancing unobserved.[1] His distaste was shared by Lord Francis Leveson-Gower, the second son of the Marquess of Stafford, who, as he was destined to inherit the Bridgewater income on his father's death, had the chief financial interest in the future of the Canal. He wrote to James Loch on 26 September 1824:

You will be glad to hear that Lady F(rancis) was safely delivered of a boy yesterday, and that both are as well as possible. As if to counterpoise this event, I have just received a letter from the Birmingham and Liverpool Rail Road Company requesting my support. I had some thoughts of forwarding them a statement of the event of yesterday and a request for theirs.[2]

When, therefore, the railway Bill came before Parliament, the Trustees petitioned against it, and helped to procure its overthrow in committee in June 1825.[3] Their attitude was not, however, as unyielding as it has often been represented. After the initial setback in the House of Commons the Liverpool railway promoters began to prepare for a second attempt to gain their Bill. Sensibly they took steps to soften the opposition. They planned to construct a tunnel which would avert their having to interrupt streets in Liverpool; they abandoned their proposal to cross the River Irwell into Manchester, agreeing instead to terminate in Salford; they modified their route so as to avoid interfering with the property of great landowners like Lord Derby and Lord Sefton.[4] When their second prospectus came out on 26

[1] J. S. Jeans, *Jubilee Memorial of the Railway System*, pp. 55–6.

[2] Lord F. Leveson-Gower to J. Loch, 26 Sept. 1824, S.E.P.

[3] *J.H.C.* lxxx (1825–6), 236 and *passim*.

[4] Booth, op. cit., pp. 25–6; J. Moss to W. Huskisson, 26 Nov. 1825, Liverpool Parliamentary Office Manuscripts, 1792–1836.

December 1825, it omitted the language offensive to the canals which had characterized their first. 'In regard to the existing means of conveyance,' it proclaimed, 'the Committee are desirous to state that they are actuated by no hostile feeling to their interest and property.'[1]

Once the hand of conciliation had been shown, Bradshaw moderated his hostility to the measure. He wrote to Loch on 27 September 1825:

> The Manchester and Liverpool railroaders are certainly going to Parliament again next session. Their existing surveyor has just been here to show me their new plans, etc., and ask permission to go over our lands; to which (you will scarcely believe it) I have consented; but the man behaved so fairly and openly that I really could not refuse; am I not a Liberal? Their new line is certainly a better one and much less objectionable than their former. They avoid Lord Sefton entirely and Lord Derby as much as possible. They do not cross the River Irwell at all, but terminate in our land in Salford, and they profess their great object to be the getting over our canal (which they must cross) with the least possible injury or inconvenience to us.[2]

The words 'in our land' were underlined by Bradshaw, probably to indicate the advantage the Trustees hoped to gain by selling or leasing land to the railway company.

It was still not clear how far Bradshaw was prepared to go in meeting the railway promoters, whether, for example, he would not oppose them when they again came before Parliament. Financial considerations might well have prompted such restraint, if nothing else had. The Trustees had already spent little short of £10,000 on the railroad fight. Owing to their having extended lengthy credits, they found themselves unusually short of cash, at a time when the life tenant was making clear his desire to have as large and as prompt a payment of his income from the Trust as possible,[2] in order that he might lend Lord Reay £100,000 on his estate in Sutherland.[3] What rendered certain a withdrawal of the Trustees' opposition was the decision, taken by the Marquess of Stafford late in December 1825, to buy into the Liverpool and Man-

---

[1] Booth, op. cit., p. 28.
[2] R. H. Bradshaw to J. Loch, 27 Sept. 1825, S.E.P.
[3] J. Loch to R. H. Bradshaw, 25 Sept. 1825, ibid.

chester Railway to the amount of £100,000, one fifth of the required railway capital.

The taking of this step is not easy to explain, for the Marquess was the beneficiary of the Bridgewater Canal, the revenues of which would probably be damaged by competition from the railway. Bradshaw, who suspected a *rapprochement* between Lord Stafford and the railway people twelve months before it actually occurred, suggested as a motive that the Marquess wished to damage the late Duke of Bridgewater's concerns in order to ensure that his second son, Lord Francis, did not enjoy a higher income than his eldest son, Lord Gower.[1] This seems improbable, for there is evidence that Lord Stafford originally planned to give Lord Francis the option of purchasing the railway shares upon his death.[2] It may be true that the knowledge that the income from the Trust estates would pass from the hands of the main line of the Leveson-Gower family when he died caused the Marquess to be less solicitous for the interests of the Duke of Bridgewater's Canal than he would otherwise have been, but this can have been no more than a permissive factor and not the spur to action. Nor can the explanation be found, as has been suggested more recently,[3] in a hostility between Loch, the Marquess of Stafford's adviser, and Bradshaw, the Superintendent of the Canal, for the Sutherland Estate Papers show that the relations between the two were very cordial, and that each relied upon the other for assistance in difficult business transactions. Some weight may be attached perhaps to the attractiveness of the purchase. The Liverpool railway promoters were so anxious to enlist the Marquess on their side that they offered him the shares at the prime cost, which, according to Mrs. Arbuthnot, was only a half of what they were really worth.[4]

It may be doubted, however, whether the answer to the riddle is wholly or even mainly to be found in any such simple economic motive. There was too much at stake upon the other side, and the Marquess of Stafford was not over anxious to

[1] R. H. Bradshaw to J. Loch, 25 Dec. 1824, ibid.

[2] J. Loch to Lord Stafford, 18 Jan. 1826, ibid.

[3] Pollins, op. cit.

[4] F. Bamford and Duke of Wellington (eds.), *The Journal of Mrs. Arbuthnot, 1820–32*, vol. ii, p. 388.

conclude. As Loch afterwards explained to Vernon-Harcourt, Archbishop of York, who was one of the Trustees, 'this decision was come to after the most mature deliberation'. What had tipped the scale was the intervention of William Huskisson, who had talked round not only the Marquess but his second son, Lord Francis.[1] 'I have been so idle with all my boys that I omitted to say that Huskisson's opinion was so much in favour of compromise that it was agreed to', Loch told Lord Gower on 29 December 1825.[2] Some credit must be given, however, to Loch himself, who had been preparing the minds of Lord Stafford and Lord Gower for a possible future compromise with the railways some twelve months earlier,[3] and who had been the medium through which the railway negotiators, Lawrence, Moss, and Robert Gladstone, had been brought into touch with the Marquess.[4]

The motives underlying Huskisson's decisive intervention and the reasons for its effectiveness were more personal and political than economic. Huskisson had been a close friend of Lord Stafford since the days of the French Revolution, when the Marquess had been ambassador from the Court of England to the French government, and the future President of the Board of Trade, then a young medical student in Paris, had become his secretary. He later accompanied the ambassador back to England and resided in his house in Wimbledon.[5] His support of the railway between Liverpool and Manchester stemmed largely from his position as Member of Parliament for Liverpool.

Called upon, as I have been, by most of the commercial associations of Liverpool to present petitions to Parliament in favour of the Manchester and Liverpool railway, [he wrote], and being satisfied by the evidence which has been laid before me that, in some shape, additional accommodation is wanted for the purpose of ensuring, and if possible with diminished expense, more regularity and dispatch in the immense and still increasing traffic between these two towns, I feel it incumbent upon me, as member for Liverpool,

---

[1] J. Loch to the Archbishop of York, 29 Dec. 1825, S.E.P.
[2] J. Loch to Lord Gower, 29 Dec. 1825, ibid.
[3] J. Loch to Lord Gower, 1 Jan. 1825, ibid.
[4] Veitch, op. cit., p. 51.
[5] J. Loch, *Memoir of George Granville, Late Duke of Sutherland*, pp. 8–9.

to support any plan brought forward by my constituents for the purpose of conferring these advantages upon their trade.[1]

No doubt also, though he protested that his adhesion was given in his capacity as parliamentary representative of the great Lancashire seaport only, his determination to uphold the railway promoters was strengthened by the fact that the government in which he served was bidding, from about 1820 onwards, for the allegiance of the mercantile interests in the country to counterbalance a revolt of the agriculturalists against it.[2]

Once the deal in the railway shares had been clinched, the Bridgewater opposition which had proved so damaging to the first Liverpool and Manchester Railway Bill collapsed. A second Bill was brought forward early in 1826, and in that session it passed both Houses. This time the Duke of Bridgewater's Trustees did not petition against it. Whatever his personal feelings, Bradshaw would have found it difficult to order a formal opposition to a measure which was so fully supported by the life tenant of the Trust estates. He might even have found it impossible, as the other two Trustees, Sir Archibald Macdonald and the Archbishop of York, whose signatures would be required to any petition submitted by the Trust, were brothers-in-law of the Marquess of Stafford, and were kept carefully informed by Loch of all that passed.

One cannot be certain what Bradshaw's immediate reaction was. His son, Captain James Bradshaw, convinced an agent of the Mersey and Irwell Navigation Company at the beginning of January 1826 that the arrangement between Lord Stafford and the Railway Committee 'had been entered into contrary to Mr. Bradshaw's advice and opinion and in direct opposition to his feelings and that it would have the effect of making him a more strenuous opponent of the measure'.[3] His statement may have been made, however, merely with a view to assuaging the wrath of a deserted ally, for the Old Quay Company and the Trustees had previously been leagued in opposition

---

[1] Draft of letter by William Huskisson, 18 Feb. 1825, Huskisson Papers, British Museum, Add. MS. 38746.

[2] W. R. Brock, *Lord Liverpool and Liberal Toryism, 1820 to 1827*, ch. vi, *passim*.

[3] M. & I.N.C. Order Book, 1821–8, p. 142.

to the railway. What we do know is that steps were promptly taken to soften the blow to the irascible Superintendent of the Trust and to reassure the life tenant to be, Lord Francis Leveson-Gower, as to the future welfare of his inheritance. At the time that he decided to invest £100,000 in the Liverpool and Manchester Railway, Lord Stafford agreed to advance £40,000 towards the improvement of the Canal. The outlay seems to have been made somewhat grudgingly, for in the arrangements for the future which he started to make immediately after the purchase of the railway shares, the Marquess insisted that upon his death his second son, Lord Francis, should pay back to his executors so much of the £40,000 as had already been laid out upon the Canal, as a condition of inheriting the railway shares.[1] Nevertheless, it went some of the way towards meeting the suggestion which Bradshaw had made to Loch twelve months earlier, that £150,000 should be spent on the Duke's Canal to strengthen its competing power.[2] Yet another gesture was made towards the Canal. Under the terms of the agreement with the Railway Committee, Lord Stafford had received the power to nominate three directors, one fifth of the Liverpool and Manchester Railway Board. Two of these seats were given to persons intimately connected with the management of the Bridgewater Canal–Bradshaw's son and deputy, James, and James Sothern, who was later to succeed the elder Bradshaw as Superintendent.[3] All the indications are that the olive branch was accepted. The younger Bradshaw took his place on the Railway Board,[4] and his father became sufficiently reconciled to the railroad by the autumn of 1826 to be desirous of obtaining the contract for cutting the tunnel at Liverpool.[5] It seems probable, therefore, that although R. H. Bradshaw did not exactly like the outcome of the battle with the railway promoters, he determined, in a businesslike manner, to make the best of a bad job.

[1] J. Loch to Lord Stafford, 18 Jan. 1826, S.E.P.

[2] See above, p. 35.

[3] C. F. Dendy Marshall, *Centenary History of the Liverpool and Manchester Railway*, p. 14.

[4] He attended a meeting of the directors on 19 June 1826. J. Bradshaw to J. Loch, 24 June 1826, S.E.P.

[5] J. Bradshaw to J. Loch, 10 Oct. 1826, ibid. See below, p. 49.

The opening round in the fight between rail and water had ended in compromise, but it was for the future to reveal what the real substance of the agreement was. There were those who believed that it was mainly a victory for the Canal, which had taken the new leviathan of steam and iron for a servant. J. B. Hollinshead, a critic of the railway party in the Liverpool Corporation, expressed the view that 'the public, by this "monstrous coalition" between land and water carriage, the Duke's Canal and the railroad, would be worse off than ever'. 'For a time', he remarked, 'like the effect produced by opposition coaches, the rates of carriage might, indeed, be reduced, but only afterwards to be raised again.'[1] On the other hand, there were the undisputed facts that a new line of communication directly competitive with the Bridgewater Canal had been opened between Liverpool and Manchester, and that the prime beneficiary of the navigation had been given a counterbalancing interest in the prosperity of the railway. For the outcome, much would depend on how the Marquess of Stafford and his advisers interpreted their interests, much also on the still undecided question of the extent to which railways as such could outclass waterways in speed and cheapness of carriage. In the unfolding of an answer to these problems lies much of the interest of rail–water relationships in north-west England in the years when the railways were being built and opened to traffic.

[1] *Liverpool Mercury*, 6 Jan. 1826.

CHAPTER III

The Rival Springs to Life

ALTHOUGH the passing of the Liverpool and Manchester Railway Bill made it appear reasonably certain that the Duke of Bridgewater's Trustees would have to share their traffic with a rival, the parliamentary victory did not of itself determine how formidable the rival would be. That would depend on the ingenuity, as yet incompletely revealed, of engineers like Stephenson. It would depend also upon the decisions of hardheaded business men sitting round the table of a board room in Liverpool or Manchester, men like Charles Lawrence, Joseph Sandars, and John Moss, who had fought and intrigued to prevent their offspring from being strangled at birth and now looked forward to nursing it through childhood and adolescence to a sturdy manhood. When the directors assembled for business towards the beginning of June 1826, many of the most vital questions affecting the success of the undertaking awaited an answer. Who were to be the engineers entrusted with the pioneer work of tunnelling under the town of Liverpool for a mile and a half's length or traversing the 'impossible' Chat Moss? What form of traction was to be adopted upon the line? The case for the locomotive, though powerfully pleaded by George Stephenson, was not as yet irrefutable, and the stationary engine and even the old-fashioned horse found advocates among the directors. Even the route to be followed was as yet not absolutely fixed, especially at the extremities, for it was unlikely that the company would rest long content with an Act of Parliament which made them terminate at Salford and forbade them to cross the river into Manchester. In short, the situation remained fluid, and there were ways in which the Bridgewater Trustees and the Marquess of Stafford, armed with a representation on the railway board, could have influenced events to the advantage of the Canal and the associated coal-mines had they been so minded.

In fact they made little attempt to do so. The directors appointed by the Marquess of Stafford were in no sense an organized party within the board. More often than not they were absent from its meetings. James Sothern never qualified as a director.[1] This was probably his way of showing contemptuous hostility towards the new concern. Captain Bradshaw attended board meetings quite regularly at first, but felt uncomfortable in the double capacity of Railway director and Deputy Superintendent of the Duke's Canal. An honest and scrupulous though rather unstable character, he 'felt hampered in his exertions in favour of the Canal from having some knowledge of what were the views and objects of the Railway Directors'.[2] With the increase in his Canal commitments consequent upon the commencement of new works at Runcorn and upon the deterioration of his father's health, his attendances soon began to fall away.[3] Loch, too, appears to have been a perpetual absentee, treating with the board from a distance through fellow directors such as John Moss and Captain Bradshaw. Towards the beginning of December 1828 Moss communicated to Loch the expressed wish of certain members of the Railway Board that a director should be appointed in Lord Stafford's interest who could attend their meetings, and it was only then, more than two and a half years after the company had been established, that the useless Sothern was replaced by Currie, one of Loch's Liverpool friends.[4]

Furthermore, even when attending to railroad business, these Stafford directors displayed little inclination to exploit their position in favour of the Bridgewater Canal. They never allowed themselves to forget that the interest which they represented on the Board was not a canal interest but the

[1] J. Loch to Lord Stafford, 1 Dec. 1828, S.E.P.

[2] J. Loch to W. W. Currie, 30 Sept. 1831, ibid.

[3] In August 1826 he told Loch that he had been absent from the two last meetings of the Railway Board, on account of his father's visit to Runcorn to inspect the works in progress there. J. Bradshaw to J. Loch, 20 Aug. 1826, ibid.

[4] J. Loch to R. H. Bradshaw, 2 and 16 Dec. 1828 ; J. Loch to Lord Stafford, 1 Dec. 1828, ibid.

interest of Lord Stafford and his family in the railway. It is true that they could never entirely rid their minds of the remembrance that the Marquess was also the beneficiary of the Canal and that his second son, for whom Loch must provide a livelihood, would be largely dependent upon the Trust properties for an income when his father died. As railway directors, however, they relegated this consideration to a place of secondary importance. Caught on the horns of the evangelical dilemma of serving two masters, or rather one master with two conflicting interests, they reacted by having recourse in the main to the New Testament precept of not letting the right hand know what the left hand was doing. In a letter to Currie written in 1831 Loch made clear the limits of his willingness to employ his railway influence on behalf of the Canal. These were exceedingly narrow and in matters relating to the internal affairs of the Liverpool and Manchester company they allowed almost no scope at all:

My opinion is, that our duty is to promote the objects of the railway without any reference to any other concern whatever— by that I don't mean to say that if the matter under discussion is one of little moment to it and might in its effect be very injurious to the Duke's Canal that I would not then endeavour to get such a measure put aside—nor do I mean that when the interests of two third parties are concerned that I would not greatly prefer the interest of that concern—nor would I lastly be the person to suggest or promote any scheme which would be decidedly injurious to the Canal though beneficial to us. So far I would abstain, but beyond this our duty is to consider and forward every measure that is submitted to our consideration for the benefit of the Railway. . . . We are not only, therefore, not bound to communicate privately to Mr. Bradshaw what we learn confidentially as Directors, but we are as much restrained from doing so as he refrains and properly and fitly refrains from communicating to me his views and sentiments, and when he does, I consider that as confidential and not as what I may state to my brother directors.[1]

He stated explicitly that this had also been Captain Bradshaw's view when he had been a director. Bradshaw had by that time relinquished his seat on the Board, in favour of Gilbert Winter, one of his father's cronies, and the veracity

[1] J. Loch to W. W. Currie, 30 Sept. 1831, S.E.P.

of Loch's assertion is confirmed by the fact that the elder Bradshaw rejoiced at the change, saying, according to Currie, that 'now he should always learn the truth as to our (Liverpool and Manchester) motions'.[1]

Bent on promoting Lord Stafford's interests as a shareholder in the company, James Loch and James Bradshaw participated a good deal in the early deliberations of the directors of the Liverpool and Manchester Railway concerning the manner of financing the early constructional work and the appointment of engineers to superintend it. Anxious to begin building their line as soon as possible and finding difficulty in borrowing money in the monetary stringency which followed the financial crisis of 1825, the Liverpool directors applied to the Exchequer Loan Office for the loan of £200,000. Bradshaw dissented from this proceeding and wrote earnestly to Loch explaining the grounds of his objection. He felt that it was against the Marquess of Stafford's interests to raise the money by any other means than a reasonable call on the shareholders, as in the event of the failure of the concern, which he considered by no means unlikely, the Marquess might be saddled, as one of the few subscribers able to pay, with heavy and awkward responsibilities. Events were to decide the issue in favour of Bradshaw's preference, for the Exchequer Loan Office demurred at making the loan on the grounds that the undertaking was private, not public, and the board had to order a call of £11 per share on the subscribers.[2]

Next came the question of the engineers. The first thought of the directors was to offer the posts of engineers in chief to the Company to George and John Rennie, who had conducted the survey preparatory to their second and successful application to Parliament. Before the appointment had been made, however, the Board quarrelled with the Rennie brothers over the appointment of a resident engineer which the latter wished to retain in their own gift, untrammelled by interference from the board room, and at a meeting on 19 June 1826 Josias Jessop was appointed consultant engineer in Rennie's stead.[3] A minority of the directors, however, had

[1] W. W. Currie to J. Loch, 10 Sept. 1831, ibid.
[2] J. Bradshaw to J. Loch, 17 and 24 June 1826, ibid.
[3] L. T. C. Rolt, *George and Robert Stephenson: the Railway Revolution*, p. 114.

upheld Rennie and this had included Captain Bradshaw, who doubted the competence of the Board to interfere in matters of a technical character. He attended the meeting and expressed regret 'that so improvident a course should have been taken', stating that he washed his hands of its consequences.[1] A great deal turned on this decision, for the Rennies were opposed to appointing George Stephenson to act under them, and had they had their way the Liverpool and Manchester Company would have lost the services of the genius who was to subdue the intractable Chat Moss and demonstrate the invincibility of the locomotive. The Stafford influence continued to work against Stephenson after he had been appointed operative (or local) engineer to act under Jessop's direction. Captain Bradshaw disliked him, claiming that he had been discharged from his previous employment with the Company for his faults.[1] James Loch, too, viewed him with no unmixed admiration. When Booth consulted him as to Stephenson's capacity and understanding displayed in the construction of a railway on the Earl of Carlisle's estate in Cumberland, Loch replied that 'as Mr. Thompson, Lord Carlisle's agent had taken the levels and had superintended the execution of His Lordship's Railway, I could not ascribe the whole merit of that work to Mr. S.'.[2]

Stephenson flourished without Loch's support. By February 1827 he had gained complete engineering control of the Liverpool and Manchester Railway, and together with his son Robert he began to prepare the way for the ascendancy of the locomotive upon that line once it was completed. To achieve this he was obliged to do battle with a number of the directors who advocated other modes of traction.[3] James Loch was among them. In October 1826, having inspected the Stockton and Darlington line, he reported to Henry Booth through Captain Bradshaw in a sense favourable to horses rather than locomotives for passenger transport. He had been impressed by the sight of carriages for thirty or forty people drawn each by a single horse for a distance of twelve miles in an hour and thirty-five minutes. In fairness to Loch it should be stated

[1] J. Bradshaw to J. Loch, 24 June 1826, S.E.P.
[2] J. Loch to J. Bradshaw, 5 Sept. 1826, ibid.
[3] Rolt, op. cit., ch. viii, *passim*.

that the locomotives which he also witnessed travelled at only 5½ miles per hour, and that his report showed other features of unusual perspicacity. Among them was the realization of the immense profit which passenger traffic would one day bring to the railways and an appreciation of the problems of traffic control. Noting the delays on the Stockton and Darlington line from the inability of carriages to overtake, he suggested as a remedy that there should be four parallel tracks upon a line of railway, two for the quicker and two for the slower carriages.[1] The potentiality of locomotives, however, he could not recognize. Two years later, in August 1828, he was arguing the case with Booth for stationary engines against steam locomotives 'where the distances are not great and no passengers are to be carried'.[2] Even after the *Rocket* had made a speed of 25 or 30 miles per hour at the Rainhill trials of 1829, he could still see no necessity for the Liverpool and Manchester Railway's committing itself to the device.[3]

The influence exerted upon railway policy by the Marquess of Stafford's directors was for the most part, therefore, unbeneficial. It was, nevertheless, disinterested. There are no serious grounds for believing that Loch and Bradshaw adhered to a policy which was to prove unprogressive in the hope of holding back the railway for the sake of the canal. When it came to a matter where the interests of the Bridgewater Trustees were more immediately involved, they were strangely slow to seize the opportunity. Shortly after work had commenced on the construction of the line in the late summer of 1826, R. H. Bradshaw expressed a desire to obtain the contract for cutting the tunnel at the Liverpool end 'in order to keep his colliery miners and other men in employ (everything being very dull here)', as his son explained. The job, however, was advertised in lots. Captain Bradshaw contented himself with reporting this disinterestedly to Loch as a piece of railway news.[4] His letter displays no sign that he had exerted himself on his father's behalf or that he wished to persuade Loch to do so.

---

[1] J. Loch to J. Bradshaw, 12 Oct. 1826, S.E.P.
[2] J. Loch to H. Booth, 2 Aug. 1828, ibid.
[3] J. Loch to W. W. Currie, 4 Nov. 1829, ibid.
[4] J. Bradshaw to J. Loch, 10 Oct. 1826, ibid.

No doubt it was commendable to avoid jobbery, but impartiality was sometimes carried to absurd lengths. Lord
Stafford's nominees were slow to employ their position as
railroad directors to avert foreseeable clashes between the
railway and the canal. This was made evident by what happened when the Liverpool and Manchester Company sought
an entry into Manchester. By the original Act of Parliament
passed in 1826 the eastern terminal of their line was to be in
Irwell Street, Salford, where it would be separated from the
centre of Manchester by the River Irwell. This arrangement,
made with a view to assuaging the opposition of the Duke of
Bridgewater's Trustees, carried disadvantages for the company. Irwell Street and the New Bailey Bridge across the
river were both too narrow to afford a satisfactory access to
the station from the town. Moreover, most of the factories
were on the Manchester side of the river, owing to the fact that
the canals were there, and if the railway line was to end in
relative isolation in Salford, the waterways would have a
decided edge upon it in terminal facilities.[1] It was not to be
expected that the Company would remain content with such
a handicap, and sure enough, about the beginning of 1828,
whilst their line was still a long way from completion, the
directors took steps to remove it. They acquired the site for a
station in Liverpool Road, next door to the Duke of Bridgewater's wharves at Castlefield, and began to consider how they
might bridge the river in order to reach it. Although these
proceedings were known to the Superintendent of the Bridgewater Trust and were viewed by him with considerable
hostility as being likely to injure the Duke's Canal, Captain
Bradshaw made no attempt to attend the Railway Board and
raise objections whilst the plans were being matured.[2] It was
left to John Moss to raise the issue with Loch on behalf of the
Liverpool and Manchester directors, and in the long run the
dispute was only settled by a direct confrontation between
Moss and R. H. Bradshaw in much the same way as any deal
might have been effected between two quite separate firms.

[1] J. Moss to J. Loch, 29 Feb. 1828, S.E.P.
[2] John Moss complained of this to Loch, when the elder Bradshaw afterwards objected to the crossing of the river. J. Moss to J. Loch, 19 Sept. 1828,
ibid.

It is fair to add, however, that once the question had been opened, James Loch contributed substantially to the new *entente* by his belated mediation, and that his influence was no doubt enhanced by the fact of his having a foot in both camps.

What Moss wanted principally was to ensure that the Bridgewater Trustees did not oppose the crossing of the river by the Railway Company. He wrote to Loch on 29 February 1828 requesting him to use his good offices with R. H. Bradshaw to prevent such an opposition.[1] Four months later he followed this up with an inducement, throwing out a suggestion that the Trustees might themselves make available a terminal for the railway on the Manchester side of the Irwell by letting his company into Castlefield. There could then be an agreement for dividing the Manchester and Liverpool traffic at that point between the two concerns. '. . . I think not improbable,' he observed, 'but there are goods which we might advantageously spare for each other.' Honey, however, was mixed with gall, for Moss's letter contained a hint that if the Trustees did not seize the opportunity, the railway might cross the river on land belonging to the New Quay Company, a large carrying company operating upon the Mersey and Irwell Navigation, in return for that company's being admitted as carrier upon the railway when it was completed. Overtures had already been received from the New Quay Company to that effect.[2] Loch, believing that his fellow directors had some proposition to submit, immediately broached the subject to Robert Bradshaw,[3] who received the intimation without enthusiasm, but equally without intransigence. He could not see how the alteration in the Railway Company's parliamentary line could have anything but an ill effect on the Trustees' property and concerns. Nevertheless, he expressed his willingness to grant full consideration to any distinct proposition accompanied by a plan or sketch that might be submitted to him by the directors.[4] His caution was not unwarranted, for no proposal followed. The furthest Moss would go was to reopen the negotiations with Loch as

[1] J. Moss to J. Loch, 29 Feb. 1828, ibid.
[2] J. Moss to J. Loch, 30 June 1828, ibid.
[3] J. Loch to R. H. Bradshaw, 7 July 1828, ibid.
[4] J. Loch to J. Moss, 14 July 1828, ibid.

intermediary two months later. With his connivance Loch put up to James Bradshaw in September a plan for making a connection between the Duke's Canal and the Liverpool and Manchester Railway in Manchester, either by extending the Canal into the railway premises or by extending the railway into Castlefield. It was coupled this time with a project for using the Bridgewater Canal to supply the as yet uncompleted railway with lime for constructional purposes. The Trustees were to reduce the lockage duty on limestone entering their waterway from the Rochdale Canal, and were to feed the commodity to the railroad at its western end via Duke's Dock in Liverpool. In return for this they were to have a site allocated to them in the Liverpool railway station.

Bradshaw continued to act coolly. He told Loch that he had objections to the proposed deviation from the parliamentary line, but that he was willing to meet a railway deputation.[1] What he feared was that, once across the Irwell, the Liverpool and Manchester Railway would be speedily linked to the Ashton Canal or the Cromford and High Peak Railway, and a way would be provided for the canal trade with Yorkshire and the east Midlands to leak away to the rails. Nor were his apprehensions groundless, for at this very time the engineer Jessop was submitting to Henry Booth proposals for a line joining the parliamentary line of the Liverpool and Manchester Railway near the New Bailey in Salford to the Cromford and High Peak Railway.[2] Loch, who was bent upon carrying through the deal between the Trustees and the Railway Company, encountered difficulties not only from Bradshaw but also from Moss, who, when apprised by Loch of Bradshaw's willingness to receive a deputation, began to qualify his earlier suggestions and stated that his company had no proposition to make to the Trustees.[3] His aim appeared to be to induce Bradshaw to refrain from opposing the crossing of the Irwell and to assist in supplying the railway with lime, whilst giving in return as little as possible. Eventually, however, after Loch had employed his persuasive powers upon Moss,[4] the Railway Board

---

[1] J. Loch to J. Moss, 15 Sept. 1828, S.E.P.
[2] J. Loch to R. H. Bradshaw, 20 Sept. 1828, ibid.
[3] J. Moss to J. Loch, 19 Sept. 1828, ibid.
[4] J. Loch to J. Moss, 20 Sept. 1828, ibid.

appointed two of its members to wait upon Bradshaw at Worsley. One of these was Moss himself, the other Gilbert Winter.[1] The interview, which was held late in October, lasted for three hours. It was a protracted trial of strength between men almost equally matched in stubbornness and endurance. Gradually, however, Bradshaw was worn down by his opponents. At the end of the argument he virtually withdrew the declaration of his intention to oppose the bridging of the Irwell which he had made at the beginning of it, without receiving any specific promise from the railway delegates that the junction between the railway and the canal would be made at Castlefield. He began by accusing Moss and Winter of coming to ask a favour, and ended by proposing himself an agreement for the interchange of traffic between rail and water, such as Moss had propounded to Loch a month or so earlier. He would even undertake on his own account the work of constructing the links that would be required.

It was not, however, an unconditional surrender, for the Superintendent of the Bridgewater Trust extracted from his adversaries at the interview a statement that their company entertained no hostile designs upon the Trustees' Yorkshire trade, and did not purport extending beyond Manchester.[2] The credit for this deal, if such a phrase can be used to describe a transaction at the public's expense, was not his alone. Loch had prepared the way for it. He had received an assurance from Moss about a month earlier that if Bradshaw agreed to his company's crossing the Irwell, the Duke's Canal should have some security against its going further, and had communicated the same to Bradshaw.[3] Before he met Bradshaw, Moss was able to tell Loch that he had sounded his committee and that its members had not 'at present any intention either collectively or individually to assist the junction of the Cromford Railway with ours'.[4] In future years the railway directors held themselves pledged to Bradshaw on this point. When another group of promoters came forward in 1829 with a plan for joining the L. & M.R. at Water Street, Manchester, to the

---

[1] J. Moss to J. Loch, 30 Sept. 1828, ibid.
[2] Memorandum enclosed in J. Moss to J. Loch, 22 Oct. 1828, ibid.
[3] J. Loch to J. Moss, 20 Sept. 1828, ibid.
[4] J. Moss to J. Loch, 30 Sept. 1828, ibid.

Cromford and High Peak at Horwich End in Derbyshire by what was to be called the Stockport Junction Railway, they hindered the project in every conceivable way, until finally it was defeated in Parliament on Standing Orders early in 1830. They restrained Stephenson from assisting it with his engineering skill and dismissed one of his sub-engineers for doing so.[1] Not until 1844 was the Liverpool and Manchester Railway connected at its eastern extremity to any line running east or south of Manchester.

But the Duke of Bridgewater's Trustees did not employ the breathing space between the passing of the Liverpool and Manchester Railway Bill and the opening of the line four and a half years later wholly in fighting a rearguard action against plans for improving the competitive efficiency of the railroads. They also set about the very necessary and long overdue task of putting their own house in order, so that they might withstand the storm, when it broke, with greater effect. Lord Stafford's advance of £40,000 for the improvement of the Canal works had made this effort possible. Supplemented by a further £20,000 taken from the fund established by the Duke of Bridgewater in his will, it furnished the basis of an ambitious building programme undertaken in the later 1820s. The most important item was the construction, at an estimated cost of more than £35,000, of a new line of locks at Runcorn, where the Duke's Canal descended to the Mersey estuary, together with a tidal dock or basin at its lower end. Already in progress in August 1826, these works were nearing completion in September 1828, by which time the locks were in operation. They were ready only just in time, for no sooner had they been opened than one of the older locks built by Brindley had to be withdrawn from action for repair. They were also much more efficient than the existing line, easing the task of working the traffic upwards and downwards between canal and river, reducing the delays which had made the waterway so unpopular just before the Railway Bill had been passed. '. . . it is incalculable the facility they afford to the trade', Loch explained to Lord Francis Leveson-Gower just after they had come into operation. Other improvements included a ware-

[1] J. Loch to J. Bradshaw, 9 Jan. 1830; J. Bradshaw to J. Loch, 13 Jan. 1830, S.E.P.

house at Manchester built in 1826 at a cost of £5,760 and an iron warehouse at Liverpool costing £3,062 and designed to secure the Staffordshire trade for the Duke's Canal.[1] Altogether the Canal installations were in much better shape when the Liverpool and Manchester Railway opened than when its promoters had first gone to Parliament five years earlier.

Much, it is true, still needed to be done. Duke's Dock at Liverpool urgently required the expenditure of some £40,000 to put it into a reasonable state of repair, and to carry out the much needed enlargement, if the delays which its present condition occasioned were to be avoided.[2] The Trustees were certainly alive to the need. In 1828 they submitted to Lord Stafford a plan for extending the dock by embanking further into the river, and later in the year Captain Bradshaw pressed upon Loch's attention the dilapidated condition of the river walls.[3] What stood in the way of remedial action was a financial problem and a divergence of opinion as to the mode of solving it. At that time the greater part of the fund set aside for improvement in 1826 was exhausted by the works which had already been carried out. Even on Loch's estimate, which Bradshaw challenged as being too low, there could have been no more than £25,000 left. James Loch favoured a policy of expedients. He thought that the outlay on the Duke's Dock should be made partly by drawing on the purse of the beneficiary to be, Lord Francis Leveson-Gower, and partly by coaxing the Corporation of Liverpool to subscribe in order to free themselves of certain obligations to the dock forced on them by the late Duke of Bridgewater.[4] He talked Lord Francis into agreeing to borrow £15,000 for the new works.[5] This was no easy task, as Lord Francis was still smarting under the recollection of his father's treachery in purchasing the railroad shares to the detriment of his own inheritance. As Greville, his brother-in-law, testified, he took a pessimistic view of the future,[6] and shrank from incurring additional

---

[1] J. Loch to Lord F. L.-Gower, 17 Sept. 1828; R. H. Bradshaw to J. Loch, 6 Dec. 1828; J. Bradshaw to J. Loch, 20 Aug. 1826 and 13 Dec. 1828, ibid.

[2] J. Loch to Lord F. L.-Gower, 17 Sept. 1828, ibid.

[3] J. Bradshaw to J. Loch, 4 Sept. 1828, ibid.

[4] J. Loch to Lord F. L.-Gower, 17 Sept. 1828, ibid.

[5] J. Loch to J. Bradshaw, 25 Nov. 1828, ibid.

[6] *Journal of the Reigns of King George IV and King William IV*, vol. ii, p. 43.

obligations at a time when he faced the prospect of making provision for his wife and children. It was half under protest that he gave way to Loch's persuasions stating that he gave 'carte blanche as to our falling house in Liverpool and that he has no objection to do anything he reasonably can to delay the final consummation and dessication of the Canal'.[1] His decision did not, however, resolve the problem. Bradshaw wanted a more radical attack upon the financial difficulties of the Trust. He and his son desired an Estate Bill to break the restriction upon the Trustees' powers of borrowing. As Loch would not agree to this, they deferred the enlargement of the dock, restricting themselves to ordering 'just so much to be done but no more as will secure the walls and dock gates from falling down'.[2]

Encouraged by these improvements, Bradshaw approached the future opening of the Liverpool and Manchester Railway with a modest self-confidence. 'With respect to the Railways, which he says will cost a million of money, and have an interest of £50,000 per annum to begin with, and the locomotives,' his son explained to Loch in November 1829, 'he hopes to be able at least to *exist* if he cannot live.'[3] There might be, as James Bradshaw conceded elsewhere, 'a very material alteration in the mode and rate of conveyance of goods etc. on canals' and a material lessening of profits, but he and his father lived 'in hopes that the practice of railroads will not be found so overpowering as its friends so sanguinely anticipate'.[4] Bradshaw was right in thinking that the Liverpool and Manchester Railway would start life burdened with heavy costs. Defending the policy of the Company against the attacks of Dr. Dionysius Lardner in 1832, Hardman Earle was yet bound to admit that the large expenditure, especially on moving power, had alarmed the timid and the cautious.[5] Moreover, there is evidence that the directors themselves viewed with consternation the high level of the regular outlay. The General Balance Sheet ending 30 June 1831 showed that the ordinary expenditure of the Railway Company amounted

---

[1] J. Loch to J. Bradshaw, 25 Nov. 1828, S.E.P.
[2] R. H. Bradshaw to J. Loch, 6 Dec. 1828 ; J. Bradshaw to J. Loch, 13 Dec. 1828, ibid.　　　　　　　　　[3] J. Bradshaw to J. Loch, 4 Nov. 1829, ibid.
[4] J. Bradshaw to J. Loch, 6 Dec. 1829, ibid.
[5] H. Earle to D. Lardner, 16 July 1832, ibid.

to rather more than 50 per cent on the receipts,[1] and the proportion did not diminish as the traffic expanded.[2] On his estimate of his opponent's costs Bradshaw founded his plan of campaign. He would slash rates, further if necessary than the Railway Company, in order to retain the trade. Thus by a single action he would both demonstrate the superiority of canals over railways in point of cheapness and avenge himself on Lord Stafford as a railway shareholder for his perfidy in deserting the Canal.

The notion of reducing rates had already taken shape in Bradshaw's mind when he interviewed Moss and Winter over the proposed extension of the railway into Manchester in October 1828. Stung by the firmness of the railway negotiators he threatened that 'he would count the railway waggons from his window and if they got much trade he would lower his price so that Lord Stafford should not gain by both canal and rail'.[3] This was the answer to those who vaunted the superior velocity of railroads. Canals could still compete with them in price, 'upon which, with respect to goods', as James Bradshaw observed, 'will ultimately be the fight'.[4] The Superintendent of the Trust was still nursing this plan in January 1830, for when John Moss of the Railway Company visited him at Worsley towards the end of that month, obviously sufficiently impressed to be seeking assurances, he explained that if he did reduce prices it would not be to oppose the railroad but to protect his canal. He promised to give warning of any reduction.[5]

Eight months later the event which all had been expecting happened. On 15 September 1830, with much pomp and ceremony, the first train made its progress along the Liverpool and Manchester Railway. Not even the fatal accident which marred the festivities could damp the enthusiasm which greeted the event. At first the traffic on the line was mainly in passengers, but before the end of the year the first load of merchandise had been drawn from Liverpool to Manchester by a locomotive known as the *Planet*.[6]

[1] J. Loch to G. Winter, 2 Aug. 1831, ibid.
[2] W. W. Currie to J. Loch, 21 Oct. 1833, ibid.
[3] Memorandum enclosed in J. Moss to J. Loch, 22 Oct. 1828, ibid.
[4] J. Bradshaw to J. Loch, 6 Dec. 1829, ibid.
[5] J. Moss to J. Loch, 26 Jan. 1830, ibid.
[6] Marshall, op. cit., p. 64.

Inevitably the arrival of the newcomer meant a certain reduction of the rates of carriage between Liverpool and Manchester, for the Railway Company was bound by its Act of Parliament to a scale of maximum charges lower in some cases than those which ruled in the market before it appeared. It was not long, however, before the principal carriers began to consider how they could control and regulate this fall. The Mersey and Irwell Navigation Company entered into negotiation with the Trustees and the Railway Company towards the beginning of May 1831 to engineer an agreement that all should reduce to the level of the Liverpool and Manchester Railway. The railway directors were quite willing to come to terms. John Moss pledged his company not to charge less than the full rates which it was authorized to receive by Act of Parliament unless it should be obliged to do so by any other carrier's charging a lower rate. W. T. Jackman's capacious generalization that railways deliberately put a low rate of carriage into force in the hope of bringing the canal proprietors to terms does not grip the facts of this case. It was R. H. Bradshaw who wrecked the incipient agreement. The Mersey and Irwell Committee learned on 4 May that he 'declined to give any pledge, thinking it better that each party should be left at liberty to exercise his own discretion'.[1] He had already lowered on cotton early in January to a rate of 1s. per ton below the railway maximum of 11s.[2]

It was Bradshaw, too, who intensified the contest by slashing the Canal tolls, thereby encouraging the private carriers on the Duke's to solicit more trade by lowering their charges to the public. Not wishing to take the irrevocable step of a formal reduction in the rate of tonnage, he began by making partial allowances to particular firms. Complaints that he had done so to the Grocers Company first reached the ears of the Mersey and Irwell Navigation Committee in June 1831. There appears to be little doubt that the Trustees had taken the lead in the matter, for the Mersey Company deferred following suit until it had been convinced of the correctness of the complaint,[3] and it was not until December 1831 that

---

[1] M. & I.N.C. Order Book, 1828–34, pp. 128–9, 4 May 1831.
[2] Ibid., p. 106, 14 Jan. 1831.
[3] Ibid., pp. 134, 136, 138, 141, 145, 17 June–24 Oct. 1831.

allegations were brought before the committee of that concern that the Railway Company, too, was making allowances to carriers.[1] In the following June the Trustees proceeded to a general reduction of tonnage, by 1*s*. 2*d*. per ton to 2*s*. 6*d*.,[2] at the same time lowering freight charges still further. This step, which was taken somewhat reluctantly in view of its permanent character, and was suggested initially by James Loch,[3] was not solely or even primarily directed against the Liverpool and Manchester Railway. It was a response to the general depression of trade which had settled upon the economy in 1831[4] and to an increased competition arising from the canal system. The new Macclesfield Canal, which gave the Grand Trunk an independent access to Manchester without going through the Duke of Bridgewater's Canal, was opened to traffic in November 1831.[5] About the same time the Grand Trunk Canal Company conducted a survey of proposed locks at Dutton to join its canal to the River Weaver and thus free itself altogether of dependence upon the Duke's for an outlet into the Mersey.[6] Menacing as they did the Preston Brook trade of the Bridgewater Canal, these developments displaced for the time being even new railway projects as a source of consternation to the Trustees.

The railway, however, was there to be fought, and Bradshaw still refused to come to terms with it. About the beginning of October 1832 he again rebutted an attempt by the Old Quay Company to arrange concerted action between water and rail, this time on the question of whether the rents of the Manchester warehouses should be remitted to the carriers as an indirect means of making an allowance to them. He declined 'having anything to do with any meeting of carriers which may be held upon the subject, intending to pursue such course as circumstances may render necessary and advisable'.[7] When all has been considered, therefore, it is difficult to resist the conclusion that Robert Haldane Bradshaw was, himself, one of the principal demolitionists of the system of price-fixing

---

[1] Ibid., p. 150, 7 Dec. 1831.   [2] Ibid., p. 174, 4 July 1832.
[3] J. Loch to J. Bradshaw, 28 Dec. 1831 and 5 Jan. 1832, S.E.P.
[4] J. Bradshaw to J. Loch, 24 Sept. 1832, ibid.
[5] G. Winter to J. Loch, 7 Nov. 1831, ibid.
[6] J. Bradshaw to J. Loch, 1 Jan. 1832, ibid.
[7] M. & I.N.C. Order Book 1828–34, p. 182, 3 Oct. 1832.

agreements for which his name has hitherto been chiefly remembered.

Bradshaw's methods were successful to approximately the extent which he had prophesied. The Canal held on to its trade and even began to increase it again after a year or two had elapsed. The total weight of traffic conveyed along it dropped only slightly, from 716,568 tons in 1830 to 705,527 tons in 1831, rose a little to 707,552 tons in 1832, and then leapt swiftly forward to 764,860 tons in 1833.[1] These figures include trades which were not as yet challenged by the railways—long-distance traffic from the Midlands and south, joining the Canal at Preston Brook, and traffic with places lying along the Canal intermediate between Liverpool and Manchester. The pattern in the Liverpool and Manchester trade was similar, but there was a marked relative gain by the railway after 1832, as the ensuing figures show:[2]

	Trade carried on the Liverpool and Manchester Railway	Trade carried on the Bridgewater Canal
	tons	tons
1831	77,271	91,793
1832	76,075	89,276
1833	113,248	105,572

Even the passenger services along the Canal survived, and continued to yield a substantial revenue to the Trustees. The receipts for the years immediately after the opening of the Liverpool and Manchester Railway were as follows:[3]

	£	s.	d.
1830	4340	9	5
1831	3245	12	4
1832	3754	13	3
1833	5292	0	0

Survival, however, was purchased at a price, for much as the Bradshaws had anticipated, there was a sharp decline in profitability. Its energies absorbed in the struggle to exist, the beleaguered goose no longer laid its golden eggs in such

[1] See below, Appendix B.
[2] J. Loch to R. Smith, 11 May 1837, E.B.C.
[3] Bridgewater Trust, General Abstracts of Accounts, 1830–7, Lancs. C.R.O.

rich profusion at Lord Stafford's door. The profits accruing
from the navigation, which had stood at £47,650 in 1830, fell to
£24,026 in 1831 and to £17,473 two years later.[1] Part of the
decrease may be accounted for by the cutting of the rates of
toll and carriage which brought down the total receipts by
about 19 per cent in the three years subsequent to the opening
of the railway.[2] In certain important respects, however, costs
were also rising, as the Trustees endeavoured in the face of
railway competition to improve their service to the public.
A letter from James Bradshaw to Loch written on 22 June
1833 shows that it was at that time that they placed steamers
on the Mersey estuary. These were used to tow vessels, and
probably to carry passengers, between Runcorn and Liverpool.
Bradshaw wrote of his father's 'being forced by circumstances
into the adoption of steam on the River'.[3] As it was the habit
of the Trustees in the earlier years to hire steamboats for
these purposes at so much per week for twelve months or other
short periods,[4] this item must have swelled the running costs
of the concern.

Although the Canal continued to pay even in the depths of
the depression of 1831–2, the impressions to be derived from
the letters which Captain Bradshaw wrote to James Loch are
those of a gloomy and fast deteriorating situation.

Trade is wretchedly bad not only with us but generally, [it was
claimed in April 1832], and from what I hear not likely soon to be
better. We have several of our flats tied up and must look to
making large reductions in our establishment if the prospect does
not speedily brighten.[5]

Six months later the position was much the same. 'We creep
and that is all.'[6] Trade depressions come and go. What was
more disturbing was the hint that even when trade revived
early in the following year, the Canal could not go on yielding
a profit without substantial capital investment such as the

---

[1] See below, Appendix A.
[2] Bridgewater Trust, General Abstracts of Accounts, 1830, p. 5; and 1833
p. 5.
[3] J. Bradshaw to J. Loch, 22 June 1833, S.E.P.
[4] F. Smith to J. Loch, 25 July 1842, L.E.P.
[5] J. Bradshaw to J. Loch, 23 Apr. 1832, S.E.P.
[6] J. Bradshaw to J. Loch, 22 Oct. 1832, ibid.

constitution of the Trust rendered it extremely difficult to provide.

Our trade is much increasing, [wrote Bradshaw in February 1833], and we are experiencing great detention and loss from the want of necessary accommodation in warehouses etc. to meet it, cargoes of our vessels lying for days together on board for want of room to discharge, and it is absolutely necessary if the concern is to be carried on to profit, that means should be found to make the requisite conveniences and afford facilities to our trade.[1]

Events were fast moving towards a crisis which could only be met by a drastic intervention of the life tenant in the affairs of the Trust. Before that action can be understood, however, in its full perspective, our steps must be retraced by several years, to study the response which the Bridgewater interest had made to the many new railway schemes which came before the public about the time when the Liverpool and Manchester line embarked upon its active life.

[1] J. Bradshaw to J. Loch, 27 Feb. 1833, S.E.P.

CHAPTER IV

New Foes to Face

IF railways did not engross the goods traffic, they certainly captured the imagination of the British public. Samuel Smiles observed: 'People flocked to Lancashire from all quarters to see the locomotive running upon a railway at three times the speed of a mailcoach, and to enjoy the excitement of actually travelling in the wake of a steam engine at that incredible velocity.'[1]

Enthusiasm expressed itself not only in sightseeing but in the promotion of new ventures. In north-west England and the northern Midlands, the catchment area of the Duke of Bridgewater's Canal, this had begun to happen even before the Liverpool and Manchester line reached completion. The experiments of the two Stephensons, the demonstrations of the prowess of the locomotive at the opening of the Bolton and Leigh Railway in August 1828 and at the Rainhill trials in the following October, the low price of iron, all tended to this result. Two new Lancashire railways, the Kenyon and Leigh Junction and the Warrington and Newton branch, received the assent of Parliament in May 1829, and other schemes were in the wind. Mention has already been made of one, the Stockport Junction Railway, but there were also plans for connecting the Liverpool and Manchester Railway with Wigan and Bolton to the north and with Birmingham and London to the south.

Most of these projects threatened the late Duke of Bridgewater's interests in some way or other. They could hardly escape doing so, for many and scattered were the regions from which the Canal drew its trade. Nevertheless, the Duke's Trustees no longer imagined that they could crush their rivals

---

[1] *The Story of the Life of George Stephenson*, p. 230.

in an open fight as they had tried to do with the Liverpool and Manchester Railway four years earlier. Their attitude was now more cautious. The Deputy Superintendent, Captain Bradshaw, expressed to Loch in December 1829 his considered opinion that 'as the fashion of the day is "Railroad" and I apprehend there is no chance whatever of preventing their establishment, the Canals can only hold up by competing with them in price'.[1] He and his father, however, were still prepared to intrigue with the powerful railway promoters at Liverpool against the smaller and less strongly backed schemes. That was how they disposed of the Stockport Junction line.[2] For this purpose they could generally rely on the support of the Leveson-Gower family, for James Loch, who administered that family's affairs, was less squeamish about using his influence in the Liverpool and Manchester Railway Company to the profit of the Bridgewater Canal when the affairs of a third party were under discussion than when what was at stake was the vital interest of the Company itself. He spelled out this distinction very carefully to Wallace Currie in the letter already quoted, outlining to him his conception of the function of one of Lord Stafford's directors in relation to the Railway Board.[3] It was to humour Loch that John Moss, one of the most active of the Liverpool directors, interviewed a deputation from the committee of the Warrington and Newton Branch Railway Company in February 1830 and persuaded the committee to delay its plans for prolonging the Branch's line to Sandbach.[4] Nothing further was heard of this scheme, which was intended to be the start of a line of railway connecting Liverpool and Manchester with Birmingham. Had it materialized it would have threatened the water traffic between these places with severe competition. But the Warrington and Newton Branch Railway was dependent upon the Liverpool and Manchester Company. A word from Moss was, therefore, enough to cause its directors to desist.[5]

---

[1] J. Bradshaw to J. Loch, 6 Dec. 1829, S.E.P.
[2] See above, pp. 53–4.   [3] See above, p. 46.
[4] J. Moss to J. Loch, 2 Feb. 1830, S.E.P.
[5] A further obstacle to proceeding with the line in face of Lord Stafford's opposition was that the Company's engineer was Robert Stephenson, son of the engineer of the Liverpool and Manchester Company. L. T. C. Rolt, *George and Robert Stephenson*, pp. 210–11.

There were limits, however, to the extent to which the Stafford railway influence could be used to block new railroad projects. It was powerless against schemes on which the Liverpool promoters had themselves set their hearts. One such was the proposal for a line from Liverpool to Birmingham, which was revived in 1829 after hanging fire for about three years. Liverpool had not shown much interest in the earlier enterprise, leaving the men of Birmingham to make most of the effort, but when the Birmingham party moved again, in 1829, certain members of the Liverpool group decided to move with them. As Moss, who was foremost among them, freely admitted to William Huskisson, 'pecuniary advantages' formed 'no inconsiderable part' of their expectations. The Liverpool and Manchester line was well advanced with every prospect of success, and the time was, therefore, ripe for new endeavours. Moreover, additional urgency was given to the proceeding by the need to forestall action by the Birmingham group or some other 'wild adventurer' who might not content himself with building from Birmingham to Liverpool but might also throw out a branch to Manchester which would compete for traffic with the Liverpool and Manchester line.[1] In the atmosphere of heightened enthusiasm for railways which followed the Rainhill trials, the Liverpool promoters were coming to think of themselves as a sort of railroad aristocracy, distinct socially and politically as well as on grounds of economic interest from others in the field. Moss observed of Liverpool: 'The majority of its inhabitants are not of the class of Liberals who seek a change at all risks; at the same time they will have the best mode of conveyance.'[2] It was natural, therefore, that they should have sought to deepen the alliance with the vested interests in the canal world against interlopers in the railway camp, thus offering to the former an escape by compromise from the dilemma which confronted them when opposition could not be made effective.

Moss made the first move when he wrote to Loch towards the end of October 1829 outlining a bold and ambitious plan

---

[1] J. Moss to W. Huskisson, 14 Dec. 1829, in C. R. Fay, *Huskisson and his Age*, pp. 24–6.

[2] J. Moss to J. Loch, 19 Dec. 1829, S.E.P.

for interweaving the interests of railway and canal,[1] and this was elaborated during the ensuing month into a formal proposition put to Lord Stafford and to Lord Clive, who acted on behalf of the Ellesmere and Chester and Birmingham and Liverpool Junction Canal companies. The gist of it was as follows. Lord Stafford was to take shares in a line from Liverpool to Birmingham which might afterwards be extended to London. This was to leave the Liverpool and Manchester Railway at Huyton, tunnel under the River Mersey at Runcorn, then follow the line of the Duke's Canal to Preston Brook en route for Nantwich, from which place the path of the as yet uncompleted Birmingham and Liverpool Junction Canal would be adopted as far as Wolverhampton, and so, on to Birmingham. The railway was to take advantage of the existing Birmingham and Liverpool Junction Canal works, and between Preston Brook and Runcorn it was to be built either along the Bridgewater Canal itself or along its towing path. Moreover, the last-mentioned section of the line would become the property of the Duke's Trustees.[2]

The offer placed Loch, as the Marquess's business manager, in a quandary. He had no attachment to canals as such, and would gladly have sacrified them to the interests of the canal owners. His main concern was to look to the welfare of the Marquess of Stafford's two sons who would shortly succeed to their respective inheritances, their father being advanced in years. On first approach the plan submitted by the railway promoters appeared to provide for both. The elder son, Lord Gower, would benefit as heir to the Stafford holdings in the Liverpool and Manchester Railway, which would be increased in value by the rail connection with the Midlands. In due course, too, he would inherit his father's shares in the proposed Birmingham Railway, and this would recompense him for the loss of the Junction Canal, in which the family also had an interest. Meanwhile his younger brother Lord Francis would be compensated for the loss of canal traffic by the receipts from a section of the new railway transmitted to him by the Bridgewater Trustees as part of the regular payment which

---

[1] J. Moss to J. Loch, 24 Oct. 1829, S.E.P.

[2] J. Loch to Lord Stafford, 20 Nov. 1829; J. Loch to Captain Bradshaw, 19 Nov. 1829, ibid.

they made at the moment to his father and would soon make to him. Moreover, that part, the greater part, of the Duke's Canal which was not to be taken for the railway need not be rendered useless by the great surgical operation to be performed at its western end. It could feed the new line with goods from Manchester and with coal from Worsley, and might itself be converted into a railway if the money could be found for carrying out the change. As John Moss observed, it was well equipped to provide the bed of a new line from Manchester. 'It is a dead level,' he remarked to Loch, 'the nearest road to Wales, would be the best road to London and even to Liverpool, so little round as to get much traffic and prevent what is now talked of, another railroad company from Manchester to Liverpool.'[1]

As soon as the practical implementation of the scheme was considered, however, the difficulties became apparent. Most of them stemmed from the divided responsibility for the Canal, a situation which accounts for James Loch's perplexity and provides most of the explanation of the subsequent failure to effect the compromise. Lord Stafford simply did not possess the authority to sanction most of the things which the railway promoters wished to see done. He was not even empowered to authorize the conversion of the Runcorn branch of the Duke's Canal into a railway. That was Bradshaw's prerogative, and right from the start Loch assumed that the old man's consent could not be obtained.[2] Perhaps he was too quick to assume it. There are grounds for thinking that although the Superintendent of the Trust would have been difficult to convince, he would not have been utterly immune to suasion. Moss, who visited him privately at Worsley in January 1830 and sounded him on the subject of the Birmingham and Liverpool Railway project, reported afterwards:

I found him disposed to discuss that subject very fairly, decided against the measure this year but promising to look into it with fairness whenever we could show him facts and convince him that railroads were more advantageous than Canals, told me what he had the power to do, and said what part of the line he should expect.[3]

[1] J. Moss to J. Loch, 24 Oct. 1829, ibid.
[2] J. Loch to Lord Stafford, 20 Nov. 1829, ibid.
[3] J. Moss to J. Loch, 26 Jan. 1830, ibid.

Loch, however, was not prepared to make the effort of wrangling with him. Essentially a reasonable and liberal-minded man, he lacked the patience, perhaps even the courage, to have the matter out face to face with one whose outlook differed so markedly from his own and who was likely to defend his position with more doggedness than logic. All that he would do was to mention the railway proposal to Captain Bradshaw in a half-hearted manner, not even specifying who were the authors of it,[1] and was easily put off when the Captain returned a scathing answer which revealed that he and his father believed the suggestion to have emanated from Telford, to whom they imputed all manner of base motives.[2]

Whether Loch could have succeeded in persuading Bradshaw must remain uncertain, but the effort would have been worth making. For without the inclusion of the Duke's Canal, the proposal that the Marquess of Stafford should support the Liverpool and Birmingham Railway merely amounted to asking him to favour one of his sons at the expense of the other. This aspect of the matter worried Loch a good deal. He wrote to Currie, in whom he was disposed to confide far more than in others: 'If I had Lord Gower only to advise, my task would be easier, but when I am also expected to think of his brother's interest, my task is more, nay most difficult.'[3]

There was a further problem, concerning the Birmingham and Liverpool Junction Canal which was still in course of construction. This had been planned as a link in a chain of waterways connecting the Birmingham area with Merseyside, and it was scarcely practicable to turn it into a railway without doing the same to the remaining links. Loch put this point to Lord Stafford in a lengthy memorandum:

> ... if it was converted into a R.R., it would not serve its original purpose of forming a junction between the Old Birmingham and the Ellesmere and between both with the Trunk and the Duke's unless they are likewise converted into R.R. . . . the Ellesmere might be also made a R.R., then this would in some degree injure the trade to Liverpool on the Liverpool and Manchester Railway in

---

[1] J. Loch to J. Bradshaw, 29 Oct. 1829, S.E.P.
[2] J. Bradshaw to J. Loch, 4 Nov. 1829, ibid.
[3] J. Loch to W. W. Currie, 18 Nov. 1829, ibid.

which your Lordship is also so deeply interested, to which it might be replied that the transhipment at Port Ellesmere would render this interference unimportant and it would be made up by the Liverpool and Manchester securing the Birmingham, Shropshire and Welsh trade with Manchester and which by the way and on the other hand was intended to go by the Middlewich branch through the Duke to Manchester and be its indemnity for that portion of the Liverpool and Birmingham trade which would find its way through the Ellesmere to Liverpool.[1]

Unable to answer for the proprietors of other canals in the chain, Loch was inclined privately to dismiss that part of the railway plan which related to the conversion of the Junction Canal, though he passed the proposition to Lord Clive with Lord Stafford's recommendation to accede to it.[2]

In fact Lord Stafford's agent had no very clear idea of what to advise his master to do. Only two things appeared fairly certain to him. One was that a line of railway between Liverpool and Birmingham could not be prevented. If the present promoters did not carry out the work, someone else would. The other was that, this being the case, it was better to compromise in some way with Moss and his associates than to allow the railroad to be constructed by men whose interests were opposed to those of the Marquess and over whom the latter would possess no control.[3] He called in others to help him reach a decision. His brother and W. Adam constituted his informal 'cabinet', and the Edinburgh engineer Jardine was also asked to give an opinion.[4] Having consulted his authorities, Loch eventually reached the conclusion that the best advice he could offer to Lord Stafford was to ask the railway promoters to delay proceeding with their plans for one parliamentary session, at the end of which time the Liverpool and Manchester Railway would be open and would have demonstrated 'what the Rail Roads are really capable of doing in point of speed, economy and arrangement'.[5] The railway men consented to this through their solicitor G. Pritt.

---

[1] J. Loch to Lord Stafford, 20 Nov. 1829, ibid.
[2] J. Loch to H. D. Lowndes, 25 Oct. 1830, ibid.
[3] J. Loch to Lord Stafford, 20 Nov. 1829, ibid.
[4] J. Loch to W. W. Currie, 18 Nov. 1829; J. Loch to Lord Gower, 21 Nov. 1829, ibid.
[5] J. Loch to Lord Stafford, 20 Nov. 1829, ibid.

They would give notice of a line from Liverpool as far as Runcorn just to secure the ground against interlopers and to prevent the unemployed capital of the neighbourhood from being lured into rival projects, but they would not go on with their plans in Parliament without obtaining the assent of the Marquess of Stafford.[1] On to this agreement James Loch grafted the further provision that the government should be approached to move in Parliament for a general moratorium on all railway schemes for a single session until the Liverpool and Manchester Railway had proved its worth.[2]

As the year 1829 drew to its close, the two parties proceeded with their joint plans. The railway people held a meeting of their supporters in Liverpool late in December, when it was decided to form a company, to approve the principle of co-operation with the canals, and to offer 'extraordinary inducements and privileges' to the canal owners to become shareholders in the new line.[3] Arrangements were also made for supplying the Marquess of Stafford's advisers with information from Henry Booth, the treasurer of the Liverpool and Manchester Company, as to the cost of carrying heavy goods by rail, in order that the former might be assisted in judging the propriety of converting their waterways into railroads.[4] To the railway promoters also fell the task of preparing a case to lay before the legislature. Pritt drew up a memorandum which was to furnish the basis of a paper to be distributed among M.P.s and ministers before the opening of Parliament. This is worth quoting *in extenso*, for it shows how far the Liverpool railway group had gone in accepting one of the leading arguments advanced by the canal proprietors in their opposition to railways—what the historian Jackman called 'the constant plea of vested interests':

The country is greatly indebted to inland navigation for her prosperity and wealth.

An immense amount of capital is invested in canals: it is difficult to form an estimate, but probably to the extent of 20 millions sterling and upwards.

---

[1] J. Loch to W. Huskisson, 25 Dec. 1829, in Fay, op. cit., pp. 26–8.
[2] W. W. Currie to J. Loch, 9 Dec. 1829, S.E.P.
[3] Jackman, op. cit., pp. 540–1.
[4] W. W. Currie to J. Loch, 9 Dec. 1829, S.E.P.

The present proprietors of canals generally, cannot be said to have had their reward, in the increase value of shares; because most of them have invested at high prices, so as to yield but a moderate return on their capital.

Amongst the present proprietors are widows, orphans and small annuitants.

The alteration of Canals into Railways would avoid that interference with private property and private rights—which the construction of new Railways would occasion.[1]

Whilst the railwaymen were thus employed, Loch was carrying out his part in the campaign. This was of a twofold nature. His first task was to bring round the proprietors of the Midland canals to the notion of a compromise with the railway. In this he failed, and his failure underlines the immense difficulty of getting the canal owners to act in unison. As we have seen, he submitted the proposition as to the conversion of the Birmingham and Liverpool Junction Canal into a railway to Viscount Clive for the approval of the Ellesmere and Birmingham and Liverpool Junction Canal companies. The offer was compromised from the start by Loch's inability to pledge the Duke of Bridgewater's Canal to the scheme, and in due course, as might well have been expected, a discouraging reply was received from Lord Clive. This stung Loch into an angry rejoinder.

I fear the anecdote which Your Lordship mentions as to Telford [he wrote on 26 January 1830] betokens fear on behalf of the canals and a blindness as to enquiry which I have always seen attend the losing party, and may prevent any arrangement, if that should hereafter be thought right until too late.[2]

To adopt such a tone was ill advised, for Clive's letter, though rude and disobliging, merely asked for a delay before being called upon to decide.[3] Again, as in his dealings with Bradshaw, Loch had proved that despite his having a foothold in both camps, he was not the man to succeed in bringing rail and water together in harmonious co-operation. He lacked the patience and the sympathy to carry with him the canal

[1] 'Heads of a Statement to be Submitted to the Public on Behalf of Canals' in Pritt to Loch, 19 Dec. 1829, ibid.

[2] J. Loch to Lord Clive, 26 Jan. 1830, ibid.

[3] Lord Clive to J. Loch, 20 Jan. 1830, ibid.

owners whom he had described a little earlier as 'a set of antiquated persons who will sit quietly still until their concerns are swept away from under them'.[1] After the exchange with Clive nothing went right with the negotiations, though Loch persisted in them for another three months. The proposal to convert the Junction Canal into a railway was finally rejected as impracticable,[2] and Clive would not even agree to Loch's suggestion that he should meet Bradshaw and Lord Harrowby, who was acting for the Grand Trunk Canal, round a table to consider what action should be taken by the canals with regard to the railway proposals.[3] It is an instructive commentary upon the close connection between aristocracy and water transport in north-west England and the northern Midlands that the effort to promote concerted action among the waterways should have been made by the land agent of a marquess in an approach to an earl and a viscount, but the common bond of nobility was powerless to counteract the divisions in the canal world, and the attempt, therefore, failed.

The other main responsibility of James Loch was to get the assent of the government and Parliament to the proposed moratorium. To this end he wrote to Huskisson as the leading parliamentarian with a knowledge of Liverpool interests, and he both solicited and, on 21 December 1829 obtained, an interview with the Home Secretary, the Rt. Hon. Robert Peel.[4] The case which he argued was a respectable one. It went beyond the pursuit of an officially imposed delay on railway legislation and raised the wider issue of a planned economy in transport. He wrote to Peel:

I cannot help mentioning, however, what a very deliberate consideration of all the points that have been of late forced on my attention by the conflicting interests of Rail Roads and Canal owners has suggested to me which is this.—When a set of gentlemen unite together to make a canal or a railroad or a turnpike, there are so many conflicting interests to consult and to [conceive ?], it generally happens that they only attempt a portion of their

[1] J. Loch to W. Lewis, 18 Dec. 1829, S.E.P.
[2] J. Loch to H. D. Lowndes, 25 Oct. 1830, ibid.
[3] Lord Clive to J. Loch, 25 Mar. 1830, ibid.
[4] J. Loch to W. Huskisson, 25 Dec. 1829, in Fay, op. cit., pp. 26–8.

scheme first and very possibly obtain power to do that which is not a part of their future main object or they modify their main object so much as to make it a very imperfect measure. Both turnpikes and canals have suffered by this extremely and they have thus been made on the most circuitous and inconvenient routes. The same thing will happen to railroads unless some general board could be established to say that they think the plan is well suited for the purpose, and that some such controuling power should be named appears not inadvisable. When a new and most important system of communication (which must call for the expenditure of many millions) is about being begun, how provoking, for example, it would be if for some such reason as I have named, twenty miles or even ten miles should be lost between this (London) and Liverpool. I am aware of all the difficulties of the question, but cannot help thinking it worthy of consideration. I will obtrude no further.

The formation of such a board could hardly be said to be an interference with private or individual enterprise and speculation, for that would be only strictly true if such a controul was to be exercised over a person in the management of what is his own. In all such cases as above, the interference would only be to regulate the manner in which one class of persons is to be permitted to deal with the property of another class and which they cannot touch without the authority and intervention of the legislature.[1]

Loch's ideas were well in advance of his time. He must have been one of the earliest advocates of state control of railways, earlier in fact than James Morrison, the Member for Ipswich, who is usually regarded as a pioneer. It was not until 1844 that a government department competent to scrutinize railway Bills was established, and then its powers were inadequate. In the England of 1829 even the more modest demand for delaying action was unlikely to be heeded. France indeed in the ensuing decade postponed her railroad development until she had thought out a plan for it, but England was not France. *Laissez-faire* ideas were here in the ascendant, and M.P.s, subject as never before to the pressure of opinion outside the House, were being pestered with requests to support railway schemes. Already unpopular with its own erstwhile supporters and bereft of a solid party backing, the Wellington government was in no position to stand boldly athwart the

[1] J. Loch to the Rt. Hon. Robert Peel, 14 Dec. 1829, S.E.P.

rising enthusiasm for railroads. Peel listened politely to Loch and requested him to put his opinions in writing, but that was as far as it went.[1]

Failure to obtain the moratorium compelled Loch to accelerate his plans with regard to the proposals from Liverpool. The railway promoters remained true to their word and refrained from bringing forward a Bill in Parliament during the 1830 session. They were becoming increasingly impatient, however, as the months rolled by and put strong pressure upon Lord Stafford to accept their terms. Anxious to have the financial support of the Marquess and the other great canal magnates even if they could not annex the canals, they threatened as an alternative to appeal to the general public with the promise of a low maximum charge and a clause fixing a ceiling of 10 per cent on dividends.[2] It was just such a policy of lowering rates that Loch was seeking to avoid. Indeed, to be able to prevent it was one of the principal advantages to be expected from an arrangement which would give his master and the other canal proprietors some say in the management of the railway. Moreover, he knew that the Birmingham group was discontented with the movement to ally with the canals and was anxious to launch an independent venture, fighting the battle out with the navigation owners in the arena of Parliament.[3] He was obliged, therefore, to act quickly, and this meant that he must face the question which he had earlier shelved, that of how to fit Lord Francis and the Duke's Trustees, from whom he would derive an income, into a compromise with the Liverpool men. Unable to sanction the conversion of the Duke's Canal into a section of the line, he worked out a variant of the railway proposal which he thought capable of being carried without Bradshaw's approval. Instead of providing the track between Runcorn and Preston Brook, the Duke's Trustees were to erect over the Mersey at Runcorn a bridge which would carry not only the Liverpool and Birmingham Railway but also a turnpike road. In return

---

[1] J. Loch to W. Huskisson, 25 Dec. 1829, in Fay, op. cit., pp. 26–8.

[2] J. Moss to J. Loch, 8 May 1830, S.E.P.

[3] 'I presume that you know the Birmingham people have had a meeting, appointed a committee, and opened a subscription for a railway from Birmingham to Liverpool, not only independent of but declared to be hostile to canals' (G. Pritt to J. Loch, 19 Dec. 1829, ibid.).

for this they were to levy a toll on all goods wagons and passenger carriages traversing the bridge whether by rail or road, and were to be authorized to borrow money on the credit of the tolls for the purpose of financing the work of construction. The plan which was agreed by Moss was to be authorized on behalf of the Bridgewater interest by Lord Francis Leveson-Gower. Bradshaw was merely informed of it by Loch as practically a *fait accompli* on 25 May 1830.[1]

This was a foolish, if not a positively illegal, proceeding. Moss thought so, for although he assented to the scheme as a concession to Loch's wishes, he observed to Pritt: 'I wondered that Loch and you, knowing the character of Old Bradshaw, should propose a discussion in his absence.'[2] The outcome was what might have been anticipated. Bradshaw dissociated himself from the whole idea,[3] deeming it contrary to the Duke of Bridgewater's will.[4] Even after that, Loch persisted in the notion that Bradshaw's decision did not in any way bind the life tenant.[5] It is difficult to see, however, how in practice the project could then have been implemented. Bradshaw was supreme in the management of the Trust, and without his direction not a stone of the bridge could be laid, nor a penny of the toll collected.

In fact, the issue was not to be put to the test, for within a week or two of the announcement of the Runcorn Bridge project, the alliance of the Marquess of Stafford and the Liverpool railway party began to fall apart. From a letter of Loch's written on 13 June, John Moss concluded that negotiation was practically at an end,[6] and although his committee reserved shares in their enterprise for Lord Francis as an alternative mode of compromise to the building of the bridge,[7] the Leveson-Gower family lost interest in the Liverpool and Birmingham Railway. The main reason for the estrangement was that the Liverpool promoters had altered their plans as to the routes to be followed. They now proposed to run straight

[1] J. Loch to R. H. Bradshaw, 25 May 1830, ibid.
[2] J. Moss to G. Pritt, 14 June 1830, ibid.
[3] R. H. Bradshaw to J. Loch, 31 May 1830, ibid.
[4] J. Moss to J. Loch, 5 July 1830, ibid.
[5] J. Loch to W. W. Currie, 28 June 1830, ibid.
[6] J. Moss to J. Loch, 5 July 1830, ibid.
[7] G. Pritt to G. Loch, 11 Dec. 1830, ibid.

into Liverpool instead of first joining the Liverpool and Manchester line. A letter of Pritt's suggests that one reason for the change was to avoid blocking the latter with traffic to and from the south,[1] but there may also have been a deeper motive, that of preventing Lord Stafford from gaining an indirect control over the line without investing in it, through his representation on the Liverpool and Manchester Board.[2] Whatever the reason for it, Loch opposed it on the grounds that it threatened the Marquess's interests both as a railway shareholder and as the beneficiary of the Duke's Canal. His belief was that the construction of a line direct to Liverpool would encourage someone to connect that line with Manchester, thus raising up a competitor with the Liverpool and Manchester Railway and the Bridgewater Canal.[3]

The breach was by no means complete. Lord Stafford maintained a benevolent neutrality towards the Liverpool promoters when they came before the House of Commons in February 1831 for permission to construct a line from Liverpool to Chorlton near Crewe, there to join up with one which was initiated from the Birmingham district. He held aloof from the opposition which was presented to the Bill by the proprietors of the Weaver and Mersey and Irwell Navigations and the 'several owners and masters of flats, boats, and other vessels' plying upon those waterways,[4] and Loch, his agent, endeavoured through Lord Granville and Lord Clive to persuade the Ellesmere, Grand Trunk, and Birmingham and Liverpool Junction Canal companies to do the same.[5] The Bill was eventually abandoned by its promoters,[6] but when, in 1833, the Liverpool party came forward again, this time in union with their counterparts in Birmingham, and successfully carried a Bill for constructing the Grand Junction Railway from the short Warrington and Newton line at Warrington via Preston Brook and Crewe to Birmingham, the Marquess reaped a small reward for his neutrality. Loch was able to

[1] G. Pritt to J. Loch, 7 July 1830, S.E.P.
[2] W. W. Currie to J. Loch, 30 June 1830, ibid.
[3] J. Loch to W. W. Currie, 21 June 1830, ibid.
[4] J. Loch to W. W. Currie, 13 Dec. 1830, ibid. W. H. Chaloner, *The Social and Economic Development of Crewe, 1780–1923*, p. 18.
[5] J. Loch to H. D. Lowndes, 25 Oct. 1830, S.E.P.
[6] Chaloner, op. cit., p. 18.

persuade the promoters to amend their Bill so as to ensure that the railway would not gain any connection with the Duke's Canal in passing it at Preston Brook.[1] Presumably the object was to guard against a possible abstraction of the trade of the Grand Trunk Canal from the water to the rails at that point. But the gain was dubious. Within a few years the Trustees had come to see that they might themselves exchange a profitable traffic with the Railway Company there, and were treating for the making of the junction which they had sought previously to prevent.

After the rupture of the negotiations with the Liverpool group in 1830, the custodians of the Bridgewater interest refrained for a while from diversifying further their commitments to railways. This was not for want of attempts to draw them in. Early in 1831 a deputation from Birmingham, accompanied by the engineer Giles, twice waited upon Loch, offering to give Lord Stafford an interest in the proposed railway from Birmingham to London amounting to no less than one half of the whole. Its members expressed anxiety to put the Marquess into the control and management of the concern in the same manner as in the Liverpool and Manchester Company or even to a greater extent. That such an offer should have been made shows the prestige which the Leveson-Gower name carried in railway circles, but James Loch advised his master to decline the proposition, tempting as it was, on the grounds that it rested 'upon no basis for Your Lordship's support'.[2] Loch's strategy was always conservative at bottom, designed to protect existing interests or to seek compensation for unavoidable injuries inflicted upon them, not to promote the extension of those interests into completely new spheres.

If the protectors of the Duke's Canal did not rush headlong into alliances with railways, neither did they exert themselves

---

[1] In its amended form the Bill tied the Railway Company down not to deviate from its prescribed route before tunnelling under the Canal, and not to use any of the Trustees' lands at Preston Brook for wharves (J. Loch to J. Bradshaw, 21 Mar. 1833, S.E.P.). Captain Bradshaw had expressed himself vehemently against the railway's forming a junction with the Canal, which, he argued, 'would be far worse than the Cholera', and would damage the Trust to the amount of several thousands a year, presumably by drawing trade off the Canal at that point (J. Bradshaw to J. Loch, 17 Mar. 1833, ibid.).

[2] J. Loch to Lord Stafford, 9 July 1831, ibid.

much to oppose the new form of transport. Where they
fought, it was for limited objectives which stopped short of the
annihilation of the enemy. The only serious parliamentary
campaign to be undertaken by the Duke of Bridgewater's
Trustees in the early 1830s was that of the 1831 session
against the Sheffield and Manchester Railway Bill. A joint
enterprise of groups of business men in Sheffield, Manchester,
and Liverpool, this measure provided for the building of a
line from Sheffield through the heart of the Peak District to
Manchester, where it was to join the Liverpool and Manchester
Railway at Oldfield Road, Salford. The Trustees assailed it
vigorously, carrying their opposition from the House of
Commons to the House of Lords,[1] where they could draw upon
the resources of aristocratic connection available to the Leveson-
Gower family. They circularized no fewer than twenty-seven
peers in order to gain their support. The titles of those who
were approached were mentioned in a letter written by Loch
to Lord Francis Gower. They ran as follows: Howard de
Walden, Bristol, Seaford, Dover, Cawdor, Clanricarde, Clanwilliam, Clarendon, Combermere, Ellenborough, Prudhoe,
Gosford, Ravensworth, Haddington, Chesterfield, Jersey,
Rosslyn, Talbot, Grosvenor, Stuart de Rothesay, Wilton,
Manvers, Harrowby, Beaufort, Northumberland, Wellington,
and Salisbury.[2] It might have been imagined that so great an
expenditure of effort would not have been undertaken for any
purpose short of defeating the Bill entirely, but such was not
the case. The Trustees aimed merely at preventing the railway
from being carried through the heart of their own Manchester
terminus at Castlefield, and to divert it to the east side of the
road by Hulme church.[3] After a hard fight in Parliament they
eventually accepted the award of an arbitrator, which adjusted the route to be followed by the railway across their
estates, restricted the path of the line to a band 31 feet in
breadth, specified the dimensions of the bridge by which the
railway was to be carried over the Canal, made the promoters
of the Bill liable for any obstruction or damage caused to the

[1] *J.H.C.* lxxxvi, Pt. 1, 1830–1, p. 292; George Dow, *Great Central*, vol. i,
pp. 6–9.
[2] Lord F. L.-Gower to J. Loch, July 1831, S.E.P. The Duke of Norfolk's
name also appeared in the list, but was crossed out in pencil.
[3] J. Bradshaw to J. Loch, 13 Apr. 1831, ibid.

navigation, and compelled the same to build a bridge over their line in order that the Canal people might get from one side of their severed estate to the other.[1] In view of the importance of Castlefield, with its great wharves and warehouses, as the hub of the canal trade, these emendations do not appear to have been unreasonably exacted, and the episode of the Sheffield Railway serves as a reminder that the opposition of canals to railroads was not always so devoid of moral justification as it has often been portrayed.

To speak, however, of a Bridgewater policy towards railways, still less of a general canal policy towards them, is misleading. Loch and Bradshaw stood for different things, and the other personalities connected with Lord Stafford and the Trust, Captain Bradshaw, Gilbert Winter, and Wallace Currie, also differed markedly in their views, the first two of them tending to align themselves with R. H. Bradshaw and the last usually with Loch. Loch was a born compromiser. Though sensitive to the interests of Lord Stafford and his second son Lord Francis in the Duke's Canal, he recognized that the spread of railways over the country could not be permanently prevented, if only because of the strength of public opinion in their favour. He wrote to Currie in 1830: '. . . as to the public and Parliament we don't attempt to oppose our interests to theirs, we only ask for a hedge.'[2] Currie's own outlook was even more friendly to railways than was Loch's. As a railway director appointed in Lord Stafford's interest, he did not consider himself bound, even in considering a proposal by a third party to construct a new line, ' to look to any other consideration but what was for the advantage of his Lordship as a proprietor in the Liverpool and Manchester Rail Road '.[3] R. H. Bradshaw's attitude was the direct opposite of this. He did not think himself obliged to look to any interests other than those of the Bridgewater Trust, and his policy, whilst he was still capable of forming one, was that of opportunism. To a considerable extent too he could rely on the support of one of Lord Stafford's directors on the Liverpool and Manchester Railway, viz. Gilbert Winter.

[1] *J.H.C.* lxxxvi, Pt. 2, 1831, pp. 750–2.
[2] J. Loch to W. W. Currie, 28 June 1830, S.E.P.
[3] W. W. Currie to J. Loch, 10 Sept. 1831, ibid.

From 1831 onwards the division in the Bridgewater interest became increasingly apparent and was fraught with consequences prejudicial to the strategy which Loch was pursuing. Bradshaw became with advancing years more unmanageable and more unpredictable than ever. In November 1831 he had a paralytic stroke, lost the use of his left arm and leg, and displayed the extreme of excitement and irritability.[1] The illness permanently impaired his judgement. In view of what had happened in the affair of the Runcorn Bridge project, it would have required from Loch great tact and diplomacy to control him, and with these qualities Loch was not superlatively well endowed. By failing to inquire sufficiently after the old man's health,[2] he rendered his own task more difficult than it need have been.

Disagreement among Lord Stafford's advisers came to a head in September 1831, when the Liverpool and Manchester Railway Board received a proposal from a rival group of promoters intent on constructing a new line into Liverpool across central Lancashire. They had already taken powers under an Act of 23 August 1831 to convert the Manchester, Bolton, and Bury Navigation into a railway, and intended to protract the resultant line westwards to Liverpool. There seems also to have been some intention of extending eastwards into Yorkshire, for the scheme was at one stage described as the Leeds and Liverpool Railway. At first, in December 1830, the authors of the plan proposed to enter Liverpool at its northern end,[3] as this area of the port was not well served by the railway between Manchester and Liverpool authorized in 1826. Nine months later, however, they changed their minds and approached the Liverpool and Manchester Company for permission to feed into their line between Newton-le-Willows and the incline at Sutton. Loch and W. W. Currie both welcomed the proposal as a satisfactory compromise with a project which could not ultimately be resisted. They were thinking entirely of the interests of the Liverpool and Manchester Railway which would be benefited by an accession of

---

[1] See batch of letters from J. Bradshaw to J. Loch, Nov. 1831–Jan. 1832, S.E.P.

[2] J. Bradshaw to J. Loch, 28 (?) Dec. 1831 ; J. Bradshaw to J. Loch, 24 Sept. 1832, ibid.

[3] G. Pritt to J. Loch, 11 Dec. 1830, ibid.

traffic from its erstwhile rival.[1] Gilbert Winter on the other
hand opposed it on the grounds that he thought 'a very great
proportion of the water conveyance must and would be taken'.[2]
In view of the division of opinion among the other members of
the Railway Board, his vote was sufficient to tip the scale
against acceptance. Six directors voted in favour of granting
permission to the promoters of the north line to open up
negotiations for the junction, six voted against, and the proposal was declined, the Chairman having presumably cast his
vote in favour of the *status quo*.[3]

There is no actual evidence that Winter was prompted to
this course by R. H. Bradshaw, but he may well have been so
influenced, for the two men were 'on very good terms'.[3] Two
years later, however, Loch was to receive more definite proof
of Bradshaw's intractability. Somewhere about the beginning
of August 1833 the latter remarked to a Mr. Bibby, one of
the promoters of the Manchester, Bolton, and Bury Canal and
Railway Company, that if that concern moved again to
construct a north line of railway to Liverpool, he personally
would take 500 or 1,000 shares in it. Bibby reported the remark
to his committee,[4] to the embarrassment of Loch, who wished
most of all to prevent the building of an independent north
line to Liverpool, for the sake of both the Liverpool and
Manchester Company and the Duke of Bridgewater's Canal.
It is difficult to understand why Bradshaw should have gone
out of his way to encourage a project which would not only
introduce another fierce competitor into the Liverpool and
Manchester trade but would also, both by itself and by its
ultimate extension into Yorkshire, challenge the forward trade
by water between Liverpool and Bolton (to which goods were
carried overland from the banks of the Canal at Worsley)
and between Liverpool and the towns of the West Riding,
besides opening up the Wigan coalfield still further as a rival
to the Worsley mines. The most charitable explanation that
can be given is that advanced senility had released the pent-
up resentments which he had been harbouring against Loch

[1] J. Loch to W. W. Currie, 30 Sept. 1831; W. W. Currie to J. Loch, 10 Sept.
1831, ibid.
[2] G. Winter to J. Loch, Sept. 1831, ibid.
[3] W. W. Currie to J. Loch, 10 Sept. 1831, ibid.
[4] W. W. Currie to J. Loch, 24 Sept. 1833, ibid.

and to a much greater extent against Lord Francis Leveson-Gower, with whom he had been on bad terms for years,[1] and had caused him to avenge the slights of the past by striking at the roots of the latter's income. For just before reports of Bradshaw's indiscretion reached the ears of Loch, the elderly Duke of Sutherland, hitherto described as Marquess of Stafford,[2] had breathed his last, and Lord Francis had entered upon the inheritance which the third Duke of Bridgewater had long before marked out for him.

In fine, when the years since the passing of the Liverpool and Manchester Railway Bill are viewed retrospectively, they can be seen to have brought to the Bridgewater concerns less than the expected benefit, both from the voice which the controllers of the same had obtained in the railway management and from the residual strength of the concerns themselves. The reasons for the failure were various. It was no unmixed blessing for the Canal to be tied to the interests of one railroad company, for thereby manœuvrability in the railway world at large was diminished. Undoubtedly, however, the paramount factor was the division within the Bridgewater interest, which paralysed so many exertions for self-defence. It was becoming abundantly clear that the assertion of a single control over the policies which were to be framed and then pursued stood in the highest order of priority if the welfare of the properties was to be secured. Fortunately, the opportunity to effect the change lay close at hand.

----

[1] Towards the end of 1829 Loch had alluded to the embarrassing position in which Lord Francis was placed 'owing to the little intercourse between him and Bradshaw' (J. Loch to Lord Gower, 21 Nov. 1829, S.E.P.).

[2] George Granville Leveson-Gower, second Marquess of Stafford, was created first Duke of Sutherland on 28 Jan. 1833.

CHAPTER V

The Struggle for Mastery

In the early summer of 1833 events portended a dramatic change in the arrangements for governing the Duke of Bridgewater's vast legacy. Enforced expenditure on installing steam traction on the Mersey estuary had swept the Trust into an acute 'ways and means' crisis, such as has been known to precede revolution in affairs of state. Capital was urgently needed for building warehouses and for improving the Duke's Dock at Liverpool, and the Trustees were obliged to appeal to the Duke of Sutherland for extraordinary measures to raise it. The sale of Brackley and the mortgaging of the canal were the chief alternatives to be considered, but Lord Shaftesbury, the Chairman of Committees and Deputy Speaker of the House of Lords, gave an opinion, when consulted, that the Upper Chamber would not sanction such a breach of trust as the first proposal.[1] The situation called for statesmanship and co-operation, but these qualities were at a discount, for the Superintendent of the Trust was becoming increasingly irresponsible. His insistence, bred of ingrained habit, on transacting all the important business himself was intensifying his 'paralytic affections',[2] to the consternation of James, his son, who trembled for the security both of the Trust properties and of the Bradshaw private estates near Worsley. Indeed, it was Captain Bradshaw who first raised the cry against his father's management. At his wits end, he wrote privately to Loch early in July warning him that the position was critical, and that unless he intervened 'there will be an end of any profit from this concern'.[3]

[1] J. Bradshaw to J. Loch, 22 June 1833; J. Loch to J. Bradshaw, 5 July 1833; and J. Loch to D. Le Marchant, 9 July 1833, S.E.P.
[2] J. Bradshaw to J. Loch, 20 Apr. 1833, ibid.
[3] J. Bradshaw to J. Loch, 2 July 1833, ibid.

It was the death of the Duke of Sutherland, however, that brought matters to a head. On this event, which occurred at Dunrobin Castle in Sutherlandshire on 19 July 1833, the Leveson-Gower family estates and the holdings in the Liverpool and Manchester Railway passed, together with the ducal title, to the eldest son, but the life interest in the Bridgewater properties went to the second son Lord Francis Leveson-Gower, who changed his name to Egerton to comply with the conditions of his inheritance. James Loch continued as agent to both brothers, thus maintaining the link between the railway and the Canal. In view of past relations Bradshaw cannot have welcomed the change of beneficiary. He became more cavalier than ever in his willingness to risk income in a desperate bid to keep trade on the Canal. At a board meeting of the Liverpool and Manchester Railway on 5 August he was said to have offered to take goods 'on any terms, so as to pay'.[1] The final straw came when he received a letter from James Loch on 10 August telling him to send Lord Francis Egerton that part of the income from the Trust which was owing to the Duke of Sutherland at the time of his death, for the Sutherland will had left it so. The missive explained further that by the terms of Lord Francis's marriage settlement, one half of the yearly income would henceforth have to be paid into a fund to raise portions for his younger children and a jointure for his wife.[2] Bradshaw evidently viewed these demands in the context of the acute shortage of capital for the Canal, for he seems to have gone berserk. The tone of his rejoinder was such as to cause Loch to lay before Lord Francis Egerton certain reports which had lately reached him casting doubt on the Superintendent's fitness for command. One was an anguished appeal from Captain James stating that 'matters press both officially and privately and both are now arrived at a crisis'. The other was what he had gleaned from a conversation in London with Gilbert Winter, a meddlesome and two-faced old gossip.[3]

It is difficult to know how much truth reposed in these

---

[1] W. W. Currie to J. Loch, 8 Aug. 1833, S.E.P.

[2] J. Loch to R. H. Bradshaw, 10 Aug. 1833, ibid.

[3] J. Loch to J. Bradshaw, 21 Aug. 1833, and J. Bradshaw to J. Loch, 12 Aug. 1833, ibid.

allegations. Gilbert Winter, when asked to confirm his statement in writing, attributed to Bradshaw a failure of the powers of concentration, irritability, obstinacy, and a dash of impropriety—'Report says he has made an addition to his stock of females whom he accompanies to church every Sunday'— but little else that was seriously detrimental. He even entered a word of praise for the judiciousness of his improvements and expenditure on the Canal and works, and maintained that he was 'very desirous of promoting the interest in which he is engaged'.[1] Later in the year Loch went out of his way to invite complaints from the public about the quality of the service rendered by the Trustees, but received none. From Joseph Sandars, the corn merchant who had inveighed against the Canal monopoly in 1825, came the reply that the management was 'very good'. The only criticism he would venture was that the Trustees were creating too much warehouse room at Manchester and that their docks at Liverpool needed enlargement.[2] Alexander Maxwells had 'no reason whatever to complain'. Their clerks spoke 'of the civility they meet with and the dispatch which any thing we do by that mode of conveyance receives'.[3] If, on the other hand, we look at balance sheets rather than the satisfaction of the consumer, the case against Bradshaw becomes more impressive. The income from the Canal in 1833 was only £17,000, far lower than at any time since the Duke of Bridgewater's death.[4] Had he been allowed to proceed further with his rashly competitive policies he might, indeed, have brought ruin on the whole concern.

The events which followed were stage-managed by Loch. Lord Francis Egerton, on whose behalf he acted, remained on holiday in Paris until all had been settled. The negotiations, which were designed to procure Bradshaw's retirement and to get him to exercise his power of nomination in favour of a suitable successor, stretched over most of September and October, and were conducted behind a veil of secrecy which it is difficult to pierce. It was lifted for one macabre moment when, on 25 September, Captain James Bradshaw, who by

---

[1] G. Winter to J. Loch, 27 Aug. 1833, ibid.
[2] J. Sandars to J. Loch, 5 Nov. 1833, ibid.
[3] A. Maxwell to W. W. Currie, 4 Nov. 1833, ibid.
[4] See below, Appendix A.

seniority was the man best qualified to succeed his father, committed suicide. Loch had no hesitation in ascribing the tragedy to 'the old gentleman's conduct'.[1] The other son, William Rigby Bradshaw, who had been recommended for the succession in the Duke of Bridgewater's will, was then eased out by Loch. '. . . up to a certain point', the latter told Gilbert Winter afterwards, 'I endeavoured to protect the interest of William and Captain Bradshaw as well as Lord Francis. . . . And the moment I saw they were incompatible I distinctly told William Bradshaw that this was the case and begged of him not to depend on my advice but to consult a friend of his own.'[2] Eventually, with the authority of the second Duke of Sutherland who was acting for his absent brother, Loch proposed to the elder Bradshaw 'that he should retire upon his full salary and that he should . . . name Mr. Sothern his successor'.[3] Bradshaw agreed to these terms, and James Sothern was appointed Superintendent by a deed of 3 February 1834.[4] The former had much to congratulate himself upon, for Sothern was a trusted member of his own staff. Son of the late Benjamin Sothern, he had been Bradshaw's personal amanuensis as early as 1813 and had become Principal Agent of the Trust in December 1832.[5] Bradshaw could also rejoice in having disposed of his private estates in Lancashire to Lord Francis Egerton for £127,000. These consisted of lands in Tyldesley and Little Hulton acquired over a period of about a quarter of a century, perhaps for the purpose of making the coal measures underlying them available to the Bridgewater Trustees for exploitation. Lord Francis Egerton raised the purchase money on mortgage from Drummonds,[6]

---

[1] *The Times*, 30 Sept. 1833; J. Loch to Lewis, 29 Sept. 1833, S.E.P.

[2] J. Loch to G. Winter, 1 Nov. 1833, ibid. This may have been because, had he appointed his son William, Bradshaw would have been empowered by the Bridgewater will to appoint the latter's successor also, thus staving off the time when the life tenant would gain control of the nomination.

[3] J. Loch to J. Moss, 28 Oct. 1833, ibid.

[4] List of deeds enclosed in Gatley and Turner to J. Loch, 15 Feb. 1842, B.T.P. (Mertoun).

[5] R. H. Bradshaw to Wrottesley, 17 Nov. 1813, B.T.P. (Mertoun), File 131; Salaries Journal, Bridgewater Trust, 1824–37, Lancs. C.R.O.

[6] J. Loch to F. Smith, 22 Nov. 1837, L.E.P. The General Abstract of Accounts for 1829 (Lancs. C.R.O.) shows that the Bridgewater Trustees paid out £1,049 in royalties during that year for 'four foot' coal got under the lands of R. H. Bradshaw and the Trustees of Warrington School. Bradshaw had

and the properties became the nucleus of the Egerton private estates.

It is clear that Lord Francis had not entered this transaction merely to replace one autonomous Superintendent by another. As Loch explained to his friend John Moss, the nomination of Sothern was to be 'subject to such restrictions as the Trustees of the Will and Lord Francis should fix, the object being in short to give Lord Francis a controul'. 'To ensure this the more', he continued, 'the mansions at Worsley Hall and Runcorn are reserved for his Lordship's own residence.'[1] Another of his letters shows that Sothern was trusted no more than Bradshaw had been, and that Loch was looking for the earliest opportunity to get rid of him. Meanwhile, he proposed to appoint 'a fit deputy to have the resident management'. 'He must know something of the course of the trade and the country, at the same time firm and prudent.'[2] Confident that his master had already gained control, the life tenant's agent began to air his plans early in November 1833 for reforming Trust policies on lines which would include a *rapprochement* with the Railway Company. 'Where is my friend Sandars?' he wrote to W. W. Currie. 'Ask him if he has no complaint to make against the Duke that may be rectified. There should be some Grand Alliance.'[3]

In this he miscalculated. Sothern had no intention of being a puppet. He saw himself as 'equally a donee' under the Canal Duke's will 'as Lord Francis himself'.[4] Moreover, he had the advantage over the latter of being already in possession, for Bradshaw had appointed him Deputy Superintendent on 9 November, in advance of the formal transfer of authority.[5] Friction occurred right from the beginning, for Sothern impounded a crucial deed drawn up by his predecessor (perhaps the one detailing the restrictions on his power), and Loch was obliged to take legal advice on how he might be made to

purchased the leased estate of Chaddock and Booths, together with part of the Warrington School land, in 1810 (J. Lunn, *A Short History of the Township of Tyldesley*, p. 105).

[1] J. Loch to J. Moss, 28 Oct. 1833, S.E.P.

[2] Copy of letter from J. Loch, 19 Nov. 1833, ibid.

[3] Extract from letter to W. W. Currie, 3 Nov. 1833, ibid. It was almost certainly written by Loch.

[4] *Manchester Guardian*, 27 Feb. 1836.

[5] Salaries Journal, Bridgewater Trust, 1824–37, Lancs. C.R.O.

surrender it. The advice suggested that, in the event of litigation, Sothern would take refuge in the uncertainties of the Court of Chancery.[1] There was nothing for it, therefore, than that the two parties should endeavour to live side by side with as much harmony as was possible. This they did for just over two years. In July 1834 Loch and Sothern met in Manchester and agreed upon an application to Parliament for power to sell Brackley and arrange with the Corporation of Liverpool about docks and to dispose of land for building purposes. Sothern differed from Loch over the details, but deferred to the latter's judgement.[2]

It was Lord Francis Egerton who first broke the truce. Bursting to take possession of his estate, he sent his house steward John Brass to Worsley in January 1836 to install his furniture in the Old Hall. Sothern was established at the New Hall, where he regaled himself with the pleasures of gracious living, holding Grand Balls and other festivities. Unwilling to admit a rival centre of influence to develop in what he regarded as his own demesne, the Superintendent had proceeded as slowly as he could with the repairs to the Old Hall which were requisite if Lord Francis was to occupy it in accordance with the arrangement made with Bradshaw. Eventually he had let the house to tenants. This was the situation when Brass arrived, and when he deposited his luggage in the Old Hall preparatory to installing the furniture, Sothern resolved to act. He took eight strong men along to the house, and ejected the intruder and his bags by main force.[3] On hearing of this, Lord Francis and his advisers declared instant war on Sothern.

Joseph Varey of the firm of Tindall and Varey, solicitors, was the man they principally employed to conduct the offensive. He made a determined bid to come to terms with Sothern's enemies, to detach his friends, and to amass the sort of information that could be used in a Chancery suit for his removal. Negotiations were opened with the Mersey and Irwell Navigation Company for a settlement of differences on

---

[1] Edward Gatty to J. Loch, 14 Nov. 1833, S.E.P.
[2] J. Loch to Lord F. Egerton, 24 July 1834, B.T.P. (Mertoun), File 134.
[3] J. Brass to Lord F. Egerton, 15 Jan. 1836; Lord F. Egerton to J. Sothern, Jan. 1836, ibid.

which Sothern had been preparing to fight. Lansdale, the cashier, was approached directly to get him to act against his superior,[1] and the independent carriers on the Bridgewater Canal were wooed with a declaration given by Lord Francis in April that their tonnage rates were reduced by 1*s*. per ton.[2] Within a day or two of this statement about tonnages, strongly worded affidavits showing the determination of the carriers to have left the navigation, had the reductions not been made, were being filed away by the life tenant's lawyers for use in the action pending against Sothern.[3] James Loch afterwards denied emphatically that the concession was made to the carriers as a bribe,[4] but the effect was much the same as if it had been.

Varey outlined to Lord Francis the kind of evidence which he was seeking against the Superintendent. It included such matters as 'the expenses of the game establishment, Mr. Sothern's personal expenses, the connection of benefits derived by Mr. John Sothern and others of the family, the collieries and various other matters'.[5] Obviously the main obstacle to this quest was Sothern's refusal to allow Messrs. Tindall and Varey to examine the Trust accounts. He would permit, however, a personal inspection by Lord Francis, who took advantage of the opportunity to submit them to an accountant for a report.[6]

Sothern responded to the attack by withholding the life tenant's income. For the rest, however, he pursued a mainly defensive strategy and was slowly pushed back. By the end of March Lansdale had turned against him and was refusing payments. 'This must soon have an end,' Loch announced jubilantly, 'now the supplies are stopt.'[7] The first round of

---

[1] J. Loch to Lord F. Egerton, 31 Mar. 1836, ibid. This letter reports that Lansdale is 'acting in unison with your wishes' and states that he has 'got your letter'.

[2] M. & I.N.C. Order Book, 1834–41, pp. 38–9.

[3] J. Loch to Lord F. Egerton, 5 Apr. 1836, B.T.P. (Mertoun), File 134.

[4] J. Loch to F. Smith, 28 May 1837, L.E.P. He claimed that the carriers had convinced him that without the concession they would be forced to leave the Canal, but admitted on further reflection that the allowance was greater than was necessary.

[5] J. Varey to Lord F. Egerton, 6 Feb. 1836, B.T.P. (Mertoun), File 134.

[6] J. Varey to Lord F. Egerton, 11 Feb. 1836, and J. Loch to Lord F. Egerton, 5 Apr. 1836, ibid.

[7] J. Loch to Lord F. Egerton, 31 Mar. 1836, ibid.

the Chancery suit, when it was eventually launched, also went against him. By an order of the Master of the Rolls given early in August he was compelled to pay over to Lord Francis within three days the balance of the income from the Trust estates down to 26 December 1835, a sum amounting to £60,594, and to allow the life tenant to depute anyone, barring James Loch or Messrs. Tindall and Varey, to inspect the account books and other papers at Worsley on his behalf.[1] Thereupon, Lord Francis appointed Loftus Lowndes, a Chancery barrister, and Richard Smith, a mining engineer from Staffordshire, to carry out the investigation. They went about their work with painstaking thoroughness, and, not content with viewing the Worsley books, went on to inspect those at Liverpool too.[2] Moreover, whilst they were at work, a timely scandal came to the life tenant's aid. Sandars disclosed on 11 October that William Eaton, receiver of corn for the Duke's Trustees at Manchester, had been defrauding his employers by releasing grain for sale by his cousin, a Manchester corn merchant. The Eatons were related to James Sothern, and the informant was able to comment pungently: 'I do not think there ever was such a snug family concern as this.'[3]

It seems probable that the imputations cast upon Sothern's management contained much exaggeration. Even Lord Francis Egerton's own agents came to realize, as they proceeded with the inspection of the accounts, that no active dishonesty could be charged against him.[4] This was in line with the impression formed three years earlier by Edward Gatty, one of his Lordship's legal advisers who judged him to be 'a straightforward, plain-dealing man'. 'His physiognomy is greatly in his favour', he added.[5] The faults in the running of the concern, and they were legion, seem to have stemmed more from the Superintendent's negligence and from his having allowed antiquated procedure to go unreformed than from positive corruption. The accounts were unsystematically

---

[1] Order marked 'Lord F. Egerton and Others v. Sothern', 8 Aug. 1836, B.T.P. (Mertoun), File 134.

[2] See various letters on the subject from Loftus Lowndes and Richard Smith to James Loch, Sept. and Oct. 1836, ibid.

[3] J. Sandars to J. Loch, 11 Oct. 1836, ibid.

[4] Loftus Lowndes to J. Loch, 11 Sept. and 20 Oct. 1836; J. Loch to Loftus Lowndes, 1 Nov. 1836, ibid.   [5] E. Gatty to J. Loch, 14 Nov. 1833, S.E.P.

kept. The accountant who first examined them found them 'so confused as to lead to no conclusion practically'. Further investigation by Loftus Lowndes showed that an entry for £8,000 relating to a deal at Manchester had been lost in the process of transfer from ledger to ledger.[1] Moreover, as Sandars implied, family connection had been allowed to become the basis of appointment and promotion in the Trustees' service to an alarmingly unhealthy extent. No fewer than seven Eatons, headed by James Eaton, the Principal Agent at Runcorn, who was a near relative of Sothern, occupied positions of profit under the Trust. Two Sotherns who were nephews of the Superintendent held clerkships at Preston Brook, whilst David Bromilow, son of a business partner of the Superintendent's brother, was the principal land agent at Worsley.[2] The worst case was that of the brother himself, John Sothern, who was allowed the free run of the Duke's wharf and warehouses at Liverpool to sell coal from his own Rushy Park colliery near St. Helens, to the exclusion of the Worsley coal, which he was also responsible for selling.[3] It is by no means certain, however, how far James Sothern was personally responsible for creating this situation, for his father had held office under the Trust before him. The concessions to his brother went back to Bradshaw's time, and may have been adopted, in the first instance, in good faith, perhaps as a means of reducing selling costs. It seems likely that his own responsibility was mainly that of conniving at abuses which he did not fully understand. With the vanity of an underling who had been suddenly advanced to lordship, he shut himself up at Worsley 'in the midst of his self sufficiency, acting upon the avowed principle of obtaining all his information from spies, surrounded by his own relations only and those whose whole object was to keep him ignorant of everything and to misinform him as suited their purposes'.[4] That, at least, is how James Loch came to see it.

If Sothern was not wholly a rogue, he was certainly less resourceful than the men who surrounded Lord Francis

---

[1] J. Loch to Lord F. Egerton, 5 Apr. 1836, B.T.P. (Mertoun), File 134.

[2] List of Clerks, etc., under Mr. Sothern, B.T.P. (Mertoun), Doc. no. 70.

[3] R. Smith to J. Loch, 22 Oct. 1836, B.T.P. (Mertoun), File 134; J. Loch to F. Egerton, 27 Mar. 1837, E.B.C.

[4] J. Loch to Loftus Lowndes, 1 Nov. 1836, B.T.P. (Mertoun), File 134.

Egerton. In his dealings with other concerns he adhered to the largely negative policy of obstructing all encroachments on the Trustees' privileges. They adopted a more subtle and sophisticated approach, aiming to replace the knock-neighbour attitudes of the past by a spirit of conciliation and arrangement.

The events of the middle thirties offered plenty of scope for ingenuity, for the time when the Bridgewater Trust was riven by internal strife was also the time when it faced a particularly determined offensive from its ancient rival the Mersey and Irwell Navigation Company. The quarrel turned on two main issues. The first was the Runcorn Island dispute. This arose because the Duke of Bridgewater's Trustees and the Old Quay Company had opposing interests in regard to the navigation of the Mersey estuary. To the former it was always a matter of acute concern that the deep water channel should be kept as close as possible to the Cheshire bank, so as to provide the shortest route for flats and coasters coming up the river to their docks at Runcorn, and that the area in front of the Duke's locks should be kept free from sediment.[1] Vessels bound for the Old Quay docks, about a mile further upstream than those of the Trustees, were severely discomfited, however, when navigating along the southern shore of the estuary on a flood tide, by the strong currents which sucked them into the rocky mouth of the narrow channel or Gut which had been made by the Duke of Bridgewater between Runcorn Island and the mainland for the purpose of strengthening the scouring effects of the tide. The Mersey and Irwell Navigation Company first attempted to combat this nuisance by taking steps to transfer the navigable channel to the northern shore. In June 1830 the Bridgewater Trustees had to apply for an injunction to restrain them from cutting down some rocks projecting into the river on the Lancashire side which served to divert the scouring ebb tide to the Cheshire banks. Though the Vice-Chancellor declined to interfere, these operations, which had been in progress for about three years when the injunction was sought, failed to change the course of the navigable channel. Eventually, the directors of the Old Quay Company revised their tactics. In June 1835 they applied to

[1] See above, p. 20.

James Sothern for permission for their vessels to sail through the Gut on their way to the Old Quay docks. Previously this had been closed to navigation on the very plausible grounds that traffic through it would impede the passage of vessels in and out of the Duke of Bridgewater's locks. Sothern made difficulties and, in order to force his hand, the Company brought an action for nuisance against the Trustees at the Liverpool Spring Assizes in 1836.[1] Lord Francis Egerton's solicitor, Joseph Varey, took a different view. Quite independently of Sothern, he approached the Old Quay Committee for an amicable adjustment of the question, and got them to agree in principle to a postponement or an abandonment of the prosecution.[2] But this did not settle the matter at issue. Varey appears to have misunderstood the objects for which the directors were working, thinking that they would be satisfied with a rounding of the northern edge of Runcorn Island as a substitute for opening the Gut to shipping.[3] The dispute dragged on.

The other question at issue between the two water companies was that of the proposed Manchester and Salford Junction Canal. In July 1835 the Mersey and Irwell Navigation Company decided to support an application to Parliament for powers to construct a short line of canal through Manchester from the River Irwell, just above the place where it was joined by the Manchester, Bolton, and Bury Canal to the Rochdale Canal about half a mile east of its junction with the Bridgewater at Castlefield. This project originated with the inhabitants of Bolton, who merely sought an improved communication across Manchester for Bolton goods in transit through the town, but the Old Quay Committee adopted it with hostile designs upon the large and growing traffic exchanged between the Duke of Bridgewater's Canal and the Rochdale, which was a principal link with Yorkshire.[4] The

---

[1] This summary of the origins of the dispute is based on 'The Brief Indictment and Case for the Defendants in the Case of the King against James Sothern Esq. and Others at the Liverpool Spring Assizes, March 30th 1836', and 'The Brief Proofs for the Defendants' in the same action; B.T.P. (Mertoun).

[2] M. & I.N.C. Order Book, 1834–41, pp. 32–3.

[3] Tindall and Varey's report on the Runcorn Island question, 17 Sept. 1838, B.T.P. (Mertoun).

[4] M. & I.N.C. Order Book, 1834–41, pp. 19–21.

Duke's was in a strong position to resist this encroachment, for, by the terms of the Rochdale Canal Act of 1794, it had obtained the right to receive the waste water supplies of the Rochdale Canal,[1] with which a new canal was now to be connected. Sothern resolved to oppose the scheme, but was checkmated by Lord Francis Egerton, who agreed to a compromise by which, in return for allowing the Manchester and Salford Junction Canal to be constructed, the Trustees were to be permitted to make a cut joining their own canal at the Manchester end to the Old River, in such a way as to enable them to share in the Bolton trade passing down the Manchester and Bolton Canal. Sothern petitioned alone against the proposals. The two other Trustees, viz. the Archbishop of York and the Earl of Devon, who sided with the life tenant, followed this up with a further petition dissociating themselves from their colleague, who promptly retaliated with a lengthy plea informing the House of Commons that they were mere 'nominal trustees' with no power of veto upon his actions, and accusing Lord Francis Egerton of acting in bad faith.[2] The outcome of this bickering was that the Bill authorizing the construction of the Manchester and Salford Junction Canal was carried on 4 July 1836, and the canal was duly cut, travelling underground for a distance of 476 yards. T. O. Lingard, the principal agent of the Old Quay Company, afterwards explained that the difficulties standing in the way of it 'could never have been overcome but at the very time the Act was obtained'.[3] The Trustees also proceeded in due course to make their own communication with the river through the Hulme Locks, which were opened on 20 September 1838.[4]

Lord Francis Egerton's growing reputation for liberality soon won the public to his side. In the press he was hailed as a new Josiah bent on effecting a reformation of the Canal management and on bringing to the public a much improved service.[5] This undoubtedly helped to strengthen his position

---

[1] J. Priestley, *Historical Account of the Navigable Rivers, Canals, and Railways of Great Britain*, p. 544.

[2] *J.H.C.* xci (1836), 129, 140, 201–2; *J.H.L.* lxviii (1836), 310.

[3] T. O. Lingard to the Proprietors of the Mersey and Irwell Navigation, 31 May 1841, M. & I.N.C. Order Book 1834–41, p. 177.

[4] *The Manchester Historical Recorder*, p. 111.

[5] *The Times*, 17 and 18 Feb. 1836.

against Sothern. Nevertheless, it became increasingly clear, the more his advisers pondered the matter, that more was to be gained by compromising with the latter than by pressing for an unqualified victory over him. Three main reasons prompted such a course.

The first was the damage which was being done to the internal efficiency and reputation of the concern by the protraction of the dispute. Writing to Lord Francis Egerton on 3 November 1836,[1] James Loch listed twelve grounds for a compromise. The first three of these ran as follows:

1. The present condition of affairs hangs up the whole business of the Canal, which is now crippled in its management in every way.

2. The late exposure of the several clerks and sub-agents makes this state of affairs more serious and the more necessary to be attended to.

3. The junction with the Old Quay—the whole warehouse system to require an immediate consideration and arrangement.

Secondly there were the impediments presented by the quarrel to negotiations with outsiders. 'The carriers don't know whom to look to. The Old Quay has no-one to deal with. . . .'[2] Loch, who wrote these words, was, no doubt, especially concerned that his plans for stabilizing the rates of carriage between Liverpool and Manchester were being hindered by the uncertainty. As agent to both the Leveson-Gower brothers, the one a railway shareholder and the other a canal proprietor, he had clearly hoped that the first fruits of Bradshaw's removal would be an ending of the ruinous competition which the former Superintendent had so rashly maintained. One of his earliest actions after that event had been to bring the Bridgewater Trustees, the Old Quay Company, and the Liverpool and Manchester Railway Company together in an arrangement for raising freight charges. This agreement took effect from 28 February 1835,[3] but was ruptured four months later by discord between the Mersey and Irwell Company and the Railway Board, and the rates

---

[1] B.T.P. (Mertoun), File 134.

[2] J. Loch to Lord F. Egerton, 1 Nov. 1836, ibid.

[3] M. & I.N.C. Order Book, 1834–41, pp. 1–3, 10–12; J. Loch to F. Smith, 6 May 1837, L.E.P.

were again slashed.[1] For some time after that, tension between the two last-named parties remained strong enough to preclude any further attempt to bring them directly together. Nevertheless, the Old Quay Committee did attempt to treat with the Bridgewater Trustees in October 1836 for fixing the Liverpool and Manchester rates at their existing level and for raising the Runcorn and Manchester charges slightly. But the discord between Sothern and Lord Francis Egerton prevented any firm negotiation. All that the Committee could do was to write to both parties in the divided Bridgewater interest. James Loch replied, promising to lay the proposal before Lord Francis; Sothern merely sent a messenger to acknowledge receipt of the communication.[2]

A third inducement to a coming-to-terms with Sothern was that the alternative, persistence in the Chancery suit for his removal, was likely to bring nothing but delay and ruinous expense. Loftus Lowndes informed Loch in October 1836:

> . . . I think there will be little difficulty in establishing a case for his suspension, but the weapon to be used for effecting that is so fearful a one that if it can be obtained without its aid, it should be, even at great sacrifice of feeling and otherwise. That Court of Chancery kicks more in the discharge than any great gun I ever heard of.[3]

Better proof could scarcely be required of the veracity of Charles Dickens's famous satire of early nineteenth-century Chancery procedures in the case of *Jarndyce* v. *Jarndyce*, or of the importance of this factor in restraining a resort to law in disputes about property.

The terms first proposed to Sothern about the middle of October 1836 were that he should continue as Superintendent for another two years, but should act under Lord Francis Egerton's instructions in the leading principles of management. These principles were afterwards defined by Loch as 'whether the collieries should be let or kept in hand, whether the farms ought to be let or not, whether the Trustees should continue carriers and to what extent and so on'. The Superintendent was also to give up the house and game at Worsley

---

[1] M. & I.N.C. Order Book 1834–41, pp. 18, 22.
[2] Ibid., pp. 50–1, 53–6, 62.
[3] Loftus Lowndes to J. Loch, 22 Oct. 1836, B.T.P. (Mertoun), File 134.

to Lord Francis. Sothern accepted the proposed restrictions on his liberty, but demurred at the further condition that Lord Francis should have the option of demanding his retirement on a pension after two years.[1] After further negotiation it was agreed at the end of the year that Sothern should resign immediately 'on or before 1 March 1837'. For this he was to receive the sum of £45,000, and Lord Francis was to write him a letter of reference, setting his character right and repudiating the various imputations which had been cast upon it.[2] On 1 March following, the Archbishop of York and the Earl of Devon, with the consent of Lord Francis Egerton, appointed James Loch to be Superintendent according to the procedure laid down in the Duke of Bridgewater's will.[3] The struggle for mastery was over. Having to buy out two Superintendents in a period of three years was a heavy price to pay for overcoming the disadvantages of a divided control inflicted upon the Canal and coal-mines by that curious instrument. But the appointment of Loch, who remained Lord Francis's agent, took care that the embarrassments of the past should not recur. Henceforth, to all intents and purposes, the ultimate control of policy rested with the man who drew the profits, and there was scope for a consistent policy to be framed.

[1] L. Lowndes to J. Loch, 20 and 22 Oct. 1836 ; J. Loch to L. Lowndes, 30 Oct. 1836, ibid.

[2] R. Smith to J. Loch, 27 Dec. 1836, and J. Smith to Gatty, 21 Jan. 1837, B.T.P. (Mertoun), Files 134, 135.

[3] Duplicate Conveyance and Assignment, Bridgewater Canal, 27 June 1872, p. 9.

CHAPTER VI

New Brooms Sweep Clean

JAMES LOCH's first task on assuming control of the Bridge-water Trust was to find someone who could manage the Canal and coal-mines for him. Himself a land agent, with more than enough on his hands already, he recognized from the start that he had neither the time nor the expertise to undertake the detailed administration of a vast and complex industrial concern. He looked, therefore, for an experienced aide-de-camp, and his choice alighted initially on Richard Smith, mine agent to the Trustees of the first Earl Dudley in the Black Country. Smith was a mineral agent of the highest distinction. Son-in-law and one-time partner of the great Staffordshire ironmaster Samuel Fereday, whose name is linked with that of John Wilkinson, he had successively managed the Rothschilds' mines in Wales, exploited the resources of bituminous coal and anthracite at Figara in Portugal, and opened up the Nova Scotia coalfield for the General Mining Association during seven exciting and fruitful years which he spent in the country from 1827 to 1834.[1] Loch offered him the post of Deputy Superintendent with a salary of £1,200 per annum, £200 more than he was getting from his present employers, together with free house and coals and travelling expenses.[2] This was sheer poaching, for he had encountered Smith through his own appointment as auditor to Lord Dudley's Trustees. It put the Dudley Trustees—Lord Hatherton, Benbow, and the Bishop of Exeter—into a towering rage which culminated in a dramatic scene at the House of Lords, when Hatherton proposed to his colleagues that they should raise Smith's

---

[1] See R. P. Fereday, 'The Career of Richard Smith', *The Acorn* (Journal of the Round Oak Steel Works, Ltd.), Summer 1966–Summer 1967.

[2] J. Loch to Lord F. Egerton, 30 Jan. 1837, E.B.C.

salary to £1,200 and force the offending Loch out of the auditorship.[1]

The outcome was that Richard Smith declined the offer from the Bridgewater Trustees, but recommended his son George Samuel Fereday Smith for the post, promising to assist him with his own experience for a great portion of every fortnight. In March 1837, therefore, Fereday Smith was appointed Deputy Superintendent with a stipend exactly half of that intended for his father. He was at the time only twenty-five, but James Loch did not count this a disqualification. 'At twenty-five years', he wrote to Lord Francis Egerton, 'Pitt and Napoleon had been at the head of their respective countries. A young man will have more activity and fewer prejudices than a more elderly one, and having the father's aid, we start without an interregnum.'[2] Moreover, Fereday Smith had much to compensate for his lack of years. As his name proudly proclaimed, the blood of two families famous in coal mining and iron manufacture, the Feredays and the Smiths, ran in his veins. His education had been an unusual mixture of the traditional and the technical. From Charterhouse and University College London he proceeded to Queen's College, Oxford, where he graduated Bachelor of Arts in 1835, and was afterwards sent abroad to study mining and geology in Germany. On his return he gained practical experience of mining and surveying in Staffordshire, and at the beginning of 1837 he was employed as engineer on the Birmingham and Gloucester Railway, which was then under construction.[3] He brought to his new duties, therefore, both the equipment of a gentleman and a scientific bent which was to gain for him eventually both an F.R.S. and an F.R.G.S. His was, indeed, a fortunate appointment. He was to serve the Trust as Deputy Superintendent or General Manager[4] for fifty years, during which time he, rather than the Superintendents whom he

[1] Staffs. C.R.O., diary of E. J. Littleton, first Baron Hatherton, Feb. 1837. I owe this reference to Mr. R. P. Fereday.

[2] J. Loch to Lord F. Egerton, 3 Mar. 1837, E.B.C. In the Bridgewater Trust Salaries Book, 1838–42, Fereday Smith is described as Deputy Superintendent with a salary of £600 per annum (Lancs. C.R.O.).

[3] J. Foster, *Alumni Oxonienses, 1715–1886*, vol. iv, p. 1313; J. Foster, *Men at the Bar*, p. 432; J. Loch to Lord F. Egerton, 30 Jan. 1837, E.B.C.

[4] For details of his subsequent demotion from Deputy Superintendent to Principal Agent or, in effect, General Manager, see below, p. 268.

served, was the originator of the more progressive initiatives which were taken in its affairs.

Having installed his deputy, Loch was now free to carry through some long-overdue changes in the management of the Trust properties. For these the time was eminently ripe. As we have seen, public opinion expected from the young life tenant and his agent a radical transformation, the first fruits of which would be a new spirit of enlightenment dedicated first and foremost to the service of the navigation user. Newspapers and individuals seeking employment under the Trust vied with each other in putting forward suggestions as to how these purposes might best be advanced. What was achieved fell considerably short of what was expected, short also of the absolute reversal of policies which later writers have imagined to have taken place. It cannot without exaggeration be described as a complete abandonment of Bradshaw's tight-fisted policies.[1] Nevertheless, reforms ranged over a wide front, and a great deal was done in the early years of the new regime to remove outstanding abuses and to render the concern efficient.

In the first place there was an overhaul of the administrative machinery of the Trust in accordance with the tenets of mid nineteenth-century liberalism, the creed which found its principal spokesmen in Jeremy Bentham and Adam Smith, its trusty henchmen in the English and Scottish middle classes, and which was to become under Gladstone the guiding principle of English government. We find Loch applying to the management of the Canal and coal-mines the notion of centralization which Edwin Chadwick brought contemporaneously to the Poor Law and to the administration of public health. Before the fall of Sothern, authority had been divided between two superior agents, at Worsley and at Runcorn, who superintended the trading arrangements on the eastern and western halves of the Canal respectively. Their responsibility extended from trade to maintenance. With the assistance of the engineer, Sothern as Worsley agent had controlled the works at Worsley and Manchester, whilst James Tonge as Runcorn agent had managed those at Liverpool and Runcorn. In the reorganization which occurred when Loch became Superintendent,

[1] Cf. Bernard Falk, *The Bridgewater Millions*, p. 128.

Fereday Smith took charge of the whole concern from head-quarters at Manchester. The Worsley and Runcorn agents became mere trading agents like those at Liverpool and Preston Brook, and a Civil Engineer's Department headed by the engineer was created to take over their responsibilities for maintenance.[1]

There was also a very characteristically liberal onslaught on jobbery, inefficiency, and wasteful expenditure. By March 1838 the new masters had succeeded in getting rid, for one reason or another, of the family connections of James Sothern, but this was not done merely to replace one corner of patronage by another. Vigilance was exercised by Loch to prevent Edmund Smith, the engineer, from becoming a 'medium of application and of influence' in obtaining promotions.[2] Care was also taken to restore the impartiality of the Trustees' servants in order to ensure that they would, in future, serve the Trustees' interests and not those of private individuals. James Tonge, the Runcorn agent, was dismissed in February 1838, ostensibly because of the general reorganization, but really because he had become connected with parties whose interests were adverse to those of the Bridgewater Trust.[3] Nearly two years later notice of dismissal was served on Edmund Smith on account of some underhand conduct in the letting of contracts.[4] Loch insisted on the highest standards of personal probity among the Trustees' employees. 'I would not keep a very bad man if he was the best possible workman', he wrote in 1842.[5] One of the grounds for discharging Edmund Smith, alluded to in the letter of dismissal cited above, was that he had concealed the fact that he had once been subject to personal arrest.

In the quest of efficiency measures received attention no less than men. Official procedures were reorganized in such a way as to effect a tighter control over the actions of individual officers. In October 1837 Loch introduced a rule, which he had imposed on previous managements under his control, that no documents should be allowed to leave any of the Bridgewater

[1] J. Loch to F. Smith, 19 Apr. and 5 June 1837, L.E.P.
[2] J. Loch to F. Smith, 16 and 17 Mar. 1838, ibid.
[3] J. Loch to F. Smith, 1 Feb. 1838, ibid.
[4] J. Loch to E. Smith, 13 Jan. 1840, ibid.
[5] J. Loch to F. Smith, 10 June 1842, ibid.

offices without a written receipt being entered in a book.[1]
Administrative costs were carefully watched, and scarcely a
detail was allowed to pass unnoticed. 'I wish you would tell
Varey to give you his reports on foolscap closely written on
both sides', Loch wrote to his General Manager in June 1838.
'The forms he sends them in', he added, 'are inconvenient and
cannot be put into my pocket, and must be more expensive
than necessary.'[2] Regular meetings were instituted at Worsley
to control the rate of expenditure, and Loch was quick to
bring home to heads of departments any excess of spending
which occurred within their spheres.[3] No doubt these measures
were fully justified, when they were first introduced, by the
need to check prevailing laxity, but in the course of time they
were so extended as to be detrimental to the best interests
of the concern. The system of controls became so rigid as
practically to debar initiative, whilst economy was carried to
such lengths as to become a vice, being directed against
expenditure which was essential for the maintenance of the
Canal and coal-mines in good working order.

Nevertheless, the essential liberalism of the reforms carried
out at the beginning of James Loch's administration was
signified by the emphasis which was placed on competition
as a revitalizing force. Competitive tendering was proposed
for the ordering of hay for the Canal boat horses at the
different stations along the navigation in June 1837[4] and for
the work of the engineer's department in April 1842. At that time
Loch gave orders that repairs to the Canal at Manchester and
all new works at the Manchester, Broadheath, Burford Lane,
Stockton Quay, and Preston Brook stations should be arranged
by bargaining with a number of contractors, instead of as
previously by the Trustees' own men detached from Worsley
Yard or Runcorn in workshop boats.[5]

Competition was not merely an ingredient of administrative
reform; it was also a principle to be applied to the trade of the
Canal. The new Superintendent set his face against restrictive
practices. It has been alleged against Bradshaw that, in his

[1] J. Loch to F. Smith, 27 Oct. 1837, ibid.
[2] J. Loch to F. Smith, 1 June 1838, ibid.
[3] J. Loch to F. Smith, 25 June 1842, ibid.
[4] J. Loch to F. Smith, 21 June 1837, ibid.
[5] J. Loch to F. Smith, 19 Apr. 1842, ibid.

time, the Bridgewater Trustees kept their competitors out of the carrying trade by monopolizing nearly the whole of the land and warehouses at Runcorn.[1] Loch did his utmost to ensure that a similar design could not be charged against his management. In July 1838 he jibbed at sanctioning the purchase of land in Manchester for the purpose of impeding other firms of carriers from establishing themselves upon it.[2] Lord Francis Egerton, he explained, would not even attempt to prevent ' all or any other concern obtaining all the advantages which the improvement of their natural resources will admit of, his property and interests not being immediately touched '.[3] It was legitimate to buy land in order to forestall a rival bent on monopolizing it for himself, but not with a view to creating one's own monopoly.

For a navigational concern, monopoly of land was but a stepping-stone to monopoly of trade, and Loch aspired to the latter no more than he aimed at the former. He set his face against all proposals for extending the trading responsibilities of the Trust, whether by leasing railway companies or by conducting new trades in the Trustees' own boats. Circumstances would compel him to relax his attitude a good deal before much more time had elapsed, but for the moment this was where he stood. 'You see the boundaries to which the Trustees are restricted', he observed to Fereday Smith in May 1838. 'To administer well and efficiently what they have charge of, is quite enough for any one person to undertake.' On these grounds he rejected Fereday Smith's suggestion in May 1838 that they should lease the Bolton and Leigh Railway.[3] Two months earlier he had spurned a proposal that they should carry in their own boats as far as the Potteries.[4] So far from accepting the plan unfolded to him on his accession to the superintendentship by a merchant in search of employment, that the concern should carry on such terms as would drive every other carrier off the water and underbid the Mersey and Irwell Navigation Company,[5] he offered every inducement

---

[1] W. T. Jackman, *The Development of Transportation in Modern England*, p. 518.   [2] J. Loch to F. Smith, 11 July 1838, L.E.P.

[3] J. Loch to F. Smith, 10 May 1838, ibid.

[4] J. Loch to F. Smith, 8 Mar. 1838, ibid.

[5] James Loch's Memorandum of Interview with John Crowther, 5 Mar. 1837, E.B.C.

in his power to the independent carriers on the Duke's to get them to stay on the line and to expand their trade. Not only did he confirm the reduction of tonnage which he and Lord Francis had dangled before them as a bait prior to the change in the management; he backdated it considerably, with a view to offsetting the attempts which were being made by the Old Quay Company to draw carriers away from the Bridgewater to their own navigation.[1]

This policy of restraint was dictated by a medley of considerations. In the first place there was the thought that, because of the restraints on the Trustees' borrowing powers, the cost of extensions would have to be borne by the life tenant, whose interests James Loch was committed to protect. Then there was the belief, implanted in Loch's mind by Captain Bradshaw, that it was unprofitable to the Trustees to carry goods on freight.[2] This opinion appears to have been well founded. An analysis of the profits of the Bridgewater Trust for the years 1844–8 which distinguishes between those derived from the Canal and those from the carrying department reveals a loss in the latter for three years out of five, whilst the former showed a handsome profit of £40,000, £50,000, or £70,000 per annum.[3] But Loch's objections to expanding the concern rested not only upon private advantage but also upon the public interest. Like many of his contemporaries he had little faith in the efficiency of large corporate businesses as trading ventures, and believed that the work of carrying for the public could be performed far more beneficially by the small partnerships which already carried on the Duke of Bridgewater's Canal. Thus in 1840 he wrote:

I have ever held, publicly and privately, that no company can carry as economically as an individual. I have always doubted whether railway companies do carry goods without drawing on their passenger profit. I have always dreaded their doing so and annihilating the private carriers, first on their own lines, next on canals and forcing canal companies to become carriers, and thus placing the whole carrying trade of the country into the hands

[1] F. Smith to J. Loch, 15 Mar. 1838; J. Loch to F. Smith, 22 Mar. 1838, L.E.P.

[2] James Loch's Memorandum of Interview with John Crowther, 5 Mar. 1837, E.B.C.

[3] See below, p. 189 text and n. 2.

of joint stock companies who will, of course, combine against the public, which monopoly they will retain by lowering if any attempt is made to interfere with it or by absorbing any new company. All this process must be worked out by much loss in the meantime.[1]

To avert such a disaster was a cardinal object of Loch's policy in the early years of his trusteeship.

To the principle of free competition which they sought to implement, the Trustees made one significant exception. They favoured agreement between rival carrying concerns to regulate the rates of carriage. One of the first steps which they took under Loch's superintendentship was to repair the *entente* which had been ruptured by the Mersey and Irwell Navigation Company in 1835. In November 1837 they entered into an arrangement with the Old Quay Company and the independent carriers by water to raise the average rate of freight between Liverpool and Manchester from 8s. 5½d. to 9s. 8½d. per ton and to make a corresponding increase in the charges between Runcorn and Manchester. The agreement was formalized at the beginning of 1838. The contracting parties engaged themselves by bonds to fulfil their promises and were required to give three months' notice before departing from the terms to which they had given their assent. Owing to the difficulty of getting agreement between the Old River and the Liverpool and Manchester Railway over such questions as the desirability of charging warehouse rent to customers who delayed collecting their goods, the railway was not formally included in the new arrangement, but the directors sympathized with the idea of raising freight charges. On down goods they had never lowered, and they now agreed separately with the Bridgewater Trustees to raise their rates on certain categories of up goods.[2] From that time forward to the end of the period covered by this book, the Trustees pursued consistently the object of stabilizing charges by agreements of this kind. Their efforts were being sabotaged continually by the aggressive onslaughts of rivals, whether railway companies or, as was frequently the case at first, other carriers by water. Always, however, they

---

[1] J. Loch to W. Slater, 10 Sept. 1840, L.E.P.

[2] M. & I.N.C., Order Book, 1834–41, pp. 93–4, 101. F. Smith to J. Loch, 30 Nov. 1837 and 20 Jan. 1838; J. Loch to F. Smith, 16 Nov. 1837, L.E.P.

returned at the first available opportunity to the course of patching up the old arrangement or effecting a new one.

The competition which the Trustees favoured was, in fact, a competition of services within a framework of agreed rates. This policy was explicitly enunciated by their successor in the control of the Duke's Canal, the Bridgewater Navigation Company, when it was presenting its case to the House of Lords against the Manchester Ship Canal Bill in 1885. W. H. Collier, the assistant Canal manager of the day, rebutted the suggestion that, because rates were agreed with the railway companies, there was no competition. There was competition of accommodation, he affirmed, and each touted for traffic at the same rates.[1] The point was also made by the counsel for the company in his summing up. 'I go so far as to say this,' he observed, 'that competition is absolutely impossible to be carried on for any length of time, except upon the principle of two competitors' agreeing rates.'[2] Loch thought so, too, half a century earlier. He believed that a contest over rates of carriage would ruin the independent carriers and further the monopoly which he dreaded.[3] The traditional version of the history of the Duke of Bridgewater's Canal is apt to treat rate fixing as a temporary aberration stemming from the peculiarly grasping quality of Bradshaw's rule.[4] In reality the phenomenon was much more durable. It was Bradshaw who broke from the practice of agreeing charges by adopting in the later stages of his administration an unrepentant 'go it alone' policy, and it was Loch who restored the policy of amicable arrangement among the rival carriers.

Whilst by such means the Trustees protected themselves and their carriers against the risks of excessive competition, they also devoted much of their attention in the early years of Loch's superintendentship to providing the public with an improved passenger service. Packet boats equipped with first

[1] M.S.C.C., Bridgewater Department: 'Opposition of the Bridgewater Navigation Co. Ltd., and of the Company of the Proprietors of the Mersey and Irwell Navigation to the Manchester Ship Canal Bill in the House of Lords, 1885' (printed archive copy, Bridgewater Navigation Company), Minutes of Evidence, qu. 11534.

[2] Ibid., Speech of Counsel, pp. 144–5.

[3] J. Loch to W. Slater, 10 Sept. 1840, L.E.P.

[4] See Falk, op. cit., p. 124; also H. Malet, *The Canal Duke*, pp. 173–4.

and second class cabins had plied upon the Bridgewater Canal since the Duke's own time, but these had been outclassed by the railway with its superior speed, and at the time when the management changed hands in 1837 the Trustees were under pressure from the public to raise the standard of their service. On 27 May the radical *Manchester Times* carried an article headed 'Canal and River Navigation' which took the form of an appeal to Lord Francis Egerton to adopt such improvements as would extend the carriage by canal not only of goods but of passengers. The writer urged that if boats on the river and on the canal sailed at eight or nine miles per hour, a greater number of persons would travel by that means than at present went by railway train. On particular occasions, such as the race week, 5,000 persons would journey to Altrincham each day. Archibald Prentice, the proprietor of the journal, sent a cutting of the article to Lord Francis together with a covering letter mentioning a newly invented paddle which would enable a boat to travel by mechanical propulsion without raising a swell that would damage the canal banks.[1]

The notion appealed to Lord Francis. He was anxious to stand well with the public both from a sense of paternal responsibility not uncommon in aristocratic circles and from the knowledge that the vast possessions which he had just inherited rendered him vulnerable to charges of avarice.[2] Moreover, as it was Loch's strong conviction that the railway companies drew upon their passenger profits to compete with the canals in the goods trade, there was much to be said for hitting back at the railways through their passenger traffic, forcing them by means of competition to reduce the heavy fares which they exacted from travellers.[3]

Right at the beginning of their rule, therefore, the young nobleman and his agent planned to increase the speed of passenger transport by water by reviving the use of tide boats

---

[1] A. Prentice to Lord F. Egerton, 24 [*sic*] May 1837, E.B.C.

[2] Explaining to his deputy the considerations which ought to govern the management of the Trust, James Loch adverted to 'Another thing to be avoided, which is not to raise a prejudice against him [Lord Francis], and his interests as being too grasping, a feeling which he has succeeded to with his vast possessions and which has not been lessened by the greater activity displayed in its arrangement since he came to the head of it' (J. Loch to F. Smith, 10 May 1838, L.E.P.).

[3] J. Loch to F. Smith, 5 Sept. 1839, ibid.

to carry passengers along the Canal between Manchester and
Runcorn. At Runcorn they would communicate with steamers
passing to and fro along the Mersey estuary between that port
and Liverpool. The new service came into operation in May
1838. By a slow process of experimentation involving the
exchange of horses at the several stations along the Canal—
Broadheath, Lymm, Stockton Quay, and Preston Brook—
the velocity of the tide boats was gradually levered up until,
in 1841, the entire distance of twenty-eight miles between
Manchester and Runcorn was covered in five hours.[1] Estuarial
transport was improved concomitantly. One new passenger
steamer was built for the purpose and launched in August
1839 with the name of the *Alice*;[2] another, the *Blanche*, was
acquired in 1842.[3] Previously the Trustees had relied on hiring
steamers (from merchants like John Sothern, the brother of
the former Superintendent, who charged an exorbitant rent),
both for carrying passengers and for towing flats and coasting
vessels between Runcorn and Liverpool. The existing passenger
steamer left much to be desired in both comfort and speed.
On Fereday Smith's appraisal it was 'so ill constructed
that it is impossible for persons of respectable character to feel
at ease in mixing with low society on board, who are allowed
to drink, smoke, swear, etc., etc.', and the voyage occupied
two hours where one ought to have sufficed.[4]

Assisted by the new steamers, the tide boats proved a great
success, but the Trustees did not rest content with them for
long. Bent on attaining higher speeds, they introduced swift
boats, which had been operating on some of the Scottish
canals for more than a quarter of a century. These differed
from the tide boats in that they were drawn by two horses
instead of one, one of them ridden and the other riderless.
The first swift boat to operate on the Duke of Bridgewater's
Canal was the *Water Witch* which began running between
Altrincham and Manchester on 17 April 1843. At first it left
Altrincham in the morning and returned from Manchester in

[1] F. Smith to J. Loch, 10, 30, and 31 May 1838; Pendlebury and Others
to F. Smith, 21 Dec. 1841, L.E.P.
[2] F. Smith to J. Loch, 9 and 12 Aug. and 21 Sept. 1839, ibid.
[3] The *Blanche* was hired in March 1842 and purchased in August 1843
(F. Smith to J. Loch, 11 Mar. 1842 and 28 Aug. 1843, ibid.).
[4] F. Smith to J. Loch, 23 Apr. 1838, ibid.

the evening, but the service was soon increased to two trips per day. The fare each way was sixpence 'front room' and fourpence 'back', and return tickets were issued. The journey took just under an hour for a distance just above seven miles. In order to maintain this speed, the horses had to be driven unmercifully and changed frequently. Eight were required at any one time, and three were held in reserve to cover such contingencies as lameness or incapacitation from cold. A specially hardy breed of horse was purchased for the work in the fairs of Durham, Morpeth, and Newcastle upon Tyne, and when obtained the horses had to be carefully trained. The service encountered a promising response. So many people applied for a passage on the morning of 22 April that as many were left behind in Altrincham as were taken, and two days later thirty-one passengers made the journey from Altrincham. Encouraged by this initial success, the Trustees ordered the construction of a second boat, the *Dart*, early in May and of a third towards the end of August, and extended the swift boats to the long-distance traffic. In November the *Water Witch* began to operate 'swift' between Manchester and Runcorn. Soon two boats per day were plying on this stretch of canal, one leaving Runcorn at 8.0 a.m. and returning from Manchester at 3.0 p.m., the other leaving Manchester at 9.30 a.m. The journey took about three hours and a half each way, and horse-drawn omnibuses to and from Chester connected with the 9.30 packet at Preston Brook. The fare from Manchester to Runcorn was 3s. 'front room', 2s. 'back'. The swift boats must have made an impressive sight as they moved rapidly on their course, headed by riders in jockey caps, designed to protect their heads when passing under bridges, and manned by captains and mates wearing the brown and gold livery and Duke's buttons prescribed for them by Loch.[1] The experience gained by running these craft proved that canals were still a factor in passenger transport in the early 1840s. They capitalized upon what one railway historian has described as 'the immense, unsatisfied demand for passenger

[1] These particulars of the swift boat service are derived from numerous letters in the Loch–Egerton Papers between March 1843 and April 1844, and a memorandum on 'the Operation and Finances of the Swift Boats', March 1844, in the same collection; also from *Slater's Directory of Manchester and Salford*, 1845, p. 462.

travel that must have been waiting the arrival of railways',[1] a demand which the as yet immature railroad system could not fully supply. It was the Duke's Canal (and, perhaps, the coach omnibuses) which first demonstrated the potentialities of cheap day travel between Altrincham and Manchester. The railway promoters followed, bringing forward a scheme for joining Altrincham by rail to the Manchester and Birmingham line at Levenshulme in July 1844.

But the success of the Canal venture was relatively short-lived. The rapid extension of the railway system and the marked improvement of the railway passenger service after the Cheap Trains Act of 1844[2] destroyed the case for the swift boats. By 1846 they were proving a disappointment financially; Loch described them as a 'dying experiment'.[3] Six years later they were still in operation between Manchester and the western reaches of the Canal, but were running into increasing difficulty from the facilities of getting to Warrington and Runcorn by rail from Manchester. Omnibuses were at that time running from Moore railway station to Runcorn.[4] By 1855 the swift packets had ceased to run, and in the following year the boats were sold.[5] Probably the experiment was principally designed to equip the Trustees with a weapon against future railway promotions which might be deterred, it was hoped, by the prospect of serious competition from the canals in the lucrative passenger trade. Fereday Smith admitted that he urged it upon George Loch 'as a means of crushing or resisting railway schemes', not anticipating so speedy an increase in the traffic as at first occurred.[6] In this respect, however, it

---

[1] M. Robbins, *The Railway Age*, p. 7.

[2] Fereday Smith observed in July 1845 that the L. & M.R. Company was 'now giving great facilities to third-class passengers both as regards fares and the number of trains daily' and that these had 'materially interfered with the Trustees and Old Quay Company's passenger traffic between Liverpool and Manchester' (F. Smith to J. Loch, 3 July 1845, L.E.P.).

[3] J. Loch to F. Smith, 19 June 1846, ibid. According to one financial report they were making a loss which exceeded Loch's anticipation. Fereday Smith was disposed to question this, but, even on his showing, the service had been curtailed because it did not pay. Cf. J. Loch to F. Smith, 3 June 1846, and F. Smith to J. Loch, 11 June 1846, ibid.

[4] F. Smith to G. Loch, 24 June 1852, ibid.

[5] F. Smith to G. Loch, 19 Apr. 1855; F. Smith to A. Egerton, 2 July 1856, ibid.

[6] F. Smith to J. Loch, 20 July 1844, ibid. The Old Quay swift packet service from Runcorn to Warrington was established purely 'with railway objects',

was a two-edged sword, for by demonstrating the need for improved facilities for the transport of passengers, the swift boats may well have hastened rather than retarded the making of new railroad flotations. James Loch came eventually to believe that the Altrincham boats encouraged the bringing forward of the Altrincham to Levenshulme railway project.[1] Nevertheless, once that scheme had been launched, the Bridgewater Trustees made good use of the argument that neither the railway nor the swift boats would pay in competition with each other, as a means of discouraging the public from investing in the former. To strengthen their case they reduced their own passenger fares. As will be seen, they did not succeed in preventing the construction of a railway between Manchester and Altrincham, but they reached a compromise with their opponents which seemed at first to offer them greater security for the future.[2]

One method of increasing the speed of transport by water was neglected by the Bridgewater Trustees, viz. mechanization. This was not from want of suggestions as to how the change might be brought about. From the moment that he assumed control of his Canal properties, Lord Francis Egerton was bombarded by applications from inventors anxious to propound some new scheme for applying mechanical power to the haulage or propulsion of boats. These showed the greatest ingenuity. They varied from a scheme advanced in 1839 for installing locomotives on the Canal banks to draw the boats by cables[3] to a proposal advanced by G. H. Fourdrinier in 1844 for propelling the boats by 'the forcing of columns of air under the bottom of the vessel'.[4] Most of them, however, were for steam-driven paddle-boats of various kinds, but in 1845 the Trust was invited to interest itself in 'a submerged propeller' boat patented by J. H. Patterson for use on the chain of canals between Nottingham and London.[5] Sometimes

and as soon as these were attained, it was reduced (F. Smith to J. Loch, 11 June 1846, ibid.).

[1] 'The truth is', he wrote, 'that the great success of the swift boats has developed an amount of passenger traffic as to make Altrincham an object of railroad communication' (Minute on G. to J. Loch, 13 Aug. 1844, E.B.C.).

[2] See below, pp. 171–3; also F. Smith to J. Loch, 20 July 1844, L.E.P.

[3] J. Loch to F. Smith, 5 Sept. 1839, ibid.

[4] G. H. Fourdrinier to Lord F. Egerton, 12 Mar. 1844, E.B.C.

[5] G. D. Clark to R. W. Barnes, 13 Jan. 1845, L.E.P.

the Trustees went as far as to inspect these inventions and to allow them to be tried out on the canal, but there is no evidence of their adopting any of them before 1855, when they got as far as joining the independent carriers in subscribing to the construction of an experimental steamboat invented by a Mr. Burch.[1] It appears to have been taken for granted by them that, as Lord Francis Egerton replied to Fourdrinier, 'any increase of speed to a loaded boat will produce damage to banks by mere displacement independent of the action of the propelling machinery'.[2] How far these fears were justified remains uncertain. In December 1837 R. White of Manchester claimed to have constructed a power-driven machine capable of propelling a boat at eight or ten miles per hour without materially, or at all, injuring the banks.[3] Two months later James Thompson of Altrincham put forward a plan for eliminating the swell of water by encasing the paddle wheels in boxes connected to the water at the rearwards by means of a pipe. He argued that the water displaced by the paddle within the box would have to be replenished through the aperture of the pipe, thus setting up two currents within the pipe and preventing a swell.[4] Probably, however, the application of steam power could not have raised speeds with safety above the levels attained by the horse-drawn swift boats, but it is arguable that it could have been employed to reduce the costs of conveyance for both passengers and goods. On 31 July 1838 a steamboat with a paddle propelling-wheel invented by a Mr. Herrick was tried out on the Bridgewater Canal in the presence of Lord Francis Egerton, James Loch, and the Canal engineer, Edmund Smith. Smith's report on the vessel was highly favourable. It referred to 'the steady course of her movements' and estimated that the device would enable 25 tons to be carried in two narrow boats at a cost of 1s. 11d. per ton and at a speed of five miles per hour, making five trips per fortnight. By comparison, horses would convey 30 tons for 2s. 9d. per ton, making three trips per

[1] G. Loch to F. Smith, 1 Mar. 1855, L.E.P.
[2] Lord F. Egerton to G. H. Fourdrinier, 14 Mar. 1844, E.B.C.
[3] R. White to Lord F. Egerton, 14 Dec. 1837, ibid.
[4] J. Thompson to Lord F. Egerton, 6 Feb. 1838 and enclosure, ibid.

fortnight.[1] Five years later the Trustees looked at a steam tug known as the *Powis* designed by a Mr. Davies for use on the Birmingham and Liverpool Junction Canal and driven by a high-pressure disc engine. They were impressed by its durability, its cheapness, and its economy in fuel consumption, and found that it could draw a train of five boats at a speed of just under four miles an hour without raising any wave that could possibly damage the banks. It was used on the Birmingham and Liverpool Junction Canal to draw trains of sixteen boats at two miles per hour, but the Trustees did not order a similar craft for their own use.[2] In the question of using steam power to raise speeds they showed a complete lack of interest. Lord Francis Egerton told an inventor in October 1844 that 'whether it be possible or not to combine safety in canal conveyance with something like the expedition of railroad conveyance, it is not an object worth attaining with respect to the articles with which Canal traffic is mainly concerned'.[3]

In attending to the basic installations of the Canal and coal-mines, however, the Bridgewater Trustees displayed greater zeal and foresight, and the early years of Loch's administration were characterized by a large investment of capital to repair the ravages of past neglect and to bring the installations up to a reasonable standard of competitive efficiency. In the years 1837–9 there was a heavy outlay on the collieries, which had fallen into acute disrepair.[4] The cost was increased by the need to equip the pits with the means of entering into the race to supply the newly opened railways of the Midlands and south as well as those of Canada and the U.S.A. with coke. In August 1839 Lord Francis Egerton authorized the immediate erection of twelve new coking ovens at Worsley and the sinking of a new pit, and within three months the ovens were almost ready for use.[5]

Work on the canal took mainly the form of extending the terminal and trans-shipment facilities. Between 1837 and 1839 the Trustees made a new dock at the southern end of the Liverpool waterfront for the purpose of attracting the timber

[1] E. Smith to J. Loch, 1 Aug. 1838, ibid.
[2] Thistleton to F. Smith, 2 and 10 Nov. 1843, L.E.P.
[3] Lord F. Egerton to E. Lang, 4 Oct. 1844, E.B.C.
[4] F. Smith to J. Loch, 11 July 1846, L.E.P.
[5] F. Smith to J. Loch, 13 and 23 Aug. and 21 Nov. 1839, ibid.

trade, which was moving southwards from the central dock area where the Duke's Dock was situated. The new venture was known as the Egerton Dock after Lord Francis Egerton, who provided the capital.[1] A few years later they turned their attention to the Duke's Dock itself, and constructed a half tide basin between the dock and the river estuary. Opened in October 1845, it afforded great advantages to the Canal trade and appreciably strengthened the power of the waterway to compete with the rails. By enabling the flats which arrived from Runcorn at half tide to go straight into dock and to leave again by half tide on the same day, it saved them a delay of twenty hours and gave reason to believe that in future the trade could be worked by about two-thirds of the number of flats previously in use. Furthermore, the entrance gate to the basin was made large enough to admit Irish and coasting vessels, so that these might take advantage of the economy of being able to discharge their goods straight into the flats, which would thus be able to capture the up traffic before any rival carriers laid their hands upon it.[2] Other improvements undertaken in the early 1840s included the provision of extended warehouse accommodation for the private carriers at Liverpool, the construction of market sheds for the potato trade at Manchester,[3] and the formation of a new dock at Runcorn known as the Francis Dock. Work on the last-named of these enterprises was proceeding in the years 1841–3. An outstanding feature of it was that the gates of the communicating locks were equipped with extra paddles so as to enable vessels to descend to the river more quickly than before.[4] Moreover, plans were afoot for building yet another dock at Runcorn, to be called the Harriet Dock after Lady Francis Egerton, though work on this was held up by the obstinacy of a landowner who declined to make the necessary land available.[5]

[1] F. Smith to J. Loch, 17 Aug. 1839; J. Loch to F. Smith, 24 Aug. and 4 Sept. 1837, L.E.P. The dock was reaching completion in Nov. 1839 (F. Smith to J. Loch, 21 Nov. 1839, ibid.).

[2] J. Loch to W. Cubitt and F. Smith, 16 July 1842; Pendlebury's Report to F. Smith, 22 July 1842, ibid.; J. Loch to Lord F. Egerton, 19 Oct. 1845, E.B.C.

[3] J. Loch to W. Cubitt and F. Smith, 16 July 1842; F. Smith to J. Loch, 2 Sept. 1842; Hathorn to F. Smith, 4 Oct. 1842; F. Smith to J. Loch, 8 Oct. 1841, L.E.P.

[4] J. Loch to F. Smith, 3 Oct. 1841; F. Smith to J. Loch, 5 Apr. 1843, ibid.

[5] J. Loch to F. Smith, 27 Sept. 1841 and 1 Feb. 1843, ibid.

In the matter of investment, the departure from past practice should not be overstressed. The new masters of the Duke's Canal did not embark upon their task equipped with anything in the nature of a building programme. They were forced along step by step by the pressure of changing circumstances, more especially by the growing competition from railway companies and from other navigations. Loch's first thought, in March 1837, was not to improve the dilapidated Worsley mines but to lease them out, so as to throw the cost of improvement upon the lessees.[1] In 1841 he carped at the expenditure on the Francis Dock, complaining that he supposed it was 'constructing on our usual plan of expenditure with such work as would be bestowed on a dock at Portsmouth'.[2] During the summer of that year Fereday Smith practically had to bludgeon him into agreeing to allow the plans for the new entrance gates at Liverpool, the market sheds at Manchester, and the second dock at Runcorn to go forward, by pointing to the growing rivalry of the railway companies, the Old Quay Company, and the carriers through Ellesmere Port.[3] Even then he vetoed outright Cubitt's proposals for a new dock at Liverpool, and insisted that the Harriet dock at Runcorn should be lined with the planks of an old ship—'constructed', as he observed, 'in the way that all Dutch and many French docks are done at this day, and which it was the fashion to build formerly in England also, until we became so horribly fine and expensive'.[4] Nor were fresh capital outlays the only things to be stinted. In 1842 a savage attack was made upon ordinary running costs. Men were discharged and horses sold, though this could only be accomplished at the expense of abandoning the old practice of changing the boat horses at every station. At the collieries all head work that could be stopped was stopped,[5] and the mines were allowed to slip back during the next four years into the state of neglect in which they had languished when Sothern gave up the superintendentship and from which they had been

[1] J. Loch to F. Smith, 22 Mar. 1837, ibid.

[2] J. Loch to F. Smith, 27 Sept. 1841, ibid.

[3] F. Smith to J. Loch, 31 July 1841; J. Loch to F. Smith, 3 Aug. 1841, ibid.

[4] J. Loch to Cubitt, 23 Sept. 1841, ibid.

[5] F. Smith to J. Loch, 6 May and 8 Sept. 1842, ibid.

redeemed by a heavy expenditure undertaken in the later thirties.[1]

Some warrant for this parsimony was to be found in the continuing legal impediments to the accumulation of capital by the Trust. As the trustee of a will Loch did not enjoy the discretion of a private industrialist to plough back profits or the power of a joint-stock company to appeal to the public for funds. Instead he found it necessary to draw upon the private resources of the life tenant for the cost of improvements. Lord Francis Egerton himself financed the construction of the Egerton Dock in Liverpool. His principal asset being his income, he spread the cost over a period of seven years by leasing the property from builders and stone-masons who undertook, in return for a charge additional to the rent, to execute the works which Lord Francis required.[2] In 1838 he spent £10,000 in purchasing the Union Company's warehouse in Manchester, later advancing a further £1,471 for rebuilding it to suit the Trustees' needs. In 1841 he bought a portion of the Runcorn foreshore for £308 to assist with dock building, and in that and the succeeding year he laid out more than £4,000 on new offices for the Bridgewater Trust in Manchester.[3] He also made himself responsible for providing the sheds at the Manchester market dock.[4] By August 1841 the Trustees' own powers of purchase were exhausted, and it was clear that all future purchases, including the land at Lymm which was required for widening the Canal, would have to be made by the principal beneficiary.[5] Dependence upon personal finance necessarily set limits to what could be achieved, especially as in this case capital outlays had to be defrayed from an income which fluctuated markedly from year to year. Moreover, the life tenant embarked upon his control of the Bridgewater properties burdened with certain heavy charges which exercised a first claim on his resources. In 1837 and 1838 he paid

[1] See below, p. 314.

[2] Lease of land, dock, and premises, part of the Herculaneum Pottery Estate, Toxteth Park, to Lord Francis Egerton, 1 Jan. 1839, B.T.P. (Mertoun), File 138.

[3] Receipt and Accounts Made on the Account of Lord F. Egerton by Messrs. Drummond, Staffs. C.R.O., D. 593/N.

[4] J. Loch to F. Smith, 3 Aug. 1841, L.E.P.

[5] J. Loch to F. Smith, 25 Aug. 1841, ibid. ; J. Loch to Lord F. Egerton, 6 June 1838, E.B.C.

out £110,000 to reduce, notably his debts, the mortgage on Bradshaw's estate; nevertheless £30,000 of the mortage remained outstanding in March 1845.[1] Unlike the third Duke of Bridgewater, who had scraped and saved successfully to build the Canal, he was also a family man, with a wife and seven children to support. On his marriage in 1822 he had pledged himself to pay one half of his income, when he first came into it, into trust to provide a jointure for his wife and portions for his younger children.[2]

But the difficulties must not be exaggerated. Given careful management Lord Francis Egerton's revenues were princely enough both to meet these liabilities and to make a handsome provision for the needs of the Canal and coal-mines. A private account, preserved in the Staffordshire Record Office, shows that the income from all sources paid into his account at Drummonds in the early 1840s was never less than £57,000 per annum and rose in 1841 to £81,000. The annual charges upon this for interest and repayment of debt and for the future of the family did not exceed £5,000.[3] The financial stringency which caused James Loch to economize heavily upon the Canal was mainly the result of mounting personal expenditure. Lord Francis was a man of culture and humanity, enlightened in his views and generous in his subscriptions to provide churches and schools for his work-people. His taste, however, like his munificence, was lavish, and he quite lived up to the large income which he received. His household and travelling expenses rose from £8,366 in 1834 to £24,660 in 1842.[3] By the accepted standards of the time £10,000 per annum was enough to afford a man 'all the conveniences and comforts that London and the country could give'.[4] Like the Canal Duke he was a

[1] Receipt and Accounts Made on the Account of Lord Francis Egerton by Messrs. Drummond, Staffs. C.R.O., D. 593/N; J. Loch to Lord F. Egerton, 6 Mar. 1845, E.B.C. See also below, p. 192.

[2] These payments were only to be made until a sum of £50,000 had been accumulated. See R. Du Cane to Lord Ellesmere, 26 July 1855, B.T.P. (Mertoun), File 152. The private account with Drummonds shows that this had been achieved by the end of 1836. After that smaller payments were made into this fund, to clear the mortgage on the private estate at Worsley, against which the portions and jointure were secured. For details see below, p. 192.

[3] Receipt and Accounts Made on the Account of Lord Francis Egerton by Messrs. Drummond.

[4] F. M. L. Thompson, *English Landed Society in the Nineteenth Century*, pp. 25–6.

patron of the arts. During 1837 he paid £400 for a Landseer and nearly £600 for a Paul Delaroche. Both in 1835 and in 1836 his total outlay on books and pictures exceeded £3,000. In 1839 he spent £4,350 on a yacht. It was in building, however, that he displayed his greatest profusion. Having paid £33,000 for the Hatchford and St. George's Hill estates in Surrey in 1839, he proceeded to pull down the existing eighteenth-century mansion at Hatchford and to expend more than £10,000 in 1841 and 1842 in rebuilding it according to the design of Edward Blore. During the years 1840–2 he advanced £41,000 for rebuilding the New Hall at Worsley, again under Blore's direction,[1] notwithstanding the fact that at that time the Trustees faced a large bill for replacing Bridgewater House in London, demolished in 1840 on account of dry rot.[2] James Loch was not primarily responsible for this ambitious budgeting. At times he intervened to restrain it. In view of the restrictions which were placed upon the development of the Canal and the coal-mines, however, it is arguable that he should have done far more than he did to persuade his master to give prior attention to these basic sources of his wealth. He had the authority to intervene with effect when he chose to exercise it.[3]

Moreover, there was a loop-hole in the restrictions on the borrowing powers of the Trust. The Trustees could go to Parliament for an Estate Act, authorizing them to borrow money on the security of their estates and to take other actions not specifically authorized by the Duke of Bridgewater's will. They did so in 1840, obtaining authority to sell land for building purposes and to grant coal leases,[4] and again in 1842, when they were permitted to borrow up to £50,000 for rebuilding Bridgewater House, for improving the Canal, and for other purposes.[5] James Loch, however, showed the greatest

---

[1] For the above items of expenditure see Receipt and Accounts Made on the Account of Lord Francis Egerton by Messrs. Drummond.

[2] *Personal Reminiscences of the Duke of Wellington by Francis, the first Earl of Ellesmere, edited with a Memoir of Lord Ellesmere by His Daughter Alice, Countess of Strafford*, p. 44.

[3] David Spring, *The English Landed Estate in the Nineteenth Century*, p. 95.

[4] *J.H.C.* xcv (1840), 607.

[5] Ibid. xcvii (1842), 548. The amount authorized to be borrowed is mentioned in the Estate Act of 1865 (28 and 29 Vict. (Private) c. 50), the text of which is available at the House of Lords Record Office.

Worsley New Hall, built 1840-6 to the design of Edward Blore, with the Duke of Bridgewater's Canal

reluctance to resort to this course. He it was who postponed application for the second Bill in April 1840, his reason being that Lord Francis Egerton needed more time to consider his plans for Bridgewater House.[1] The needs of the Canal and of the docks at Runcorn and Liverpool were apparently a secondary purpose of the proposed measure, and could be laid aside when the main purpose, that of rebuilding the ducal residence in London, was shown not to be ripe for fulfilment. It is difficult to avoid the conclusion that, on the whole, Loch begrudged expenditure upon the Canal works,[2] though he was open-minded enough to allow himself to be reasoned into it by experienced subordinates.

To be fair, however, it must be admitted that an Estate Act was not easy to obtain. The parliamentary procedure for passing such Bills was forbiddingly solemn and formal, as befitted an interference with the dispositions of a dead testator. It required the giving of an opinion on the Bill by two English judges. Until 1845 it demanded also the personal attendance of all who were affected by the provisions of the Bill before a committee of the House of Lords to signify their assents. As by the middle 1840s there were fourteen tenants for life in addition to Lord Francis Egerton interested in the Bridgewater properties, most of them to a very limited or remote extent, and as the beneficiaries seemed likely to double in number in no long period, the Duke's Trustees could not hope to carry such a measure without inconveniencing a widening range of persons, many of whom had little to gain from what was proposed. The Harcourt family protested in 1845 when they were called upon to present themselves in the Lords to give their consent to a Bill introduced by the Trustees to enable them to purchase the Mersey and Irwell Navigation, and James Loch was driven to suggest an approach to the Lord Chancellor to allow beneficiaries who were not themselves heirs to Lord Francis Egerton's body to assent in writing to all future Bills.[3]

[1] J. Loch to F. Smith, 10 Apr. 1840, L.E.P.
[2] The impression is confirmed by his remark to Fereday Smith regretting the purchase of the Egerton Dock at Liverpool on the grounds that this action had stimulated rival canal companies to improve their premises (J. Loch to F. Smith, 3 Aug. 1841, ibid.).
[3] J. Loch to Lord F. Egerton, 13 May and 21 June 1845, E.B.C.

A further difficulty was that the House of Lords was apt to scrutinize very carefully any proposals to allow the Trustees of a will to run up a debt. When in 1851 the Bridgewater Trustees applied for a Bill to enable them to borrow two sums, one of £150,000 and the other of £50,000, for the purpose of improving their navigations, they were obliged to abandon their claim to the second sum on account of objections raised by Lord Redesdale, the Chairman of Committees, who also insisted that a sinking fund should be established to extinguish the additional debt as it was created. James Loch's account of the event implies that there had been doubt as to whether the Bill would pass, and that the knowledge that the Trustees had already created a sinking fund voluntarily to reduce their existing indebtedness weighed heavily in its favour.[1]

The position was slowly changing to the Trustees' advantage. By 1851 beneficiaries outside the Egerton–Ellesmere family had been relieved of the necessity for personal attendance,[2] and the 1851 Estate Act conferred a much wider borrowing discretion on the Trustees than they had previously possessed, as well as enlarging their power to grant building leases. In the early forties, however, the state of the law relating to trusts still presented real obstacles to the development of the industrial properties.

[1] J. Loch to the Earl of Ellesmere, 23 June 1851, B.T.P. (Mertoun), File 147.
[2] J. Loch to the Earl of Ellesmere, 5 June 1851, ibid.

CHAPTER VII

The Years of Equipoise (1837–1844). I

THE early 1840s were once considered to have been the crucial years for the overthrow of the canals by the railways. Clapham maintained that 'down to about 1840 railway competition developed so slowly that the canals made no attempt to improve their own competitive capacity', but that 'then in six years the whole weight of railway competition . . . fell upon the unprepared canals'.[1] Jackman also subscribed to this opinion. 'By 1845 . . . ,' he claimed, 'the railways had grown to be the predominant party in the contest, completely overshadowing most of the canals.'[2] The experience of the Duke's diverges from this pattern. The fiercest and the most devastating assaults by the railroads upon this waterway came not at the beginning but at the end of the fifth decade of the nineteenth century. Although in the years 1837–44 the Bridgewater Trustees went through a difficult period and lost certain categories of trade, they continued on balance to hold their own, and the challenge which confronted them came more from other navigations than from the rails.

It was a view prevalent in canal circles about this time that the long-distance or through traffic by canal was immeasurably more vulnerable than that passing over short distances. James Loch accepted as probable the opinion which was put to him by Baxendale, of the firm of Pickfords the carriers, at the opening of the Great Western Railway in June 1838 that 'long railways will beat long canals but that short canals will keep their ground with railways'.[3] The distinction was a sound one, for the disparity was amply illustrated in the traffic of the Bridgewater Canal, which was of two kinds—that which was

---

[1] *An Economic History of Modern Britain*, vol. i, pp. 396, 398.
[2] *The Development of Transportation in Modern England*, p. 638.
[3] J. Loch to F. Smith, 4 June 1838, L.E.P.

transacted jointly with adjacent waterways and passed over considerable distances, and the relatively short-distance trade between Liverpool and Manchester and between Runcorn and Manchester.

The history of the long-distance trade in the seven years after Loch became Superintendent of the Trust falls broadly into three phases. During the first of these, which lasted for approximately two years, railway competition was negligible; nevertheless, a powerful opposition from newly constructed canals and from recently improved older navigations threw into relief the weaknesses of the traditional channels through which the trade of the Duke of Bridgewater's Canal passed, the very weaknesses, in fact, which the railways were later to exploit.

Notwithstanding Clapham's assertion to the contrary,[1] the 1830s witnessed a marked improvement in the 'competitive capacity' of the northern and the north Midland canals. Railways and the threat of railways, together with the pressure of expanding trade, had by that time shattered the old complacency and caused canals to compete with canals in lowering their rates to the public and extending the facilities which they offered to the trade. The result was that when Loch assumed command in 1837, the Duke of Bridgewater's Canal confronted a fierce rivalry from six other water routes.

The first of these was that of the Mersey and Irwell Navigation Company, which had long been competitive with the Duke's in the Liverpool and Manchester and Runcorn and Manchester traffics, and was now seeking to burst into the through trade (with Yorkshire, with Stockport and Macclesfield, and with the northern parts of Derbyshire) which was fed into the Bridgewater Canal through the Rochdale Canal lock. With this end in view the company had, as we have seen, obtained from Parliament in July 1836 powers to cut a short canal through Manchester from the Old Quay wharfs near the lower end of Quay Street to the Rochdale Canal at a point a little to the south of Great Bridgewater Street.[2] The cut was opened on 28 October 1839, and for a brief spell it looked as if the Old Quay Company would remit all charges on its line between Runcorn and Manchester for the week following completion

---

[1] See above, p. 121.   [2] See above, pp. 93–4.

as a means of drawing traffic through it away from the Bridge-water Canal. This did not happen, however,[1] and in the event the Manchester and Salford Junction Canal proved a costly failure. The works involved the construction of a tunnel which occupied about a half of the route. Soon after the opening one of the locks collapsed, temporarily disrupting the traffic and helping to discredit the concern. The Bridgewater Trustees added further to the difficulties by denying the new canal water from the Rochdale Canal and forcing the proprietors to the expense of reconstructing their summit lock so as to prevent any abstraction of the same from taking place. By the terms of their Act of 1794, the owners of the Rochdale Canal were obliged to turn their waste water into the Duke's at Castle-field. By August 1841, therefore, the Manchester and Salford Junction Canal was in so unflourishing a state that the Mersey and Irwell Navigation Company had to take it over from the subsidiary company which had built it to save it from being closed entirely. As a threat to the through traffic of the Bridge-water Canal, it proved to be of negligible importance. Popular 'prepossessions' remained in favour of the long-established line of traffic,[2] and as a reward for their consent to the making of the canal the Trustees won the agreement of the Old Quay to their cutting the Hulme Locks between the Canal and the river. Opened on 20 September 1838[3] these locks provided the Canal for the first time with a continuous water communication with Bolton. Previously the Trustees had had to rely on overland cartage from Worsley or more recently upon the Bolton and Leigh Railway for access to that town.

The Duke's Trustees were less successful, however, in checking the aggression upon their southern trade through Preston Brook. The attack came from five different directions. The canals leading inwards from the Bristol Channel competed

---

[1] F. Smith to J. Loch, 3, 16, and 28 Oct. 1839, L.E.P.

[2] M. & I.N.C. Order Book, 1834–41, pp. 164–7, 173–6, 179–80. See also volume entitled 'Acts Relating to the Third Duke of Bridgewater's Canal Schemes, etc. Collected by Lord Francis Egerton' (Manchester University Library), pp. 808–14, for the terms of the Act (3 Vict. (Local) c. 15, s. 6) compelling the Old Quay Company to reconstruct the summit lock. The later history of the Manchester and Salford Junction Canal was unfortunate. By the end of 1846 the tunnel had started to collapse, and the Canal was partially filled in under the terms of an Act of 1875.

[3] *The Manchester Historical Recorder*, p. 111.

for the privilege of supplying Birmingham with sea-borne oil, alkali, brimstone, and tar pitch,[1] whilst those of Yorkshire operating in conjunction with the coastal voyage along the east coast of England challenged the Duke's in its Manchester and London trade.[2] The three most serious rivals, however, were the Macclesfield Canal, the Weaver Navigation, and the Ellesmere and Chester Canal.

Opened as recently as 1831, the Macclesfield supplied a much shorter route from the Midlands to Manchester than that which went by Preston Brook. By December 1837 it had abstracted nearly all the Manchester traffic in Wolverhampton iron. Two years later the interest of the Duke's was to see Scottish and Welsh iron rather than Staffordshire iron sold in Manchester.[3]

The River Weaver was a much older rival. Improved and partially canalized in a series of schemes carried into effect over the years 1720–1807, this great water highway of the county of Chester had long possessed facilities for trans-shipping traffic to and from the Grand Trunk Canal at Anderton near Northwich, and thus constituted an alternative route to the Duke's and the Trunk for trade passing between Liverpool and the Staffordshire Potteries. An inclined plane, perhaps one by which wagons running downwards to the river hauled up others ascending to the Canal, had been installed at Anderton by 1813.[4] The trans-shipment of pottery materials was brought to an end in 1807, however, and in 1828 clay, flints, and lime for the Potteries were carried exclusively by Preston Brook.[5] But the tide was soon to turn. A fresh burst of improvement in the early 1830s permitted the firm of Alexander Reid & Co., which first put its boats on the Weaver in February 1829, and changed its name to the Anderton Carrying Company in 1836, to build up almost from nothing in the intervening seven years an extensive traffic in pottery goods and raw materials.[6] The Weaver Trustees assisted its

[1] Prichard Brothers to J. Loch, 16 May 1839, L.E.P.

[2] F. Smith to J. Loch, 25 Sept. 1838, ibid.

[3] F. Smith to J. Loch, 9 Dec. 1837 and 30 Dec. 1839, ibid.

[4] T. S. Willan, *The Navigation of the River Weaver in the Eighteenth Century*, pp. 115–17, 130–2.

[5] Minutes of the Committee of the Weaver Trustees, Book no. 480, p. 140. See also the Northwich and Acton Bridge Tonnage Books of the Weaver Trustees, nos. 130–4.

[6] Weaver Trustees: Northwich and Acton Bridge Tonnage Books, nos. 130–4.

rise by enlarging the trans-shipment basin at Anderton in the
years 1829–30, equipping it with two entrances, and by building in 1832 a new inclined 'railway' which was to convey
first coal and later salt and other merchandise between the
river and the Canal. In 1835 the Company was authorized to
construct its own rails for trans-shipping timber.[1] Encroachment upon the Bridgewater Trustees' pottery trade was
assisted by the shortcomings of the Preston Brook route.
When Fereday Smith visited the Staffordshire Potteries in
September 1837 to investigate complaints voiced by the
potters through a local M.P., he was told a piteous tale that
clay was left exposed to the elements on the wharfside at
Runcorn, thereby gaining so much in weight from the absorption of moisture that it was sold by the clay merchants to the
manufacturers for more than it was worth. He also learned
that crates of pottery ware suffered from delay, exposure, and
rough handling both there and at Liverpool, and that the
potters felt neglected because the Duke's Trustees and the
Grand Trunk did not send agents to visit them.[2]

At the time when Loch became Superintendent of the Trust,
the threat from the Weaver was intensifying. The Weaver
Trustees planned to build docks at Weston Point, where the
Weaver Canal entered the Mersey estuary. As yet there was
merely a single entrance basin between the Canal and the
estuary for the use of sailing flats passing from one to the other,
but it was feared that by the construction of docks Weston
might be raised to the status of a river port competitive with
Runcorn. The Weaver authorities also proposed an enlargement of their shed and wharf accommodation at Anderton.[3]
Meanwhile the Anderton Carrying Company extended its trans-
shipment trade to include Burton ale, and started to build up
a Macclesfield trade through Red Bull in competition with that
which passed along the Duke's to Manchester and thence via the
Ashton, Peak Forest, and Macclesfield Canals to Macclesfield.[4]

[1] Minutes of the Committee of the Weaver Trustees, Book no. 480, pp. 190,
222, 229, 291, 365, 368–9, 385.   [2] F. Smith to J. Loch, 8 Sept. 1837, L.E.P.
[3] J. Davenport to J. Loch, 22 Sept. 1837; F. Smith to J. Loch, 8 Sept. 1837
and 11 Oct. 1838, ibid. See also map of the River Weaver deposited 29 Nov.
1828, Cheshire C.R.O.
[4] J. Loch to F. Smith, 27 Nov. 1837; F. Smith to J. Loch, 6 Apr. 1838 and 5
Oct. 1839, L.E.P.

Like the Weaver, the Ellesmere and Chester Canal was of respectable antiquity, having been completed as long ago as 1805. It was only, however, the construction of two new canals, both completed in the 1830s, that brought this water-way into a direct competitive relationship with the Duke's. One was the Birmingham and Liverpool Junction Canal, finished in 1835, which opened a new path for Staffordshire iron to Liverpool by way of Ellesmere Port; the other was the Middlewich branch of the Ellesmere and Chester system which was opened two years earlier from Barbridge Junction on the Ellesmere to the Grand Trunk at Middlewich. This made it possible for the Trustees to think of attracting to Preston Brook not only the iron from south Staffordshire which passed down the Birmingham and Liverpool Junction Canal, but also the traffic in slates and agricultural produce coming down the Welsh branch of the Ellesmere. Could they but capture the carriage of these commodities from Preston Brook to Liverpool and Manchester, they need not fear what the superior Birmingham and Liverpool Junction Canal might do to the ancient canal route from the Midlands to the north by way of Haywood Junction, where the Staffordshire and Worcestershire Canal joined the Grand Trunk some thirty miles further south than Middlewich. The Ellesmere Canal Company, however, had an obvious interest in passing the traffic, or at least that portion of it which was bound for Liverpool through Ellesmere Port, and towards the end of 1836 it bestirred itself to improve the efficiency of the last-named route. Previously the Company had not carried upon its own line, preferring to leave the work to independent carriers whose boats had plied up and down half empty and had frequently been held up, waiting for goods to arrive. Now, however, it established a carrying committee, appointed agents at Liverpool, Chester, and Ellesmere Port, and engaged a steam tug company to tow its flats across the Mersey estuary from Ellesmere Port to Liverpool. Eight months later it advertised for tenders to build a steam tug of its own.

The venture was a great success, for the carrying trade made a profit of more than £3,000 in the year of its inception.[1]

[1] E. & C.C.C. General Committee Order Book, 1827–46, pp. 148–9 and 249–51 ; Minutes of Carrying Committee, 1836–8, pp. 1–2, 6, 10.

Inevitably the Duke's suffered. The Trustees could neither sustain the old trade through Haywood in competition with the Birmingham and Liverpool Junction Canal, which was both shorter and less heavily locked than the Trent and Mersey Canal route; nor could they build up a new traffic along the Middlewich branch, for this was blocked partly by a discriminatory toll (3*d.* per ton per mile as compared with 1*d.* on the main line) levied for understandable reasons by the Ellesmere Company,[1] and partly by a prohibitory charge made by the Grand Trunk for the use of the junction lock at Middlewich in the vain hope of driving the Birmingham and South Staffordshire traffic to Haywood Junction on its northward path.[2] The Grand Trunk Committee sadly miscalculated. The only result of their action was to send not only the South Staffordshire trade but also the traffic from the Welsh branch of the Ellesmere scudding to Ellesmere Port. By March 1837, to the Bridgewater Trustees' immense alarm, the 'most considerable carrier' via Preston Brook had deserted to Ellesmere Port.[3] The Trunk was altogether a most unfortunate partner for the Trustees to be yoked to. It throttled the through trade, not only by its Middlewich Junction Toll but also by the inflexibility of the tonnage charges on its own main line. Like the Oxford Canal, which also formed part of the chain by which long-distance traffic reached or emanated from the Duke's, it had a substantial local trade as yet unchallenged by any competitor, in addition to what it passed through to the Duke's. Forbidden by clauses in their Acts of Parliament to lower upon the latter without also reducing on the former, these two canals presented an almost insurmountable obstacle to concerted reductions of toll designed to foster a through traffic.[4] To a large extent their policies were irrational and out of date. In June 1838 Fereday Smith observed to Loch that

the Trent and Mersey Company are a set of persons who are not yet awake to their real interests, or who are unwilling to deviate

[1] J. Loch to F. Smith, 14 Apr. 1837, L.E.P.

[2] The charge on timber, slates, iron ore, potatoes, and grain was 10½*d.* per ton (F. Smith to J. Loch, 8 Sept. 1837, ibid.).

[3] J. Loch to F. Smith, 20 Mar. 1837, ibid.

[4] J. Loch to Lord F. Egerton, 5 Oct. 1841, E.B.C.

from the course which was successfully (perhaps) pursued some years back when circumstances were in a different train to those under which all canal owners are now compelled to act, and who, moreover, are particularly sluggish in their motions.[1]

Although the Ellesmere Company could reasonably hope to send its Liverpool traffic mainly through Ellesmere Port, its prospects of building up a substantial Manchester traffic that way were less impressive. Thomas Stanton, the manager of the concern, turned therefore to devise a means of dispatching merchandise from Wales and the Midlands to Manchester down the Middlewich branch. Unhappily for the Trustees, the plan which he hit upon seemed likely to deal a further blow at the trading prospects of the Duke's Canal. In order to bypass the existing circuitous route from Nantwich to Manchester by way of Preston Brook and to avoid the notorious Middlewich junction lock, he and his son-in-law, W. A. Provis, an engineer who had worked under Telford, brought forward in September 1837 a proposal for a new canal. It was to be driven through the heart of rural Cheshire, from a point on the Middlewich branch a little to the west of the junction lock through the Knutsford area to the Duke of Bridgewater's Canal just to the north-east of Altrincham. The project, known as Provis's Scheme, though supported by Lord Clive and the Birmingham and Liverpool Junction Canal Company, was deeply offensive to the Duke's Trustees, who saw in it the possibility of a further extension into Manchester, eliminating their navigation altogether. They feared among other things the probable diversion to Middlewich of the profitable Chester and Manchester trade which they conducted partly overland and partly by water, for Chester was the great emporium for Manchester goods *en route* for North Wales and for Welsh flour, malt, grain, and minerals destined for Manchester.[2]

Despite the encumbrance of unworthy allies, the Duke's Trustees confronted their problems boldly. The vigour of the

---

[1] F. Smith to J. Loch, 7 June 1838, L.E.P.

[2] Prospectus and Plan of the Proposed Manchester and Birmingham Junction Canal 1838, B.T.P. (Mertoun), Bundle 49 (Railways and Canals 1837–9); F. Smith to J. Loch, 18 Sept. 1837, L.E.P.; J. Loch to Lord F. Egerton, 9 Dec. 1837 and 29 Nov. 1838, E.B.C.

new management was displayed in a scheme to knock the
Anderton Company out of business and to deter the Weaver
Trustees from building docks at Weston Point. Convinced that
it was from the profits of the clay and crate trade that the
Anderton people were financing their entry into the traffic in
general goods at lower prices than were charged by their own
carriers, the Bridgewater Trustees resolved to undercut them
in this supposedly very lucrative branch of their commerce.
In December 1837 they engineered an agreement with Henshall
& Co., carriers for the Trent and Mersey Canal Company, to
effect jointly a drastic reduction in the rates of freight on clay
from Liverpool to Etruria, which had previously been equal
whether the clay went by Preston Brook or by Anderton.
The plan depended for its success on the Trustees' being able
to induce the coasting vessels to discharge their cargoes of
clay at Runcorn instead of at Liverpool, thus saving themselves
the cost of freighting the material up the estuary in their own
flats and enabling them to reduce charges to the minimum
necessary to cover steam towage for the coasters on the
estuary, docking and unloading expenses at Runcorn, and
canal tolls between Runcorn and Preston Brook. Among their
grounds for hoping that they would be successful in this was
the fact that captains of vessels might cook their dinners on
board ship in the dock at Runcorn but not at Liverpool.
Under the new agreement the Trustees were to come down by
10*d.* per ton, whilst Henshalls, who carried the clay from
Runcorn to the Potteries along the Bridgewater and Grand
Trunk Canals, were to reduce by another 10*d.*, and were also
to lower by 1*d.* per crate on the return cargo of earthenware.
This was a substantial abatement of the original joint charge
of 9*s.* per ton on clay from Liverpool to Etruria.[1]

Somewhat inconsistent with the high moral and competitive
tone which Loch endeavoured to impart to the Trust's affairs
on becoming Superintendent, this arrangement was engineered
by the young and energetic Fereday Smith, whose outlook
was always bolder and more opportunistic than that of his
superior. Loch, who was a busy man, seems not fully to have
understood what was at stake, for he wrote later to his
Deputy: '. . . I certainly was not aware, to the extent at least

[1] F. Smith to J. Loch, 8 Sept. 1837, 22 Feb. 1838, and 9 Mar. 1839, L.E.P.

that I am now, that the arrangement which was adopted was framed to try to knock up the Anderton Company, but that it was only meant to enable us to enter into more active competition with them.'[1]

Whilst they schemed against the Weaver, the Trustees also strove to remove the obstacles to the use of the Middlewich branch of the Ellesmere Canal. To accomplish this they were obliged to play a double game. They acted with the Grand Trunk Committee to compel the Ellesmere Company to desist from making partial tonnage charges on its Middlewich branch and from varying the rate which it charged for conveying goods across the Mersey from Ellesmere Port to Liverpool, seeking in the early spring of 1837 to amend a Bill which the company had itself brought before Parliament to these effects.[2] Shortly afterwards, however, they wrangled with the Trunk directors to procure the abandonment of the Middlewich Junction toll on timber, grain, iron ore, and potatoes and an effective reduction of the tonnage dues payable on these articles between Middlewich and Preston Brook. They were prepared to go a long way to conciliate the Trunk, offering in September 1837 to bear the reduction on the through trade in their own charges between Preston Brook and Runcorn on condition that the Trent and Mersey Committee would compensate them for doing so. This was to obviate the difficulties arising from the other concern's inability to charge a partial tonnage rate.[3] At the same time, however, they were obliged to consider what they would do if in the last resort the unreliable Trent and Mersey Committee refused to yield. This led them to cultivate support among the Shropshire canal proprietors. As yet they would have nothing to do with Stanton and Provis and their pet project of a canal from the Middlewich branch to the north-east of Altrincham. They did, however, open a negotiation at the end of the year with Lord Clive, a wavering supporter of Stanton, who from motives of aristocratic obligation was anxious not to injure the property of Lord Francis Egerton. They put to him first the idea of a canal from Wardle Green to Preston Brook, and when he

---

[1] J. Loch to F. Smith, 18 Apr. 1839, ibid.
[2] J. Loch to F. Smith, 14 Apr. 1837; F. Smith to J. Loch, 15 Apr. 1837, ibid.   [3] F. Smith to J. Loch, 8 Sept. 1837, ibid.

refused this, they continued to treat with him for the making of a cut from the Trent and Mersey at Northwich to the River Bollin at Bollington, a little to the west of Altrincham. They had themselves taken geological soundings a few months earlier for a tunnel at Mere through which the latter was intended to pass.[1]

In consenting to a Bollington line which would short-circuit Preston Brook, the Bridgewater Trustees had made a substantial concession. They were to concede more in the ensuing year. During the months of May and June 1838 they moved from the advocacy of the Bollin Canal to a full support of Provis's Scheme. In July Fereday Smith joined the provisional committee. He was even offered the chair, which he refused.[2] Outwardly there were good grounds for supposing that they had scored a victory over their opponents. Lord Francis Egerton was promised an allocation of shares in the company and the power to nominate to the board of directors.[3] It seemed to be 1826 and the Liverpool and Manchester Railway affair all over again. Moreover, a survey of the land between Altrincham and Manchester convinced the Trustees that there was little danger of the new canal's being continued eastwards to join the Rochdale Canal in Manchester. The difficulties and the expense would be too great.[4] Beneath the surface, however, there was evidence of weakness in the Trustees' volte-face. The Bollington line was abandoned because the opposition of local landowners was likely to be fiercer to that than to Provis's Scheme.[5] There was a feeling, too, that the demand from the manufacturing and commercial interests of Manchester and Birmingham was too strong to be resisted. Lord Francis Egerton's reputation as a public and political figure

---

[1] J. Loch to Lord F. Egerton, 5 Dec. 1837, E.B.C.; F. Smith to J. Loch, 18 and 28 Sept. 1837, L.E.P.; F. Smith to J. Loch, 12 Oct. 1837, B.T.P. (Mertoun), Quarto Letter Book, Apr. 1837 to Feb. 1838.

[2] F. Smith to J. Loch, 18 July and 5 Sept. 1838, L.E.P.

[3] In October 1838 Loch envisaged that Lord Francis should subscribe £31,250, one-sixteenth of the total capital, and receive the power to nominate one director (J. Loch to F. Smith, 3 and 5 Oct. 1838, L.E.P.). A deposit of £1,250 was actually paid by him on 16 October. Receipt enclosed in Jones Loyd & Co. to Lord F. Egerton, 16 Oct. 1838, B.T.P. (Mertoun), Bundle 49 (Railways and Canals 1837–9).

[4] F. Smith to J. Loch, 3 July 1838, L.E.P.

[5] J. Loch to F. Smith, 28 May 1838, ibid.

was at stake. 'You will have done your duty to the public',
Loch reassured his master, once the decision had been taken.[1]
Besides this, there were economic considerations to be re-
spected. The Grand Trunk Company had proved every bit as
obdurate in the matter of the junction toll at Middlewich and
in that of its own tonnage to Preston Brook as it was expected
to be. It had agreed in April 1838 to reduce the charge on
timber passing through the junction lock from $9\frac{1}{2}d.$ to $1d.$ per
ton, but that was as far as the Committee was prepared to
go.[2] The Trustees knew, however, that the Macclesfield Canal
was eating away their iron traffic between South Staffordshire
and Manchester. Only a bold reappraisal of policy could
conceivably reverse the trend.

On other sides, too, the Trustees' position was crumbling.
The Anderton Carrying Company parried the supposedly
lethal thrust against its Potteries trade by reducing the charge
on the clay which it freighted to north Staffordshire by $10d.$
per ton. As Henshalls had declined after some deliberation to
continue their reduction of $10d.$ on that portion of the clay
that was landed by the coasting vessels in Liverpool, this
move gave the Anderton Company the trading advantage of
being $10d.$ below the carriers by Preston Brook on this trade,
for the Trustees had never undertaken to reduce upon it.[3]
The latter had no answer. Presumably their hopes of attracting
the coasters to Runcorn, which was the only way in which
they could now hope to underbid the Anderton, had been
unfulfilled. By April 1839 they were negotiating with the
Anderton Company for a restoration of the clay rates to the
level existing before the reductions were commenced.[4]

A new phase opened in the spring of 1839, when to the still
intensifying competition from rival waterways was added the

---

[1] J. Loch to Lord F. Egerton, 13 Nov. 1838. E.B.C. See also J. Loch to Lord F.
Egerton, 29 Nov. 1838, ibid. In the latter Loch told Lord Francis how he had
explained to a deputation of canal owners hostile to the Altrincham Canal
scheme 'that it was a difficult matter for a person with a public character, as
you are, and in the prominent situation which you hold, to oppose yourself
to any great public improvement called for by any great body of the public'.
Lord Francis was Member for South Lancashire in the Parliament of 1837.

[2] F. Smith to J. Loch, 27 Apr. 1838, L.E.P.

[3] F. Smith to J. Loch, 9 Mar. 1839, ibid.

[4] F. Smith to J. Loch, 27 Apr. 1839, ibid.

hostility of railways. The attack when it came was many-sided, for owing to the huge extent of its hinterland the Canal was vulnerable to railroad development in many different parts of the country. The 1830s, which included the first great railway mania, had seen great advances, and although at the close of the decade not even the framework of the national system was complete, lines which had been planned in the preceding years were rapidly coming into operation to the discomfiture of the canals which had so long held the stage.

The Duke of Bridgewater's Canal began seriously to feel the pinch when the Grand Junction Railway attacked the canal trade between Birmingham and Liverpool and Manchester by a series of reductions of charges culminating in one made on 1 June 1839, which was of the order of 5s. per ton.[1] The reasons for the outbreak of hostilities deserve examination, for they were more complex than might appear on first consideration to have been the case. Historians of transport have been too frequently content not to raise the question of causation in studying disputes between rail and water, tacitly assuming that railways were born with a 'manifest destiny' to crush canals.[2] There is a danger, however, of using too much hindsight in interpreting the motives both of railway directors and of canal proprietors. If conflicts came, it by no means follows that this was because the men in control planned several stages ahead that they should come. Contingency or accident sometimes figure largely as agents of change even when economic necessity appears to the outside observer clearly to point the way. The Grand Junction Railway was opened on 4 July 1837. The facts of geography placed it in a position to compete with the canal route via Preston Brook for the traffic from the Midlands to Liverpool and Manchester. Yet there were those on both sides who saw the relationship between the railway and the Duke's Canal in terms of alliance rather than enmity. Coke was the principal bond. In July 1837 the Grand Junction Company contracted to take from the Trustees a hundred tons per week to supply its locomotives

---

[1] Memorial of Canal Carriers sent to F. Smith by J. Loch, 1 Aug. 1839, ibid.
[2] Clapham made the point explicitly: 'Everywhere the canal interest was in natural opposition to railway projects' (*An Economic History of Modern Britain*, vol. i, p. 396).

with fuel. There was a possibility also, however, of a trading link, for the two parties discussed a proposal that the Trustees should be allowed to construct a railway–canal junction at Preston Brook, where the newer and the older forms of transport come together.[1] It was envisaged that this should be used not merely to feed coke to the railroad from the Canal but also for an interchange of goods. Had the plan been carried out the Duke's Canal might have become the outlet of the Grand Junction Railway to Merseyside, and the struggle between the two concerns for the Birmingham traffic might have been for some time warded off. It is impossible with certainty to state how seriously the Grand Junction directors took this project. That they were dissatisfied with their existing egress along the Liverpool and Manchester line from Newton is beyond all doubt. Joseph Locke, the company's engineer, favoured the idea of a junction with the Trustees,[2] and John Moss, the chairman, was at least prepared to keep the question open provided that the Trustees would supply him with confidential information about the costs of water carriage between Preston Brook and Liverpool.[3]

Too much suspicion of the motives of the railway directors ruled in the hearts of James Loch and Fereday Smith for this proposal to be readily accepted, and in the early months of 1838 the Bridgewater authorities transferred their interest to a different and incompatible plan. In February the Grand Junction Railway Company went to Parliament for power to construct a branch line across the River Mersey at Fiddlers' Ferry with the object of shortening their access to Liverpool. Lord Francis Egerton agreed to take charge of the Bill in Parliament. The Trustees' object in encouraging the life tenant to take this step was of a twofold character. They hoped on the one hand to prevent the Mersey and Irwell Navigation Company from proceeding with its proposal to render the Mersey navigable to coastal vessels as far inland as Warrington. The railway bridge at Fiddlers' Ferry would be built in such a way as to see to that. On the other hand, they looked upon the

---

[1] F. Smith to J. Loch, 26 July 1837, L.E.P.

[2] F. Smith to J. Loch, 19 Oct. 1837, B.T.P. (Mertoun), Quarto Letter Book, Apr 1837–Feb. 1838.

[3] J. Loch to F. Smith, 23 Mar. 1838, L.E.P.

Fiddlers' Ferry line as a guarantee against an alternative scheme to join Warrington to Liverpool by rail.[1] This held out the threat of an extension from Warrington to Stockport which would cut further into their east–west traffic. In turning from the Preston Brook junction to the Fiddlers' Ferry line the Bridgewater Trustees were sacrificing a possible protection for their south-bound traffic for the sake of obtaining a safeguard for their Liverpool and Manchester trade. They were the more ready to do so in that Fereday Smith believed firmly that the Grand Junction Railway would not 'ever be extensive carriers or carry many heavy goods'.[2] This was a serious miscalculation. In the event the Trustees lost both objectives. The Fiddlers' Ferry branch was lost in committee. The Bill proposing it was greeted in Parliament by a barrage of opposition from aggrieved navigation owners, boatmen, salt works proprietors, and coal-owners. Already at the end of March Moss was suggesting privately to Loch that the Bill should be abandoned in favour of a return to the Warrington project. His letter provoked a bitter rejoinder accusing him of bad faith.[3]

For the remainder of the year relations between the Trust and the Grand Junction Railway slowly deteriorated, and an attack upon the rates of carriage between Birmingham and the north was hourly expected. Fereday Smith stated in July that the directors were falling dangerously under the influence of their Birmingham agent, Ghorall, who favoured an aggressive course.[4] The conflict was eventually precipitated, however, by the support which was given by Lord Francis Egerton and James Loch to the Stone and Rugby Extension Railway Bill when it came before the Commons in May 1839. Promoted by the Manchester and Birmingham Railway Company, of which Lord Francis Egerton and his brother the Duke of Sutherland were supporters, this measure ran dead against the interests of the Grand Junction Railway Company, whose Manchester to London traffic it challenged. On 21 May 1839, a week after the

---

[1] F. Smith to J. Loch, 28 Mar. 1838; J. Loch to F. Smith, 15 Feb. 1838, ibid.

[2] F. Smith to J. Loch, 28 Feb. 1838, ibid.

[3] *J.H.C.* xciii (1837–8), 411, 551–2; J. Loch to J. Moss, 25 Mar. 1838, L.E.P.

[4] F. Smith to J. Loch, 7 July 1838, L.E.P.

Bill had passed its second reading, James Loch warned his deputy: 'Be on your guard as to the Grand Junction, and take care of our old customers for coke. They have taken much offence, I am told, at His Lordship and my supporting the Manchester Junction. Be prepared for a very serious lowering of rates on goods.'[1] Eleven days later occurred the savage reduction to which reference has already been made.

The contest, once started, lasted for about two years, further reductions following in February 1840 and in February 1841. The Trustees sustained heavy losses. The traffic passing along their canal on its way between Birmingham and Liverpool and Manchester fell by 12,253 tons in the half year ending in June 1840 from the level of the corresponding period of the preceding year. The losses were not undiscriminating. Over the same period the London traffic through Preston Brook actually rose slightly (by 583 tons),[2] and as late as 1844 the Grand Junction Railway Company was finding the tonnage rates charged by the Bridgewater, Grand Trunk, and Birmingham and Liverpool Canals on Manchester packs going south to London too low for comfort.[3] One disturbing feature of the situation, however, was the power of the railroad to steal from the Canal its most profitable traffic. A comparison of the trade of the Duke's Canal during three consecutive weeks of the summer of 1839 with that which passed during the same period of 1838 reveals that while merchandise carried at a low rate of tonnage had increased both in weight and in monetary yield, goods conveyed at a higher toll had diminished in both respects.[4] The heaviest tolls were those payable on valuable or perishable goods or on goods liable to risk. Birmingham hardware was especially vulnerable. The contest with the Railway Company had not proceeded for very long before the carriers of this by water began to threaten to withdraw their boats. Worthington's did withdraw at the end of July 1839, finding, as they explained to the Trustees, that 'all the best paying goods between here (Birmingham) and Manchester and

---

[1] J. Loch to F. Smith, 21 May 1839, ibid.

[2] F. Smith to J. Loch, 19 Aug. 1840, ibid.

[3] The Company threatened to reduce its own rate on pottery crates unless the Duke's and the Grand Trunk agreed to raise their tonnage on packs from $\frac{1}{2}d.$ to $1d.$ per ton per mile. F. Smith to J. Loch, 4 Mar. 1844, ibid.

[4] F. Smith to J. Loch, 22 Aug. 1839, ibid.

Liverpool are going by the Railway'.[1] The railroad had in this case the advantage not only of speed but also of cost. The Bridgewater Trustees had to charge a high rate for freighting hardware down the Mersey estuary from Runcorn, because they knew that they would be held responsible for the loss of so valuable a cargo if one of their flats sank in the river.[2]

It was not against the Grand Junction alone that the Trustees contended. As the months passed the area of the conflict widened, bringing in other lines. To the north of Manchester the Manchester and Bolton and North Union Railways, both opened in 1838, encroached steadily upon the traffic on the Worsley branch of the Duke's Canal with places like Preston, Blackburn, and Wigan. By 1841 the Manchester and Leeds, Cromford and High Peak, and Birmingham and Derby Junction Railways were all engaged in attacking some part of the through trade of the Duke of Bridgewater's Canal.

Some trades were easily lost. Foremost among them were those encumbered by disadvantages built into the Canal system at the time of construction. Such defects were especially apparent in hilly country where water routes tended to be circuitous and heavily locked. Before the coming of the railways goods were sent from Blackburn to Manchester by way of the Leeds and Liverpool and Lancaster Canals and the Leigh and Worsley branches of the Duke's. The distance travelled by the carriers' boats was forty-three miles, though as the crow flies Blackburn and Manchester were less than twenty-five miles apart, and no fewer than thirty-six locks had to be negotiated. When, therefore, the railway from Manchester to Bolton was completed, several Blackburn manufacturers began to send their products in carts overland to Bolton, where trans-shipment into railway wagons took place. They found that by doing so they could cut the length of the journey by more than a half. Goods could be dispatched many hours later than hitherto and still reach Manchester for market or Exchange hours. Hargreaves, the carrier by water, saw his trade steadily dwindle away. Cut to three boats per week by September 1840, it suffered a further decline during the first nine months of 1841. In October Hargreaves gave notice of his intention

[1] Worthington to F. Smith, 31 July 1839, ibid.
[2] F. Smith to J. Loch, 8 Sept. 1838, ibid.

to quit his rooms in the Castlefield warehouse altogether by Christmas.[1]

It would be misleading to suppose, however, that the loss of through traffic on the Duke's Canal stemmed entirely from defects inherent in the Canal system from the outset. The situation was made worse than it need have been by a want of enterprise and adaptability on the part of the Canal proprietors. This was to be seen notably in the failure to quote economical rates. The Trustees themselves were reasonably active and vigilant in these matters. Even they, however, occasionally allowed a tonnage charge appropriate to the old days before the railways came to remain unchanged amidst very different conditions. The decline of the Blackburn and Manchester canal trade was hastened by the fact that a tonnage of 2s. 6d. (2d. per ton per mile) was payable for the use of the fifteen miles of Bridgewater Canal from Leigh to Manchester. On the remainder of the route the carrier paid 1½d. per ton per mile to the Leeds and Liverpool Canal Company and the same to the proprietors of the Lancaster Canal, but it was not until the trade had started to leak away that the Trustees decided to lower their toll by an amount not exceeding 1s. per ton.[2] The owners of other canals forming part of a chain with the Duke's were often, however, more rigid than the Trustees themselves. The Grand Trunk and the Oxford Canals, for instance, maintained the same intransigence in the face of railway competition that they had already shown in the struggle against the Ellesmere Canal and the Weaver Navigation.

It was the inflexible charges of the Trent and Mersey which, as Loch explained to Lord Francis Egerton, brought the Cromford and High Peak Railway into serious competition with the Duke's for the Shardlow trade.[3] In the early 1840s large cargoes of malt, flour, and grain from Nottinghamshire and Lincolnshire still travelled up the Grand Trunk from Shardlow, the busy trans-shipment point for traffic from the River Trent, to Preston Brook, whence they were taken to Manchester via the long arm of the Duke's Canal. Weekly accounts

---

[1] F. Smith to J. Loch, 10 Sept. 1840 and 13 Oct. 1841, ibid.

[2] F. Smith to J. Loch, 10 Sept. 1840; J. Loch to F. Smith, 15 Sept. 1840, ibid.

[3] J. Loch to Lord F. Egerton, 5 Oct. 1841, E.B.C.

recording quantities of 100, 200, and sometimes nearly 300 tons exist for the later months of 1841, when the trade had already come under attack. The boats conveying this produce returned laden with Manchester packs which were in due course transferred to the Trent barges for transport to Nottingham, a large centre of the cotton hosiery and lace-making industries.[1] Ever since 1831, when the Cromford and High Peak Railway linking the Cromford Canal to the Peak Forest Canal had been opened, there had existed an alternative route for the traffic to take, thirty-five miles shorter in distance than the Preston Brook route. Nevertheless, despite Bradshaw's fears, the High Peak line did not at first prove a serious rival to the Duke's. For the first ten years of its existence it failed to pay, carrying mainly limestone.[2] The situation was radically altered, however, by the opening of new lines of railway in the early forties. About the middle of June 1841 the Manchester and Leeds Company, whose line had been completed from Normanton to Manchester in the previous March, reduced its rates of carriage. The directors no doubt hoped to be able to attract the through traffic between Manchester and Shardlow to an easterly route using their own line, for they had a connection through Selby with the river system feeding into the Humber and through the Humber into the Trent. The intervention of the newcomer triggered off a chain reaction. The Yorkshire canals followed suit; so also did the Ashton and Cromford Canals and the High Peak Railway. Sutton's, Soresby's, and Barrow's, three carrying firms operating by Preston Brook, went immediately to the Grand Trunk Committee to request a reduction of toll, and on being refused determined to go in future by the Cromford and High Peak route.[3]

This decision owed little if anything to the technical superiority of the latter. A good deal more than half of the journey by the new route would be by canal, and the High Peak railroad itself possessed few of the advantages of a railroad over a canal. Because of the steep gradients (reaching

---

[1] Mitchell to F. Smith, 2 November 1841, L.E.P.

[2] D. J. Hodgkins, 'The Origin and Independent Years of the Cromford and High Peak Railway', *Journal of Transport History*, vi (1963–4), 39–55.

[3] F. Smith to J. Loch, 15 and 26 June and 7 July 1841, L.E.P.

a maximum of one in seven) which had to be negotiated, locomotive traction alternated with that of stationary engines drawing wagons up inclined planes. Nine such planes existed on the thirty-three mile long stretch, and their presence imparted an element of delay and high cost comparable to that which was produced on the canals by locks.[1] It was simply a matter of rates. In August 1841 the total amount of tonnage payable on packs travelling from Manchester by the High Peak route was 4s. 7d.; by way of Preston Brook the charge was 9s. 9d. On general merchandise the figures were 10s. and about 13s. respectively. The Trustees did what they could by unilateral action to reduce the disparity. By slashing their own toll on packs between Manchester and Preston Brook to the absurd level of ½d. per ton per mile, they reduced the total charge by that route to 6s. 4½d. per ton. They also lowered on flour, malt, and grain of all kinds.[2] Without the co-operation of the Grand Trunk, however, they could not hope to equalize the charges, and the traffic leaked steadily away.

Soon the contest extended from the Shardlow trade to the traffic in general goods between Manchester and London. This had previously gone by the Duke's, the Grand Trunk, and the Coventry, Oxford, and Grand Junction Canals. In September 1841, however, the proprietors of the Cromford, Erewash, and Union Canals meeting at Matlock agreed to reduce the tonnage on general goods from Manchester to Nottingham from 10s. to 6s. 5d. per ton. This achieved the desired effect of diverting the London trade to a route which followed the High Peak Railway, the Leicestershire canals, and the Grand Union to the Grand Junction Canal. The proprietors of the latter assisted the diversion by introducing a heavy discrimination into their tolls against traffic fed into their waterway from the Oxford Canal and in favour of that which came from the Grand Union. This step was conceived as a measure of retaliation upon the Grand Trunk for obstructing the through traffic by heavy charges, but the Duke of Bridgewater's Canal suffered too.[3]

The unyielding attitude of the Grand Trunk Committee

---

[1] Hodgkins, op. cit.; H. G. Lewin, *Early British Railways*, p. 13.
[2] Marsden to F. Smith, 17 and 27 Aug., 20 Sept., and 19 Oct. 1841, L.E.P.
[3] F. Smith to J. Loch, 20 Sept. 1841, ibid.

towards all proposals to reduce tolls is partly explained by jealousy of the independent carriers. In June 1839 Trubshaw and Ruscoe, two gentlemen connected with the Company, told Fereday Smith that their committee had no present intention of reducing the Canal rates 'in consequence of their having discovered that on former occasions of reductions the carriers had pocketed the reductions'. Devoid of any sense of the urgency of the situation introduced by the opening of competing railways like the Grand Junction, they seemed more concerned to harass the carriers with stringent regulations about gauge plates and about declarations of weight than to collaborate with them against the common foe.[1] Such conduct, though it was just, was liable to induce the canal carriers to sell their boats and transfer their traffic to the railways, continuing to profit as collectors and distributors of goods whilst inflicting severe injury upon the canal owners whose capital was less mobile. It was by no means unknown for canal carriers thus to further the decline of the waterways. Hargreaves, a substantial carrier by water to places north of Manchester, made a strong line of business in leasing short stretches of railway with a view to building up an exclusive trade upon them. He leased first the Bolton and Leigh railroad and later the North Union line.[2] Manifestly the division of interest between the carrying trade and the ownership of the track was a serious weakness to the canals in the struggle with the railways.

It would be a mistake, however, in dealing with this early period to emphasize too strongly the superiority of the railways over the canals. Communications by rail were so disjointed that railway companies often depended upon adjacent canals for power to enter into competition for the long-distance traffic. The Cromford and High Peak Railway furnished one example; the Manchester and Leeds supplied another. That company entered upon a very violent quarrel with the Duke of Bridgewater's Trustees in the autumn of 1841, but it was only able to make headway because it could align itself with the Trustees' old enemy in the canal camp, the Mersey and Irwell Navigation Company. The dispute did not arise from

[1] F. Smith to J. Loch, 5 June 1839, ibid.
[2] F. Smith to J. Loch, 4 May 1838 and 15 Sept. 1840, ibid.

any well-defined clash of economic interests, for the Bridge-water Canal stood more in an 'end on' than in a 'parallel' relationship to the railway. It was a product of a mainly accidental factor—the involvement of the Principal Trustee James Loch in the management of the Liverpool and Man-chester Railway. The object of Captain Laws, General Manager of the Manchester and Leeds Company, in attacking the Trustees was to compel the Liverpool and Manchester Railway board to co-operate in constructing a connecting line through Manchester which would join its own track to that of the Manchester and Leeds. When the Leeds Railway was opened in March 1841, it ended at the St. George's Street Station in Oldham Road, which was on the other side of Manchester from the terminus of the Liverpool and Manchester railroad in Liverpool Road. The Liverpool and Manchester Company had been authorized by an Act of Parliament passed in June 1839 to build a connecting line from Cross Lane, Salford, to Hunts Bank, using a section of the Manchester and Bolton line as part of its route. At Hunts Bank this would join an extension of the Manchester and Leeds, which was still to be made. The direc-tors, however, afterwards changed their minds and declined to proceed with the work. Captain Laws, anxious to remove all impediments to a through trade by rail between Liverpool and the West Riding, attributed their defection to the in-fluence upon the Board exerted by James Loch. He believed that Loch was principally motivated by a desire to retain the monopoly of a continuous through route from Liverpool via Manchester to Yorkshire for the Duke of Bridgewater's Canal.

This was an over-simplification. Loch had indeed opposed the construction of the junction line through Salford, not however with any view to obstructing a railway link-up alto-gether, but with the object of furthering an alternative route which would go round the southern side of Manchester, taking in the joint terminus of the Sheffield, Ashton, and Manchester and the Manchester and Birmingham at Store Street, Picca-dilly, on its way. He supported this project against the other on grounds which stemmed as much from the interests of the Liverpool and Manchester Railway as from those of the Bridge-water Canal, though he hoped to be able to sell some of the Trustees' spare land at Castlefield for building the south line

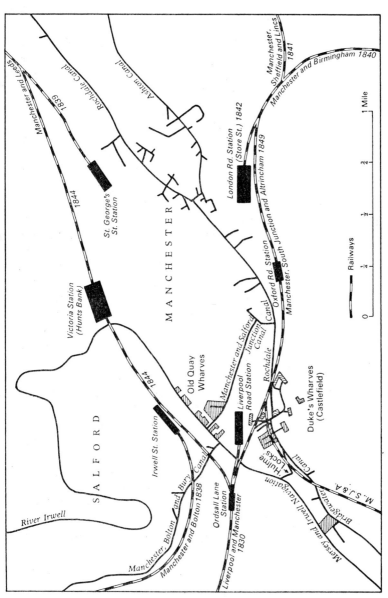

Map 3.   Principal Rail and Canal Connections in Manchester, c. 1850.

and to create a railway–canal junction at that place. Moreover, his was not the only influence upon the Board working in this direction.

The correctness or otherwise of Captain Laws's diagnosis matters less perhaps than the action which he took in furtherance of his opinion. Thinking to intimidate Loch, he threatened in October and November 1841 that he would ruin the Duke's Trustees by flooding the Manchester market with cheap coke (in opposition to that from Worsley) and by diverting the through traffic between Liverpool and Yorkshire away from the Duke's Canal and towards the Mersey and Irwell Navigation.[1] To show that this was no idle boast, he made an agreement with the Old Quay Company in February 1842 for exchanging traffic in Manchester, and arranged to discriminate in favour of the River trade in his own charges. The M. & L. was to carry Liverpool goods to and from the West Riding at a lower rate per ton if they travelled west of Manchester by the River than if they used the Duke's Canal. It would quote a low through rate on down goods which adopted the Old Quay route, paying the Navigation Company for the use of its boats, whilst assuming no responsibility beyond Manchester for traffic which went forward by the Bridgewater Canal. This arrangement immediately unsettled the carriers on the Duke's. It was reported to Loch on 22 February that Pickfords had deserted the Canal.[2]

It should also be remembered that side by side with the competition from the railways, the threat from opposing canals continued to grow. The Anderton Carrying Company and the Ellesmere and Chester Canal encroached steadily upon the southward trade of the Bridgewater Canal, continuing the offensive which they had mounted in the preceding decade. By the end of 1841 the former had gained a complete monopoly of the Congleton and Macclesfield trades and carried twice as many boatloads of pottery crates each week as Henshalls conveyed along the Duke's.[3] In October James Loch wrote to

---

[1] J. M. Laws to J. Baxendale, 31 Oct. and 14 Nov. 1841; J. to G. Loch, 6 Dec. 1841, 'Bundle Marked 1841 Mr. Loch's Correspondence with Captain Laws About Connection Railway,' L.E.P.

[2] F. Smith to G. Loch, 10, 17, 19, and 22 Feb. 1842, ibid.

[3] F. Smith to J. Loch, 7 July 1841; Mitchell to F. Smith, 10 Nov. 1841, ibid.

Lord Francis Egerton: 'There has taken place a great revolu
tion in the Preston Brook trade. The low charges of the Railway and the low tonnages of the Ellesmere Canal have
absorbed the greater part of the London and Birmingham trade
with Liverpool and Manchester.'[1] His letter makes clear both
the extent of the crisis into which the Trustees' affairs had
passed at this time and the fact that it had come about not
because of railways alone, but because the threats from the
rail and from the water coincided.

Under the pressure of increasing competition the Trustees
found it necessary to modify one of the most cherished principles imposed by James Loch as Superintendent—the notion
that it was desirable to restrict to a minimum their commitments as carriers and to maintain a free and equal competition
upon their canal. Experience was soon to teach them that in
any sustained contest for the long-distance trade the independent carriers went to the wall. To protect their own interests as canal proprietors, therefore, as well as to preserve
their existing carrying business on the Mersey estuary, they
were obliged to assume extended responsibilities for carrying.
They moved very cautiously, for Loch kept a watchful and
discouraging eye upon the process. Nevertheless, they did
move. In October 1839, as a thrust against the Anderton
Company, they established Thomas Jackson, once the Company's manager at Macclesfield but now a freelance, in the
Macclesfield trade, by granting him a drawback from the tolls
on the Bridgewater Canal. Despite his known aversion to
partial arrangements Loch sanctioned the deal.[2] Two years
later, in November 1841, the Trustees sent their own boats
south from Preston Brook along the Grand Trunk to the
Staffordshire Potteries and along the Ashton, Peak Forest,
and Macclesfield Canals. This was a radical departure from
past practice. Even in the Old Duke's day, when a far larger
proportion of the traffic of the Canal had been carried on
freight, the boats owned by the Duke had seldom traded on
waterways other than his own. It was only adopted as an
emergency measure designed to save the trade in general goods

---

[1] J. Loch to Lord F. Egerton, 5 Oct. 1841, E.B.C.
[2] F. Smith to J. Loch, 5 Oct. 1839; J. Loch to F. Smith, 20 Oct. 1839,
L.E.P.

(groceries, soap, wines and spirits, etc.) from annihilation, for Kenworthy, a carrier to North Staffordshire via Preston Brook, had just withdrawn from the traffic, leaving to the Anderton Company nearly the whole of the groceries trade to the Potteries. This, at least, was how Loch saw it. The local agents, with some support from Fereday Smith, seem to have welcomed the event as an excuse for indulging in expansion for expansion's sake, for they exceeded their instructions. An agent was appointed in Macclesfield, and both there and in the Potteries the most earnest endeavours were made to solicit a traffic not only in groceries but in iron and Manchester packs and trusses by quoting rates which were below those of the Anderton Company.[1]

It was Loch's view, however, that prevailed. The Trustees simply acted as primers of the pump of independent enterprise. Their action put the remaining carriers upon their mettle. Sutton & Co. engaged an additional Potteries agent and reduced their rates to compete with those of the Anderton Company. Pickfords agreed to adopt the Anderton Company's charges in their trade with both Macclesfield and North Staffordshire. As soon as the private carriers bestirred themselves, the Trustees retreated. They abandoned the carrying trade with the Potteries on 15 December 1841, little more than a month after they had begun it, and in 1842 they handed over the resuscitated Macclesfield trade to Pickfords.[2]

The successful intervention of the Duke's Trustees in the carrying trade marks in some respects a turning-point in their fortunes. During the third phase in the history of the struggle for the through trade, a phase which extended over the years 1842–4, they appeared to have surmounted the worst crisis, and although they were still involved in many bitter conflicts, they were returning the fire of their opponents with much greater effect.

A feature of the situation which contributed materially to the easement of their position was that a lull occurred in the incipient battle against the railways. The edge was removed

---

[1] F. Smith to J. Loch, 11 Nov. 1841; Heathcote to Mitchell, 16 Nov. 1841; J. Loch to F. Smith, 2 Dec. 1841, L.E.P.

[2] F. Smith to J. Loch, 13 and 16 Dec. 1841 and 6 Jan. 1842, ibid.

from the quarrel between the Trustees and the Manchester and Leeds Railway when in July 1842 the Liverpool and Manchester railroad directors went to Parliament for powers to build the northern connecting line, which Captain Laws desired, along a somewhat less objectionable route than the one which was first envisaged.[1]

By February 1844 the General Manager of the M. & L. had completely changed his tune towards the Trustees, giving his opinion that railways and canals ought not to fight.[2] With the Grand Junction Railway relations underwent a complete reversal. The idea of an exchange of traffic at Preston Brook which had been discussed in 1837 was revived, and an agreement for effecting a junction at that place was signed on behalf of the Trustees on 9 October 1841.[3] The Trustees hoped that the deal would free them from dependence upon the obtuse Grand Trunk Committee for their lifeline to the Midlands and the south. They were especially keen to have iron included in the list of commodities which were to be transshipped, hoping to win back by means of the Grand Junction Railway the traffic which they lost to Ellesmere Port through the obduracy of the directors of the Trent and Mersey. They were also attracted by the prospect of using the railway to feed coal to the salt works at Wharton near Winsford and to bring back a loading of salt which might be distributed by the Canal to Liverpool, Manchester, Bolton, and Yorkshire.[4] High in hopes, they pressed on with their part of the bargain, and within a month or two of the signing of the agreement the shed at Preston Brook was in course of erection.[5] The Railway Company, on the other hand, was slow to perform its promises. By March 1842 it had, indeed, stationed a clerk at Preston Brook with the necessary books,[6] but the trade in

---

[1] *J.H.C.* xcvii (1842), 291, 547.
[2] F. Smith to J. Loch, 14 Feb. 1844, L.E.P.
[3] F. Smith to J. Loch, 6 Oct. 1841 ; J. Loch to F. Smith, 9 Oct. 1841, ibid. By this arrangement the Railway Company agreed to sell to the Trustees a strip of land lying between their own line and the Trustees' land at Preston Brook. In return for this the Trustees were to erect a shed for trans-shipment purposes. F. Smith to J. Loch, 16 Sept. 1841 ; J. Loch to F. Smith, 10 Oct. and 28 Nov. 1841, ibid.
[4] F. Smith to J. Loch, 13 Feb. 1841 and 31 May 1842, ibid.
[5] F. Smith to J. Loch, 7 Dec. 1841, ibid.
[6] F. Smith to J. Loch, 2 Mar. 1842, ibid.

Staffordshire iron which the Trustees impatiently awaited failed to materialize for almost a year. The railroad directors had some shadow of an excuse for this delay in that they did not as yet possess the necessary links with the ironworks at the southern end of their line. To establish these they needed to obtain a connection with the network of canals which spread out from Birmingham into the heart of the Black Country. At the end of the year, however, a shed for trans-shipping iron from canal to railway was in course of erection in Birmingham.[1] After that, for a little while, the agreement with the Trustees seemed about to bear fruit. Early in February 1843 a trade in iron goods and chains began to be passed by the Grand Junction Railway to the Bridgewater Canal at Preston Brook, and the Railway Company made offers to the Staffordshire ironmasters to deliver their iron at very low rates alongside vessels in the Liverpool docks by means of the Trustees' flats.[2] Just as it was developing, however, the Grand Junction Company cut it short. In July Captain Mark Huish, the Company's General Manager, expressed himself in favour of leaving it to the iron-masters to decide whether to send by rail to Preston Brook only or all the way to Liverpool. Shortly afterwards Fereday Smith heard that a shed for accommodating iron was about to be erected at the railway terminus in Liverpool. His opinion was that the company favoured sending all such iron as was intended for immediate sale or use in Liverpool (and not dis-patched to order) all the way by rail.[3]

It is difficult to tell whether the directors of the Grand Junction Railway ever seriously intended to promote an exchange of traffic at Preston Brook, or whether, as Loch came eventually to believe, they were simply using the project as a diplomatic weapon against the Trustees themselves or against some other party.[4] The object may have been to force terms upon the Liverpool and Manchester Railway, which stood to lose by any diversion of traffic at Preston Brook. On the other hand, the Grand Junction Company may have toyed seriously with the idea of annexing the trade which came into England

---

[1] B. Poole to F. Smith, 9 Dec. 1842, L.E.P.
[2] F. Smith to J. Loch, 12 Jan. and 10 Feb. 1843, ibid.
[3] F. Smith to J. Loch, 22 July and 1 Aug. 1843, ibid.
[4] J. Loch to F. Smith, 20 June 1844, ibid.

through the port of Runcorn and via the Duke's Canal and of using the facilities which the Trustees possessed at Liverpool for loading directly into sea-going vessels. On balance the former explanation carries greater weight than the latter. In either case, however, the point remains that a large canal undertaking such as the Duke's still counted for something in the calculations of a railway company. It could neither be ignored nor crushed, but must on the very lowest estimate be temporized with.

Unhappily for the Trustees the slackening of the contest with the railways was offset by the continued growth of the hostility of other canals. The principal rivals were those which had been causing anxiety in the later 1830s, viz. the Anderton Carrying Company and the Ellesmere and Chester Canal, but to these was now added the Leeds and Liverpool Canal, which by its low tonnage charges competed for the Yorkshire to Liverpool traffic in 1842. The competitive strength of the Ellesmere Port route to Liverpool was vastly increased at this time, partly by the opening of a new dock at Ellesmere Port in September 1843 and partly by the new carrying ventures of the Ellesmere and Chester and Birmingham and Liverpool Junction canal companies. Even before Parliament intervened in 1845 with general legislation designed to remove the legal disabilities which hindered canal companies from acting as carriers, some of the leading navigation proprietors had begun to take up the business perhaps through an intermediary or under an assumed name. The Grand Trunk Company had long carried as Hugh Henshall & Co., but the desire to compete more effectively with the railways now drove others to follow its example. In August 1842, in pursuance of a private Act of Parliament, the General Committee of the Ellesmere and Chester Company resolved in favour of carrying by deputy to and from places on their Llanymynech and Llangollen branches. Early in the following year the company was preparing to enter the trade between the Potteries and Liverpool which it had previously left to the Anderton Company and to Henshalls, the carriers by Preston Brook. Its boats were to go by the Middlewich branch.[1] In the spring of 1842 the Birmingham

[1] F. Smith to J. Loch, 6 Sept. 1843; W. S. Thistleton to F. Smith, 6 Feb. 1843, ibid. E. & C.C.C. General Committee Orders, 1827–46, pp. 242–3, 248–56.

and Liverpool Junction Canal also obtained carrying powers, under which the Company's superintendent Samuel Skey put trains of boats drawn by steam tugs upon the Junction and Ellesmere Canals in a determined bid for the traffic in iron and other merchandise between the Black Country and Lancashire. Both the Bridgewater Trustees and the Grand Junction Railway viewed his activities with intense alarm. The former made a desperate bid to divert Skey from Ellesmere Port to Preston Brook, but were foiled in their purposes partly by the refusal of the Grand Trunk committee to grant the necessary permission for a train of boats to operate upon their waterway.[1]

Events moved forward to a climax in the second half of 1843 when a sharp contest occurred between the Ellesmere Port and Preston Brook routes to Liverpool. The Bridgewater Trustees hit back sharply at their opponents. Their powers of retaliation were strengthened by a newly found ability of the canals sharing the route with them to act in unison. In July 1843 they reduced their charge for freighting iron from Preston Brook to Liverpool from 2s. 4d. to 2s. per ton. This was part of a plan concerted with the Staffordshire ironmasters, the Staffordshire and Worcestershire Canal, and the Grand Trunk Canal, under which was to be effected not only a reduction of charges but a reorganization of the trade which would dispense with the private carriers. The ironmasters were to carry the iron in their own boats to Etruria, where it would be transshipped into the boats of Henshalls, the carrying department of the Grand Trunk. Henshalls would then convey it to Preston Brook, where the boats of the Bridgewater Trustees would take over.[2] The Ellesmere Company replied by ordering a great reduction in the freight of pottery goods, clay, and flints to and from Ellesmere Port and Liverpool and through the Middlewich branch.[3] Both companies were acting aggressively, for the Ellesmere Canal had no pottery trade to defend and the Bridgewater Trustees had no longer any iron trade to speak of between Preston Brook and Liverpool. The contest was a simple trial of strength between two giants to discover

[1] J. Loch to F. Smith, 1 May 1842; F. Smith to J. Loch, 12 May 1842 and 18 Apr. 1844, L.E.P.; C. Hadfield, *The Canals of the West Midlands*, p. 188.

[2] F. Smith to J. Loch, 22 and 28 July 1843; J. Loch to F. Smith, 21 July 1843, ibid.

[3] E. & C.C.C. General Committee Orders, 1827–46, pp. 268–72.

which could first be brought to its knees. It would not be long before the issue was decided, in the Trustees' favour, but the victory when it came would be upon a wider front than this. Before we can appreciate its full extent we must review developments relating to the short-distance traffic upon the Duke's Canal.

CHAPTER VIII

The Years of Equipoise (1837–1844). II

So far we have seen that even in the through trade, where the defects of the canal system were acknowledged to be the greatest, railway competition, though for a while serious, was by no means the only problem confronting the Duke of Bridgewater's Trustees in the years 1837–44. It was of smaller importance for the traffic which travelled only along the twenty-eight miles of Bridgewater Canal between the Top Locks at Runcorn and the Castlefield wharves in Manchester, originating or ending in the immediate vicinity of the great metropolis of the Lancashire cotton manufacture. Some of this trade, notably the grain and flour which were imported straight into Runcorn by coasting vessels, was not subject at all to competition from railways except in so far as an excessive canal rate between Runcorn and Manchester might cause the produce to be landed at Liverpool. Most of it passed, however, through the port of Liverpool and had the option of using the Liverpool and Manchester Railway instead of the Canal. Nevertheless, despite the fact that the railway had been open since 1830, the Trustees' most dangerous rival at this period was not the Railway Company but the Mersey and Irwell Navigation Company.

The hostility of the Old Quay displayed itself in many ways. The Company continued to haggle with the Trustees about the passage of Runcorn Island. Despite protracted negotiation, the question seemed at the beginning of 1840 as far from settlement as ever.[1] Undeterred by falling profits, perhaps

---

[1] See above, pp. 92–3, for the commencement of the dispute.
At the end of 1838 the Bridgewater Trustees agreed to the opening of the Gut, on condition that they might be allowed to make some alterations at the western end of it, to facilitate the entrance of vessels into their own locks. The terms, however, were unacceptable to the Old Quay Company. Negotiations

indeed because financial difficulties had made them reckless, the directors of the Company, led by the young and energetic Thomas Ogden Lingard, planned also in the later 1830s to make their river system navigable to vessels of 150 tons burthen. In 1841 they toyed with the idea of cutting a ship canal from Garston to Runcorn Gap, intending that it should be continued along the Sankey Canal to Warrington.[1] Fortunately for the Trustees, whose traffic depended upon the coasting vessels' proceeding up river no further than Runcorn, these schemes came to nothing. Nevertheless, in the years 1840–1 the Old Quay Company did extend the navigability of the Irwell at its Manchester end, making it possible for some ships to reach Victoria Bridge. The estimated cost of the improvement was up to £2,600.[2] In June 1838 the Old Quay Committee placed upon its waterway a steamboat called the *Jack Sharp* propelled by a twelve horse-power engine and capable of carrying 150 passengers.[3] They competed vigorously with the Trustees for the traffic in potatoes carried from Aston, Ince, and Preston Brook into Manchester, and planned in 1841 to construct a potato market dock in the last-named town to match the dock which had been built by the Bridgewater people two years earlier.[4]

It was in their attitude towards rate-fixing agreements, however, that the controllers of the Mersey and Irwell Navigation Company manifested their aggressiveness in the form which the Trustees feared most. Unlike the long-distance traffic which joined the Canal at Preston Brook, at Leigh, and at Manchester, the Liverpool and Manchester and Runcorn and Manchester trades were regulated trades. Competition

were reopened in September 1839 for rounding off the outside of the island as a substitute for opening the Gut, but the two concerns could not agree upon an engineer to superintend the works. The Trustees committed their interest to Cubitt; the Old Quay Company consulted Bateman. Eventually a compromise was reached. Bateman and Cubitt conferred, with the authority of their respective employers, and reached agreement in August 1840. J. Loch to F. Smith, 24 Dec. 1838, 24 July and 17 Sept. 1839; F. Smith to J. Loch, 14 Feb. 1840, L.E.P.; M. & I.N.C. Order Book, 1834–41, pp. 121, 148, 151.

[1] M. & I.N.C. Order Book, 1834–41, pp. 114, 133. F. Smith to J. Loch, 6 Mar. and 3 Apr. 1841, L.E.P.

[2] M. & I.N.C. Order Book, 1834–41, pp. 144, 150, 168.

[3] *The Manchester Historical Recorder*, p. 112.

[4] F. Smith to J. Loch, 21 Nov. 1839, 16 Oct. 1841, and 26 May 1843, L.E.P.; M. & I.N.C. Order Book, 1834–41, p. 161.

in the sense of bidding for traffic by reducing rates was now the exceptional rather than the normal state of affairs. Because a substantial amount of the carrying business was in the hands of three large carrying establishments which were able to combine (the Trust, the Old River, and the Railway Company), the rates of carriage were determined by the agreement of these parties.[1] The Liverpool and Manchester Railway Company accepted on the whole the principle of regulation, striving merely to shift the terms of agreement in its own favour as it grew in strength. The Bridgewater Trustees stood mainly for the maintenance of the *status quo*. It was the Old Quay Company and to a lesser extent the independent carriers by water that played increasingly the role of the *enfant terrible*, over-turning arrangements at the slightest pretext and snatching traffic by means of rebates and reduced rates.

One agreement for raising and maintaining freight charges had been made by the water carriers at the beginning of 1838, and was accompanied by an informal understanding with the Railway Company to the same effect. It lasted for about two and a half years. On 30 June 1840, however, the Mersey and Irwell Navigation Company, which was running deeper into financial difficulties, gave notice of an intention to withdraw from the agreement on 1 October. The effect of this action was to unsettle the trade. Rumours were soon flying that both the Old Quay Company and the private carriers upon the Duke's were attracting trade by abandoning customary charges for porterage and for cartage in Manchester and by other means which the directors of the Liverpool and Manchester Railway Company deemed unscrupulous. The latter complained of a very serious diminution of their carrying trade, especially in cotton, and on 1 October they lowered their charge on eggs from 12s. 6d. to 10s. per ton, and on loose grain, flour, and madder from 9s. to 8s. 4d. per ton, announcing the changes to the

[1] Some figures quoted by W. T. Jackman indicate that in the years 1839–41, about one-third of the traffic by water between Liverpool and Manchester was carried in the boats of the Canal proprietors, notably in those of the M. & I.N.C., which in 1839 conveyed more than three times as much trade as was carried by independent firms along its waterway. The Bridgewater Trustees, the Old Quay Company, and the L. & M.R. Company appear from the same statistics to have assumed responsibility for between 50 and 60 per cent of the combined railway and Canal traffic. From 1842 onwards, however, the proportion fell sharply (*The Development of Transportation in Modern England*, p. 741).

public without prior communication with the Canal carriers.
The Mersey and Irwell Navigation Company retaliated without delay. Not only did it match the reductions effected by
the Railway Company; it went a step further, lowering grain
in sacks from 8*s.* 4*d.* to 7*s.* 6*d.* per ton and wines and spirits
from 10*s.* 10*d.* to 9*s.* 2*d.* Hitherto wines and spirits had been
almost entirely a railway traffic.[1] The carrying firms now stood
on the brink of a serious contest, but at this point the community of interest between the Bridgewater Canal and the
Liverpool and Manchester Railway created by the Marquess of
Stafford's purchase of railway shares fourteen years earlier was
called into play to save the situation. James Loch's son George,
a director of the Liverpool and Manchester Railway appointed
by the Duke of Sutherland, worked hard to keep open the door
to negotiation. At a board meeting on 19 October 1840 he
swung the decision against an immediate reduction of rates
and procured the appointment of a deputation, consisting of
Henry Booth, the Secretary and Treasurer of the Company,
and himself, to see Lingard of the Old Quay. When the Old
Quay Committee declined a proposal to restore the *status quo*,
he fought another rearguard action at a meeting of the railway
directors on the 22nd and succeeded in getting the question of
rates left to Booth, who was on his side. Against him were
arrayed powerful personalities—Sandars, Rotheram, Lawrence, Hornby, Earle, all strongly opposed to delay in retaliation. Moss was especially vehement. Loch was surprised to find
him so decidedly bent on destroying the private carriers and
impairing Lord Francis Egerton's income.[2] Being chairman of
the directors of the Grand Junction Railway as well as a
member of the Liverpool and Manchester board, he had not
forgotten Lord Francis's earlier support of the Manchester
and Birmingham Railway Company's proposed extension to
Rugby.

Whilst the younger Loch worked for peace within the
Railway Company, the elder as principal trustee of the Bridge-
water Canal endeavoured to bring the water carriers into line.
Fereday Smith was instructed to warn the independent carriers

---

[1] M. & I.N.C. Order Book, 1834–41, pp. 149–50, 153–4; F. Smith to J. Loch,
19 and 22 Aug. and 7 Oct. 1840, L.E.P.
[2] G. to J. Loch, 19 and 22 Oct. 1840, S.E.P.

operating upon the Duke's that they were being watched by some of the railway directors, and that if they provoked a contest the Trustees would stand by and allow them to be ruined by it.[1] Eventually, at a meeting of the Liverpool and Manchester board on 5 April 1841, George Loch, assisted by Langton, his fellow Sutherland director, succeeded in aligning the Railway Company with the Duke's Trustees in putting pressure on the Mersey and Irwell Navigation Company to undertake with other carriers a joint retracing of steps. The manœuvre succeeded. On 22 April the Mersey and Irwell Navigation Company, the Bridgewater Trustees, and the Liverpool and Manchester Railway Company met by delegation and agreed to return to the scale of rates charged immediately before the disruption of the late agreement.[2]

It is not to be supposed that the solicitude shown by the Loch family for the maintenance of rates of carriage stemmed purely from concern for the Bridgewater Canal. One motive was to save the Duke of Sutherland's large holdings in the Liverpool and Manchester Railway from the losses of a contest.[3] Nevertheless, it was also apprehended by both father and son that a battle with the railway would either ruin the carriers by water or force upon the Trustees a reduction of tolls. In the first case there would be a serious risk that the business handled by the carriers would be in great measure lost to the canals, as there was no guarantee that the carrying department of the Trust would be able to annex it; in the second the Trustees would find themselves bearing more than their fair share of the loss. This would be the case even if the reduction of toll was only a portion of the fall in freight charges 'inasmuch as it would be a contest of carriers, and carriers' profits not highway tolls ought to be affected'.[4]

The agreement of April 1841 was not, however, a permanent settlement. On 6 December it was denounced. This time the aggressor was the Liverpool and Manchester Railway, which

[1] J. Loch to F. Smith, 17 and 22 Dec. 1840, L.E.P.

[2] G. Loch to J. Loch, 5 and 12 Apr. 1841; H. Booth to J. Loch, 5 and 12 Apr. 1841; extract from Minutes of L. & M.R. Board, 5 Apr. 1841; J. Loch to H. Booth, 12 Apr. 1841, S.E.P. F. Smith to J. Loch, 23 and 24 Apr. 1841, L.E.P.   [3] J. Loch to H. Booth, 12 Apr. 1841, S.E.P.

[4] Extract of letter from George Loch, 31 Aug. 1840; J. Loch to F. Smith, 9 Sept. 1840; J. Loch to W. Slater, 10 Sept. 1840, L.E.P.

reduced the freight charge on cotton from 10*s*. 6*d*. to 9*s*. per ton and made an allowance of 2*s*. per ton to carriers to and from Yorkshire. The railroad directors were fighting, however, not to smash the canals but to achieve a parity with them. They claimed that the independent carriers by water were depriving them of the trade in raw cotton, and that only 13 per cent of the total quantity of that commodity passing from Liverpool to Manchester went by rail.[1] This was almost certainly an exaggeration, but even the figures drawn up by the Bridgewater Trustees to rebut the allegation show that in the week ending 2 December 1841 the railroad carried only a quarter of the cotton conveyed to Manchester, the remaining three-quarters being divided almost equally between the Bridgewater Canal and the Mersey and Irwell Navigation.[2] In the down trade in Manchester manufactured goods even more than in the up traffic in cotton, the canals appear to have had the edge upon the railway. George Loch wrote to his father in March 1842:

It has been observed that of late the canals have been obtaining a much larger share of the down goods trade than formerly by means of the facilities they offer in sending their flats into dock and discharging their goods at once into the ship. This is productive of convenience in every way, saves breakage and damage to packages, etc., and combined with the rapidity of delivery now attained by means of steam tugs, has deprived the Railway of any superiority in the competition for the down trade.[3]

Nevertheless, under the existing agreement the carriers by canal were allowed to charge less than the Railway Company for the carriage of goods in order to compensate them for supposed disabilities. On down goods the differential was as much as 1*s*. 8*d*. per ton.[4] The railroad directors had certainly a case for being discontented.

A vigorous contest now ensued, for the Duke's Trustees and the Old Quay Company matched the reductions of freight charge made by the Railway Company. By the middle of February 1842 raw cotton was down to 7*s*. per ton, grain to

---

[1] H. Booth to F. Smith, 6 Dec. 1841; J. Loch to F. Smith, 7 Dec. 1841; F. Smith to J. Loch, 7 Dec. 1841, ibid.

[2] F. Smith to J. Loch, 7 Jan. 1842, and enclosure, ibid.

[3] G. to J. Loch, 2 Mar. 1842, S.E.P.

[4] F. Smith to J. Loch, 11 Mar. 1842, L.E.P.

6*s*., and eggs in crates to 8*s*. Both sides made losses. As Loch anticipated, the independent carriers by water were the weakest link in the chain on the Canal side. Veevers and the Merchants Company made as if to throw in the sponge, and the Trustees hesitated to come to their assistance by reducing tolls, fearing that if they did so they would never be able to raise them again and preferring, therefore, to offer help in the form of drawbacks from the tonnage charge, which could be made for only a limited period.[1] Nevertheless, the first feelers for peace came from the railway. John Moss wrote to the elder Loch on 26 February: '... I wish the carriers question was left to you and I [*sic*]. We have settled more difficult ones before now. It would save some thousands a week now thrown away.'[2] The Company's terms were twofold, viz. that the differential between the railway and canal charges on down goods should be dropped and that the navigation owners should guarantee the performance of the new agreement by the private carriers.[3] A new obstacle to the making of peace had now appeared, however—the Mersey and Irwell Navigation Company, which, although it did not start the battle, seized the opportunity to abstract the potato trade from the Bridgewater Canal by promise of a toll-free passage for the hauliers. Lingard would not even negotiate at first. He spoke of making the fight as bloody as possible. Eventually, however, after much tangled diplomacy had been gone through, a new settlement was agreed by representatives of the Old Quay, the Trustees, and the Railway Company meeting in Liverpool on 21 April 1842.[4] James Loch had done more than anyone to bring this result about. He had softened up the railway directors by hinting at a possible withdrawal of the Duke of Sutherland's holdings from the Company should the contest continue, and had intrigued behind Lingard's back with some of the directors of the Old Quay Company—Shakespeare Philipps, Buckley, and G. W. Wood.[5] The terms of the agreement were as follows. Freight

---

[1] F. Smith to J. Loch, 25 Jan., 15 and 17 Feb., and 26 May 1842; Holt, Murgatroyd, & Leah to J. Loch, 2 Feb. 1842, L.E.P.

[2] J. Moss to J. Loch, 26 Feb. 1842, S.E.P.

[3] G. to J. Loch, 2 Mar. 1842, ibid.

[4] F. Smith to J. Loch, 15 Mar. 1842 and 23 Apr. 1842, L.E.P.

[5] J. Loch to C. Lawrence, 25 Mar. 1842, S.E.P. J. Loch to F. Smith, 16 Mar. 1842, L.E.P.

charges were to be raised to a level higher even than before the contest started. The exact rates were to be fixed by subsequent negotiation, but it was laid down that the differential between rail and water should be reduced to 1*s.* per ton on down goods and that it should be abolished altogether on some of the principal up goods—cotton, grain, flour, madder, dyewoods, sugar, and tallow. The water carriers were to make an additional charge of 10*d.* per ton if their flats went alongside sea-going vessels to discharge down goods, and 1*s.* per ton if they entered the public docks or basins at Liverpool to receive up goods directly from the ships. Canal owners were to undertake for the adherence of their carriers to the agreement 'so far as they have the power'. By the third week in May the new rates of freight were agreed and printed. To the Trustees' disappointment, however, the railway directors had declined to go above 10*s.* per ton for cotton.[1]

The next bid to subvert the agreed structure of rates came from the private carriers on the Canal. During the latter half of 1842 these parties, whom Loch was so anxious to protect from the blast of a full-blown contest with the railways, began to find loop-holes in the restrictions which were imposed upon them by the canal owners supposedly in their own interests. Because there was no agreement with the railways for maintaining charges in the forward traffic (i.e. between Liverpool and towns east of Manchester), they were permitted to grant drawbacks from the rate of carriage by water between Liverpool and Manchester to manufacturers from Ashton, Oldham, and Stalybridge who made their own provision for carting cotton from the carriers' warehouses in Manchester. It was but a short step, however, from this to the illicit and fraudulent practice of granting such drawbacks to Manchester mill-owners who dishonestly consigned their cotton to forward towns whilst collecting it in Manchester. The fraud was difficult to detect, for many mill-owners had factories both in Manchester and outside, and it was almost impossible to distinguish between cotton sent to their Manchester mills and that which was dispatched to their establishments in Oldham

---

[1] F. Smith to J. Loch, 23 and 26 Apr. and 20 May 1842, L.E.P. Minutes of the Board of Directors of the L. & M.R., 1842–5, p. 19. B.T.H.R.

or Ashton.[1] By this device the Liverpool and Manchester rates could be indirectly lowered. In January 1843 the firm of Patchett & McKay, carriers on the Duke's, was arraigned before a disciplinary committee operating under the carriers' agreement and convicted of conveying merchandise to Manchester at 3s. per ton less than the agreed rates. A few days later Garstang, Almond & Co., another firm of carriers by water, was similarly condemned for a breach of the agreement.[2] It was now the duty of the Bridgewater Trustees to punish the offenders by turning them out of their warehouses, suspending their credit, and declining to tow their vessels down the Mersey estuary. Fearful, however, of destroying the carriers or of driving them on to the rails, they failed to carry out the sentences properly, seizing upon alleged irregularities in the trial of Patchett & McKay's case to postpone withdrawal of credit to that firm. Neither would they agree to a proposal of Henry Booth's that tonnage charges should be raised by the canals in order to impose restraint on the carriers in future.[3]

The situation rapidly got out of hand. The private carriers led in reductions; the Trustees' carrying department and the Mersey and Irwell Navigation Company followed, this being the only way to save the traffic which they carried in their own boats from being taken away from them by the carriers. By 8 March down goods were as low as 5s. per ton, and the contest extended from the Liverpool to Manchester to the Runcorn to Manchester freight charges.[4] Events took an even more serious turn when the Old Quay Company, whose manager Lingard had at first stood out for stringent measures against the defaulting carriers, suddenly changed its tune, and proposed to assist them by a full remission of tolls on the up trade whilst freight charges remained so low. Lingard had for some time harboured the design of handing over the entire carrying business on the Mersey and Irwell Navigation to

---

[1] McKay to F. Smith, 17 Jan. 1843; F. Smith to J. Loch, 30 Jan. 1843, L.E.P.

[2] F. Smith to J. Loch, 28 and 31 Jan. and 2 Feb. 1843; J. Veevers to F. Smith, 26 Jan. 1843, ibid.

[3] F. Smith to J. Loch, 2 Feb. 1843, and enclosures; F. Smith to J. Loch, 17 Feb. and 4 Mar. 1843, ibid.

[4] Mason to Marsden, 8 Mar. 1843, and J. Loch to F. Smith, 27 Feb. 1843, ibid.

private carriers, and was probably using the crisis as an opportunity to further his ambition. To retain the carriers on the Bridgewater Canal the Trustees were obliged with the greatest reluctance to follow suit.[1] The Liverpool and Manchester Railway Company held aloof from the struggle as far as it was able, hoping to see the independent carriers by water, whom it disliked far more than the canal companies, ruin themselves by internecine warfare. The railroad directors followed the example of the canal carriers in making reductions on the up trade, whilst keeping their charge for down goods steady at 10*s.* per ton.[2] Eventually they reaped the reward of their restraint by acting the part of mediator between the disputants. James Loch also contributed individually to the pacification by renewing his approaches to certain of the Old Quay directors. The new settlement which was agreed by Henry Booth, Lingard, and Fereday Smith on 1 May 1843 embodied important concessions to the railway point of view. It was, in fact, a compromise between the old type of rate-fixing agreement which had prevailed in the past, and an arrangement for dividing the traffic between the principal participants, such as the railroad directors were disposed to favour. All parties were to raise freight charges to the level of April 1842. For the future the navigation owners undertook to insist on the payment of full tolls and other charges by their respective carriers. The Railway Company, on the other hand, did not bind itself to any particular set of charges to the public; it simply undertook not to carry along its line a greater share of the trade than the average proportion which it had conveyed during the five preceding years, and to compensate the Canal authorities at the rate of 3*s.* 6*d.* per ton for any surplus of traffic above that ratio.[3]

The new arrangement was merely a truce. The participants scarcely understood what they were signing. Hardly was the ink dry upon the document embodying it before the Liverpool and Manchester Railway Company, finding that it had by no means its allotted share of the trade, embarked upon a series

---

[1] M. & I.N.C. Order Book, 1842–4, p. 6. Marsden to F. Smith, 22 Apr. 1843, and F. Smith to J. Loch, 25 Apr., 6 May, 1 and 27 June 1843, L.E.P.

[2] Marsden to F. Smith, 22 Apr. 1843, ibid.

[3] F. Smith to J. Loch, 3 May 1843, ibid.

of reductions of freight, lowering upon porter and ale from
10s. to 6s. per ton and upon butter from 10s. to 8s. 4d. per ton
in June 1843 and on cotton by 20 per cent in the following
August.[1] The directors were quite within their rights so to act,
for they had bound themselves merely to charge as high a
rate as was consistent with the object of maintaining their
correct proportion of the trade. This was not fully compre-
hended, however, by the carriers on the canals, at first not
even by the Bridgewater Trustees, for Fereday Smith took up
the question of the cotton reductions with Henry Booth on
behalf of the carriers on 19 August.[2] It was the Mersey and
Irwell Company, however, that reacted with the greatest vehemence. On 24 August the Old Quay Committee decided to
terminate the agreement of 1 May on account of the construction which the Railway Company placed upon it. Shortly
afterwards the Company and its carriers advertised a reduction of freight charges by 50 per cent on goods removed from
the warehouses within ten days of their arrival.[3] This was far
more than a mere retaliation against the Railway Company.
The plain fact was that under Lingard's brash leadership the
Old Quay Company was bent on competing desperately for the
last morsel of trade and at the lowest possible rates. It was
attacking not only the Liverpool and Manchester charges but
those which were in operation on the Runcorn and Manchester
trade in which the Railway Company was not involved. It
had thrown open the Runcorn trade to private carriers in
July 1843.[4] Lingard told Fereday Smith that the Company was
bankrupt, and therefore cared nothing for the maintenance of
rates, and James Loch concluded, probably with every justification, that he was deliberately making the concern a nuisance
in the hope of getting it bought up by a competitor.[5]

Loch and Fereday Smith tried every method known to them

[1] F. Smith to J. Loch, 1 June 1843, 17 and 19 Aug. 1843, and T. O. Lingard
to F. Smith, 27 June 1843, L.E.P.

[2] F. Smith to J. Loch, 19 Aug. 1843, ibid.

[3] M. & I.N.C. Order Book, 1842–4, pp. 55 et seq; J. Loch to G. W. Wood,
30 Aug. 1843, and F. Smith to J. Loch, 2 Sept. 1843, L.E.P.

[4] This meant charging a toll per mile and a rate for dockage, wharfage, and
towing between Liverpool and Runcorn similar to that made to the carriers
between Liverpool and Manchester (M. & I.N.C. Order Book, 1842–4, pp. 52–3).

[5] F. Smith to J. Loch, 28 Aug. 1843; J. Loch to F. Smith, 29 Aug. 1843,
L.E.P.

of bringing the Mersey Company to reason. By working upon sympathetic directors, notably G. W. Wood and E. J. Lloyd, they persuaded the Committee at its meeting on 13 September to agree to a restoration of the freight charges of 25 April 1842. Lingard, however, managed to frustrate the carrying out of this resolution. He was assisted by the sudden death, on 3 October, of G. W. Wood, Loch's greatest friend among the Old Quay directors.[1] All hope of raising freight charges now vanished, and to save their carriers from ruin the Duke's Trustees adopted the unpalatable course of remitting tonnages to their carriers with effect from 14 October. In authorizing this step, Loch expressed his regret that the present excellent state of trade should afford no remuneration to those engaged in it.[2]

The time had come to put an end to the rogue elephant course on which the Old Quay Company had launched itself, and with this end in view Loch determined upon acquiring the river navigation for the Trustees. The deal was forced upon him, for it ran contrary to his oft-asserted prejudices against extending the concern. Although the possibility of the Trustees' making such a purchase had been commented upon by an outsider as early as April 1843, it was not until the death of G. W. Wood had banished all prospect of conciliation that Loch decided to press the subject above all other matters. He acted in the full knowledge that, if the Bridgewater interest did not annex the Old Quay, one of its rivals might do so, for Lingard had offered the concern to the Liverpool and Manchester Railway Company in July.[3] The transaction was concluded on 21 December and the change of ownership took effect from 1 January 1844.[4] To circumvent legal restrictions upon the power of the Trustees to borrow money or to add to their commitments a large undertaking which formed no part

---

[1] T. O. Lingard to F. Smith, 13 Sept. J. Loch to G. W. Wood, 31 Aug. F. Smith to E. J. Lloyd, 16 Sept. 1843, and F. Smith to J. Loch 2 Nov. 1843, ibid. Wood, who was President of the Manchester Literary and Philosophical Society, died suddenly at the Society's rooms (W. E. A. Axon, *The Annals of Manchester*, p. 223).

[2] J. Loch to F. Smith, 14 Nov. 1843, L.E.P.

[3] F. Smith to J. Loch, 17 Apr. 1843 ; F. Smith to J. Loch, 12 July 1843 ; and J. Loch to F. Smith, 26 Oct. 1843, ibid.

[4] Axon, op. cit., p. 224. 'Duplicate Conveyance and Assignment of the Bridgewater Canal, the Runcorn and Weston Canal and Divers Lands, Hereditaments, etc., dated 27 June 1874' (M.S.C.C., Bridgewater Department).

of the inheritance from the third Duke of Bridgewater, Lord Francis Egerton made the purchase in the first instance. He paid out the existing shareholders in bonds carrying an interest payment of not more than 4 per cent per annum and redeemable by himself at intervals during the ensuing ten years. In 1845, however, the Trustees obtained an Estate Act authorizing them to take over the shares from the life tenant and to raise the money on mortgage from the Law Life Assurance Society. They then proceeded to redeem the bonds in instalments by drawing periodically upon the insurance company. Not until December 1853 had they paid out the Old Quay bondholders,[1] but the control was theirs from the moment of the purchase by Lord Francis. James Loch became Principal Agent of the Mersey and Irwell Navigation on 30 December 1843.[2] Henceforth all the important decisions relating to that concern were taken by him, assisted by Fereday Smith.

The Bridgewater people paid a heavy price for subduing a rival. The burden of debt which they shouldered was £550,800. Of this £402,000 was for obtaining the shares at £800 each,[3] an exorbitant sum to pay in view of the fact that eight months earlier Old Quay shares stood at £380.[4] The balance was bonded debt built up by the Navigation Company itself over a long period. Such a weight was not speedily shaken off. The Trustees still owed £327,000 to the Law Life Assurance Society in the early seventies, and in addition £93,100 of bonded debt.[5] In return for this commitment they had acquired a rather dubious asset. The river navigation was in a bad state of disrepair. No sooner had the deal been clinched than the Barton lock fell in, stopping the traffic almost completely for three months.[6] Moreover, the boats of two independent

---

[1] M. & I.N.C. Order Book, 1842–4, pp. 75–6, 79, 83–102; 'Duplicate Conveyance and Assignment', 1874, pp. 15, 16, 18, 23, 25, 26; *J.H.C.* lxxvii (1845), p. 1138.   [2] M. & I.N.C. Order Book, 1842–4, p. 77.

[3] 'Opposition of the Bridgewater Navigation Co. Ltd., and . . . the Mersey and Irwell Navigation, to the Manchester Ship Canal Bill in the House of Lords, 1885', Minutes of Evidence, qu. 11552 (M.S.C.C., Bridgewater Department, archive copy); 'Duplicate Conveyance and Assignment', 1874, pp. 15–16; M. & I.N.C. Order Book, 1842–4, pp. 75–6.

[4] F. Smith to J. Loch, 2 May 1843, L.E.P.

[5] 'Duplicate Conveyance and Assignment', 1874, p. 48.

[6] F. Smith to J. Loch, 29 Dec. 1843 and 21 Mar. 1844, L.E.P.

carrying concerns on the Old Quays, were not gauged, thus enabling the firms to under-declare their weights. It was to this cause that the Trustees mainly ascribed the great losses made by the waterway under its former management, and they hastened to correct the omission.[1] By these means, as well as by promoting economies in running costs, sometimes at the expense of future efficiency, they managed to wring a profit of £23,000 out of the navigation in 1849, though the return fell again afterwards.[2]

If in itself the Mersey and Irwell Navigation was hardly worth the price which was paid for it, possession of the concern conferred upon the Duke's Trustees certain immediate advantages. In the first place it enabled them to end the disastrous contest which had developed in the trade west of Manchester. The last act of the Old Quay Committee was to join with the Bridgewater Trustees and the Liverpool and Manchester Railway Company in restoring the rates of carriage to those of May 1842. It was an express condition of the purchase that they should so participate in order to camouflage the fact that the increased charges had arisen from the purchase of the Mersey and Irwell Navigation by Lord Francis Egerton.[3] A great public and political figure, Lord Francis had no wish to be pilloried as a scheming monopolist. The agreement of December 1843 was not a final settlement of the disputes between the carriers in the Liverpool and Manchester trade. It was an armistice rather than a peace treaty, and for some months afterwards the Duke's Trustees, the independent carriers, and the Railway Company had to devote a great deal of attention to hammering out their differences. Nevertheless, the chief impediment to negotiation had been removed by the disappearance of the Old Quay as an independent entity, and in July 1844 a more permanent agreement as to rates was made between the water carriers and the Liverpool and Manchester Railway. It was understood that this would be accompanied by an arrangement for the division of the traffic. The details of the latter were not as yet fixed, however, for there was

---

[1] Orders were issued to the carriers to have their boats gauged early in 1844 (J. Loch to F. Smith, 12 Apr. 1844 (two letters), ibid.).

[2] See below, Appendix A.

[3] H. Booth to F. Smith, 20 Dec. 1843, L.E.P.; M. & I.N.C. Order Book, 1842–4, pp. 75–6.

disagreement between the participants as to the shares which they were to be allocated. The railway directors were beginning to demand a higher proportion than would be justified on the basis of the average of earlier years, for they could now offer improved facilities owing to the construction of their new Manchester terminus at Hunts Bank.[1] Sixteen months earlier they had been content to accept a division of the traffic based on the averages of the past five years. The rise in their expectations is a measure of the extent to which railway power had increased in the years in which the waterways had been fighting each other with so much ferocity.

A second advantage which the Trustees reaped from the purchase of the Old River was a more realistic appraisal of their relationship to the independent carriers. In the past they had pampered and cossetted the carriers upon their own line, declining to face the unpleasant truth that owing to the thrusting competitiveness of the latter, this policy could not be squared with the maintenance of agreed rates of freight. When, however, they examined the records of the Mersey and Irwell Navigation Company, they discovered how effectively in the past the carriers had played off one canal against another in their quest of allowances and reductions of tonnage charges.[2] Their suspicions were increased when the carriers on the Old River seized the opportunity of the interregnum to annex the traffic formerly carried in the boats of the Mersey and Irwell Navigation Company, whilst those on the Bridgewater Canal responded to the removal of the threat from the Old Quay by embarking upon a fresh onslaught upon the rates.[3] A new and tougher line was discernible on the Trustees' part in January 1844, when Loch gave orders that the Old Quay Company's carrying trade should be recovered and that of the Bridgewater Trustees extended, with a view to obtaining a firmer hold on the private carriers.[4] By October the machinery of the carriers' association had been revised to assist disciplinary action against carriers who broke the rules. A paid

---

[1] F. Smith to J. Loch, 13 July 1844; G. Loch to F. Smith, 4 Aug. 1844, L.E.P.

[2] J. Loch to F. Smith, 28 Feb. 1844, ibid.

[3] J. Loch to F. Smith, 8 Jan. 1844; F. Smith to J. Loch, 26 Feb. 1844; H. Booth to F. Smith, 28 Feb. 1844, ibid.

[4] J. Loch to F. Smith, 8 Jan. and 21 Mar. 1844, ibid.

secretary was appointed to investigate all accusations.[1] It was still highly doubtful whether the usual weapon of discipline, withdrawal of credit, would prove at all effective, but the will to impose it was now present in the Trustees.[2]

Thirdly, the Trustees were able to profit from the successful take-over by availing themselves of the economies which came from operating upon a larger scale. To save duplication of effort the Old Quay repair yard at Manchester was closed down, and the work of refitting the boats which used the Mersey and Irwell Navigation was transferred to Worsley Yard. A single officer was placed in charge of the Bridgewater and Old Quay agencies at Runcorn and at Manchester, and reductions in the Old Quay establishment were projected. The merger was not complete, however, for Loch intended that there should be competition for trade between the river and the Duke's Canal. He insisted, therefore, on the retention of separate goods solicitors for the two concerns which he now controlled.[3]

The purchase of the Mersey and Irwell Navigation signalized an easing of the situation for the Duke of Bridgewater's Trustees. The sharp struggle with opposing waterways which had absorbed their attention during the previous seven years was drawing to a close, and they were emerging as the victors. Manifested first in the acquisition of the Old Quay, this victory was shortly to be displayed in the Trustees' dealings with their competitors in the long-distance trade through Preston Brook. The conflict with the Ellesmere and Chester Canal Company, which as we have seen drew to a climax during the latter half of 1843, terminated in the following June when an agreement was made between the two concerns, by which the Trustees leased from the Ellesmere Company the whole of its carrying trade across the River Mersey estuary (except that which was conducted to and from Chester) together with its docks, wharfs, cranes, warehouses, and stables at Ellesmere Port, its two steam tugs, and all its flats and

---

[1] F. Smith to J. Loch, 1 Oct. 1844, ibid.

[2] Veevers had their credit stopped by the Trustees in October 1844 (J. Loch to F. Smith, 5 Oct. 1844; see also F. Smith to J. Loch, 18 Dec. 1844, ibid.).

[3] J. Loch to F. Smith, 4, 13, and 20 Jan., 9 and 18 Apr. 1844; Rippon to F. Smith, 10 Apr. 1844; F. Smith to J. Loch, 16 Feb. and 22 Apr. 1844; G. Loch to F. Smith, 6 June 1844, ibid.

floats, except those which were retained for the conduct of the
Chester trade. The arrangement was to be terminable upon
two years' notice.[1] On the Bridgewater side the enthusiasm
for the arrangement came from Fereday Smith, the Deputy
Superintendent of the Trust, who was less cautious than Loch
of involving the Trustees in new combinations and interests.
He was influenced on his own admission by the trend towards
amalgamation which was already beginning to appear upon
the railways and with which he held it necessary for the canals
to keep pace.[2] He and the permanent staff of the Trust may
have harboured secretly the design of using the control of the
exit from the Ellesmere Canal to drive all the Midlands traffic
bound by canal for Liverpool on to the Preston Brook route,
but the official arrangement which was concluded was such
as to make this well nigh impossible. The Trustees contracted
to maintain the freight charge between Ellesmere Port and
Liverpool at 4*d.* per ton less than between Preston Brook and
Liverpool.[3] Nevertheless, even if the Bridgewater Canal seemed
unlikely to benefit, there was a reasonable prospect that the
Bridgewater Trustees, as carriers of goods on the Mersey
estuary, might win back through Ellesmere Port the trade
with the Midlands which they had lost through Preston Brook.
They also increased by the transaction their stock of steamboats available for drawing flats along the river mouth. In
1843 they had possessed only two—the *Alice*, an iron steamer
of 70 horse-power, and the *Blanche*, a similar vessel of 74
horse-power which was originally acquired mainly for working
the passenger trade. The purchase of the Mersey and Irwell
Navigation added four more—the *Hercules*, the *Tower*, the
Pilot, and the *Rival*—all wooden ships and mostly inferior in
horse-power to those already in the Trustees' possession.[4]
When from the Ellesmere Company they hired the *Earl
Powis* and the *Clive*,[5] the Trustees could not unfairly boast of
having their own steam fleet on the Mersey. Possession of it

[1] E. & C.C.C. General Committee Orders, 1827–46, pp. 268–72, 281–5.
[2] F. Smith to J. Loch, 2 Nov. 1843, L.E.P.
[3] E. & C.C.C. General Committee Orders, 1827–46, pp. 268–72, 281–5.
Minutes enclosed in F. Smith to G. Loch, 16 Dec. 1843, L.E.P.
[4] R. Rawlinson to F. Smith, 26 Apr. 1844, ibid.
[5] E. & C.C.C. General Committee Orders, 1827–46, pp. 268–72, 281–5;
F. Smith to G. Loch, 11 Jan. 1850, L.E.P.

would increase their bargaining power in the subsequent conflicts with the railways.

At approximately the same time as the Trustees reached
their agreement with the Ellesmere company, they also came
to terms with another old rival in the long-distance trade,
viz. the Anderton Carrying Company. From the middle of
1843 onwards, this company had been extending its ambitions
from the Midland trades to the traffic between Liverpool and
places to the east of Manchester. It had planned initially to
carry between Liverpool and Stockport and between Liverpool
and Ashton-under-Lyne, forwarding by the Liverpool and
Manchester Railway as far as Manchester and thence by its own
boats plying upon the Ashton Canal. This would have rendered
it competitive with the Duke's in yet another area. Twelve
months later, however, it announced its intention to carry
between Liverpool and Manchester along the Duke's with
effect from 1 July 1844.[1] This was only the first step in a
rapprochement which was to be carried further. In 1848 Lord
Ellesmere (formerly Lord Francis Egerton) purchased the
Anderton Company (which had by then run into financial
difficulties, and was anxious to be taken over) for the Trustees,
to prevent it from falling into the hands of either the London
and North Western or the North Staffordshire Railway Company. This deal, like the arrangement with the Ellesmere
Company four years earlier, was much more the idea of
Fereday Smith and the agents than that of James Loch.[2]
It brought to the Trustees extensive premises at Anderton,
including two steam-engines for hoisting and lowering between
the Weaver and the Grand Trunk Canal, sheds and warehouses at Liverpool, Manchester, Northwich, Macclesfield,
and Congleton and at various wharfs in the Potteries, and a
carting establishment at each of the main stations. It added a
further steamer, the *Thomas Royden* (145 h.p.), to the fleet
on the Mersey. An annual traffic of some 61,853 packs of

[1] Mitchell to F. Smith, 22 June 1843, and F. Smith to J. Loch, 28 June 1844,
ibid.

[2] F. Smith to G. Loch, 27 Oct. 1847, 2 Feb. and 11 Mar. 1848, ibid.
For the financial arrangements for the purchase see G. Loch to the Earl of
Ellesmere, 23 July 1848, B.T.P. (Mertoun), File 141, and G. to J. Loch, 18 Feb.
1848, ibid. File 140. The property was to be paid for partly in cash but mainly in
bonds secured against the personal estate of Lord Ellesmere and his eldest son,
Lord Brackley.

earthenware and 24,713 tons of clay between Liverpool and the Potteries passed also to the Trustees, restoring them to a dominant position in the pottery trade.[1] In the four years after the purchase, the up trade through Anderton leaked slowly away to Preston Brook. The Trustees, however, were chary of lending too much encouragement to this change from a fear of injuring the traffic of the River Weaver. For reasons which were political as well as economic, James Loch always displayed a certain deference towards the Weaver Trustees. He wished to avoid alienating the County of Chester.[2]

When, therefore, Lord Francis Egerton and his servant Loch surveyed the scene as it presented itself to them in the year 1844, they had grounds for congratulating themselves. They appeared to have weathered the storm which had pressed so severely upon them three years earlier and to have emerged into the sunshine. The Duke of Bridgewater's Canal had never been more prosperous than it was in the boom years of the middle forties. The Canal and the carrying department together showed a profit of £76,410 in 1844,[3] a figure but rarely attained even in the golden age before the building of the Liverpool and Manchester Railway. Some trades had been lost either to railways or to cheaper or more efficient canal routes, but the total volume of traffic carried on the Canal was greater than ever before. From 716,000 tons in 1830 it had risen to 1,280,000 tons in 1844.[4] The greatest increase was in the traffic carried on toll, and this was also overwhelmingly the largest source of profit. In 1844 only £3,157 of the £76,410 yield from the Canal came from the carrying department.[5] It was the independent carriers who had been winning traffic for the Canal, and the results obtained seemed fully to vindicate Loch's policy in encouraging them.

All, however, was not well, for the triumph over opposing canals was partly offset by a revival of the threat from the rails. As yet the danger was not overpowering, but the situation contained disquieting features which boded ill for the

[1] F. Smith to G. Loch, 11 Mar. 1848. Statement enclosed in F. Smith to G. Loch, 12 Apr. 1848; Fawcett & Co. to Pendlebury, 30 Oct. 1848, L.E.P.

[2] J. Loch to F. Smith, 2 July 1849; F. Smith to G. Loch, 12 Aug. 1852, ibid.

[3] See below, Appendix A.

[4] See below, Appendix B.

[5] Bridgewater Trust General Accounts, 1844–50.

future, and the Trustees' self-confidence suffered a severe
shock. On the one hand there was evidence of increased
hostility from existing railroads. In March 1844 the Grand
Junction Railway, under the active and vigorous leadership
of its general manager, Captain Mark Huish, began to threaten
the Bridgewater Trust and other canal proprietors who controlled the routes between Lancashire and the Midlands that
if they did not raise their tonnage charge on light goods, such
as Manchester packs going south to London, he would reduce
freights on heavy goods such as crates from the Potteries to
Liverpool.[1] The incident is evidence of the power of the canals
to harry the railways even in a comparatively long-distance
traffic in manufactured goods, but it also marked the end of
the period of good feeling between the Grand Junction
directors and the Trustees. A further cause of disagreement
arose in July when the Trustees, now virtually the owners of
the Mersey and Irwell Navigation, resisted an attempt by the
Railway Company to throw a railway bridge across the
Mersey at Marsh Gate in its renewed quest of a shorter access
to Liverpool.[2] It was even doubtful whether the alliance with
the Liverpool and Manchester Company would endure, for the
amalgamation movement was already in train, and James
Loch's son George was fighting a battle on the board to prevent
the company's being absorbed by the Manchester and Leeds.[3]

Even more alarming, however, than these developments
among existing railways were certain plans for the construction of new lines in the Manchester area. In 1844 England was
moving slowly towards the second great speculative mania
connected with the building of railroads. At the beginning of
the year the Sheffield, Ashton, and Manchester and the
Manchester and Birmingham Railway Companies, anxious to
enjoy the privilege, already won by the Manchester and Leeds,
of a continuous communication through Manchester to the
Liverpool and Manchester line, broached to the Bridgewater
Trustees a plan for constructing a link. This would run round
the south side of Manchester from their joint station at Store
Street, Piccadilly, to the Liverpool Road terminus of the

[1] F. Smith to J. Loch, 4 Mar. 1844, L.E.P.
[2] F. Smith to J. Loch, 20 July 1844, ibid.
[3] J. Loch to Lord F. Egerton, 24 Aug. 1844, E.B.C.

Liverpool and Manchester Railway, passing through the Trustees' land at Castlefield on the way. Several months later, in July 1844, a scheme for joining Altrincham to the Manchester and Birmingham line at Levenshulme via Didsbury and Burnage was brought before the public by two Manchester promoters, Wheeler and Lawton, acting in concert with certain of the directors of the M. & B. This plan had been influenced, it would appear, by the success of the swift boat service on the Bridgewater Canal between Altrincham and Manchester. The Trustees disliked both projects, and visited the second of them with the severest opposition, whipping up the local landowners such as Sir Thomas de Trafford, Egerton of Tatton, and Tatton of Wythenshawe against it and discouraging subscription by slashing the swift boat fares. Their hostility stemmed partly from a desire to prevent the Liverpool and Manchester Railway from getting access to Bank Top (Piccadilly), a valuable commercial site, where one of the Trustees' coal wharves and some of their carriers' warehouses were located, and partly from the simple motive of protecting the through trade by canal from the competition of yet another continuous line of railway communication through Manchester. Mainly, however, it arose from the fear that these lines, once constructed, would be extended westwards towards Runcorn, Chester, and Liverpool, making fresh inroads into the traffic of the Canal to and from those regions.[1] Eventually, however, the Trustees were driven to a compromise. On 24 August James Loch recommended to Lord Francis Egerton an arrangement which his son George had negotiated for him with the S.A. & M. and M. & B. Railway Companies. The two Manchester projects were to be fused into the Manchester, South Junction, and Altrincham Railway, the Altrincham line becoming a branch of the southern connecting line, leaving it at Castlefield Junction near Knott Mill. Control of the enterprise was to be shared equally between the S.A. & M. and M. & B. railroad companies and Lord Francis Egerton. Lord Francis was to be allotted shares in the company to the extent of £50,000 and was to have the right to nominate a third of the directors.

---

[1] F. Smith to J. Loch, 22 Jan., 3 Feb., 16, 20, and 23 July and 12 Aug. 1844; Slater to F. Smith, 23 July 1844; J. Loch to F. Smith, 29 May 1844, L.E.P. G. to J. Loch (and enclosed heads of agreement), 13 Aug. 1844, E.B.C.

A further safeguard to the Trustees was to be found in the provision that the unanimous consent of the board should be required for any extension of the line west of Altrincham. The need for unanimity was only to be waived if the Manchester and Leeds Company gained control of the Liverpool and Manchester line, in which case a simple majority was to suffice. It was also laid down that the Trustees should either remove their swift packets between Altrincham and Manchester or forfeit the guaranteed interest on the capital subscribed by Lord Francis Egerton. George Loch had recommended the proposals to his father as the best possible compromise for the Trustees' interests, pointing out that they could not hope to frustrate the making of a continuous communication by rail through Manchester, and that unless the Altrincham branch was included in the scheme, a similar line would be constructed later by the S.A. & M. and M. & B. Companies outside the Trustees' control. The public and the government figured largely in his calculations, for he added: 'The new element of the Board of Trade is a very important one, but I don't think it would assist the Liverpool and Manchester and the Bridgewater Trustees in extinguishing a line to Altrincham unless they had something better to propose as a substitute.'[1]

The arrangement was adopted. It was a further application of the Loch family's ideal of compromise and conciliation which had been tried on several occasions previously. But it was not a success. The provision as to the necessity for a unanimous concurrence of the directors gave no effective guarantee against a westward extension of the line. Even before the end of 1844, the committee of the new line was discussing such a scheme, assuming that as the Liverpool and Manchester railroad was almost amalgamated with the Grand Junction, a simple majority would serve to authorize it.[2] In 1847, some two years before the South Junction line was completed, Lord Francis Egerton, now first Earl of Ellesmere, sold out his holdings to the London and North Western Railway, despairing of their being any further use to him.[3]

---

[1] G. to J. Loch, 7, 12, 13, 20 Aug. 1844; J. Loch to Lord F. Egerton, 24 Aug. 1844, E.B.C.

[2] J. Loch to F. Smith, 12 and 13 Nov. 1844, L.E.P.

[3] F. Smith to G. Loch, 24 May and 23 Oct. 1847, ibid.

It must have been apparent to James Loch right from the outset that the Trustees' cause had suffered a setback. On the very day that he advised Lord Francis Egerton to agree to invest in the South Junction Railway, he also suggested that the life tenant might consider selling his two navigations to a joint stock company which would be formed for the purpose, and which might proceed to convert the Bridgewater Canal into a railway and the Old River into a ship canal. He mentioned the cheap money conditions of the time as being conducive to the flotation of such an undertaking.[1] The idea seems to have been put into his head by a paragraph inserted in the *Manchester Guardian* early in April intimating that the Duke's Canal would be turned into a railway. It is not clear who was responsible for this article. Loch suspected the salt manufacturers—'these salt fellows' as he called them—and it was hinted that the scheme would be in opposition to the Grand Junction Railway.[2] As the Trustees' difficulties in the railway world deepened, Loch became increasingly attracted to the notion of a sale. His son George discussed it with Fereday Smith, who advised a figure of not less than £2,000,000.[3] It was not that Loch despaired of the future of the Canal. He still held to the view that whilst 'long canals, if not too circuitous, having no local trade, will cease or become railways', short ones 'such as the Bridgewater, with a very large local trade will continue to flourish'.[4] He did anticipate, however, that though trade might increase, income would probably fall, and was influenced in his recommendation by the desire to secure to Lord Francis 'a permanent though probably a somewhat diminished income'.[5]

The life tenant rejected his agent's suggestion, and the navigations remained in the Trustees' hands for a further twenty-eight years. Nevertheless, a turning-point in their history had been reached, for the thought of selling them was from that time forward seldom absent for long from the minds of the men to whom their custody was entrusted. Though

[1] J. Loch to Lord F. Egerton, 24 Aug. 1844, E.B.C.
[2] F. Smith to J. Loch, 13 Apr., and J. Loch to F. Smith, 14 Apr. 1844, L.E.P.
[3] G. to J. Loch, 20 Aug. 1844, E.B.C.
[4] J. Loch to Lord F. Egerton, 10 June 1844, ibid.
[5] J. Loch to Lord F. Egerton, 19 Oct. 1845, ibid.

nothing like a complete collapse of the canal trade was in fact experienced, there was a fixed conviction at the highest levels of control that the best years were over, and that the wisest course was to dispose of the property whilst it was still saleable at the earliest convenient opportunity.

CHAPTER IX

The Bridgewater Trustees and the Railway Mania (1845–1847)

THERE was no respite for the Duke of Bridgewater's Trustees. Scarcely had they emerged from the successful struggle with other canals than they were called upon to protect their interests against a torrent of railway schemes. During the years 1845–7, which opened with the notorious speculative mania, when £100,000 per week was expended on advertisements, meetings, and railroad matters generally,[1] Parliament was inundated with Bills which in their totality transformed the English railway system and greatly increased its power to outdo the canals. For the latter, therefore, this was a time of trial. Fereday Smith sensed the approaching crisis in July 1844. He wrote to Loch:

> My sincere conviction is, from the turn events are taking, money may be raised during the next two or three years very readily, and parties may be found to undertake almost any new railway project, however absurd, but that, if the Bridgewater Canal can overcome competition for the next four years or thereabouts, it may do so for many years afterwards. . . .[2]

The object of this chapter is to outline the character of the developments in the railway world which affected the interests of the Bridgewater Canal, to show how the Trustees confronted the thrust against them and also how they fared economically during the period of the struggle.

The first outstanding change to be implemented by the railway Bills of the middle forties was a vast extension of the railway network. More new track was authorized during 1845 than all the length of rail in operation at the end of the preceding

---

[1] E. F. Carter, *An Historical Geography of the Railways of the British Isles*, p. 91.   [2] F. Smith to J. Loch, 16 July 1844, L.E.P.

year, and the additions sanctioned in 1846 were even more extensive than those of 1845—4,500 miles as against 2,800.[1] Many additional lines were planned in the catchment area of the Duke's Canal. Of these none raised a greater alarm than those which threatened to introduce fresh competition into the Liverpool and Manchester trade, a treasured preserve, which in the Trustees' eyes could only be safely shared with the Liverpool and Manchester Railway. The Liverpool, Warrington, Manchester, and Stockport Direct Railway, popularly known as the 'Spinners Line' because it was supported by the cotton manufacturers of Lancashire, was expressly designed to break into the traffic. It was brought before Parliament by petition on 6 February 1845, but to the Trustees' intense relief was withdrawn by its promoters after a stormy reception to which the Bridgewater Trust, the Marquess of Salisbury, and the Earl of Derby all contributed.[2] The Liverpool and Bury line, however, was not to be disposed of. Authorized in July 1845, it provided by virtue of its connections with the Manchester, Bolton, and Bury and the Manchester and Leeds systems an alternative route, not only to Manchester but also to the West Riding. It soon became part of the Lancashire and Yorkshire Railway, and was all the more dangerous in that it was linked with promoting groups traditionally hostile to the Trustees and the Leveson-Gower interest. The elements of a third line of railway between Liverpool and Manchester were supplied by the efforts of the St. Helens Canal and Railway Company to extend westwards and eastwards. In 1846 the company obtained powers to build from Widnes to Garston, a place on the Mersey estuary only four miles from Liverpool. Twelve months later it was authorized to join Widnes and Warrington by a line running along the course of the Sankey Canal. Even the attenuated gap between Warrington and Manchester seemed likely to be closed by the Birkenhead, Lancashire, and Cheshire Junction Railway, which as originally sanctioned in

---

[1] Hamilton Ellis, *British Railway History, 1830–76*, pp. 154–5, 163.

[2] *J.H.C.* ci, Pt. 1, (1846), pp. 75, 183, 229, 530. There may have been a political factor in the struggle, for Fereday Smith once alluded to the project as 'the [Anti-Corn Law] League or Spinners Line' (F. Smith to G. Loch, 23 Jan. 1846, L.E.P.). To break the combined rail and water 'monopoly' between Liverpool and Manchester would be a task congenial to the followers of Cobden and Bright.

June 1846 was designed to run from Hooton on the Chester and Birkenhead line through Warrington and Altrincham to Stockport.

Proposed new lines between Liverpool and Manchester did not exhaust the worries of the Duke's Trustees. In the flood of promotions which came before the public, hardly any of their remaining interests escaped attack. The Chester trade, one of their most highly valued prizes, was challenged by the Birkenhead, Lancashire, and Cheshire Junction and the abortive Chester and Manchester Direct line which was brought to the notice of the House of Commons in March 1846. Meanwhile the North Staffordshire Railway, formed in 1845 by the amalgamation of three as yet unbuilt lines in the northern half of the county of Stafford, pointed a dagger at the Trustees' traffic in pottery materials. Eventually limited to a localized network in Staffordshire and the adjacent portions of Cheshire and Derbyshire, the company at first intended to build a line northwards from Harecastle to Liverpool.[1] Had it done so it would have possessed a continuous and direct communication by rail between Stoke-on-Trent and Merseyside.

The years which witnessed the launching of so many new projects were also years of consolidation in the railway world. In a few rapid shifts the scene confronting the Duke's Canal took on an appearance much more like that of the early twentieth century, with a few giant companies operating upon a regional or supra-regional basis in the place of the numerous tiny, localized concerns. The Midland Railway was the first of its kind. It appeared in 1844, and was followed two years later by the London and North Western, an amalgam of the London and Birmingham, the Manchester and Birmingham, and the Grand Junction, which had itself swallowed the Liverpool and Manchester line together with three other railways of Lancashire in August 1845. The London and North Western Bill received the royal assent on 16 July 1846. In the same year occurred the amalgamation of the Manchester and Leeds, Manchester, Bolton, and Bury, and Liverpool and Bury lines into a single company which took the name of the Lancashire and Yorkshire Railway in 1847, and the founding of the Manchester, Sheffield, and Lincolnshire Railway by the fusion

---

[1] F. Smith to G. Loch, 18 Sept. 1845, L.E.P.

of the Sheffield, Ashton, and Manchester with three other companies. The Duke's was to find in these great concerns competitors of a more formidable kind than it had hitherto encountered. They were better equipped to promote a long-distance traffic by rail, and by virtue of their larger resources and more varied interests they could sustain a contest of rates with greater ease. They were also less amenable to control. The disappearance of the little Liverpool and Manchester Railway Company robbed the Trustees of their most powerful means of exerting an influence in railroad quarters. Although the Duke of Sutherland had some power of nomination to the London and North Western Railway Board—he appointed the Marquess of Stafford a director on 11 March 1854—his nominees must presumably have carried less weight there than in the smaller and less heavily capitalized Liverpool and Manchester Company.[1]

A third category of railway Bill which threatened the interests of the canals consisted of those which transferred stretches of waterway to railway ownership. It was at this stage more than at any other that railway companies came into the control of a number of vital links in the canal system. Almost two-thirds, in fact, of the waterways which were acquired by railroads down to the year 1872 changed hands between 1845 and 1847.[2] Several navigations with which the Duke's exchanged a trade were either absorbed or threatened at that time. The Rochdale Canal and the Shropshire Union (a compound of the Ellesmere and Chester and Birmingham and Liverpool Junction Canals effected in 1845) were for the time being reprieved, though Bills to transfer them to the Manchester and Leeds and London and North Western Railway Companies respectively came before Parliament in 1847.[3]

---

[1] L. & N.W.R. Board Minutes, no. 3, Minute 2288. A Mr. Loch, presumably George Loch or his father, attended meetings of the L. & N.W.R. Board frequently down to 14 July 1849, but only very occasionally afterwards. He attended, it may be assumed, as the Duke of Sutherland's nominee, and after a while decided that nothing useful could be achieved by his continued presence.

[2] E. Cleveland Stevens, *English Railways, their Development and their Relation to the State*, p. 91.

[3] *J.H.C.* cii (1847), 622, 761, 785. The Shropshire Union–L. & N.W.R. Bill received the royal assent, but the House of Lords inserted an amendment which placed difficulties in the way of completing the transaction, and the lease was not signed until 1857 (C. Hadfield, *The Canals of the West Midlands*, p. 234).

Moreover, the Shropshire Union Company was itself partly a railway company, being authorized to construct three lines in the Midlands and Wales and to turn part of the canal into a railway. Other canals, however, were actually transferred— the Trent and Mersey to the North Staffordshire Railway Company by an Act of 1846 which implemented an arrangement made with the canal company on 12 July 1845,[1] the Huddersfield to the London and North Western under the terms of an Act of 1847, the Manchester, Bolton, and Bury to the Lancashire and Yorkshire grouping in 1846, the Peak Forest and the Macclesfield to the Manchester, Sheffield, and Lincolnshire Railway by legislation of the year 1846, and the Ashton Canal to the same company by an Act which was eventually passed in 1848 after attempts to carry it in the two preceding sessions had been defeated. By 1849 the Bridgewater navigations were hemmed in on almost every side by railway-controlled canals. The Rochdale remained a notable exception. Some safeguard for the through trade by water was offered, it is true, by the 'impartiality' clauses (designed to prevent the companies from discriminating against their canal traffic for the benefit of their railway trade) which had been introduced into some but not all the amalgamation Bills, but it was not clear that these were proof against evasion.[2] The future must have seemed rather uncertain.

In 1845, however, the situation was still fluid. The Bills introducing these momentous changes were only beginning to come before Parliament, and it was open to all who had the necessary means to endeavour to resist them. The Bridgewater Trustees were aware of the opportunity and bestowed much attention on watching, and in some cases fighting, adverse schemes.

Their opposition was not lacking in intelligence or resourcefulness. It relied in the first instance on diplomacy. In September 1844 railways were threatening to break into another cherished preserve of the canals—the port of Runcorn and the adjacent agricultural districts hitherto dependent upon the Bridgewater navigations for their communications

---

[1] 'Manifold', *The North Staffordshire Railway*, pp. 20–1, 26.

[2] Particulars of the parliamentary history of these and other Bills mentioned in this chapter are taken from the *J.H.C.* unless otherwise stated. See G. Loch to E. Ryan, 19 May and 24 Sept. 1849, on the working of 'impartiality' clauses, B.T.P. (Mertoun), File 144.

eastwards with Manchester and the smaller cotton towns round about it. Two new lines were proposed. One, a forerunner of the later Birkenhead, Lancashire, and Cheshire Junction Railway, was to link Birkenhead with Manchester by way of Runcorn, tunnelling under the Duke's Canal at that place; the other was a scheme of the Grand Junction Railway Company to improve its access to Liverpool by throwing a branch over the River Mersey at Runcorn.[1] Fearing a concerted invasion of Runcorn by the Grand Junction and the promoters of the Birkenhead project, the Trustees planned to divide their opponents and to offer a sop to the public. Early in October George Loch hoped to arrange that the Grand Junction should agree to modify its plans so as to cross the River higher up, opposite Cuerdley Marsh, and should then join Lord Francis Egerton and the Liverpool and Manchester Railway Company in opposing the Birkenhead. To satisfy the demand for the latter, Newall's rival scheme embodying a line from Chester to Preston Brook was to be supported, Lord Francis taking shares in it.[2] The plan miscarried. At a meeting in Liverpool on 9 November the G.J. and L. & M. Companies agreed to a crossing further upstream, but turned down a proposition from Newall. This gave Loch, who was already cooling towards the latter's project on account of protests from one of the sub-agents that it would damage the market goods trade by canal, the opportunity to withdraw Lord Francis's support from it. The Trustees' bargaining position was weakened by suspicions as to their duplicity. Whilst they were ostensibly working against the Birkenhead scheme, George Loch was toying with the idea, not wholly approved by his father, that Lord Francis should actively participate in another scheme for building railways westwards across the Cheshire plain, the proposed extension of the Manchester and Altrincham line to Preston Brook or Warrington.[3] What the Trust suffered from was not a dearth of ideas of how to come to terms with the railways, but a surfeit of them.

[1] G. Loch to Lord F. Egerton, 27 Sept. 1844, E.B.C.

[2] G. Loch to Lord F. Egerton, 2 and 8 Oct. 1844; J. Loch to Lord F. Egerton, 5 Nov. 1844, ibid.

[3] J. Loch to Lord F. Egerton, 5 and 10 Nov. 1844; J. to G. Loch, 20 Nov. 1844; ibid.

Moreover, the approaching consolidation with the Liverpool and Manchester did not immediately kill the Grand Junction Company's desire for a shorter ingress to Liverpool than was furnished by the use of the former's track between Earlestown and Liverpool. The proposal to cross at Runcorn was revived in January 1845.[1] By then, however, the Trustees were ready for it. Two months earlier they had themselves surveyed for a line of railway from Runcorn to Preston Brook, partly to prevent the Birkenhead people from occupying the ground, partly to enable better terms to be struck with the G.J.R. should that company again move in the matter.[2] On 3 March the preliminaries of a very advantageous agreement with the latter were signed. In return for permission to cross the Mersey at Runcorn and for the free cession of land, the Grand Junction Company contracted to assume from Lord Francis Egerton the responsibility for effecting the line from Runcorn to Preston Brook. They were to refund him all expenses of the undertaking, to pay him a toll on all goods carried by rail from Runcorn to Preston Brook *en route* for places south or east, and to vest in him the ownership of the branch which was to connect the new line with Runcorn docks, thus enabling him to ensure that too much traffic passing through the docks was not diverted from the Canal. The Railway Company also agreed to construct its bridge over the river at such a height as would not interfere with the passage of masted vessels, and to shoulder almost the whole of the expense of executing a cut through Runcorn Island, a proceeding which was designed to improve the navigation in the upper part of the river.[3] Some such improvement was urgently needed, for in 1840 Bateman, the engineer, had compiled a report suggesting the bringing of a larger volume of the tide through the Gut between Runcorn Island and the mainland 'for the purpose of deepening and improving the navigation in the upper part of the river'.[4]

Assuming that the railway must come to Runcorn, these were perhaps the best terms on which its approach could be

[1] J. Loch to Lord F. Egerton, 10 Jan. 1845, E.B.C.

[2] J. Loch to Lord F. Egerton, 9 Nov. 1844; G. Loch to Lord F. Egerton, 27 Jan. 1845, ibid.

[3] J. Loch to Lord F. Egerton, 4 Mar. 1845, ibid.

[4] J. Loch to Captain Beaufort, R.N., 9 Jan. 1845, ibid.

permitted. Whilst providing some protection for the canal trade, they promised to benefit the Trustees both by fostering the general growth of the commerce of Runcorn and by promoting the passenger traffic which the Trustees conducted on the Mersey estuary between Runcorn and Liverpool. Their hope was that the Grand Junction Railway, which was planning to extend into the Staffordshire Potteries, would feed them with a continued supply of earthenware at Runcorn, thus increasing the quantity of backloading available to vessels sailing to the port; moreover, that it would bring up passengers from Birmingham and the Potteries, who would break their journey to Liverpool to inspect their properties upon the wharves at Runcorn and travel to their ultimate destination in the Trustees' steamers.[1] Accordingly, in March 1845 Lord Francis Egerton moved in the House of Commons for power to construct the railway. His Bill was overthrown, however, in the Lords in the following July by the opposition of Sir Richard Brooke, a powerful Cheshire landowner, and of the Trent and Mersey Canal Company.[2] Fifteen years elapsed before an almost identical opportunity occurred again; then, however, the plans were carried into effect.

It is a curious paradox that in their desire to forestall competition, the Duke's Trustees also had recourse to encouraging that process of consolidation in the railway world which was to raise up in due course far more powerful rivals to the canals than had ever before existed. James Loch claimed that it was his son George who had first induced John Moss of the Grand Junction to think seriously of the amalgamation with the Liverpool and Manchester which was soon afterwards realized. George's immediate object was merely to prevent another merger which was then impending and which constituted a more serious threat to the Trustees' interests—that of the Liverpool and Manchester with the traditionally hostile Manchester and Leeds.[3] He afterwards referred, however, writing to Lord Francis, to 'protection' for canals 'against

---

[1] F. Smith to J. Loch, 18 Apr. (and enclosed answers to questions respecting Runcorn and Preston Brook Railway) 1845; G. Loch to F. Smith, 8 May 1845, L.E.P.

[2] *J.H.C.* c (1845), 143; *J.H.L.* lxxvii (1845), 889–90.

[3] J. Loch to Lord F. Egerton, 24 Aug. 1844, E.B.C.

idle rival schemes'—he was thinking presumably of railway schemes—that 'was hoped might follow from the united strength and interests of the amalgamated railways'.[1] Similarly, the elder Loch, thinking thereby to put an end to the proliferation of railway schemes in Cheshire resulting from the endeavours of the Manchester and Birmingham to gain an independent access to Merseyside,[2] worked energetically to procure the inclusion of that company in the amalgamation. He approached Charles Lawrence, the Chairman of the Liverpool and Manchester, with that end in view in November 1844.

I stated shortly to you yesterday [he informed his son], that Mr. Lawrence had come here and spent the whole forenoon with me, my impression being that he had come to speak to me on the subject of my letter of an amalgamation with the Manchester and Birmingham. I began with that subject. I, however, found that I could make but little way with him, and we then talked of a variety of other matters.[3]

Perhaps the policy of encouraging amalgamations was more James Loch's than George's. Certainly George was swifter than his father to perceive that dangers as well as benefits would accrue to the canals from the creation of mammoth railway companies. He observed to Lord Francis that the same extension of power and resources and the same identity of purpose which were relied on for the repression of rival railways might at the same time make them more formidable competitors in case of a quarrel between them and the canals. Using a hint which he had privately received that governmental opinion was adverse to consolidation, he swung the Trust in favour of reliance instead upon Board of Trade protection against new and unwanted projects. On 28 November 1844 he took advantage of a private interview, the ostensible object of which was to present notice of the proposed Runcorn to Preston Brook line, to harangue Lord Dalhousie, the head of a newly created department of the Board which was appointed to sift railway Bills, for twenty minutes on the lack of necessity for the Birkenhead railroad project. He stated that the port of Birkenhead was 'altogether a great bubble'

[1] G. Loch to Lord F. Egerton, 28 Nov. 1844, E.B.C.
[2] J. Loch to Lord F. Egerton, 14 Nov. 1844, ibid.
[3] J. Loch to G. Loch, 20 Nov. 1844, ibid.

and sought a postponement of the railway Bill until it had proved its capacity to acquire trade. Lord Dalhousie, however, made polite but non-committal noises,[1] and when the Board of Trade produced its recommendations in February 1845, these were not to the Trustees' liking. The report was in favour of 'the Salop, Shrewsbury and Chester lines' and of the long dreaded 'North Line', proposed by the Manchester and Leeds Company from Bolton through Wigan to Liverpool. At the same time it rejected all the schemes of the Grand Junction Railway, a company with which the Trustees' relations were relatively good.[2]

The Trust was, therefore, thrown back on what it could do to protect its own interests in Parliament. The battle which was on an unprecedented scale required much careful planning in advance. At the beginning of each of the parliamentary sessions, 1846 and 1847, Fereday Smith was required to submit to George Loch, who was by this time acting for his father in most matters relating to the Canal, a list of impending schemes which affected the interests of the Bridgewater properties and needed to be watched and possibly petitioned against. The 1847 list mentioned twenty-four private Bills, some of them being railway projects, and others proposals for waterworks, gasworks, docks, and markets.[3] It was James Loch's original intention that the strategy of opposition should be co-ordinated by the appointment of a general parliamentary agent instead of being left to the several solicitors, town and country, and to separate agents appointed by them, as had been the case in the past. In January 1846 he authorized his son George to offer the post to his other son William, who was also to be asked to undertake a similar responsibility on behalf of the Duke of Sutherland.[4] The plan appears to have misfired, for Fereday Smith was required to desert his Manchester office for London in order that he might exert just such a co-ordinating function over the Trustees' proceedings in Parliament. In May 1846 he was told to see James Loch every morning and tell him what he proposed doing as to conduct

[1] G. Loch to Lord F. Egerton, 28 Nov. 1844, ibid.
[2] J. Loch to Lord F. Egerton, 13 Feb. 1845, ibid.
[3] J. Loch to G. Loch, 11 Jan. 1846; J. Loch to F. Smith, 11 Jan. 1846; F. Smith to G. Loch, 4 Feb. 1847, L.E.P.
[4] J. Loch to G. Loch, 11 Jan. 1846, ibid.

and clauses.[1] This wasteful use of a general manager was to some extent checked, however, in the following month when an agent named Barratt, of the firm of Wagstaff & Barratt of Warrington, was commissioned to see everything through the House of Lords in conjunction with William Loch. In February 1848 this person accepted the general charge of the Trustees' parliamentary business for the session. He may well have had it in the preceding session, too, for his name was mentioned in connection with the negotiations concerning the Liverpool Corporation Waterworks Bill in May 1847.[2]

Despite careful provision the Trustees entered the parliamentary battle with one hand tied behind their backs. At the beginning of 1846 Fereday Smith had of his own accord worked out an ingenious routine for thwarting railway Bills which were injurious to the Trustees' interests. He had set surveyors to work ferreting out inaccuracies in the plans, and proposed to use their findings as a basis for overthrowing the projects on a technicality before the Standing Orders Committee. His idea was that the proposals should have to pass a double test. Those which slipped through the net on Standing Orders would be vigorously opposed at the committee stage in the House of Commons.[3] George Loch intervened, however, to veto the procedure. He expressed reluctance to sanction an opposition on Standing Orders. The only exception to this rule was made in the case of the Liverpool, Warrington, Manchester, and Stockport Direct Railway. After a special plea had been entered by Fereday Smith, the Trustees, taking their stand as landowners on the proposed route, petitioned against it on 20 February 1846, complaining that it did not comply with Standing Orders. Smith's surveyors had unearthed many important errors as to gradients in the plans. Their industry probably contributed much to the defeat of the measure, which never got beyond the Standing Orders Committee.[4] In other cases, however, George Loch's preferences, which were also those of his father, furnished the basis for action. Where the Trustees petitioned, either in

---

[1] J. Loch to F. Smith, 11 May 1846, L.E.P.

[2] F. Smith to G. Loch, 18 June 1846, and 22 Feb. 1848 ; G. Loch to F. Smith, 1 May 1847, ibid.

[3] F. Smith to G. Loch, 21 Jan. 1846, ibid.

[4] F. Smith to G. Loch, 23 Jan. 1846, ibid ; see above, p. 177, n. 2.

James Loch's name or in that of the Mersey and Irwell Navigation Company or in that of Lord Francis Egerton, they did so when the Bill was in committee, assigning to themselves the more difficult and hazardous task of arguing a case on its merits.

George Loch's objections to an opposition on Standing Orders rested upon a twofold basis. Firstly, the expense was very great: 1846 was a year of financial stringency for the Trustees, partly, no doubt, because the burden of taking over the Mersey and Irwell Navigation from Lord Francis Egerton was beginning to fall upon their shoulders. Secondly, there was the need to preserve Lord Francis Egerton's reputation from any stain of pettiness or chicanery.[1] The moral argument did not apply only to the position of Lord Francis as a public figure. In James Loch's view the good name of the Trust was a business asset not to be lightly thrown away. When instructing Fereday Smith to see him every morning in May 1846 about the strategy to be pursued with railway Bills, he wrote somewhat reprovingly: 'And pray don't suggest anything that cannot be justified upon the broadest principles of justice and expediency. It weakens our influence.'[2]

This desire to stand well with the public affected not only the Trustees' procedure in the narrow technical sense but also the extent to which they were prepared to resist unwelcome proposals. Their opposition had to be discriminating. Much of it was of a formal character designed to procure the insertion of protective clauses into a Bill rather than the complete overthrow of the measure. The petition which they presented against the Manchester and Leeds and Liverpool and Bury Railway Bill in 1846 was of this kind. So also were those against the Manchester and Leeds Railway and Rochdale Canal, the L. & N.W.R. and Huddersfield Canal, and the M.S. & L.R. and Ashton Canal consolidations in the following sessions.[3] The clauses which the Trustees wished to obtain were prepared in advance and were sometimes not unreasonable.

[1] G. Loch to F. Smith, 22 Jan. 1846, ibid. L.E.P.

[2] J. Loch to F. Smith, 11 May 1846, ibid.

[3] Writing to George Loch on 4 February 1847, Fereday Smith mentioned that Mr. Barratt had promised to furnish clauses for the last three of these Bills. In a letter of 8 June 1846 he had sent him a copy of the clause which they intended to insert in the Liverpool and Bury Amalgamation Bill. Ibid.

It was desired to amend the Manchester and Leeds and Liverpool and Bury Bill only to the extent of preventing the united company from diverting traffic from the Bridgewater navigations by making discriminating charges on different sections of its own line.[1] The clauses to be inserted in the Rochdale Canal Bill were aimed at maintaining the free navigation of the Canal, at ensuring the provision of a constant and regular supply of water, and at fixing a differential of 2*d.* per ton between the M. & L.R.'s charges to carriers for tolls, wagons, and power and Canal rates for tonnage only.[2] Many Bills deeply affecting the Trustees' interests were not petitioned against at all, possibly in some instances from want of *locus standi*. These included the Chester and Manchester Direct Railway Bill (1846), the Widnes and Garston and Widnes and Warrington Bills (1846 and 1847 respectively), the Bill merging the Liverpool and Manchester line with the Grand Junction, Bolton and Leigh, Kenyon and Leigh Junction, and North Union Railways (1845), and the several measures transferring the Grand Trunk, Shropshire Union, Macclesfield, and Peak Forest Canals to railway control.

As the parliamentary battle proceeded, the Trustees' position weakened, and they found themselves having to compromise with proposals which they had initially intended to thwart. By September 1845 they realized that they could no longer hold at bay, as they had at first intended, the projects, of which two were then before the public, for joining Wigan and Manchester through the Worsley area, their own domain. Making, therefore, a virtue of necessity, they turned to rendering one of these subservient to the interests of the Worsley coal-mines which stood badly in need of an improved outlet for their coals.[3] This was the Manchester, Wigan, and Southport Railway launched initially by the Grand Junction and Manchester and Leeds Companies conjointly and destined eventually to become the charge of the L. & Y. With its promoters the Trustees made a number of agreements as to constructing branch lines into the collieries, which, had the main project been carried out, would have removed one

---

[1] F. Smith to G. Loch, 8 June 1846, and enclosure, L.E.P.
[2] F. Smith to J. Loch, 25 Feb. 1846, and enclosure, ibid.
[3] G. Loch to Lord F. Egerton, 19 Sept. 1845, E.B.C.

of the principal obstacles to the further expansion of the mines.[1]

Viewed in a long-term perspective, the developments of the middle forties wrought a decided shift in the balance of economic advantage between the Canal and its railway opponents. For the moment, however, there was no sign of a disastrous collapse in the Trustees' fortunes. The years of the battle against railroads in the parliamentary arena were years of continuing, though slowly declining, prosperity for the Canal as the ensuing figures show:[2]

	Profits of the Canal			Profits of the Bridgewater Carrying Department		
	£	s.	d.	£	s.	d.
1844	73,252	17	1	3,157	6	3½
1845	69,510	4	11	(−) 6,768	15	5
1846	59,816	9	5	535	5	4
1847	53,605	11	1½	(−) 1,850	14	3
1848	43,396	6	0½	(−) 5,709	4	9½

The trade returns, too, tell a favourable story. The quantity carried both on tonnage and on freight went on increasing down to 1846. In the two following years both items diminished, but the decrease in tonnage traffic was relatively slight.[3] The strongest point was the short-distance trade between Liverpool and Manchester, where the Trustees and their carriers depended upon themselves alone. Here the canals were gaining trade not only absolutely but relatively to the railways. In January 1845 the Trustees entered into an agreement with the Liverpool and Manchester Railway to partition the traffic between Liverpool, Manchester, and certain places

---

[1] See below, pp. 317–18.

[2] Bridgewater Trust General Accounts, 1844–50, Annual Profit and Loss Account. Owing to a change in the method of keeping the accounts, the figures for 1848 are not strictly comparable with those for the other years in the series, but on any computation there was a loss in that year on the Bridgewater Carrying Department. It should be noted, however, that the Trustees did not lose over all on the trade carried in their own boats, for the outgoings of the Carrying Department included a large annual payment for tolls transferred to the credit of the Canal Department. They only lost on carrying.

[3] Bridgewater Trust General Accounts, 1844–50, Summaries of Trade and Tonnage, listed under Canal Department, and 'Abstracts', listed under Carrying Department.

adjacent to Manchester in accordance with the proportions
carried in the six preceding years and to pay compensation for
any excess. By this arrangement the Duke's Canal and the
Mersey and Irwell Navigation were conjointly allocated two-
thirds of the traffic. Nevertheless, the Trustees exceeded their
proportion by 28,578 tons in 1845, by 23,296 tons in 1846, by
15,156 tons in 1847, and by 30,226 tons in 1848. They paid
out nearly £50,000 in compensation to the Railway Company
in the two years after the agreement came into effect. The
excess was due partly to the fact that the Grand Junction
Railway's share of the traffic was under-declared, but was
mainly caused by the zeal of the independent carriers by water
who snatched trade both from the Railway Company and
from the Trustees' own carrying department by making
unauthorized discounts to shippers and by offering unusual
facilities such as the insurance of goods while in warehouses.[1]
The port of Runcorn was also flourishing: 160,000 tons of
goods destined for the interior of the country were trans-
shipped there from coasting vessels in the year 1845,[2] and there
were signs of the beginnings of a foreign trade through the
port. The first foreign vessel to enter the docks of the Bridgewater Trustees at that place did so on 18 June 1846 bearing
railway sleepers.[3] The Trustees strove to encourage this
development by having Runcorn recognized as a bonding
port early in 1847,[4] by issuing a new schedule of dock
rates which assimilated the charges on the foreign trade to
those in force on coasting traffic,[5] and by making an agreement with a Winsford firm in October 1848 to send salt by
canal to Runcorn to serve as a backloading for vessels discharging in the docks.[6] They stood to gain from the growth
of the port as canal proprietors, for goods landed at Runcorn,
unlike those which were unloaded at Liverpool, had no option
but to travel inland by water.

[1] 'Statement on the Part of the Bridgewater Trustees Re Contests and Com-
petition of Railways', undated [1850] (Bridgewater Department, M.S.C.C.).
G. Loch to H. Booth, 23 June 1847; G. Marsden to F. Smith, 18 Feb. 1846,
L.E.P.

[2] F. Smith to G. Loch, 2 Jan. 1846, ibid.

[3] C. W. Rippon to F. Smith, 18 June 1846, ibid.

[4] F. Smith to G. Loch, 10 Feb. 1847, and enclosure, ibid.

[5] F. Smith to G. Loch, 19 Nov. 1847, ibid.

[6] F. Smith to G. Loch, 10 Oct. 1848; G. Loch to F. Smith, 16 Oct. 1848, ibid.

Even the canal trade which travelled over greater distances and made use of more than one navigation, fared better than it had earlier done. The Preston Brook route between the Midlands and Lancashire was winning back trade from that via Ellesmere Port in 1845 and 1846. The weight of goods using the former rose from 40,856 tons in 1845 to 43,807 tons in 1846, whilst the quantity through the latter hardly increased at all.[1] In May 1846 Pickfords gave notice to forward all their goods from Liverpool to Birmingham and Wolverhampton by way of Preston Brook instead of Ellesmere Port.[2] The improvement was due partly to uncertainty as to the future of the Shropshire Union canals whilst the plan of converting a portion of them into railways was in contemplation, but it was also the result of a change of heart in the Grand Trunk Canal Company, which joined the Trustees in lowering tolls on earthenware, ale and porter, and Birmingham hardware in November 1845.[3] No doubt the Trent and Mersey Committee was encouraged to take this step by the general Act of Parliament passed in the preceding June which enabled canal companies, like railway companies, to vary their tonnage charges between different sections of their lines. But the company's attitude had been tending towards a greater realism from about the year 1843 onwards, and the trend was not reversed by the transference of control to the North Staffordshire Railway. The legislation authorizing the merger reduced the tolls between Haywood Junction and Preston Brook by $\frac{1}{4}d.$ per ton to $\frac{1}{2}d.$ per ton per mile,[4] and the Railway Company during the period 1846–9, when its own lines were under construction, made far greater exertions to build up a through trade in co-operation with the Duke of Bridgewater's Trustees than the independent canal company had ever done.[5]

Down to the end of 1847, in fact, railways did not inflict much additional damage upon the Trust concerns. In some respects they had the reverse effect of fostering the canal

---

[1] F. Smith to J. Loch, 31 Oct. 1848, ibid.
[2] F. Smith to J. Loch, 7 May 1846, ibid.
[3] G. Loch to F. Smith, 27 Oct. 1845; F. Smith to J. Loch, 8 Oct. 1845, ibid.
[4] F. Smith to G. Loch, 1 Sept. 1847, ibid.
[5] F. Smith to G. Loch, 24 July 1847, 18 July 1848; J. Loch to F. Smith, 14 Feb. 1847, ibid.

trade. The Duke's had the privilege of carrying the stone, iron rails and chairs, bricks, and other materials used in the construction of the Birkenhead, Lancashire, and Cheshire Junction Railway authorized in June 1846.[1] Moreover, as carriers, though not as canal proprietors, the Trustees managed to turn the Chester and Birkenhead Railway to their advantage by making an agreement with its owners in 1846 (signed in September 1847) for conveying their traffic across the Mersey estuary. By this means the Railway Company obtained an access to Liverpool and the Trustees the promise of a 20 per cent share in the gross receipts of the railroad.[2] In practice, however, the gains were small—£372 in 1847 and even less in the following year.[3]

The real weakness of the Trust lay as yet not in the fierceness of its enemies without but in the unsoundness of the structure within. Even in this sphere an improvement had occurred by the middle forties. James Loch was always a better financier than a business man. His careful husbanding of resources raised the financial position of the life tenant, diminishing his need to wring the last ounce of profit out of the concern and enhancing his power to invest in it. To raise the portions for Lord Francis's younger children, he opened an account at Drummonds in his own and Lord Morpeth's name, feeding it with contributions from His Lordship's income and investing the money in government stock. Advantage was then taken of a rise in the price of the funds to dispose of the stock for a sum which paid off a part of the mortgage on Bradshaw's estate, thus helping to free this land for the support of the family. As more and more of the mortgage was redeemed, the interest which was saved was paid into the account and invested, until by adding together these payments and accumulating them half-yearly, together with the growing dividends, a sum of more than £20,000 was amassed. This stock was then sold, in 1845, and the proceeds were used to clear the remainder of the mortgage. Lord Francis Egerton's private affairs were at that time in a sufficiently healthy condition to permit the

---

[1] C. Mitchell to F. Smith, 4 Jan. 1847, L.E.P.

[2] F. Smith to J. Loch, 1 Jan. 1846; F. Smith to G. Loch, 4 Sept. 1847, ibid.

[3] Bridgewater Trust General Accounts, 1844–50, Annual Profit and Loss Account.

continuation of the fund for the purpose of building up capital into the future. The Trust properties benefited from the easement, for Lord Francis advanced between £2,000 and £3,000 towards the construction of the new entrance basin and gate at Duke's Dock, Liverpool, which was completed in 1845, the idea being that he should be later reimbursed with funds borrowed by the Trustees under the terms of the Estate Act of 1842.[1]

A decisive setback in this improvement resulted, however, from the purchase of the Mersey and Irwell Navigation. It was on 17 January 1846 that the Duke's Trustees took over from Lord Francis Egerton the shares in the Old Quay, making themselves responsible thereby for the servicing of a huge bonded debt amounting at the time to £565,000.[2] The greater part of this (£402,000) was soon converted, as we have seen, into a single consolidated loan drawn from the Law Life Assurance Society, but a substantial residue of bonds, some of which bore an interest of $4\frac{1}{2}$ per cent per annum, continued into the later 1850s.[3] Moreover, the sinking fund established to effect a gradual redemption of the debt claimed as much as £12,000 of the income accruing to the Earl of Ellesmere from the Trust estates in 1858.[4] For this reason, and also because the internal costs of the Trust rose sharply during 1845,[5] Loch inaugurated a fresh wave of retrenchment in the following year. Early in July the estimates for the Michaelmas quarter were savagely cut back—from £63,462 to £50,842.[6] Notwithstanding the fact that the Egerton Dock was choked with mud to a depth of nearly ten feet, and needed to be scoured, Loch flatly refused to sanction the erection of a pile dam. 'I wish I could get you all with the ambition of making the cheapest thing and not the finest thing', he thundered to

[1] J. Loch to Lord F. Egerton, 9 Feb. 1846, E.B.C.

[2] The date of the indenture assigning the shares to the Trustees is given in the 'Duplicate Conveyance and Assignment of the Bridgewater Canal, etc.', 27 June 1874 (Bridgewater Department, M.S.C.C.). See also, for evidence of concern about the interest burden of the debt as early as March 1846, G. Loch to F. Smith, 12 Mar. 1846, L.E.P.

[3] Enclosure in A. Egerton to F. Smith, 11 Nov. 1858, ibid.

[4] Statement of the Revenue of the Bridgewater Trust Estates for 1858, enclosed in A. Egerton to F. Smith, 30 Apr. 1859, ibid.

[5] J. Loch to F. Smith, 10 June 1845, ibid.

[6] J. Loch to Hathorn, 6 July 1846, ibid.

his deputy apropos the extension of the dock wall at Runcorn.[1]
'It lies between doing the thing cheaply or not at all.'

All this boded ill for the future. Superficially, however, once
the parliamentary battle of 1845–7 was over, the ship appeared
to be drifting into calmer waters. James Loch took note of this
in September 1848. He wrote to Smith: 'I think we must walk
a little more leisurely now seeing the state of the railway
world and the necessity there appears to be for their raising
their charges.' 'The Canals have seen the worst of their case,'
he added, 'What say you?'[2] Events, however, were soon to
prove him wrong.

---

[1] J. Loch to F. Smith, 11 July 1846; see also F. Smith to J. Loch, 15 July
1846, L.E.P.

[2] J. Loch to F. Smith, 2 Sept. 1848, ibid.

CHAPTER X

The Heat of Battle (1849–1851)

<hr>

TOWARDS the turn of the half-century the Bridgewater Trustees came face to face with the realities of the extended and reorganized railway system. In less than three years they fought two sharp contests, principally with the L. & N.W.R. and L. & Y. Companies—from April to December 1849 and from January to August 1851—and there was some desultory skirmishing in between. Severely assailed even in their Liverpool and Manchester trade, which had been hitherto their most impregnable stronghold, they fought back vigorously and effectively. These more than any other were the crisis years in the battle between the Duke's navigations and the railways. They left their mark on all that followed.

The rivalry had been slowly intensifying since 1847 as the various railway projects of the middle forties became fact. In that year the youthful East Lancashire Railway joined with the L. & N.W.R. in attacking the rates between Liverpool and Bury.[1] Soon afterwards the L. & Y. diverted Scottish iron, imported coastwise into Lancashire, from Runcorn to the railway port of Fleetwood,[2] whilst the L. & N.W.R. cut into the Macclesfield traffic by reducing charges and running extra luggage trains.[3] The trade depression of 1847 which fell with particular severity upon the Lancashire cotton industry increased the tension, for it encouraged the private carriers on the waterways, who were faced with the alternative of laying their boatmen, their horses, and their vessels idle, to redouble their efforts to attract trade by reducing rates, even those which were supposed to be fixed by agreement of the Trustees and the Railway Company. They encroached upon the L. &

---

[1] F. Smith to J. Loch, 1 July 1847, L.E.P.
[2] F. Smith to G. Loch, 21 Aug. 1848, ibid.
[3] F. Farrel to F. Smith, 1 Nov. 1848, ibid.

N.W.R. in both the Liverpool and Manchester trade and the forward traffic, giving the two navigations in 1848 a greater surplus over their allocation under the terms of the compensation agreement of 1845 than ever before.[1] The Bridgewater Trustees, though they did not benefit from most of the traffic which was taken from the Railway Company, were nevertheless slow to intervene, partly because they wished to establish a case for revising the compensation agreement in their own favour[2] and partly because they did not know how to discipline the carriers. The Lochs were disposed to veto harsh measures such as a refusal to tow their vessels on the Mersey estuary or the raising of tolls to the maximum of 3s. 4d. per ton.[3] Eventually the alarm of some of the more responsible carriers at the low level to which freight charges had been reduced (1s. 6d. per ton on down goods) helped to supply a corrective, and in August 1848 rates were raised again, whilst a compensation agreement was adopted by the carriers themselves.[4] But the delay had not improved the temper of the L. & N.W. directors. In June 1847 Henry Booth had hinted that if the Trustees did not control their carriers, 'some serious derangement' might ensue,[5] and the experience of these preliminary years helped to sharpen the contest when it came.

It was not the L. & N. W., however, but the L. & Y. that first flung the gauntlet. In April 1849 that company opened its Liverpool and Bury line. Connected at Bolton with the Manchester, Bolton, and Bury railroad, which led to Manchester, and at Bury, via the Heywood branch, with the main line of the old Manchester and Leeds running through Rochdale to the West Riding, the new route was bound to disturb the arrangement of the Trustees and the L. & N.W. for partitioning the Liverpool and Manchester trade and to intensify the pressure on the forward trade by canal from Liverpool to places north and east of Manchester. It is possible, however,

---

[1] F. Smith to G. Loch, 12 Apr. 1848, L.E.P. 'Statement on the Part of the Bridgewater Trustees Re Contests and Competition of Railways', undated [1850] (M.S.C.C., Bridgewater Department).

[2] F. Smith to G. Loch, 21 June 1848, and G. Loch to F. Smith, 22 June 1848, L.E.P.

[3] G. Loch to F. Smith, 22 June and 18 Oct. 1848, ibid.

[4] F. Smith to G. Loch, 11 and 29 Aug. 1848, ibid.

[5] H. Booth to G. Loch, 21 June 1847, ibid.

that the L. & Y. could have been brought peacefully into the existing system of regulation had the Duke's Trustees been prepared to cede to it a share of the trade. Fereday Smith heard about 22 March 1849 that the company had approached the L. & N.W.R. for a joint move to abolish the differential of 5*d.* per ton by which the water carriers were allowed to undercut the railroad, and that the L. & N.W.R. was likely to acquiesce and press the Trustees for a larger allocation of traffic.[1] No proposal appears to have been put forward at this time, but had it been advanced it would have been rejected. In George Loch's view

it would be unwise to enter into so close an agreement, embracing the principle of compensation, with such persons as conduct the business of the L. & Y. Co., as that which has generally worked agreeably and usefully with the L. & N.W. Co. At any rate no such agreement would be possible at first nor until the pretensions of the former company to participation has been tested by some experience.[2]

Previous success in attracting trade had gone to the Trustees' heads. Believing that the Liverpool and Bury line might take traffic from the L. & N.W.R. rather than from themselves, at least between Liverpool and Manchester, they hastened to abrogate the existing compensation agreement, lest they should find themselves having to reimburse the latter for trade abstracted from it by the L. & Y. At this critical juncture they seem to have been prepared even to risk a contest with both companies rather than give way on the question of proportions.[3]

Denied a place in a recognized traffic agreement, the L. & Y. began to fend for itself. In April 1849 it struck at the rates between Liverpool and the towns of Bury, Wigan, Rochdale, Oldham, Ashton-under-Lyne, and Stalybridge, at the same time raising the tolls upon its own Manchester, Bolton, and Bury Canal to the maximum level. Timber, flour, and grain destined for Rochdale were lowered from 11*s.* 8*d.* to 9*s.*, from 10*s.* 10*d.* to 8*s.* 4*d.*, and from 12*s.* 6*d.* to 9*s.* per ton respectively, and the other reductions were of a similar order. Raw cotton

---

[1] F. Smith to G. Loch, 22 Mar. 1849, ibid.
[2] G. Loch to F. Smith, 22 Mar. 1849, ibid.
[3] F. Smith to G. Loch, 21 Apr. 1849 (two letters), ibid.

for Oldham came down from 13*s*. to 10*s*. 6*d*. in June.[1] As yet
the Liverpool and Manchester trade was unaffected, probably
because the L. & N.W.R. Company, whilst keeping out of the
conflict itself, encouraged the L. & Y. not to compete with it
for the railway traffic between Liverpool and Manchester, but
to concentrate upon taking a certain portion of the Yorkshire
trade in which the L. & N.W.R. was less interested. Fereday
Smith reported an agreement to this effect between the two
railway companies at the end of March.[2] It was not, in fact,
until another company, the East Lancashire Railway, entered
the struggle that the Liverpool and Manchester rates were
assailed. The E.L.R.'s circuitous route from Manchester to
Liverpool through Bury, Accrington, Preston, and Ormskirk
had only reached completion on 2 April 1849. Towards the end
of June this railroad began to carry down goods at 2*s*. 6*d*. per
ton less than the old rate by rail and 10*d*. per ton less than
the water rate. The canal carriers and the Trustees followed
these reductions, and at length the London and North Western
Railway, abandoning its previous restraint, announced on
7 July that it would carry both up and down at the same
rates as were charged by water, thus repudiating the accepted
practice of maintaining a differential between the two.[3]

It was not long before the Trustees felt the weight of the
attack upon them. Their carriers began to desert to the enemy.
In the middle of May, Nall, whose boats plied upon the Mersey
navigation, became an agent of the L. & Y. He handed his
plant and his whole concern over to the Railway Company and
used the Old Quay docks and warehouses at Liverpool for
goods which he dispatched inland by rail. When, on the expira-
tion of notice, the Trustees endeavoured to resume possession
of the premises which they rented to him, a disorderly scene
ensued, and the Liverpool police declined to intervene. Dowling, the Police Commissioner, 'said it would be something to
do for the lawyers'.[4] Carvers and Faulkner soon followed in the
wake of Nall.[5]

---

[1] F. Smith to G. Loch, 2 and 21 Apr. and 6 June 1849, L.E.P.

[2] F. Smith to G. Loch, 30 Mar. 1849, ibid.

[3] F. Smith to J. Loch, 26 June 1849; F. Smith to G. Loch, 2 and 7 July 1849, ibid.

[4] Pendlebury to F. Smith, 2 July 1849; see also F. Smith to J. Loch, 22 June 1849, ibid.   [5] G. Loch to F. Smith, 17 May 1849, ibid.

Despite these reverses, the Trustees remained sufficiently assured to refuse at the beginning of July to discuss quantities with Captain Laws, the General Manager of the L. & Y., until 'after the L. & N.W. Company and the Bridgewater Trustees shall have together agreed on the share of the trade they will concede to him or the limit beyond which they would not accede to his demands'.[1] On the 6th they rejected a proposal from the L. & N.W.R. that the two railway companies should be jointly allocated seven-twelfths of the Liverpool and Manchester trade.[2] On the following day, as we have already seen, the L. & N.W.R. declared war upon them by equalizing the charges between rail and water. Still, however, they were not dismayed. They had cards up their sleeves which they hoped in due course to play to the detriment of all their opponents.

Some of their schemes were too ambitious and too uncertain to promise relief in the short run. They merely served to bolster up the Trustees' self-confidence. There was talk, for example, of rendering either the Canal or the Old River navigable as far as Manchester to vessels like the Yorkshire 'Billy Boys' capable of carrying 110–20 tons and drawn by a single horse or, if on the river, by Foster's steam tug; alternatively of making it possible to bring Irish and Scottish coasters straight up to Manchester by fitting the vessels with swivel masts.[3] Talk, however, it remained.

Of more immediate potential was Fereday Smith's plan of turning the independent carriers by water into commission agents of the Trustees. This was adopted in principle at a meeting in the Brunswick Hotel, Manchester, on 28 June at which C. J. Faulkner presided and eight other carrying firms, including the New Quay Company, the Grocers' Company, the Harrington Company, Kenworthy & Co., and J. & J. Veevers, were represented. The agreements into which the carriers severally entered with the Trustees were for six years, expiring on 30 June 1856. By these the carriers theoretically hired out their boats and such other plant as they possessed to the Trustees, whilst in practice continuing to work them. In

[1] G. Loch to M. Huish, 2 July 1849, ibid.
[2] 'Statement on the Part of the Bridgewater Trustees, etc.'
[3] F. Smith to G. Loch, 18 May and 12 June 1849, L.E.P.

return they received from the Trust a commission, which was calculated as a percentage of the freights, and a fixed payment of so much per ton, which was to cover the rent of boats and other working expenses such as boatmen's wages, provender for the horses, tolls payable on canals other than those of the Trustees, porterage, and the cost of finding and maintaining wagons to collect and distribute merchandise in the Manchester area. The Trustees were to fix the freight charges payable to the public and to receive the difference between these and the allowances due to the carriers.[1] The agency scheme was in the first instance limited to the short-distance traffic between Liverpool and the Manchester region, but a carrier of iron between the Midlands and Liverpool was soon admitted to it.[2] It was proposed by Fereday Smith as a means of checking the drain of carriers to the rails, for Smith believed that under the preceding system 'one inducement to the canal carriers to go upon the railway' was 'that the railway company relieves the carrier from the necessity of finding capital and enters into a definite arrangement for a term—in Nall's case it is for five years'.[3] Nevertheless, the process of working out the details with the carriers was a slow one. In November 1849 the agreements had still not been signed, though the arrangements for concluding them were well advanced.

The plan on which the Trustees mainly relied for tipping the balance in the contest against the railway companies was that of launching an attack upon them on a wider front by consolidating the canal interests involved in the long-distance traffic. Such an activity did not come naturally to them, for in the past the Lochs had cast their influence in favour of a more or less 'go-it-alone' policy. In August 1838 James had refused to send a representative to a meeting of canal delegates at Birmingham. His objections were threefold: firstly, that by being represented he would recognize the authority of the conference to inquire into the mode of management of the

[1] Copy of resolutions of meeting in Manchester, dated 28 June 1849. See also G. Loch to F. Smith, 20 Nov. 1849, and F. Smith to G. Loch, 24 Nov. 1849, for details of the agency scheme; also, for the date of the termination of the agreements, F. Smith to A. Egerton, 25 June 1856, L.E.P.

[2] F. Smith to G. Loch, 20 Feb., 15 and 27 June 1850, ibid.

[3] F. Smith to G. Loch, 18 May 1849, ibid.

constituent canals; secondly, that he would thereby also assent to the principle that 'the opinion of the majority would have the power of controuling if not influencing the conduct of all'; and thirdly, that such co-operation might involve a disclosure of partial tonnage and freight agreements with individual carriers and for particular trades.[1] The Trustees had at that time many arrangements for differential charges which they did not wish to publicize. As the pressure from the railways intensified, however, the Trustees were obliged to revise their view. George Loch wrote in April 1849:

> Does it not deserve consideration whether it would not be the wisest step for the Canals (in case the evil [of contest] cannot be peaceably averted) to unite between the two coasts in making the contest too general and too serious for the railways to sustain? Otherwise we may be beaten piecemeal.[2]

To Loch and to his father the strategy was a defensive one. They shrank from an attack upon the L. & N.W.R., which, linked as it was with the Sutherland interest, they still regarded as the natural ally of the Trust. It was their General Manager Fereday Smith who gave the new policy an offensive twist. Writing to George Loch on 10 July 1849, he defined the Trustees' first objective as

> by alliances offensive and defensive or arrangements equivalent thereto, to strengthen themselves in such a way as to be able to compete successfully with the L. & N.W.R. Co. for the long traffic and for the traffic on which that Railway Co. obtain the largest amount of revenue and profit, thus compelling them to a fair and reasonable arrangement in reference to the North and South rates and the East and West traffic.[3]

On his initiative the Trustees drove the North Staffordshire Railway Company to an arrangement about the Trent and Mersey Canal by sending their own boats south to Wolverhampton to compete with those of the company. By this agreement which was made on 18 July, the Bridgewater Trustees leased the tolls on the through traffic of the Grand Trunk for a period of seven years and took over the canal carrying

---

[1] J. Loch to F. Smith, 24 Aug. 1838, ibid.
[2] G. Loch to F. Smith, 21 Apr. 1849, ibid.
[3] F. Smith to G. Loch, 10 July 1849, ibid.

stock of the North Staffordshire Company at Wolverhampton, guaranteeing to the company in return an income of about £12,500 per annum. This was only part, moreover, of an ambitious scheme to gain control both of the canals and of the carrying trade between Wolverhampton and Liverpool and Manchester by way of Preston Brook, for Lord Ellesmere authorized Fereday Smith to open negotiations for extending the arrangement to the tolls of the Staffordshire and Worcestershire Canal.[1] The Trustees' intention was to develop a carrying trade which would be virtually toll free and could therefore be conducted at reduced rates.[2]

Shipton & Co. of Wolverhampton, who had once been carriers of a large and varied canal trade between London, Derby, Hull, and the north, were also brought into the agreement. The necessity for including them arose from the fact that since 1847 they had been closely linked with the canal carrying department of the North Staffordshire Railway Company, which had relieved them of their traffic in light goods between Lancashire and the Midlands, leaving them with the heavy trade in iron. By 1849, however, the roles had been reversed, and Shiptons were bidding to take over the carrying trade of the N.S.R. Company and to lease, in like manner to what the Bridgewater Trustees were later to propose, the tolls on the Trent and Mersey Canal. These negotiations were abandoned when the Trustees made their proposals to the North Staffordshire, and Shiptons were fitted into the new arrangement. They became solicitors of traffic for the Trustees in the South Staffordshire district and were guaranteed a minimum commission of £2,000 per year for seven years, calculated at five per cent on the freights. In return for this they relinquished to the Trustees their trade in heavy goods with Lancashire and the boats in which it had been conducted, retaining merely a London traffic along the Grand Junction Canal.[3] By their agreements with Shiptons and the N.S.R. Company, the Duke's Trustees thus became firmly established as carriers on the Midland canals, thereby obtaining a position

---

[1] Memorandum signed by J. Lewis Ricardo, dated 18 July 1849; F. Smith to G. Loch, 19 July 1849; G. Loch to F. Smith, 20 July 1849, L.E.P.

[2] F. Smith to G. Loch, 10 July 1849; G. Loch to F. Smith, 19 July 1849, ibid.

[3] F. Smith to A. Egerton, 13 Jan. 1857; see also F. Smith to G. Loch, 24 July and 14 Oct. 1847, 10, 12, and 19 July 1849, ibid.

which was to afford them unforeseen advantages in dealing with the railway companies in the years to come, as will be shown in the ensuing chapter.

The wide-ranging strategy which led to this result was not solely dictated by needs arising from the contest with the railways in Lancashire. There were many other objectives, and these were listed by Fereday Smith in his letter to G. Loch on 10 July—to compete successfully with the Shropshire Union Canal Company for the traffic between South Staffordshire and Liverpool, more especially as the Ellesmere Port agreement was in danger of falling through, and the N.S.R. Company was on the point of concluding an alliance with the Shropshire Union Company to divert a large trade from Preston Brook to Ellesmere Port; to vie with the Macclesfield Canal route to Manchester now under the control of the Manchester, Sheffield, and Lincolnshire Railway, with the Birkenhead Railway route to and from the south, and with the newly opened M.S. & L. line for trade between Lincolnshire and Manchester and Liverpool; to preserve a fair share of the Potteries trade; to guard against the possibility of a junction being made between the Grand Trunk and the Weaver at Acton; and to forestall an alliance between the L. & N.W.R. and the North Staffordshire Company directed against themselves.[1] By intervening more effectively in the Midland trades, Smith hoped to be able to drive the Shropshire Union Company and perhaps also the L. & N.W.R. into making a compensation agreement with the Trustees similar to that which was in operation between Liverpool and Manchester, and which could be accompanied by a general raising of rates.

This, however, was a long-term plan. The immediate purpose was to reduce the canal charges between London and Lancashire and by this aggression to force the L. & N.W.R. to terms between Liverpool and Manchester. 'I believe it can be done', wrote Smith to George Loch on 13 August 1849.[2] To complete the link with London it was above all necessary to bring in the Grand Junction Canal, which ran from the Oxford Canal at Braunston in Northamptonshire to the capital. Smith

---

[1] F. Smith to G. Loch, 10 July 1849; see also F. Smith to G. Loch, 19 July 1849, ibid.

[2] F. Smith to G. Loch, 13 Aug. 1849, ibid.

hoped to arrange with its proprietors, who were already carrying by water between London and the north, for the Trustees to be admitted to the whole or a portion of the trade. The latter would either look after a traffic which would be jointly conducted, at the Liverpool and Manchester end, or carry throughout in Shipton's boats with the aid of a tonnage reduction on the Grand Junction Canal. Negotiations were opened up but dragged unpromisingly. Afraid of being drawn by the Grand Junction Company into a permanent contest with the L. & N.W.R. for the London trade at cut-throat rates, the Trustees held back from committing themselves until eventually, in November 1849, the canal company, evidently suspecting that it was being made a cat's-paw for interests not its own, signified its refusal to reduce rates. According to Fereday Smith, the company representative's dislike of the project seemed to be dominated by the fear that

by way of forcing the railway to terms between Liverpool and Manchester the Trustees should reduce between Liverpool and Birmingham, and compel a reduction between London and Birmingham (by changing to the extent of the difference of freight the Liverpool and London markets of supply to the Midland counties).[1]

But this may have been merely an excuse for breaking off the negotiations.

Whilst the Trustees schemed, the contest sharpened. When the L. & N.W.R. adopted the charge of 7s. 6d. per ton on down goods, the rate which the canal carriers were quoting, the Trustees came down to 6s. 8d., insisting that a differential between canal and railway charges was essential to the maintenance of the traffic upon the water. The L. & N.W.R. promptly adopted the same rate, whereupon the Trustees quoted 5s. 10d.[2] A conference was then held on 25 July to arrange a settlement. The L. & Y. Company did not participate, but the Trustees put up to the L. & N.W.R. a proposal for admitting them to the Liverpool and Manchester trade. The Bridgewater navigations were to retain one-half of the

---

[1] F. Smith to G. Loch, 24 Nov. 1849; see also G. Loch to F. Smith, 12 Oct. 1849, and J. Loch to F. Smith, 19 Nov. 1849, L.E.P.

[2] F. Smith to G. Loch, 20 July 1849 (two letters), ibid.

traffic, whilst the two railway companies divided the remainder in the proportion of 3 : 2, the larger share going to the North Western. This concession did not satisfy the L. & N.W.R., which rejected the proposition without communicating it to the L. & Y.[1] Though they had not been the first to break the peace, the directors of the former had no intention, once it was broken, of returning to the *status quo ante* with regard to their allocation of the traffic. Braithwaite Poole told Fereday Smith on 28 August that his company was resolved to have two-fifths of the Liverpool and Manchester trade, giving the L. & Y. one-fifth and the Trustees two-fifths, and that 'he would reduce and reduce until he attained his object'.[2]

The struggle, therefore, continued, reaching its severest pitch in August and early September. Freight charges fell to ruinous levels. By 15 September the L. & N.W.R. had reduced on both cotton and down goods to 2s. 6d. per ton:[3] only when the rate on down goods was above 5s. per ton could the Trustees make a profit. According to George Loch, however, who, as a railway director, was in some position to know, the minimum level at which profitability could be sustained by the Railway Company was even higher.[4]

Nor were reductions in the rate of freight the only weapons with which the combatants fought. The L. & N.W.R. endeavoured to discredit the Trustees with their customers by issuing a circular on 1 September pointing out that goods transported along the tideway of the River Mersey were uninsured.[5] By way of retaliation the Trustees contemplated publishing a list of all the accidents and irregularities of the Railway Company's passenger traffic. 'It would perhaps not be injudicious to give Mr. Lawrence a hint that such a course was possible', Fereday Smith advised Loch.[6] The directors of the North Western also used their control of the Huddersfield

---

[1] 'Statement on the Part of the Bridgewater Trustees Re Contests and Competition of Railways', undated [1850] (M.S.C.C., Bridgewater Department).

[2] F. Smith to G. Loch, 29 Aug. 1849, L.E.P.

[3] F. Smith to J. Loch, 11 and 15 Sept. 1849, ibid.

[4] He wrote to Marsden: '. . . so long as the rate is maintained above 5s. we shall continue making some little profit, while the railway are sustaining considerable loss' (G. Loch to Marsden, 24 Aug. 1849, ibid.).

[5] F. Smith to G. Loch, 1 Sept. 1849; G. Loch to F. Smith, 4 Sept. 1849, ibid.

[6] F. Smith to G. Loch, 7 Sept. 1849, ibid.

Canal to interfere with the through trade by water. Braithwaite Poole warned Fereday Smith on 28 August that

he would show how the Huddersfield Canal could be managed, now
that the L. & N.W. Railway Company had possession of it, inasmuch as the tunnel should be declared unsafe, and that from time
to time the works should be out of repair, and there should be a
scarcity of water. He would also alter the hours of passing through
the tunnel daily so as to impede the canal traffic to the utmost.[1]

Within a week Smith reported that the company was making
some very stringent arrangements for parties navigating on
the Huddersfield and Sir John Ramsden's Canals, making
them pay on passing. The water carriers Kenworthy & Co.
expected daily to be turned out of their warehouses at Huddersfield.[2] This example, together with the raising of the tolls on
the Manchester, Bolton, and Bury Canal by the L. & Y.
Company referred to earlier in this chapter, shows that even if,
as was contended in the controversies surrounding the report
of the Royal Commission on Canals in 1909, railways did not
generally acquire canals in order to strangle them, they were
certainly not above exploiting their control of links in the
chain of waterways once it had been attained, to further their
purposes in contests with adjoining canals.

But the Duke of Bridgewater's Trustees remained strong
enough to pursue attack as the best form of defence. In the
middle of September Fereday Smith was trying to persuade
James Loch to sanction a plan for bringing coal into Manchester
from the Trustees' mines at cost price to compete with that
which was supplied by rail. His argument was that the sacri-
fice of trading profit would be partly offset by the royalties
accruing to Lord Ellesmere from increased sales, whilst the
railway companies would be placed in the position of having
not only to forego their charges but also to purchase coal from
other mine-owners with hard cash if they wished to underbid
the Trustees.[3] This scheme was propounded as a reserve
measure and there is no evidence that it was implemented.
Nevertheless, the Trustees did strike at the L. & N.W.R.

---

[1] Memorandum of a conversation between Poole and Fereday Smith,
enclosed in F. Smith to G. Loch, 29 Aug. 1849, L.E.P.

[2] F. Smith to G. Loch, 7 Sept. 1849, ibid.

[3] F. Smith to J. Loch, 12 Sept. 1849, ibid.

through that company's passenger traffic. On 21 August Smith ordered the fitting up of vessels to carry third-class passengers by canal between Manchester and Runcorn and to connect with Liverpool by means of one of the Trustees' steamers. The entire cost of the trip was to be about 5*d.* per head, and the avowed object of the enterprise was to cut into the profits of the Railway Company which was getting 2*s.* 6*d.* per head on the traffic. At first George Loch declined to sanction so blatant a departure from defensive tactics, but Fereday Smith renewed his suggestion on 11 September after the goods rate had been further lowered by the railway directors.[1] This time apparently it was acted upon, for nearly forty years later W. H. Collier, the Assistant Manager of the Bridgewater Navigation Company, produced for the enlightenment of the House of Lords an advertisement issued in 1849 for carrying passengers between Manchester and Liverpool by canal for 3*d.* each. He told how the Trustees built boats 80 or 90 feet long which were mere shells drawn by 'blood horses' and travelled exceedingly rapidly.[2] Whether this venture succeeded in injuring the Railway Company remains uncertain, but there are indications that it did so. In the month ending 8 October 1849 the proceeds of the passenger traffic of the L. & N.W.R. fell by £10,340 as compared with the same period of 1848. Reporting the same to the half-yearly meeting of the company, the directors ascribed it to the visitation of the cholera,[3] but the fact that the yield dropped sharply in the week ending 16 September (which followed immediately upon Fereday Smith's final recommendation) and again in the week ending 7 October, when the cholera was losing force, suggests a different interpretation.[4]

Whilst fighting their rivals the Trustees also sought to divide them. Surmising correctly that the L. & N.W.R. had not revealed to the L. & Y. the proposal which they had made

---

[1] F. Smith to G. Loch, 21 Aug. 1849; G. Loch to F. Smith, 27 Aug. 1849; F. Smith to J. Loch, 11 Sept. 1849, ibid.

[2] 'Opposition of the Bridgewater Navigation Co. Ltd. . . . to the Manchester Ship Canal Bill', 1885, Minutes of Evidence, qu. 11540 (M.S.C.C., Bridgewater Department).

[3] *Herapath's Railway and Commercial Journal*, 23 Feb. 1850, p. 173.

[4] L. & N.W.R. Weekly Traffic Receipt Returns, 1849–50, abstracted from numbers of the *Railway Times* for 1849.

in the preceding July for apportioning to the latter a share of the Liverpool and Manchester trade, they let slip the information through an intermediary on 17 September, and received from Captain Laws through the same medium a reassuring and friendly reply. The Captain was perfectly satisfied with the proposition and willing to arrange on all fronts.[1]

By the middle of October peace appeared to be in sight. On the 11th George Loch was greeted with such affection by the directors of the L. & N.W.R. when he met them in the refreshment room at Wolverton that he surmised that the Trustees might safely raise their terms for a new agreement, and when the Railway Company put up a proposal to the Trustees early in the following month, his father displayed no hurry to conclude.[2] After the negotiations had at length begun, on 10 December, it soon became evident, however, that the Bridgewater people had misjudged their strength. The London and North Western Company would readily join in a settlement of the southern trade with both the Duke's Trustees and its own ally, the Shropshire Union Canal Company. The three parties agreed in principle on 13 December that the L. & N.W.R. should carry undamageable iron from Wolverhampton to Liverpool at 6*d*. per ton more than the canal charge, that there should be an equalization of rates between the Preston Brook and Ellesmere Port water routes between the two towns, and that the tonnages derived from the water traffic should be paid into a common fund which would be divided between the canal owners in agreed proportions. Braithwaite Poole, acting for the Railway Company, even wanted these provisions carried into effect without waiting for a complete agreement to be reached on all points.[3] The Trustees, however, insisted upon having a comprehensive settlement which would include the east–west traffic, and here they ran into serious difficulties with both the L. & N.W.R. and the L. & Y. Companies. To a considerable extent the problems were of their own making, for they were bargaining for a privileged position. They wished to be allowed to charge 1*s*. 8*d*. per ton less than the

[1] G. Loch to F. Smith, 26 Aug. 1849; F. Smith to G. Loch, 17 Sept. 1849, L.E.P.

[2] G. Loch to F. Smith, 12 Oct., 8 and 20 Nov. 1849, ibid.

[3] F. Smith to G. Loch, 13 and 15 Dec. 1849, and enclosed memorandum and minutes, ibid.

railway companies on all the down traffic from the forward towns east of Manchester. The railroad directors conceded the principle of a differential between the two charges, but desired to restrict it to certain categories of forward trade. The L. & N.W.R., for example, wished to exclude the Sheffield trade which it exchanged with the M.S. & L. Company. There were also differences about the proposed new compensation arrangement for dividing the Manchester and Liverpool traffic between the water and the rails. These turned mainly upon the question of how the Manchester and Liverpool traffic was to be distinguished from the forward trade. Eventually, however, in the first week of the new year a truce was arranged which ended the contest for the time being. The Liverpool and Manchester rates were restored to what they had been before the conflict began, and the Trustees agreed to withdraw from their customers many accommodations and services which they had hitherto granted, such as the loan of carts and of the services of porters, and to discontinue the allowance of discounts of $1\frac{1}{2}$ per cent for prompt cash payments. The new arrangement, however, which was concluded at a meeting in Liverpool on 7 January 1850, left most of the thorniest questions about the division of the traffic and the level of the forward rates unresolved. A clause establishing a differential of 1*s*. 8*d*. between canal and railway charges was accepted, it is true, but there was a difference of opinion between the contracting parties as to whether it applied to Sheffield goods.[1]

Although the Trustees cannot be said to have driven their opponents to what was from their own point of view a satisfactory or even a durable settlement of differences, their own trading position at the end of the conflict remained largely unimpaired. The quantity of merchandise carried upon the Duke's Canal had increased rather than diminished during the contest. From 1,360,774 tons in 1848 it rose to 1,536,715 tons in 1849. The traffic on the Mersey and Irwell Navigation increased from 247,449 tons to 283,015 tons during the same period.[2] Admittedly the success in retaining trade was

---

[1] 'Statement on the Part of the Bridgewater Trustees, etc.'; F. Smith to B. Poole, 22 and 26 Jan., and B. Poole to F. Smith, 23 Jan. 1850, L.E.P.

[2] *Select Committee on the Principle of Amalgamation Applied to Railway or Railway and Canal Bills, Third Report*, Minutes of Evidence, p. 25; 1852–3 (246) XXXVIII.

purchased at a cost. The profits, mainly from tolls, of the canal department of the Trust, which had never been less than £40,000 per annum in the five preceding years, fell to £9,504 in 1849.[1] Yet, despite all the efforts of the railway companies to shake their grip on the trade, the two waterways of the Bridgewater Trust still carried, when the contest was over, rather more than two-thirds of the traffic in goods between Liverpool and Manchester, if a statement prepared by the Trustees early in 1850 for submission to an arbitrator is worthy of credence.[2] Even the through trade, especially in raw cotton, clung tenaciously to the water. A rough estimate drawn up by Fereday Smith in February gave to the canals 80,000 tons per annum of the 'forward cotton', to the railways only 30,000 tons.[3] Much of this traffic in raw materials, especially that which was designed for towns like Oldham, Ashton-under-Lyne, Stalybridge, and Stockport which were not too far from Manchester, travelled no further than Castlefield by canal. There it was collected by the spinners in the horse-drawn carts in which they brought their manufactured products to Manchester to be exhibited for sale and packed for exportation. The saving of the canal charges beyond Manchester helped to fasten the traffic upon the water west of that town, for the railway companies, owing to their more limited warehouse accommodation, were unable to offer comparable facilities for the collection of the cotton by the parties to whom it was consigned.[4] This was especially true of the L. & Y., a relative newcomer to the trade.[5]

From this position of strength the Trustees retreated voluntarily later in the year to save themselves the expense of another contest and to ensure the maintenance of profitable rates of carriage. They were driven to do so by the continuing discord between themselves and the railway companies which

[1] Bridgewater Trust General Accounts, 1844–50 (Lancs. C.R.O.). The decline was partly counteracted by a slight improvement in the yield of the Trustees' own carrying trade. The loss on the Canal carrying department fell from £5,709 in 1848 to £1,837 in 1849, whilst the profits of the (estuarial) steam towage department rose from £4,430 to £5,067. For the over-all profits of the Canal and carrying business together, see below, Appendix A.

[2] 'Statement on the Part of the Bridgewater Trustees, etc.'

[3] F. Smith to G. Loch, 12 Feb. 1850, L.E.P.

[4] 'Statement on the Part of the Bridgewater Trustees, etc.'

[5] F. Smith to G. Loch, 13 Feb. 1850, L.E.P.

the truce of 7 January did little to allay. As was to be expected, the principal irritant was the question of the forward rates which had not been adequately settled by that agreement. When the L. & N.W. and L. & Y. Companies began at their own discretion to restore these charges in January and February 1850, they fixed them at levels which did not allow a sufficient margin above the Liverpool and Manchester rates to satisfy the Duke's Trustees. The latter complained in the above-mentioned statement of the case which they submitted to an arbitrator that there was no margin at all. This was not true, at least not in every case, as the Loch–Egerton correspondence makes clear,[1] but the L. & N.W. Company appears to have infringed the January agreement, at least as far as the Trustees recalled it, in the matter of the Sheffield rates.[2] The Trustees themselves, however, were equally guilty of a breach of the arrangement, for through inadvertence they allowed their commission agents to continue granting to their customers certain accommodations which they had consented to forego.[3] Moreover, with a view to countering the low railroad charges upon the forward trade, they again permitted discounts from the standard Liverpool and Manchester rates to spinners who collected their cotton in their own carts. The effect of this action was to jeopardize the entire rate structure east of Liverpool. On 11 February 1850 Captain Laws of the L. & Y. wrote to George Loch expressing his company's determination

to consider themselves entirely absolved from any existing arrangement as regards charges between Liverpool and Manchester unless the system now regularly practised by the agents (and, as it appears, with the Trustees' sanction) of delivering goods at Manchester for less than the rates agreed upon by yourself on the part of the Trustees [ceases].[4]

Faced with a rapidly deteriorating situation, the Trustees became alarmed, and the solution of ceding traffic to the railways with a view to preserving charges on that which was

---

[1] The L. & N.W.R. Company proposed to make the Stockport rate higher than the Manchester rate by 1*s*. 8*d*. on certain classes of goods, by 2*s*. 6*d*. on a further class, and by 5*s*. 0*d*. on yet another (G. Loch to F. Smith, 4 Feb 1850, ibid.).

[2] F. Smith to B. Poole, 26 Jan. 1850, ibid.

[3] 'Statement on the Part of the Bridgewater Trustees, etc.'

[4] J. M. Laws to G. Loch, 11 Feb. 1850, L.E.P.

retained took shape in their minds: '. . . we must really consider the value of this forward trade', wrote George Loch to Fereday Smith on 9 February, 'in comparison with the importance of maintaining rates on all the other trade of the navigations.'[1] Three days later he added:

I have no fear of the L. & N.W. Co. being desirous of provoking a renewal of hostilities. They have something to lose. Not so the L. & Y. Of trade between Liverpool and Manchester I apprehend they have not gained much, and therefore they would feel less seriously the effects of contest, and it may be worth while to make some concession that shall have the double effect of benefitting them and increasing the stake they have in the continuance of peace. . . . Would giving up the Rochdale and Heywood trade satisfy Laws?[2]

In the ensuing months, therefore, the Trustees were in the ironical situation of having to contrive means of disposing of traffic which had become an embarrassment to them. At the beginning of April they decided to withdraw the allowances to road carriers by which the trade between Liverpool and places in the Rossendale area (Haslingden, Rawtenstall, and Ewood Bridge), remote from the banks of any navigation, had been retained on their canals. This step was taken partly on grounds of general principle, viz. that 'to retain a footing in that district is not to shew the capabilities of canal traffic as opposed to railway traffic, but to try and pit carting on the high road against the economy and advantages of railway transit'; partly, however, it was 'to avoid the risk of provoking the E.L. Railway'.[3] In June they withdrew the cartage allowances to the spinners which had enabled them to compete with the L. & N.W. and L. & Y. Railways for the trade between Liverpool and Heywood, Rochdale, Littleborough, Todmorden, Oldham, Ashton-under-Lyne, Stalybridge, and Stockport.[4]

Not content with merely abandoning trade, they took positive steps to transfer it to the rails. In the course of June they negotiated an agreement with the Lancashire and Yorkshire Railway Company whereby they were constituted agents of that company between Liverpool and Manchester and

---

[1] G. Loch to F. Smith, 9 Feb. 1850, L.E.P.
[2] G. Loch to F. Smith, 12 Feb. 1850, ibid.
[3] G. Loch to F. Smith, 30 Mar. and 4 Apr. 1850, ibid.
[4] Draft circular enclosed in F. Smith to G. Loch, 6 June 1850, ibid.

between Liverpool and the forward towns, Oldham, Middleton, Heywood, Rochdale, Ashton-under-Lyne, and Stalybridge. The idea of the arrangement as outlined in a memorandum which was being discussed by the parties earlier in the month was that they should place their own traffic and that of their commission agents upon the Lancashire and Yorkshire Railway either for the whole journey from Liverpool or at a junction between the Manchester, Bolton, and Bury Canal and the railroad at Ringspiggot in Salford. If they carried throughout by rail, they would receive a commission of $12\frac{1}{2}$ per cent calculated upon the prevailing Liverpool and Manchester rate. If they carried by water as far as Ringspiggot, they would pay to the Railway Company the difference between the charge to the customer and the full rate of freight usually charged between Liverpool and Manchester. The charge to the Trustees would cover the tolls on the Manchester, Bolton, and Bury Canal, and the Railway Company would allocate to them free of charge accommodation at Ringspiggot for effecting the trans-shipment. The arrangement was to be for five years.[1]

For the Duke's Trustees this agency agreement was a necessary corollary of a wider arrangement which they had made with both the L. & N.W. and L. & Y. Companies on 8 June for so dividing the Liverpool and Manchester traffic (which included that portion of the forward trade which changed bottoms in Manchester) as to give to the two Bridge-water navigations one-half of it. On any excess above the moiety the Trustees were to pay to the railway companies 5s. per ton in compensation, and as at the time of the making of the agreement they were conveying far more than a half of the trade by water, it became urgently necessary to carry some of it by rail if the payment of a large amount of compensation was to be avoided. Moreover, some of the commission agents, notably Carvers and MacKays, were beginning to send goods by the L. & Y.R. on their own initiative, and there was much to be said from the Trustees' point of view for bringing the process under their own control lest it be carried too far.[2] For

---

[1] In F. Smith to G. Loch, 7 June 1850, ibid.

[2] G. Loch to F. Smith, 9 June 1850; F. Smith to G. Loch, 24 June 1850; memorandum enclosed in F. Smith to G. Loch, 28 Nov. 1850: H. Booth to G. Loch, 15 Nov. 1850, ibid.

their own part the Trustees would gladly have steered clear of compensation agreements altogether. They would have preferred to return to the old type of rate-fixing arrangement with no provisions as to quantities, but the railway companies would not hear of this. They were obliged, therefore, to acquiesce in such an arrangement as a means of obtaining the assent of the railways to the pegging of rates, and the agreement of 8 June which embodied it also provided for the fixing of charges in the Liverpool and Manchester trade.

Thus it may be seen that the Bridgewater Trustees deliberately and of their own accord threw away canal trade for the purpose of ensuring a high return on what they kept. The policy went against the grain. James Loch at first vetoed any suggestion that the Trust should become a carrier by rail between Liverpool and Manchester. His view was that the

character of carriers is forced on the Trustees by circumstances. It should be restricted as much as possible, and rendered subordinate to their true and more important position as owners of a Navigation, and it does not seem consistent with true policy to take a ton of goods from their Canals that they can induce to remain there.[1]

It was Fereday Smith, the General Manager, who worked out the agency scheme in conjunction with Captain Laws of the L. & Y. Railway. The Lochs merely assented to it as a sad necessity, and endeavoured to ensure that the diversion of traffic from the canals to the railways should be done 'in such manner as not to weaken or diminish in any way the inherent strength and vitality' of the canals and to avoid the possibility of its being operated 'more fatally and extensively than we intended'.[2] Nevertheless, the total traffic of the Duke's Canal fell from 1,536,715 tons in 1849 to 1,460,572 tons in 1850,[3] whilst the Liverpool and Manchester portion declined from 294,595 tons to 254,680 tons.[4] The losses were not outstanding, insufficient even to cancel out the gains of the preceding year. They appear more significant, however, when it is recalled that the general trade of the country was improving during this period.

[1] G. Loch to F. Smith, 14 Feb. 1850, L.E.P.
[2] G. Loch to F. Smith, 1 Oct. 1850, ibid.
[3] See below, Appendix B.   [4] Jackman, op. cit., p. 741.

The policy reflects on the one hand the shaping of a new role for the canal proprietors as collectors and distributors of goods for the railways. Already apparent in the agreement with the Birkenhead Railway Company in 1846, this role was to be further emphasized in negotiations with the Shrewsburys and the Great Western in the early fifties. On the other hand, it signifies a failure of nerve on the Trustees' part. The sharply diminished profits of 1849 operated as a sore and bitter remembrance in their minds, and their willingness in 1850 to surrender trade in the hope of avoiding a further contest contrasts markedly with the more truculent mood in which they had approached the conflict in the early months of the preceding year. There were other indications, too, in 1850 that their confidence in the staying power of their principal asset, the Canal, was on the wane. In March they were seriously considering memorializing the Board of Trade for governmental protection in the unequal struggles between canals and railways.[1] Previously James Loch had bitterly opposed the idea of an appeal by the waterways to the government, thinking that a parliamentary enactment could only be obtained at the price of Board of Trade interference with the freedom of the navigation owners. When some of the canal companies petitioned the Board for a relaxation of the restrictions upon their power of making partial tonnage charges, he warned them against adopting such a course.[2] It was in 1850, too, that the Trustees began to devote attention to the development of their other resources. In the following year, encouraged by the return of prosperity to Lancashire, they obtained from Parliament an Act to facilitate the leasing of their estates for building purposes. Their object, as stated in a memorandum drawn up by James Loch, was to give Lord Ellesmere 'an income, upon which he can depend, especially when other means of conveyance, and the rapid changes in the progress of the district renders the income dependent upon the Canal Revenue less certain and subject to fluctuation'.[3]

Any hopes which the Trustees may have entertained that the measures which they adopted to surrender traffic to the

[1] G. Loch to F. Smith, 11 Mar. 1850, L.E.P.
[2] G. Loch to F. Smith, 12 and J. Loch to F. Smith 18 June 1844, ibid.
[3] Memorandum written by James Loch at Runcorn, 10 Dec. 1851, ibid.

railway companies would ensure the future stability of rates were quickly to be dashed. Despite all that had been done, the two railway companies failed to make good their claim to the half share of the traffic which the agreement of 8 June had accorded them.[1] This was partly, no doubt, because of the weakness of the L. & Y., which did not possess sufficient accommodation at Manchester to handle its half of the share of the Manchester traffic proper allocated to the railway companies. The situation bred dissatisfaction on both sides—in the Trustees, who resented having to compensate the railways for traffic of which they could not rid themselves, and in the L. & N.W.R. directors, who aspired to appropriate that portion of the railway allocation which the L. & Y. could not command.[2] Matters took a turn for the worse in the last three months of the year when the railway companies and the carriers on the Trustees' navigations began to accuse one another with great vehemence of filching their customers by reducing rates and offering additional facilities. The allegations do not appear to have been unfounded, and although it is difficult to be certain in the atmosphere of accusation and counter-accusation who began this cut-throat competition, the greatest suspicion attaches to the New Quay Company, a large carrying firm operating upon the Mersey and Irwell Navigation which had been excluded from the commission agency agreements and was, therefore, less amenable to discipline by the Trustees than most of the other carriers. The Trustees did their best to stop the rot. They even terminated the agency of the Grocers' Company on 12 December on the strength of allegations made against it by Captain Laws of the L. & Y.[3] But it was all to no avail. By the beginning of the new year the agreement between the Trust and the railway

---

[1] At the beginning of August 1850 George Loch drafted a letter to the L. & N.W.R. Company pointing out that the agency agreement with the L. & Y.R. had not proved sufficient to divert a half of the traffic to the railways, and requesting that the L. & N.W.R. would enter into a similar agreement with them in order to reduce their liability to an excess payment. Draft enclosed in G. Loch to F. Smith, 1 Aug. 1850, L.E.P.

[2] F. Smith to G. Loch, 4 Feb. 1851, ibid.

[3] J. Peacock to F. Smith, 13 Dec. 1850. For evidence of the charges referred to above, see copy of letter from Murgatroyd enclosed in F. Smith to G. Loch, 26 Nov. 1850; also G. Loch to F. Smith, 28 Nov. 1850, and F. Smith to G. Loch, 11 Dec. 1850, ibid.

companies was at an end,[1] and a new contest comparable with that of 1849 was under way.

Although they may not have been principally responsible for the resumption of hostilities, once the fighting had commenced the railway companies assailed the canal trade with every weapon at their command. The attack was two-pronged. On the one hand the freight charges to the public were savagely reduced so as to embarrass the Trustees and their carriers. In January 1851 the L. & N.W.R. and L. & Y. Companies lowered the charges on raw cotton for Ashton, Stalybridge, and Oldham to the same level as the Liverpool and Manchester rate, thus allowing the canals no margin at all for the forwarding expenses from Manchester if they wished to compete effectively for the trade. The cotton rates to Mossley and Stockport were also reduced by the L. & N.W.R., and by the middle of February the Liverpool and Manchester charges were seriously affected. The L. & N.W.R. was quoting 5*s.* per ton on cotton for Manchester and the same rate to Stockport, to which place the charge had previously been 10*s.* 8*d.* During the following month, March, the competition waxed more intense, reductions extending from cotton to zinc and guano.[2] At the same time as they lowered rates, however, the railway companies made a determined bid to seduce the canal carriers from their allegiance to the navigations. At the beginning of January, Captain Laws offered to allow McKay to farm the L. & Y. station at Ashton, i.e. to find clerks, porters, carts, etc., at so much per ton, if he would carry by rail. He hinted that in the event of the offer's being refused he would establish a new railway carrier at Ashton. Carvers already had a similar arrangement with the company in respect of one or two places in Yorkshire.[3] About the same time Braithwaite Poole, acting for the L. & N.W.R., went to almost all the canal carriers offering them premiums of 12½ to 30 per cent if they would put their trade on the railway and playing up the carriers' grievances against the Trustees.[4]

Thanks to the commission agency agreements, the Duke's

[1] G. Loch to F. Smith, 5 Jan. 1851, ibid.

[2] William Jackson & Sons to F. Smith, 13 Jan. 1851; F. Smith to G. Loch, 30 Jan. 1851; F. Smith to G. Loch, 15 Feb. 1851; F. Smith to G. Loch, 8 Mar. 1851, ibid.   [3] F. Smith to G. Loch, 6 Jan. 1851, ibid.

[4] F. Smith to G. Loch, 7 Jan. 1851, ibid.

Trustees were in a stronger position to control their carriers than on many similar occasions in the past. Their assent was necessary before the latter could become agents for the railway companies and, officially at least, they controlled the rates which could be quoted to the public. These powers were used in restraint of competition, for George Loch was almost indifferent to the loss of traffic. He was quite prepared to allow the carriers to transfer a certain portion of it from the water to the rails, peacefully and without a struggle, if this would serve to avoid a downward pressure upon the rates of carriage. Thus he suggested to Fereday Smith at the end of January 1851 that the Trustees might consider issuing a circular authorizing the agents to put trade on the L. & N.W.R. provided that they did so at the full rates prevailing before the reductions began.[1] He saw no objection to the railway companies' annexing one half of the traffic provided that the Trustees took every step to defend the other half.[2] His real concern was still to maintain profitable charges, and with that end in view he imposed a brake upon reductions by the carriers. He began by requiring them to give written proof that the railway companies had made abatements before following suit.[3] This stringent requirement was abandoned on 18 January when 'reasonable proofs' were admitted in the place of written evidence,[4] but the agents were not given a completely free hand. They were told by Fereday Smith late in March that they must communicate with himself or Marsden before making any further reductions, and that they must in no case go below 5*s*. per ton or below cost price.[5] In other ways, too, the Trustees interfered with the freedom of their agents to compete. When the railway companies started to enter into contracts with their customers to supply them with cotton for six months or even longer, Loch gave permission for the Trust to do likewise. He nevertheless insisted that the contracts should be 'only in particular cases and for as short a period as possible'. Though he was prepared reluctantly to revive the system of allowances to customers in the forward

[1] G. Loch to F. Smith, 28 Jan. 1851, L.E.P.
[2] G. Loch to F. Smith, 6 Feb. 1851, ibid.
[3] G. Loch to F. Smith, 5 Jan. 1851, ibid.
[4] G. Loch to Marsden, 18 Jan. 1851, ibid.
[5] F. Smith to G. Loch, 27 Mar. 1851, ibid.

towns who would cart their goods away from Manchester, he insisted that no attempt should be made by means of extravagant discounts to retain the trade with Oldham and other distant places to which the railways had a decided advantage.[1] As the struggle intensified the restraints were relaxed, but their existence implied that the Bridgewater navigations entered the contest of 1851 with less than a full determination to defeat their opponents.

Hard pressed by the railway companies and hampered in their powers of retaliation by the Trustees, the canal carriers grew increasingly favourable to the idea of carrying by rail. At a meeting with George Loch and Fereday Smith on 5 April they asked that they should all be permitted to place a portion of their traffic upon the railways. Jackson & Sons, Thompson MacKay & Co., and the Merchants' Company were each to divert 8,000 tons of merchandize; Carver & Co. and Barnby, Faulkner & Co. were to send 6,000 tons each, Kenworthy & Co. 9,000 tons, and J. & J. Veevers 4,000 tons, making a total of 49,000 tons (about one-fifth of the total Liverpool and Manchester traffic carried by water in the previous year). Though not averse to a transfer, George Loch would have preferred that some of the carriers should have withdrawn to the rails altogether, leaving others entirely upon the canals. This solution would have enabled the Trustees to keep the transaction more firmly under their own control and within the bounds which were set. Nevertheless, he assented to the carriers' proposal provided that the Trustees retained the right to stop the transference of traffic should it be carried to excess.[2] It was not long, however, before the Trustees became alarmed that too much of their trade was leaking away to the rails. Their suspicions were aroused by a series of reports from their agent Marsden giving estimates of the quantity of traffic carried by rail and by water. Espionage was resorted to as a means of obtaining information about the railway traffic, for Braithwaite Poole of the London and North Western wrote in scornful tones to the manager of the Trust at the end of May:

Withdraw the man who has been peeping from the top story of your Botany Bay warehouse in Water Street during the last two

---

[1] G. Loch to F. Smith, 6 Feb. 1851, ibid.
[2] G. Loch to F. Smith, 5 Apr. 1851; F. Smith to G. Loch, 7 Apr. 1851, ibid.

months at every train of [the] L. & N.W. and L. & Y. companies to and from Liverpool, and counting the waggons. Send him to me and he shall see the books which will be much more information for you.[1]

The statements arrived at by these means suggested that from about the beginning of May onwards, if not earlier, the two railways were carrying very much more than a half of the traffic between Liverpool and Manchester conveyed by rail and water. The figures for the week ending 7 June were as follows:[2]

	Up goods	Down goods	Total
	tons	tons	tons
By rail	4,446	3,069	7,515
By water	4,408	1,828	6,236

Moreover, if anything, they underestimated the railway weight by about 1,000 or 1,200 tons.

This represented a greater loss of traffic than the Trustees could contemplate with any equanimity, and they were disposed to blame the carriers for diverting more than their allotted share. Fereday Smith observed that the railway companies were acquiring a large increase in trade 'with the help of the Canal machinery, by which the Navigations would naturally secure the larger proportion of the traffic'.[3] Further investigation, however, rendered this conclusion suspect. A report received by the Trustees from one of their employees named Brydon early in June revealed that none of the carriers was placing an undue proportion of trade upon the railways except Barnby, Faulkner & Co. and the Merchants' Company, and when the Merchants' Company were questioned about this, they explained that the great bulk of the traffic which they were sending by the Lancashire and Yorkshire Railway would have gone by rail even if they had not been the instruments of sending it.[4] Moreover, the L. & N.W. Company complained later in the year that the Trustees' carriers had dispatched by rail a good deal less than they had promised. According

---

[1] B. Poole to F. Smith, 28 May 1851, L.E.P.
[2] G. Marsden to G. Loch, 10 June 1851, ibid.
[3] F. Smith to G. Loch, 7 May 1851, ibid.
[4] G. Loch to F. Smith, 4 June 1851 ; F. Smith to G. Loch, 14 June 1851, ibid.

to Braithwaite Poole they had undertaken to transmit 1,000 tons per week by the L. & N.W.R., but the weekly average attained over the period April to August (inclusive) had been only 348 tons.[1] A statement drawn up by the Trustees themselves for the three months ending 30 June showed a total of 9,143 tons (762 tons per week) by the L. & Y. and 6,618 tons (551 tons per week) by the L. & N.W.R.[2]

Evidence of this kind led the Trustees to revise their original assessment. By the middle of June Fereday Smith was convinced that factors other than the carrying by rail undertaken by the commission agents were responsible for the railway gains. 'The great cause . . . of the railway traffic being swollen', he wrote, 'is their cotton contracts and also the fact of their allowing the carriers as between Liverpool and Manchester a cartage out of the 5*s*. rate, while the Trustees (very properly I think) refuse to go below cost price.' He also mentioned a third influence, viz. that 'the recent state of the Liverpool cotton market had tended very much to increase the railway traffic in cotton'.[3] The price of raw cotton at Liverpool had fallen by as much as 60 or 70 per cent between January and the end of May 1851,[4] causing mill-owners to live from hand to mouth. Instead of building up stocks of depreciating material, they ordered up supplies when they were needed, and for this purpose found the speed and dispatch of the railways an advantage over the more leisurely proceedings of the canal carriers.[5]

Whilst the Trustees mulled over the reasons why the railway companies were gaining upon them between Liverpool, Manchester, and the forward towns, they found themselves confronted with railroad competition in a new and disturbing form. The growth of a national railway network was beginning to produce a re-routing of the country's export trade. Because railways cheapened and improved the long-distance traffic proportionately more than the short, London was able to reassert against Liverpool her function as an exporter of the manufactured produce of the north. The Bridgewater

---

[1] B. Poole to F. Smith, 30 Sept. 1851, ibid.
[2] F. Smith to G. Loch, 12 Aug. 1851, ibid.
[3] F. Smith to G. Loch, 14 June 1851, ibid.
[4] T. Tooke and W. Newmarch, *A History of Prices*, vol. v, pp. 260–1.
[5] F. Smith to G. Loch, 22 Apr. 1851, L.E.P.

Trustees suffered from the change both indirectly and directly. Indirectly because, as the Great Northern Company, whose line ran along the eastern side of England from London to York, was endeavouring to divert the export traffic in Sheffield steel for America from Liverpool to London by under-cutting charges, the L. & N.W.R. and M.S. & L. Companies jointly reduced their through rate by rail from Sheffield to Liverpool from 23s. 4d. to 20s. per ton. This rebounded on the traffic trans-shipped from the M.S. & L. to the Bridgewater Canal at Manchester.[1] Directly, because the L. & N.W.R. route to London was gaining on both canals and railways between Manchester and Liverpool for the carriage of bales and cases of Manchester cottons destined for India and China. On inquiry from some mercantile houses in Manchester, the Trustees gained the impression that their loss of the trade was due more to the better shipping facilities offered by the capital than to any machinations of the L. & N.W.R. board. The Londoners had put on regular lines of packets which sailed periodically and punctually, and the London shipbrokers were offering to give the merchant or broker the consignment of a vessel at the Indian or Chinese terminus provided that he furnished a certain amount of backloading for her in the capital. It was later alleged, however, that the L. & N.W.R. directors were encouraging the diversion by charging a lower rate per ton for goods sent from Manchester to London in bulk than that which they exacted on the same commodities conveyed in smaller quantities.[2]

Despite the widening of the area of the conflict, the Trustees continued to pull their punches. They accepted the threat from London with an almost fatalistic resignation, acquiescing almost without question in the view that the whole matter was outside the control of the overland carriers and that only the Liverpool shipowners could do anything to correct the balance of advantage. In the original struggle with the railways between Liverpool, Manchester, and the forward towns they were not much less nonchalant. They were prepared to act, perhaps at expense, to prevent further loss of traffic.

---

[1] Barnby, Faulkner & Co. to F. Smith, 5 May 1851, L.E.P.

[2] F. Smith to G. Loch, 14 June 1851 ; Pendlebury to F. Smith, 15 Oct. 1851, ibid.

In July they allowed, and may have assisted, their timber carriers to shoulder the cost of carting in Liverpool. This was to counter a bid by the Lancashire and Yorkshire Railway Company to capture the timber trade between Liverpool and Manchester and a number of the forward towns.[1] They were by no means disposed, however, to make sacrifices to win back the cotton trade from the railway whilst the existing low rate of freight on cotton ruled. They appeared content with their existing trade, reduced though it was, on the grounds that the present averages would yield them an income of nearly £40,000 per annum on the Liverpool and Manchester traffic after the expense of steam towage on the estuary had been deducted.[2] All was by no means lost, and their half-hearted exertions to compete during the contest of 1851 were a sign not of the paralysis of despair but of returning confidence, confidence to survive upon a modest scale.

That is not to say that the Trustees were content with the *status quo*. They earnestly desired to see a restoration of the rates of carriage to the level prevailing before the contest, and in August 1851 they were negotiating with both the L. & N.W.R. and the L. & Y. to achieve this end. At the end of the month they succeeded in obtaining agreement to raise the freight of cotton between Liverpool and Manchester to 8s. per ton plus an extra shilling per ton for delivery at the customers' premises. The arrangement took effect from 1 October, but it did not include the forward rates, on account of the opposition of the L. & Y. Company which was bent on making such charges as would drive off the spinners' carts and divert the trade permanently from the water to the rails.[3] The position as it was thus left was by no means satisfactory to the Trustees. Although about two-thirds of their entire gross trade stopped at Manchester, four-fifths of the traffic in raw cotton travelled on beyond that city to supply the mills of the outlying towns.[4] Moreover, as they saw it, the forward trade was likely to grow in importance, for the daily increasing desire to have goods from hand to mouth rendered it unlikely that Manchester

[1] Letters from the Harrington Carrying Company and Brockbanks to the Trustees, 10 July 1851 ; F. Smith to G. Loch, 14 July 1851, ibid.

[2] F. Smith to G. Loch, 14 June 1851, ibid.

[3] F. Smith to G. Loch, 2 Sept. 1851, and enclosed draft circulars, ibid.

[4] F. Smith to G. Loch, 8 May 1851, ibid.

could long remain the market for articles of consumption. Furthermore they had been forced by the railway companies to assent to a charge for down goods which was so high as to promise to divert the traffic progressively to the rails.[1] The old differential on which they had relied so much to retain their hold upon it had not been restored. Negotiations were resumed, therefore, in March 1852 and dragged on until the following October. The Trustees were working for a restoration of the original margin between the Manchester and forward rates, and as a means of satisfying the railway companies over quantities were prepared to offer to join with them in a common purse into which the freight charges drawn by the contracting parties should be paid, to be later divided between them when the working expenses had been deducted. The railroad directors preferred a different kind of arrangement— for dividing the traffic into equal parts—and those of the L. & Y. held out for an equalization of rates between the Manchester and forward trades.[2] Consequently there was never for long a meeting of minds between the negotiators, and the outcome was inconclusive.

The sharp contest, however, which opened in the first six months of 1851 slowly died down in the second half of the year. The Duke's Trustees emerged from it chastened but not routed. Their Liverpool and Manchester traffic had fallen by 63,865 tons from 1850 to 1851 (i.e. by some 15 per cent)[3] and the railways had for the first time taken the lead over the canals in the trade between Liverpool and the towns of southern Lancashire. Moreover, the agreed framework within which the traffic was conducted, had been further adjusted to the Trustees' disadvantage, and there were prospects of a further deterioration of their trading position in the future. They had also conceded to the railway companies the principle that their commission agents might carry by rail without binding the former to a satisfactory scale of charges in the forward trade. Originated as a temporary expedient to deal with a transient evil, the practice was in danger of becoming

---

[1] F. Smith to G. Loch, 24 Oct. 1851, L.E.P.

[2] G. Loch to F. Smith, 2 Mar. 1852; F. Smith to G. Loch, 8 Mar. 1852; G. Loch to F. Smith, 11 Oct. 1852, ibid.

[3] i.e. the aggregate tonnage of both the Duke's Canal and the Mersey and Irwell Navigation (Jackman, op. cit., p. 741).

permanent, and in Fereday Smith's view, at least, it threatened seriously to undermine the Trustees' ultimate position.[1] George Loch, on the other hand, with whom the final decision rested, was more confident, refusing to be rushed into any premature agreement with the Trustees' opponents for a permanent division of the traffic as a means of securing the revival of the differential on down goods.[2] He trusted to certain long-term developments in the railway world which were raising up rivals to the L. & N.W. and L. & Y. Companies, and hoped that by playing off railway against railway he would be able at length to bring the enemy to terms.[3] To grasp what lay beneath this policy of 'wait and see' we must look beyond the conflicts in the east–west traffic of southern Lancashire to happenings further south, for it was there that the Trustees' hopes principally lay.

[1] F. Smith to G. Loch, 6 Dec. 1851, L.E.P.
[2] G. Loch to F. Smith, 7 Dec. 1851, ibid.
[3] G. Loch to F. Smith, 28 Nov. 1851, ibid.

CHAPTER XI

The Quest of a New Ally (1851–1855)

THE early 1850s were still a time of opportunity for some of the larger industrial canals of Britain. Although the amalgamation movement which began in the middle of the preceding decade had called into being a number of vast railway empires which greatly intensified the pressure upon them, it had not yet proceeded far enough to create anything resembling a complete railroad monopoly, even upon a regional basis. The situation remained fluid, and there was room for one giant to encroach upon an area principally served by its neighbour. From such encroachments arose conflicts which a canal could sometimes turn to its advantage by backing one combatant against another.

The intrusion upon which the Duke of Bridgewater's Trustees relied to extract them from their difficulties was that of the Great Western into the area of the London and North Western. This was a slow, creeping development stretching over several years. In the beginning the G.W.R. directors were lured away from their natural province less by their own ambitions than by the blandishments of the Grand Junction Company which was then (in 1845) at variance with the London and Birmingham and anxious to obtain an alternative outlet to London and the south. The result was a scheme for building a railway from the Great Western's proposed Oxford and Rugby line at Fenny Compton to Birmingham. The project, known as the Birmingham and Oxford Junction Railway, was soon afterwards deserted by the Grand Junction, which executed a volte-face and amalgamated with its former enemy, but was carried forward by its other supporters and eventually incorporated into the Great Western by an Act passed in 1848. By the same measure the G.W.R. took over another as yet unbuilt line, the Birmingham, Wolverhampton, and Dudley, which would connect the Birmingham and Oxford at Birmingham with the already authorized Oxford, Worcester, and Wolverhampton Railway, the 'Old Worse and Worse', at Priestfield Junction, a mile or more south of Wolverhampton. Both Birmingham lines and the O.W. & W.R. were ordered to be built upon a mixed gauge, which could accommodate trains designed for use on either of the two conflicting systems, and their authorization promised, therefore, to carry the broad gauge of the Great Western effectively as far as Wolverhampton.

Events, however, were beckoning the G.W.R. even further north. The Shrewsbury and Birmingham and Shrewsbury and Chester Railway Companies, owners of two standard gauge lines, completed in 1849 to form a communication by rail between Chester and Wolverhampton, began, almost as soon as their lines were finished, to quarrel with the L. & N.W.R. over the traffic between Birmingham and the Black Country and Chester, Birkenhead, and Liverpool. The conflict was one of the most spectacular in railroad history, nearly resulting in a pitched battle between rival gangs of navvies at Wolverhampton. Eventually the two Shrewsbury companies turned for protection to the G.W.R., entering into a traffic agreement with that concern on 10 January 1851 and following this up early in May with an agreement for their future amalgamation with the Great Western. The eyes of Paddington were now fully open to the opportunities which presented themselves, for the Shrewsbury lines led on via the Chester and Birkenhead Railway, now part of the Birkenhead, Lancashire, and Cheshire Railway Company's system, to Birkenhead. Manchester, too, could be reached if the L. & N.W.R. would give running rights from Walton near Warrington, where the Birkenhead Company's new line from Chester (opened in December 1850) fed into what had formerly been the Grand Junction Railway. The cry of 'the Broad Gauge to the Mersey' had been raised, and to its appeal Charles Alexander Saunders, the Secretary of the G.W.R., was not immune.[1]

This ambition was one which the Duke's Trustees sought to encourage. They looked to a clash of interests between the

[1] E. T. MacDermot, *History of the Great Western Railway*, vol. i, p. 312.

Great Western and the North Western Companies, not only
to drive the latter to an amicable settlement of the issues
which had engendered the contest of 1851, but also to produce
a long-term, if not a permanent, arrangement for the future
of the Canal. For James Loch and his son George it had
become a major object of policy to dispose of some, if not all,
of the fluctuating assets of the Trust in order to secure to the
Earl of Ellesmere a more stable income. The Old River, with
its heavy burden of debt, was a liability of which they would
have been very glad to rid themselves. The idea of converting
it into a ship canal, which had been considered as early as 1840,
was revived right at the beginning of 1851, with the intention
of transferring the property to a joint stock company for the
execution of the work. There were obstacles, however, geographical and man-made, in the way of constructing the Canal,
and an alternative scheme for rendering the navigation saleable, by building a railway along its banks from Manchester to
Warrington to connect with a proposed line from Warrington
to Garston docks, was also suggested at that time.[1]

To dispose of the Duke of Bridgewater's Canal was a matter
of less urgency, but the two Lochs do seem to have considered
very earnestly the possibility of leasing the Liverpool and
Manchester traffic to either the L. & N.W.R. or the G.W.R.
Company, and it was to this aim that an encouragement of the
rivalry between the two rail concerns was relevant.

It would have been more natural and more desirable in all ways
[wrote George Loch on 25 October 1851] that some such proposal
should have proceeded from the companies already occupying the
district. This has not yet happened, and no indication has been
afforded that it is likely to happen. Whether it may spring from
the collision of interests that is about to occur consequent on the
efforts of the Great Western Co. to obtain a footing in this neighbourhood, proceeding either from the one party or the other, has
yet to be seen.[2]

An opportunity to exploit the division was first placed in
their hands not by the Great Western Company itself but by
its allies, 'the fighting Shrewsburys', as they have been called.
At the beginning of 1851 these two railways, locked in a

---

[1] E. Smith to F. Smith, 4 Jan. 1851, L.E.P.
[2] G. Loch to F. Smith, 25 Oct. 1851, ibid.

struggle with the London and North Western, were principally concerned to secure their communications with the Midlands and the south. The Shrewsbury and Birmingham line ended at Wolverhampton. The Great Western extended no further north than Banbury, to which town its Oxford and Rugby branch had been opened on 2 September 1850. If they were to carry London traffic to and from Lancashire in competition with the L. & N.W.R., the Shrewsbury companies would be obliged to span this gap. They needed help even if they were to reach Birmingham, for the Birmingham (Snow Hill), Wolverhampton, and Dudley Railway had not yet been begun, and the Stour Valley line which connected Wolverhampton with Birmingham (Navigation Street) was kept closed by the London and North Western Railway. It was clear to the Shrewsbury directors that the Midland waterways could provide a temporary solution to their problems until the links with the Great Western had been forged, for the Birmingham, Warwick, and Oxford Canals furnished a continuous line of communication by water between Wolverhampton and Banbury by way of Birmingham. Moreover, the canals could also help the railway companies by acting as collectors and distributors for them in the Midland district. The Birmingham area and the Black Country were literally honeycombed with canals and their branches which, sometimes with the aid of tramways, sometimes without, penetrated to the sites of the scattered ironworks and mines which the railways did not reach. Mr. Charles Hadfield in his comprehensive study of the canals of the west Midlands lists no fewer than sixty branch canals of the Birmingham Canal Navigations. He shows how, in the middle years of the nineteenth century, the Midland canal boats worked short distances between the collieries and ironworks and the railway interchange basins, performing the same function as a lorry working to a rail depot would now do. So useful, in fact, was the local canal network that it was still being extended in the 1840s and 1850s, and 'the fighting Shrewsburys' were not the only railway companies which attached importance to gaining a connection with it. In February 1855 the traffic manager of the O.W. & W.R. strongly supported the completion of railway basins at Tipton and Wolverhampton 'as it will be impossible to secure the heavy weight

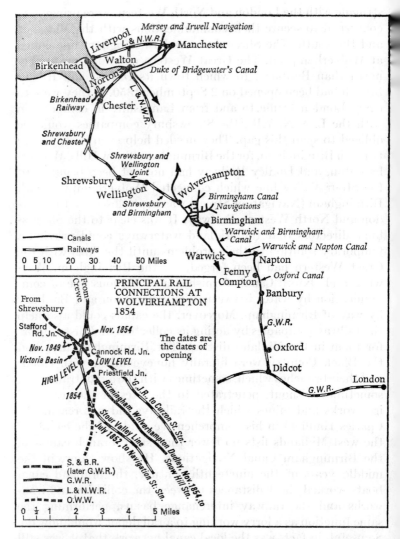

Map 4. Canal Connections of the Great Western and Shrewsbury Railways in the Midlands and North, December 1850

of traffic from works on the canals until we have the means of loading to and from the boats direct into the Railway waggons'.[1]

In pursuit of assistance from the waterways the Shrewsbury companies first addressed themselves to Shipton & Co., the carriers on the Midland canals. The negotiation was undertaken by the directors of the Shrewsbury and Birmingham Railway who approached Shiptons to carry parcels and passengers for them by van or swift packet between Banbury and Wolverhampton and to act as their general agents in collecting and delivering in the South Staffordshire area both for the northern and for the southern traffic. Shiptons, finding themselves precluded from performing the second of these functions by their agreement of 1849 with the Bridgewater Trustees, took steps at the end of January 1851 to bring the latter into the deal. It was now proposed that the Trustees should themselves become collectors and distributors for the Shrewsbury and Birmingham Railway in South Staffordshire, using for the purpose the stock of boats and carts which they had taken over from the North Staffordshire Railway Company and from Shiptons under the 1849 agreements. Shiptons would then be limited to carrying the Railway Company's through traffic between Wolverhampton and Banbury. Fereday Smith, however, seeing the possibility of extracting from the situation a larger advantage than was contemplated in the original proposition, went straight to the Chairman and Secretary of the Shrewsbury and Birmingham Company at the beginning of February, and ignoring Shipton & Co., proposed to those officers a wider arrangement which was designed to benefit the Trustees as canal owners further north. This was to the effect that all the trade between the Shrewsbury lines and Manchester and between those railways and Yorkshire should be trans-shipped from the Birkenhead railroad either to the Mersey and Irwell Navigation at Walton near Warrington or to the Duke of Bridgewater's Canal at Norton, provided that Sir Richard Brooke, a powerful landowner at the latter place, whose hostility to the Trustees was almost implacable, could be persuaded to release the land for constructing a transshipping place. It was also suggested that the Trustees should

[1] C. Hadfield, *The Canals of the West Midlands*, pp. 258–60; see also pp. 254–5.

convey the Shrewsbury Company's Liverpool trade across the Mersey estuary from Birkenhead in their flats.

Walker, the Chairman of the Shrewsbury and Birmingham Board, and Knox the Secretary responded favourably to Fereday Smith's proposal, making it clear that they preferred Norton to Walton as the place of trans-shipment because the absence of locks on the Bridgewater Canal would ensure a speedier transit to Manchester. They expressed anxiety to meet the Trustees upon it and requested Fereday Smith to attend a meeting of the joint board of the Great Western and Shrewsbury lines in London. One great inducement to them to accede was that the Bridgewater Trustees had abundant warehouse accommodation in Manchester and that, as most of the foundries lay upon the banks of the canals there, they would save themselves the cost of cartage from the railway station if they entered the town by water. Indeed, it was even doubtful whether they could get into Manchester by any other route, for their jealous rival the L. & N.W.R. refused to allow them running rights over its own line between Warrington and Manchester.[1] Fereday Smith had grounds, therefore, for congratulating himself upon the success of his diplomacy. The arrangement in which he had interested the Shrewsbury directors promised solid gains to the Duke's Trustees. It would turn the Shrewsbury lines and the G.W.R., too, into feeders of one or the other of the Bridgewater navigations and enable those waterways to recover by rail the traffic from the south of England and South Wales which had been lost as a through water trade. It would give the Trustees a line of communication with the south which would remain open when the Grand Trunk Canal was frozen. Furthermore, it would diminish the inducement to the Shrewsbury companies to support the construction of yet another line of rail communication between Liverpool and Manchester. As things stood they were disposed to favour Harrison Blair's project for a railroad from Warrington to Altrincham as a means of overcoming the L. & N.W.R.'s opposition to their entry into Manchester.[1] Finally, as the Trustees were well aware, by turning themselves into a vital link in a chain that could let the G.W.R. into Manchester,

[1] Full particulars of the opening phase of the negotiations are given in F. Smith to G. Loch, 5 Feb. 1851, L.E.P.

they would enhance their bargaining power both with that company and with the L. & N.W.R. The ultimate result might be the long-desired offer of a lease or purchase. At all events there would be a lever for bringing the L. & N.W.R. to reasonable terms in the contest which was in progress between Liverpool, Manchester, and the forward towns.[1]

Negotiations were soon placed upon a formal basis. About the beginning of March the two Shrewsbury companies and the Great Western applied for an appointment with G. Loch in London, and Fereday Smith was on the point of drawing up a proposal for submission to the former, when hopes of a speedy agreement were suddenly dashed by the intervention of the London and North Western.[2] Anxious to separate the Shrewsbury companies from the Great Western and thus to forestall the threatened broad gauge invasion of the north-west, Captain Huish, the indomitable General Manager of the London and North Western, had resorted to the device of buying up Shrewsbury and Birmingham shares and distributing them among the L. & N.W.R. employees with a view to creating a fifth column in the ranks of the Shrewsbury company. After a good deal of manœuvring stretching over several weeks, he eventually induced a special and half-yearly meeting of the proprietors of the S. & B. Company, held between 4 and 8 April, to carry a resolution handing over the company's line and rolling-stock to the L. & N.W.R. for 21 years and to appoint a batch of opposition 'directors' who could be relied upon to thwart the wishes of the true board.[3] Perceiving the incompatibility of L. & N.W.R. control with their own designs, the Bridgewater Trustees withdrew from the negotiations with the Shrewsburys.[4] They did so prematurely, at a time when Saunders of the Great Western was assuring them on behalf of the joint traffic committee of the three railways that 'there is no reason why an arrangement with the Duke's Trustees should be postponed on account of the threatened agreement between the L. & N.W. and the Shrewsbury and Birmingham companies'.[5]

---

[1] See above, pp. 216–24; also G. Loch to F. Smith, 28 Nov. 1851, L.E.P.
[2] G. Loch to G. Skey, 2 Mar. 1851; F. Smith to G. Loch, 8 Mar. 1851, ibid.
[3] MacDermot, op. cit., vol. i, pp. 363–6.
[4] G. Loch to F. Smith, 21 Mar. 1851, L.E.P.
[5] C. A. Saunders to F. Smith, 17 Mar. 1851, ibid.

During the next four months, from the end of March to the end of July, they fell back upon developing the trade which they passed along the traditional highway connecting their navigation with the Midlands and the south—the Grand Trunk Canal. With this object in view they drew closer to the North Staffordshire Railway Company, and prevailed upon the directors to reduce the toll on iron ore passing along the Trunk from 1s. 1½d. to 6¾d. per ton. They afterwards used this reduction and a similar one made by the Staffordshire and Worcestershire Canal Company to build up a carrying trade in Cumberland ores through Runcorn and Preston Brook to the Black Country. They were assisted in this by George Skey, a prominent figure in the water carrying trade of the Midlands, who established himself in business as an iron ore merchant and sent consignments to south Staffordshire in the Trustees' boats, selling them to the ironmasters at cost price. By these means they were able to compete with the Shropshire Union Canal route through Ellesmere Port and with the Shrewsbury and Chester and Shrewsbury and Birmingham Railways, which imported the ore through Saltney Wharf. The growing iron ore trade helped to fill the space in their boats left by the loss of the limestone traffic, which had previously been carried down the Trent and Mersey Canal from Froghall to the Black Country but which had recently been ousted by cheaper Derbyshire limestone brought by railway.[1] Meanwhile plans were afoot for cementing further an alliance between the Trustees and the North Staffordshire Company. Negotiations were opened for relieving the Welsh and Shropshire canal trades of the burden of the Middlewich Junction toll, for enabling the Trustees to take over the remaining carrying trade conducted by the Railway Company on the Trent and Mersey Canal, and for sundry other adjustments.[2]

The Trustees seemed incapable, however, of pursuing a single consistent line of policy for long, and in the month of August, whilst still in treaty with the North Staffordshire, they resumed the attempt to reach an accommodation with

[1] F. Smith to G. Loch, 28 June, 16 and 17 July, and 3 Oct. 1851; Bantock to F. Smith, 15 and 19 Aug. 1851, L.E.P.

[2] F. Smith to G. Loch, 20 Mar. and 22 July 1851; G. Loch to F. Smith, 21 Mar. and 30 June 1851, ibid.

the Shrewsburys, whose interests were in several important respects diametrically opposed to those of the Trent and Mersey Canal. Captain Huish's attempt to dominate the Shrewsbury and Birmingham and a later bid to command the Shrewsbury and Chester had both been defeated by 16 July, and the shareholders of the two companies had accepted terms which bound them for the future to the Great Western.[1] The three allies then prepared to resume negotiations with the Bridgewater people for filling the gaps in their system. On 26 August Robert Roy, the Secretary of the Shrewsbury and Chester Company, submitted a proposal which was virtually to the effect that the Trustees should bind themselves to transmit all their South Staffordshire traffic by the allied railways, in return for which the allies would, it was presumed, give to the Trustees all that they were able to command. This proposition surprised the Trustees. It both went beyond, and fell short of, what was contemplated in earlier discussions. It went beyond in requiring a transfer of all traffic. The very most that the Trustees were prepared to envisage was that, in addition to collecting and distributing actual railway traffic in South Staffordshire and in Lancashire, they should undertake to work the whole of their own goods traffic, and such portion of the iron trade as might be agreed upon, to the south of their own waterway by the Shrewsbury railroads. Even this was a mere suggestion put forward by Fereday Smith as a means of reaching agreement; it is by no means certain that the Lochs would have approved it. To commit themselves to such a wholesale diversion of canal traffic as the railway promoters proposed was to risk alienating the proprietors of both the Trent and Mersey and Staffordshire and Worcestershire Canals and driving them to measures of retaliation. It would certainly put an end to the policy of promoting good relations with the North Staffordshire Railway Company which had been pursued not without success of late, and it was George Loch's view that 'our natural relations will in the end be found to be on this (the North Staffordshire Railway) side'. A commitment of so binding a character to the Great Western group would, moreover, stand in the way of the Trustees' prospects of leasing the tolls of the Bridgewater Canal to the London

[1] MacDermot, op. cit., vol. i, pp. 367–9.

and North Western Railway, an enterprise on which they were disposed to look with a good deal of favour. A further obstacle to the proposed arrangement was that by the agreement of 18 July 1849, under which they leased the tolls of the Grand Trunk Canal, the Bridgewater Trustees had guaranteed to the North Staffordshire Railway Company a minimum toll of £13,000 per annum for a period of seven years. If they now diverted all their southward trade to the Shrewsbury railways, they would be diminishing the income from tolls out of which they should defray this charge.

Roy's proposition, however, also fell short of the Trustees' expectations in that it provided for an arrangement lasting only for 'a definite period'.[1] They were looking for an agreement acceptable to themselves which would be rendered permanent by an Act of Parliament. In other words, they wanted to remain free as far as possible to send goods southwards either by rail or by water whilst binding the Shrewsbury railways *in perpetuo* by statute to send all their Liverpool trade across the Mersey in the Trustees' boats.

The difference of view was sufficient to set back the negotiations for about two months, and might have ended them altogether had it not been for a dramatic change of circumstances which gave the Trustees an additional motive to conclude an alliance with the Shrewsburys. During the month of October they became aware of the danger that the North Staffordshire Railway Company might lease its properties to the London and North Western Company. The North Staffordshire directors had suddenly started to promote new lines of railway with the object either of obtaining an outlet to the north and to the south or of compelling the Great Western or the London and North Western Companies to take their concern over.[2] Early in the following month they were in actual treaty with the L. & N.W.R. To the General Manager of the Bridgewater Trust it was abundantly clear that the L. & N.W.R. Board, which, unlike the North Staffordshire, commanded a through line of railway between the Midlands

---

[1] F. Smith to G. Loch, 28 Aug. 1851; G. Loch to F. Smith, 30 Aug. 1851; cf. F. Smith to G. Loch, 15 Aug. 1851, and enclosed memorandum drawn up at Worsley on 15 Aug., L.E.P.

[2] F. Smith to G. Loch, 17 Oct. 1851, ibid. See also H. Ellis, *British Railway History, 1830-76*, pp. 194-5.

and Lancashire, would have a vested interest in obstructing the trade of the Trent and Mersey Canal. He warned George Loch that if the treaty between the two railway companies was concluded 'it is possible that the toll on iron between Preston Brook and Haywood may be raised from $\frac{1}{2}d$. to $\frac{3}{4}d$. per ton per mile . . ., which would be fatal to the Trustees' Staffordshire trade in all probability'. This threat, he argued, furnished 'the chief anxiety to bring matters to a speedy conclusion' with the Shrewsburys, if only to ensure the Trustees of the means of communicating with the Midlands should the worst befall.[1] The attempt to reach an accommodation was, therefore, resumed. The task was a difficult one, however, for the Shrewsbury companies sought power to determine whether the Trustees' trade should go by rail or by water, whilst the Trustees aimed to retain a certain discretion in the matter.[2] It was also an object of policy with the latter to get the Trent and Mersey guarantee made a charge upon the receipts of the railway traffic, a suggestion which the Shrewsbury directors resisted.[3] Proposals and counter-proposals followed one another in quick succession, and the negotiations dragged on unpromisingly and inconclusively through the autumn and winter of 1851–2. A further obstacle presented itself in March 1852, when fresh doubts appeared as to whether the projected amalgamation of the Shrewsbury companies with the Great Western could be carried through. The Bill to effect this consolidation was held up by the Wharncliffe Standing Order of the House of Lords which required the approval of any such Bill by a majority of four-fifths of the shareholders of the constituent companies, and the Huish 'fifth column' was strong enough to prevent this majority from being obtained at either of the Shrewsbury meetings.[4] The Duke's Trustees became doubly averse to committing themselves to pass trade by the Shrewsbury companies when the G.W.R. was no longer likely to be party to the arrangement, for they feared that the L. & N.W. and G.W. Companies might manœuvre to deprive the Shrewsburys of the means of carrying on a Staffordshire

---

[1] F. Smith to G. Loch, 7 Nov. 1851, L.E.P.
[2] G. Loch to F. Smith, 16 Nov. 1851, ibid.
[3] F. Smith to G. Loch, 1 Nov., and G. Loch to F. Smith, 2 Nov. 1851, ibid.
[4] MacDermot, op. cit., vol. i, p. 382.

R

and Liverpool trade. Moreover, the withdrawal of the Great Western would deprive the Trustees of the through traffic to and from London which was an important element in their calculations.[1]

Suddenly, however, in May 1852 the situation was wrenched from stalemate by the news that the North Staffordshire Railway Company had come to terms with the L. & N.W.R., thus placing the Trent and Mersey Canal tolls at the mercy of the latter.

> Pray lose no time in expediting the agreement with the Shrews-bury companies [wrote George Loch to Fereday Smith]. If what I have heard today in the street be true, it is possible enough that they may soon become our only highway for traffic to the South.[2]

His instructions were promptly acted upon. The Trustees bound themselves to transfer a certain amount of their South Staffordshire trade to the Shrewsbury railways, though less than the directors had hoped for. The Preston Brook fly boats were to be taken off and the goods traffic as far as possible dispatched by rail, but it was to be left to the discretion of customers whether iron should go by railway or canal. In return for these concessions the Trustees were to be allowed to act as feeders of the Shrewsbury and Birmingham line at its eastern extremity. They were to run a fly boat service between Birmingham and Wolverhampton and to purchase gradually one or two more wagons with horses for the purpose of collect-ing and delivering by road in the South Staffordshire area.[3] Steps were also taken to implement as soon as possible the arrangements at the northern end of the railway system. The Liverpool traffic could pass immediately across the Mersey in the Trustees' boats, and in order to connect with Manchester the Shrewsbury and Chester Company pressed on with the construction of a short branch line from the Birkenhead Railway to the Duke of Bridgewater's Canal at Norton. The branch was opened to traffic on 19 October 1853.[4]

[1] F. Smith to G. Loch, 16 Apr. 1852, L.E.P.
[2] G. Loch to F. Smith, 6 May 1852, ibid.
[3] F. Smith to G. Loch, 8 and 27 May 1852, ibid.
[4] Grierson to F. Smith, 20 Oct. 1853, ibid.

Within a few months of entering into the agreement with the Shrewsbury companies, the Duke's Trustees were given an added incentive to make use of the facilities which it provided. During the second half of 1852 the iron trade between South Staffordshire and Liverpool was booming. So great was the expansion that by November the Trustees were having to divert the traffic to the Shrewsbury and Birmingham Railway in order to relieve the Canal. The supply of canal boats was very inelastic owing to the fact that the system by which the boatmen were expected to shoulder the expense of finding horses militated against an expansion in the number both of boatmen and of horses.[1] Paradoxically, too, the Trustees were prompted to put iron on the railways by the fact that, although the traffic was easy to obtain, it could not be carried profitably by water. The rate of freight had been driven down to a wholly unremunerative level by the warfare between the London and North Western and Shrewsbury and Birmingham Railway Companies over the right of the latter to run trains on the Stour Valley line (opened in July 1852) from Wolverhampton into Birmingham New Street station.[2]

Had they wished to do so the Bridgewater Trustees could have turned the trans-shipment agreement into a full-scale alliance. Twice during the summer of 1852 Fereday Smith was offered a directorship of the Shrewsbury and Chester.[3] The two Shrewsbury boards and the Great Western sought to enlist Lord Ellesmere's political influence to counteract the opposition to their amalgamation Bill which the London and North Western Railway Company was raising among the peers. George Loch, however, shrank from a complete commitment to the Great Western grouping.[4] His reasons were

---

[1] Bantock to F. Smith, 27 Nov., and F. Smith to G. Loch, 30 Nov. 1852, ibid. 'We were never doing more than we have been doing for the last fortnight', observed Bantock, the Trustees' agent at Wolverhampton.

[2] F. Smith to G. Loch, 16 Nov. 1852; G. Loch to F. Smith, 5 Apr. 1853, ibid.

[3] F. Smith to G. Loch, 28 June and 12 July 1852, ibid.

[4] He was willing to employ Lord Ellesmere's influence to procure the suspension of the Wharncliffe Order in the case of the Great Western Amalgamation Bill, but would not allow the Trust to take an active part in the amalgamation proceedings (G. Loch to F. Smith, 13 June 1852, ibid.). He sent a telegraph message from Manchester to Fereday Smith in London, ordering him not to accompany a deputation to Lord Beaumont on a matter purely of railway policy (G. Loch to F. Smith, 11 June 1852, ibid.).

expressed in a letter to Fereday Smith pressing him to refuse
the directorship:

The principal and the most difficult relations of the Trustees
must always be with the L. & N.W. Co. You know well the view
they take of G.W. proceedings and the jealousy with which they
regard the railways which are in alliance with that company.
They . . . were not inclined to look with much forbearance on the
steps recently taken by the Trustees to secure an outlet for their
traffic over those railways, but they could not find justification
even to themselves for raising any complaints, inasmuch as it was
so obvious that no other defensive course was left open to the
Trustees in consequence of the efforts making by them, the L. &
N.W. Co., to obtain possession of the Trent and Mersey Canal,
the natural highway of the Trustees' traffic to the South. If, however, you were to become a director of the Shrewsbury and
Chester railway, not only would the L. & N.W. Co. regard the
Trustees (through you) as being directly implicated in a course of
railway policy which they consider in the last degree hostile to
them, but they would see under another aspect the recent steps
taken by the Trustees to secure the branches at Norton and Walton.

There is, too, an additional matter to be borne in mind. The
Trustees' position relatively to the Ellesmere Port arrangement
is already one of considerable difficulty, and it is impossible to say
what view the Court will take of the arguments that will be adduced
by the Shropshire Union Company in their approaching effort to
oust the Trustees on the merits of the question. Undoubtedly their
pleas, whatever they may be, would receive greatly augmented
force, were it in their power to point to the fact that anyone so
nearly connected with the Trustees' affairs as you are was a
director on the board of the Shrewsbury and Chester Railway.[1]

To grasp the influences moulding this extreme caution, we
must bear in mind both the lingering hope which the Trustees
entertained that the London and North Western Company
might be the party to relieve them of their worries by leasing
the tolls of the Duke's Canal, and also the delicacy of the
situation which prevailed with respect to the east–west trade
between Liverpool and Manchester and places east of Manchester. Relations between the Duke's and the L. & N.W.
and L. & Y. Railway Companies had certainly improved since

[1] G. Loch to F. Smith, 29 June 1852, ibid. The Shropshire Union Canal
Company gave the Trustees notice to quit the premises at Ellesmere Port in
July 1852 (F. Smith to G. Loch, 16 July 1852, L.E.P.).

1851, in that there was no return to the disastrous contests which had occurred intermittently in the three preceding years. Throughout 1852 and the greater part of 1853 the general trade of the country flourished, encouraged by the gold discoveries in California and Australia, and the widening market left the great transport undertakings of southern Lancashire and northern Cheshire more room to expand without treading upon one another's toes. At the end of 1852 the Bridgewater Trustees and the L. & N.W. and L. & Y. Companies combined once again to raise their freight charges on raw cotton. The charge on cotton taken to Manchester for delivery in the town became 10s. per ton.[1] Nine months later the L. & N.W.R. proposed a further advance.[2] For all that, however, the basis of the truce remained precarious. The threat to the maintenance of rates came, it is true, not from the railway companies, much less from the Duke's, but rather from the carriers by water whom the Trustees were unable fully to control. The principal culprit was the New Quay Company, a large and well-established carrying concern which operated upon the Mersey and Irwell Navigation. Impelled, no doubt, by the hope of selling itself out to the Trustees at an exalted price, this company pursued a piratical course of stealing traffic, both from the other water carriers and from the railways, by illicit rebates which infringed the rate agreements made between the carriers in the Liverpool and Manchester trade. At this stage the railway companies, able no doubt, now that trade had improved, to get all the traffic they needed without fighting for it, were not easily provoked. There was always the danger, however, that the privateering activities of the New Quay Company would prove the last straw and plunge the entire trade into contest once more. The quantity of cotton carried by the L. & N.W.R. fell by 46 per cent between the first six months of 1852 and the same period of 1853, and Henry Booth was disposed to attribute the loss to the offering of reduced rates, discounts, and allowances by the New Quay Company and the Bridgewater agents.[3]

---

[1] Thompson, McKay & Co. to G. Loch, 31 Dec. 1852, ibid.

[2] They suggested advancing all the rates from Liverpool to Manchester and places east of it by 10d. per ton (F. Smith to G. Loch, 28 Sept. 1853, ibid.).

[3] Extract from H. Booth to F. Smith, 23 Aug. 1853, ibid.

On a superficial view the remedy for the instability in the Liverpool and Manchester trade appeared to rest with the Trustees themselves, who should have taken steps to control their carriers. But this was easier said than done. The New Quay Company, being a joint stock company, was excluded from the agency agreements into which the other carriers on the Bridgewater navigations had entered, and was, therefore, free from the stringent penalties which could be inflicted upon recalcitrants under those compacts. The most that the Trustees could do to punish its proprietors was to withdraw the discount of 10*d.* per ton which had previously been made to them from the toll of 3*s.* 4*d.* per ton on the River. This was not a course, however, lightly to be embarked upon, for the directors of the New Quay were powerful men, highly placed in Manchester business circles and eminently capable of making trouble for the Duke's. Among them was Thomas Bazley, the Chairman of the Manchester Chamber of Commerce and an ex-Anti-Corn Law Leaguer. The Trustees were in an extremely vulnerable position. If they attempted to coerce the New Quay Company into adopting higher charges by raising the rate of toll levied upon their boats, or if alternatively they made a bid to buy up the concern, they risked being denounced as unscrupulous monopolists bent on exploiting the public. This charge had been effectively levelled against them in 1825 when the Liverpool and Manchester Railway was being projected; it would be even more devastating in the 1850s when belief in freedom of trade had become almost a national religion. It will serve as an example of the kind of blackmail which the New Quay Company was prone to levy upon the Trustees that an intermediary who was trying to arrange a purchase of the concern by the Bridgewater Trust thought it necessary to warn Loch that

Bazley, Watkins and Harter would, once seriously engaged in a contest with the Trustees, be sure to carry the public opinion with them, that they will set the machinery of the Corn Law League in motion, that they will (as they are just now well able) exercise a considerable influence on the government.[1]

Loch was not disposed to take so extreme a threat very seriously. What he feared more was that any steps taken to

---

[1] F. Smith to G. Loch, 1 Nov. 1853, L.E.P.

enforce the agreed rates upon the New Quay Company would prejudice the case which the Trustees were conducting in Parliament against the amalgamation of canals and railways.[1] They were especially concerned to fight the proposed amalgamation of the London and North Western and North Staffordshire Railways when it came before Parliament in 1853, and gave evidence before Cardwell's Committee against this and other consolidations during the same session. To attract attention to themselves by arrangements which smacked of monopoly could only damage their cause.

It should be further stated that the attempt to bring the New Quay Company into line with other carriers was not only fraught with danger to the Trustees' reputation, it was also uncertain of success. In June 1853 the Trustees succeeded by a ruse in establishing against the company a sufficient case to justify the application of punitive measures. Discovering from a former employee of the concern who had been dismissed that it was the custom of the New Quay Company to under-declare the weight of its flats by five or ten tons, they at length hit on a method of putting this information to the test. The water from the Old River was drawn off and the New Quay flats were forced on to the Bridgewater Canal, where they were weighed out and found to be in excess of their declarations. Having thus exposed the fraud by which the company succeeded in undercutting its rivals whilst still making a profit, they gave notice to the directors that they would in future be charged full toll.[2] The results of this disciplinary measure were, however, disappointing. The company simply turned from the carriage of lower-classed goods to make inroads upon the higher-classed articles which could afford to pay a toll of 3*s.* 4*d.* per ton. Instead of menacing the up trade in raw cotton, it started to attack the down goods trade, and by the end of the summer both the Trustees and the commission agents were feeling the impact upon their commerce.[3] All that the former had achieved was to goad the directors of their insubordinate underling into proceeding

---

[1] G. Loch to F. Smith, 7 Jan. 1853, ibid.
[2] F. Smith to G. Loch, 13 Jan. 1853, and enclosures; F. Smith to G. Loch, 27 June, and G. Loch to F. Smith, 27 June 1853, ibid.
[3] F. Smith to G. Loch, 22 Sept. 1853, ibid.

to further lengths of campaigning against themselves. In November 1854 Bazley got up an association to compel the Trustees to cleanse their canal, the smells arising from which were proving extremely offensive to residents in the Altrincham district.[1]

Unable then to answer for the behaviour of their own carriers in the Liverpool and Manchester trade, the Duke of Bridgewater's Trustees refused to engage themselves so firmly to the Great Western group of railways as to add the last straw of provocation to the London and North Western. Fears of a return to the anarchy of the years 1849–51 hung over them like a cloud and supplied a powerful persuasive to caution. Nevertheless, relations with the Western railways were not destined to remain frozen at their existing level. Hitherto the Trustees' dealings had been mainly with the subordinate partners in the as yet uncompleted alliance. Soon, however, they were to receive an approach from the G.W.R. itself.

On 1 October 1852 that company opened its line from Banbury to the Snow Hill station in Birmingham.[2] This event gave a tremendous fillip to the directors' ambitions to open up a trade between London on the one hand and Liverpool, Manchester, the Potteries, and South Staffordshire on the other. These designs depended partly for their realization upon the collaboration of the two Shrewsbury companies and the Birkenhead, something which could not entirely be relied upon, as the activities of a minority of Euston controlled shareholders within the Shrewsburys still rendered the amalgamation with the G.W.R. uncertain, whilst the Birkenhead Company, through the influence of its chairman Alderman Bancroft, had gone over to the enemy, the London and North Western. Nevertheless, even if formal amalgamation with lines north of Birmingham should prove impossible, the Great Western Company still had grounds for hope that it might be allowed to exercise running rights over those lines. It was to go to Parliament in the 1853 session for power to do so. In Great Western eyes there was a strong case, therefore, for enlisting the help of the Duke of Bridgewater's Trustees in

---

[1] F. Smith to G. Loch, 23 Nov. 1854, L.E.P.

[2] For passengers only. Goods traffic began in February 1853. MacDermot, op. cit., vol. i, pp. 324–7.

this great venture of northward expansion without a moment's delay, for the Trustees could supply indispensable assistance, not only by bridging the gaps in the railway system but also by placing their trading connections in Liverpool, Manchester, South Staffordshire, and the Potteries at the G.W.R.'s disposal. Accordingly, therefore, on 15 October 1852 Charles Saunders proposed to constitute them agents to the Great Western in those four towns and districts, as well as in Macclesfield, for the trade with London, Birmingham, and places on the G.W.R. line between London and Birmingham. For this service they were to receive a commission of ten per cent on goods and five per cent on undamageable iron. The trade with Lancashire was to be carried upon the Shrewsbury and Birkenhead lines between Wolverhampton and the trans-shipment stations at Norton and Walton. For the traffic named the Trustees were to cut their connections with all other carriers by rail or water, such as Shiptons or Pickfords, the agents for the L. & N.W.R., and to give all their trade to the Great Western Railway.[1]

George Loch and his father did not welcome the idea of so wholehearted a commitment to the G.W.R. Their objections were similar to those which they had raised against making too close an alliance with the Shrewsburys, that such a course might prejudice their chances of disposing of the Bridgewater Canal by sale to the London and North Western Railway Company and might also adversely affect their parliamentary campaign during the following session against the absorption of the Trent and Mersey Canal by the L. & N.W.R.[2] But the Trust was a house divided against itself, for Fereday Smith, the General Manager, enthused about the railway proposition as presenting the Trustees with an opportunity to recover the traffic between Liverpool and Manchester and the metropolis which had once passed upon the Bridgewater Canal but had later fallen an easier victim to the railways than many of the short-distance trades.[3] The following figures, which Smith had compiled,[4] illustrate the dramatic character of the decline down to 1847:

[1] F. Smith to G. Loch, 15 Oct. 1852, L.E.P.
[2] F. Smith to G. Loch, 18 Dec. 1852, ibid.
[3] F. Smith to G. Loch, 15 Oct. 1852, ibid.
[4] Cited in F. Smith to G. Loch, 18 and 20 Dec. 1852, ibid.

	Trade passing along the Duke of Bridgewater's Canal	
	Between Liverpool and places south of Birmingham, including London	Between Manchester and places south of Birmingham, including London
	tons	tons
1839	7,065	19,595
1840	6,839	19,615
1841	4,574	15,564
1842	2,519	9,127
1843	2,150	10,003
1844	2,397	8,609
1845	2,238	6,654
1846	1,373	2,297
1847	1,309	1,277

Since 1847 there had been a partial recovery as shown below:

	Between Liverpool and places south of Birmingham, including London	Between Manchester and places south of Birmingham, including London
	tons	tons
1848	1,786	7,388
1849	2,000	8,908
1850	2,369	8,354
1851	2,652	9,176
1852	2,530 (approx.)	9,041 (approx.)

Nevertheless, it was arguable that by effecting an exchange with the railway companies at Norton or Walton, the Trustees might bring about a much greater restoration of their former position, for the trade which they carried would enjoy the advantage of enhanced speed for the major part of the journey. The danger was, of course, and Fereday Smith was not unaware of it, that the Great Western Company would make use of them for a limited period, and then by degrees abstract their customers by placing its own salaried agents at Birmingham, Manchester, and Liverpool to solicit in opposition to them; but the risk would be much reduced if the Company constituted the Trustees as its sole agents in those places as it initially offered to do.[1]

The dispute within the Trust did not turn solely on questions of expediency. To the Lochs there was a matter of principle

[1] F. Smith to G. Loch, 18 Dec. 1852, L.E.P.

at stake. From the time when he assumed the superintendent-ship in 1837, James Loch had set his face against extending the scope of the Trust's activities. By the early 1850s he and his son George were becoming acutely aware that in the struggle to defend themselves against railroad competition they had drifted step by step a long way from this course of self-limitation. They had become controllers by lease or purchase of waterways other than their own. They had assumed carrying responsibilities on navigations situated at a consider-able distance from the Bridgewater Canal. Now they were being asked to take a further step away from their basic function as canal owners by becoming agents for traffic which was to travel long distances by rail. The time appeared to have come, therefore, for calling a halt to the process.

. . . it is by no means clear [observed George Loch], that it would be either wise or right in them as Trustees to attempt to compensate themselves [for losses of trade by canal] by embarking in extensive trading operations on lines of railway in which they have no interest, and to seek to replace their diminished position as proprietors of a Navigation by undertaking great transactions as mere railway carriers. . . . Strictly speaking [he added], the Trustees ought to eschew such a business entirely; the rapid and wonderful changes of the day, have to some extent compelled them to abandon this rule, and have, I believe, justified that abandon-ment. One of the most anxious responsibilities now imposed upon them is, in each case, to determine at what point the line ought to be drawn in this respect. . . .[1]

His father was much more pungent. When Fereday Smith suggested that the Trustees should undertake a carrying agency for the G.W.R. to Bristol, the elder Loch observed sarcastically that he was 'sure that Marseilles would be next suggested'.[2] To counter these objections Smith was obliged to have recourse to a different argument of principle—the argument of conciliation.

It seems certain [he wrote], that the way to make ultimate and permanent terms with the railway companies is to show them that

---

[1] The opinion was actually given in answer to a proposal that the Trustees should carry by rail to the Staffordshire Potteries, but the same logic was applicable to the proposed G.W.R. agreement (G. Loch to F. Smith, 13 July 1852, ibid.).

[2] G. Loch to F. Smith, 18 Mar. 1853, ibid.

the Trustees really have a trade some of which they have it in their power, and are willing, to place on the rail, and thus instead of the Trustees' being forever looked upon as the natural enemies of railways, they may in time be looked upon as friends and allies.[1]

In the event it was Fereday Smith who had his way. By keeping the negotiations mainly in his own hands and by tactfully prompting his superiors when they cavilled at the terms which were offered, he gradually closed the gap between the Great Western Board and the Trustees. An interim arrangement was made in January 1853, by which the Trustees were to collect and deliver goods for the Railway Company in the area round Birmingham,[2] and to facilitate this service a temporary trans-shipment station was constructed in the town, on the Birmingham Canal navigations near to the G.W.R. goods station at Upper Trinity Street, Coventry Road.[3] Three months later, on 30 April, the Trustees entered a larger and more binding commitment which turned them into agents of the Great Western Company at Liverpool and Manchester for traffic passing between those towns and the metropolis.[4] In return for this privilege they were required to suppress the canal trade which Shiptons, who were their agents, conducted on the Grand Junction Canal between Birmingham and London, such traffic being deemed competitive with that of the Great Western Railway.[5] They were also compelled to incorporate in the agency agreement the traffic between Lancashire and the Midlands which they conveyed by the Shrewsbury companies' lines. George Loch at first stood out for keeping this upon the basis established by the looser agreement of May 1852, which allowed the Trustees to fix their own charges to the public for the trade which went by rail. In the end, however, he approved the draft of an arrangement negotiated

---

[1] F. Smith to G. Loch, 25 June 1852, L.E.P.

[2] C. A. Saunders to F. Smith, 8 Jan., and F. Smith to G. Loch, 12 Jan. 1853, ibid.

[3] Bantock to F. Smith, 2 Apr. 1853, ibid.

[4] G. Loch to F. Smith, 30 Apr. 1853, ibid.; for the nature of the agreement see *Select Committee on . . . Railway and Canal Bills, Third Report*, Minutes of Evidence, p. 40; 1852–3 (246) xxxviii.

[5] An agreement was made with Shiptons on 12 May 1853. The latter sold their London stock to the Trustees in return for a guaranteed income of £1,000 per year for seven years (F. Smith to the Hon. A. Egerton, 13 Jan. 1857, L.E.P.).

by Smith, contenting himself with the observation that it weakened the Trustees' position by making them collect as agents at such rates as the Shrewsbury companies should fix.[1]

It looked at first as though the Great Western agreement would open up a new era for the Trustees, in which their income would derive as much from carrying by and with the assistance of railways in various parts of the country as from the ownership of the navigations in Lancashire and Cheshire. This at least was what the General Manager seemed by his actions to be bent on compassing. Encouraged by his success in closing with the G.W.R. for the agency in the London trade, he sought to multiply agreements with railway companies for the interchange of traffic. Wherever the opportunity existed he seized it, paying scant regard to consistency in the alliances which he projected. In the years 1853–4 he treated with the G.W.R. for an agency in the trade with Bristol and South Wales,[2] with the London and North Western for exchanging traffic between canal and railway both at Preston Brook and Walton,[3] and with the North Staffordshire for establishing a joint rail and water trade in salt and flints between Gainsborough and the Staffordshire Potteries.[4] James Loch was filled with alarm by the complexity of the web of arrangements which he appeared to be weaving. Sanctioning an exchange of land at Walton which was being undertaken to prepare the way for the making of a further canal–railway junction, he wished it to be 'understood that it may not lead to the recommendation of any new set of complicated transactions and connections with other concerns and interests'.

I have long felt, [he added], that such have been carried to the utmost verge of prudence and that the machine was, to say the least of it, sufficiently cumbrous and complicated and that its further extension would be injudicious and, therefore, injurious. It is long since I have said that what are called measures of protection far oftener become measures of weakness by multiplying points of attack,—or they are maintained at a cost beyond the value of what is sought to be preserved.[5]

---

[1] G. Loch to F. Smith, 4 Feb. and 7 Apr. 1853, ibid.
[2] F. Smith to G. Loch, 28 Jan. 1854, and enclosure, ibid.
[3] F. Smith to G. Loch, 13 Aug. 1853; B. Poole to Mitchell, 11 Aug. 1853, ibid.   [4] F. Smith to G. Loch, 29 July 1854, ibid.
[5] J. Loch to F. Smith, 12 Dec. 1853, ibid.

Loch's pessimism could scarcely have received firmer corroboration than in the Trustees' experience of implementing their compact with the Great Western Railway. The agreement of 30 April 1853 never worked as planned. Responsibility for its failure is divided between four parties—the Shrewsburys, the Birkenhead Railway, the Duke of Bridgewater's Trustees, and the G.W.R. Behind the unco-operativeness of the first two of these lay the influence of the London and North Western, which was contending with the G.W.R. for the command of the souls of both. The Shrewsbury companies dealt the first blow by declining to execute the agreement.[1] Their defection did not in theory deny the Trustees the right to send traffic southwards over their lines, for this could be done under the terms of the earlier arrangement made in May 1852. When, however, the Trustees sought to exercise this right, they were refused the necessary trucks and their river flats were detained for an unreasonable period at Birkenhead for loading and unloading. In extenuation of this the Shrewsbury directors pleaded the unsatisfactory state of their relations with the Birkenhead Railway Company.[2] The Birkenhead was undoubtedly responsible for sabotaging that part of the agreement which related to a G.W.R. trade with Manchester, for it fixed its rates between Chester and the junction with the Bridgewater Canal at Norton at so high a level as to prohibit the working of a trans-shipment traffic through that place.[3]

The Trustees' contribution to the breakdown was relatively minor. True, they had at first neither the boats, the carts, the horses, the warehouse space, nor the supervisory staff to work the trans-shipment traffic at Birmingham properly, and the G.W.R. was given grounds to complain of bottlenecks and even of pilfering.[4] Once they had discovered the deficiencies, however, they soon took steps to make them good. They ordered up new stocks of narrow boats and wagons, dismissed

---

[1] 'Draft case of the Bridgewater Trustees against the Great Western Railway Company Designed for Submission to Counsel', enclosed in F. Smith to G. Loch, 9 Aug. 1854, L.E.P.

[2] 'Draft case, etc.', enclosed in F. Smith to G. Loch, 9 Aug. 1854; F. Smith to G. Loch, 2 Mar. 1854, ibid.

[3] Grierson to F. Smith, 16 Dec. 1853, ibid.

[4] F. Smith to G. Loch, 7 Nov. 1853, and 6 May 1854, ibid.

porters who were suspected of dishonesty, and acquired the use of some railway arches to furnish additional warehouse accommodation.[1]

Undoubtedly the chief culprit was the G.W.R. At first this company had some shadow of an excuse for non-compliance with its commitments, in that it could not control the Shrewsburys. By September 1853, however, this difficulty was largely at an end, as the shareholders' meetings of both the Shrewsbury and Chester and the Shrewsbury and Birmingham had voted by large majorities to accept Saunders's terms of amalgamation. It only needed an Act of Parliament passed in the following session to formalize the union.[2] But the Secretary of the G.W.R., instead of using his authority over the Shrewsburys to bring them into line with the agreement of 30 April 1853, sought to impose upon the Bridgewater Trustees a new arrangement which would have bound them more rigidly than that which the Shrewsbury companies in their independent days had subverted. He told Fereday Smith in August 1854 that his company wished the Trustees to become their sole agents between the northern and central districts of England under an agreement which would provide for the division of the traffic. When Smith demurred, he retorted that the Trustees must at least undertake to work the traffic in such a way as to give the G.W.R. the entire control of it at one terminus.[3] Not only, moreover, did he seek to reconstruct the portion of the agreement which referred to the Staffordshire trade; he also neglected, whilst the dispute continued, to put into operation the rest of it concerning the Trustees' agency for the London trade in Liverpool and Manchester. The Bridgewater people were, therefore, obliged to dispatch such merchandise as they intended to send south by rail, across the river under the terms of their old agreement with the Birkenhead Railway Company. Instead of their commission they received merely an unremunerative river freight.[4]

The source of the disagreement was the Trustees' interest in an alternative route from Lancashire to the Midlands and

---

[1] F. Smith to G. Loch, 9 Nov. 1853, and 6 May 1854, ibid.
[2] MacDermot, op. cit., vol. i, p. 388.
[3] F. Smith to G. Loch, 8 Aug. 1854, L.E.P.
[4] F. Smith to G. Loch, 2 Apr. and 16 May 1855, ibid.

south to that provided by the G.W.R. lines, viz. the Trent and
Mersey Canal. This is clear from correspondence which passed
between the parties.

> I know not how the Duke's Trustees mean to act with regard to
> the North Staffordshire and Trent and Mersey Canal interests
> [wrote Saunders to Fereday Smith in January 1855]. It is obviously
> impossible that our Northern traffic can be placed in their hands,
> so long as they shall be competitors by Canal.[1]

There was logic in this remark from the standpoint of the
Railway Company's interests, but its enunciation revealed
that the negotiators were in a false position. George Loch
indignantly rebutted Saunders's suggestion that the Trustees
had ever 'given your company or the Shrewsbury companies
ground for expectations connected with their Canal traffic
which have not been fulfilled'. He made it abundantly clear
that 'the Trustees must always regard their Canal traffic
between Staffordshire and Lancashire as paramount to them
in interest to any that might arise in connection with the
railways'.[2] The latter was but a second string to be kept
available in case the former broke in their hands. Moreover,
the most likely cause of its breach would be the transference
of the Grand Trunk to London and North Western Railway
Company ownership. The North Western was in Parliament
in four successive sessions from 1852 to 1855 inclusive to
effect this purpose, and to oppose it was a perennial concern
of the Trustees. The latter were well aware that by tying themselves too closely to the Great Western in the conduct of the
trade between South Staffordshire and the north they would
surrender their freedom to resist. This was the reason given
by Fereday Smith for refusing Saunders's offer of a sole
agency.[3]

Throughout the negotiations with the Shrewsbury and
Great Western Companies it was the ambivalence of the
Trustees' position that militated against success. Their bargain-
ing power suffered from the fact that they were juggling with

---

[1] C. A. Saunders to F. Smith, 13 Jan. 1855, L.E.P.

[2] G. Loch to F. Smith, 17 Jan. 1855, and enclosed reply to Saunders, ibid.
No doubt the raising of the rate on iron carried by canal which was effected
in March 1854 increased the Trustees' attachment to the water traffic.

[3] F. Smith to G. Loch, 8 Aug. 1854, ibid.

too many balls. They were torn between the conflicting attractions of a G.W.R. and an L. & N.W.R. alliance and between the rival polarities of the railway trade via the Shrewsbury and Great Western lines and the canal trade via the Grand Trunk.

Even if the Trustees had been willing to commit themselves firmly to the Great Western group, however, it is extremely doubtful whether they would have extracted for themselves more than a very temporary advantage. For the railway system was continually expanding, and each successive stage of growth brought nearer the day when the Great Western Company would be able to realize its ambitions without the aid of the canals and their carrying services. Already in 1855 this lesson was being brought home to the Trustees. With the opening of the 'mixed gauge' Birmingham, Wolverhampton, and Dudley line on 14 November 1854,[1] the Great Western Company gained access by rail to Wolverhampton. It also obtained a direct link with the Shrewsbury and Birmingham, for the O.W. & W.R. line had by then been completed and a short G.W.R. stretch, joining the O.W. & W.R. to the Shrewsbury and Birmingham at Stafford Road Junction, was also opened in November 1854. No longer so dependent upon the canal boats for the collection and distribution of their traffic in the Black Country, the railway directors hastened to displace the Trustees from their remaining terminal services in that locality. Six months after the completion of the new line they instructed their Wolverhampton agent to deliver all import goods from London in their own wagons. Fereday Smith remarked bitterly that they had made use of the Trustees to originate a London traffic for them and that once it was established they had by one stroke deprived them of one-half of it at Wolverhampton, transferring the customers to their own books.[2] Other blows quickly followed. From 1 June 1855 the G.W.R. started to keep and to collect its own accounts in Birmingham.[3] Soon it was scheming with the Warrington and

---

[1] MacDermot, op. cit., vol. i, p. 336. A short stretch of line connecting the O.W. & W.R., into which the Birmingham, Wolverhampton, and Dudley fed at Priestfield, with the Shrewsbury and Birmingham at Stafford Road, north of Wolverhampton, was opened at the same time.

[2] F. Smith to G. Loch, 16 May 1855, L.E.P.

[3] G. Bowker to F. Smith, 29 May 1855, ibid.

Stockport Railway Company, whose line from Warrington to
Timperley had been opened in May 1854, to push a Manchester
trade independently of the Trustees. The last lap of the journey from Broadheath into Manchester was to be covered by
road.[1] The company also took steps to acquire dock space in
Liverpool and indicated its intention to employ vessels other
than those of the Trustees to convey its traffic across the
Mersey.[2]

It was now apparent to the Trustees that their agreement
with the Great Western Company was defunct. Nothing remained for them but to sell themselves to a different customer
whilst their trading connection was large enough to commend
them. In their extremity they turned to the L. & N.W.R.
Instructions were given to the Staffordshire agents towards
the end of June to dispatch no more London traffic by the
G.W. line but to make use of the North Western instead.[3]
Some days later they made a temporary arrangement with
the Oxford, Worcester, and Wolverhampton Railway Company, allied at that time with the Euston Confederacy, to act
as their agents at all stations north of Droitwich. Joined as
it was to the London and North Western line at Yarnton
near Oxford, the O.W. & W.R. supplied the Trustees with a
means of continuing to conduct a railway traffic between
South Staffordshire and London. It did so, moreover, on
easier terms than the Great Western was disposed to offer,
for the company controlling it made no stipulations in restraint
of the trade on the Midland canals.[4] The Trustees were left
entirely free to enter shortly afterwards into an agreement
with the Grand Junction Canal Company to cart the London
traffic of that concern to and away from the canal banks at
Birmingham, Wolverhampton, and Tipton.[5] This was the
kind of arrangement, free from restrictions as to quantities,
which George Loch was disposed to favour. Nevertheless, the
minor success scored by the Trustees in extricating themselves

---

[1] F. Smith to G. Loch, 14 June 1855, L.E.P.
[2] F. Smith to G. Loch, 23 June 1855, ibid.
[3] F. Smith to G. Loch, 25 June 1855, ibid.
[4] F. Smith to G. Loch, 29 June, and G. Loch to F. Smith, 30 June 1855, ibid.
[5] It was concluded in November 1855 but was denounced by the Grand
Junction Company three months later (F. Smith to A. Egerton, 7 Nov. 1855,
and 15 Feb. 1856, ibid.).

from their immediate difficulty cannot be allowed to obscure the fact that the latter had wasted four years on negotiations which in the end had proved almost entirely fruitless.[1] If they had succeeded in finding continued employment for the stock of boats and carts which they had acquired in the Midlands, they had done little or nothing to further the long-term interests of the Bridgewater Canal and the Mersey and Irwell Navigation, which were their principal source of profit. The permanent settlement extending perhaps to an amalgamation with one or other of the great railway companies, to which they had looked forward upon entering into the negotiations with the G.W.R. and its allies, was as far off as ever. Admittedly, the need to change the existing basis of things had diminished. The Trust and the great railway companies of the north-west were no longer locked in mortal combat as they had been in the years 1849-51. Under the chairmanship of Lord Chandos, who was favourably disposed to the interests of his fellow nobleman Lord Ellesmere, the L. & N.W.R. had been behaving since about August 1853 with greater cordiality towards the Trustees than ever before. There had been joint action to promote a trans-shipment trade at Preston Brook in August 1853[2] and to raise the rates of carriage on iron between South Staffordshire and Lancashire in October.[3] These improvements, however, owed more to favourable but transient economic conditions[4] than to any peculiar skill on the Trustees'

---

[1] But not quite fruitless. In October 1855 the Trustees made an agreement with the G.W.R. to carry the company's iron and other goods across the Mersey between Liverpool and Birkenhead on better terms than could be obtained from the Birkenhead Railway Company. This arrangement came into effect early in February 1856, when the G.W.R. started running its own trains to Birkenhead. It was still operative in 1859. See F. Smith to A. Egerton, 27 Sept. 1855, 23 Jan. and 5 Feb. 1856, 20 May and 1 Dec. 1859, ibid.

[2] G. Loch to F. Smith, 29 Aug. 1853, ibid.

[3] F. Smith to G. Loch, 13 Oct. 1853, ibid. The rates between South Staffordshire and Liverpool were not raised, however, until March 1854, when the sharp rivalry between the L. & N.W.R. and G.W.R. Companies had started to abate (G. Loch to F. Smith, 23 Mar. 1854, ibid.).

[4] Among these the boom of 1852-3 was perhaps the most important. This is evident from the fact that the return of depression in 1854-5 nearly produced a renewal of contest between the railways and the canals. In February 1855 Braithwaite Poole of the L. & N.W.R. told Fereday Smith that 'it was his fixed intention, now that he had plenty of spare waggons, to go amongst the New Quay Company's customers and reduce the rates so as to secure some of them' (F. Smith to G. Loch, 19 Feb. 1855, ibid.). The breach was averted,

part in engineering them. Altogether, when they looked back upon their diplomacy during the past four years, the latter could find little on which to congratulate themselves.

however, by action taken by the Trustees to restrain the water carriers from offering further provocation to the Railway Company, and by the slow recovery of trade as the year advanced.

CHAPTER XII

Reform and Reappraisal

For the Duke of Bridgewater's Trustees the years of negotiation with the Shrewsbury and Great Western Companies were locust years. In matters other than those which formed the subject of the railroad diplomacy they were years of caution and indecision, of unwillingness to spend money or to take risks. Thus, while the Trustees angled for a traffic which was to be handed to them by the railway companies, they let slip some important opportunities to raise the competitive efficiency of their own system.

Discussion of improvements turned largely at this stage on the question of the facilities for importing and exporting goods through Runcorn. It was not surprising that this should have been the case, for Runcorn was the point of effluence into the Mersey estuary of the two great waterways which the Trust controlled. The coming of the railways can only have increased its importance to the Trustees, for whilst the goods which were landed by sea-going vessels at Liverpool had the choice of two great railway systems for transportation eastwards to Manchester and of two, also, if their destination was the Midlands, the commerce of Runcorn had as yet no option but to be conveyed inland by canal. For canal reasons, therefore, it was more than ever the concern of the Bridgewater authorities to foster the expansion of Runcorn. But they were also interested in the town itself, for they had large quantities of capital already sunk in docks, warehouses, and other transshipment facilities there, as well as land which could be made available for further development. Economically, in fact, once the purchase of the Mersey and Irwell Navigation had been completed, Runcorn was practically in their pocket. Though it boasted a few soap manufacturing and chemical works, shipyards, and foundries, which had grown up mainly in the

1820s and 1830s, nearly two-thirds of the annual rateable value of its industrial estate was constituted in 1851 by the properties of the Bridgewater Trust,[1] which also found employment, ten years earlier, for about a half of the population.[2]

In the middle of the nineteenth century Runcorn was still a small and underdeveloped town with a population of less than 9,000 inhabitants.[3] Traces of the locality's former beauty lingered in the middle forties, for in 1845 it remained a summer resort for parties visiting 'the Cheshire coast, the Mersey and places adjacent'.[2] There were encouraging signs, however, about that time, of future growth in the trade of the port. Not all of these were destined to fulfil immediately the expectations which they aroused. The hopes of attracting an extensive foreign trade to Runcorn experienced a sudden setback, when the separate bonding privileges accorded to the town in 1847 were abruptly withdrawn as unnecessary in 1850.[4] But the traffic of the port displayed a marked buoyancy in the later forties and early fifties. The number of loaded sea vessels arriving at Runcorn docks rose from 935 in the period January to July 1850 to 1,328 in the corresponding portion of the following year,[5] and in November 1852 the pressure of business at Runcorn was so great that the Trustees were unable to provide enough canal boats to handle it.[6] The growth was especially encouraged by the efforts of the latter to build up a large backloading of coal, salt, iron, and manufactured commodities there, which was designed to serve as an inducement to foreign vessels to venture forward to Runcorn instead of stopping at Liverpool. Runcorn was already the great depot for Staffordshire earthenware. To make it a depot for salt also, arrangements were made with the Cheshire salt manufacturers to encourage them to load exportable salt in flats for Runcorn instead of, as previously, for Liverpool. In 1848 the Trustees contracted with Kay & Blackwells of Winsford to

---

[1] Charles Nickson, *History of Runcorn*, pp. 163–7.

[2] Answers to questions respecting the Runcorn and Preston Brook Railway, enclosed in F. Smith to J. Loch, 18 Apr. 1845, L.E.P.

[3] 8,688 in 1851 (Nickson, op. cit., chap. xvii).

[4] At the beginning of March 1850 Runcorn was reduced to the status of a creek within the port of Liverpool (Howarth to F. Smith, 8 Mar. 1850, L.E.P.).

[5] F. Smith to G. Loch, 24 July 1851, ibid.

[6] F. Smith to G. Loch, 12 Nov. 1852, ibid.

provide them with a warehouse for storing salt at Runcorn, agreeing to charge them 1*s*. 6*d*. per ton for freighting the commodity from Preston Brook to Runcorn on such occasions as they chose not to send it in their own vessels.[1] More important was the drawback of 2*d*. per ton from the sixpenny canal toll given to William Hayes on rock salt carried from Preston Brook to Runcorn, round about 1850. This, together with a simultaneous reduction of equivalent amount on the Grand Trunk, led Hayes to establish salt-works on the banks of the latter.[2] The export of salt from Runcorn rose from about 16,000 tons in 1846 to 83,000 tons in 1854, the difference being made up by the increased traffic through Preston Brook as distinct from that which reached Runcorn via the River Weaver, the ancient highway for Cheshire salt, and Weston Point.[3]

During 1851 the Trustees were also scheming to bring back to Runcorn the Irish grain trade which was thought to be recovering after the famine. Early in the following year they considered a plan to make the port a general depot for imported grain destined for the south, the east, and the north of England. Such a project was assured of support from the corn merchants of Manchester, who chafed under the heavy charges for storage to which they were subjected at Liverpool.[4]

By that time, however, it had become abundantly clear that these objectives could not be attained without a considerable expenditure of money on new docks and warehouses. The facilities already provided were not even sufficient for the existing trade, for the spring tides of May 1851 brought such an influx of coasters to Runcorn that the docks overflowed, and some of the vessels had to berth upon the beach, where they neaped.[5] Four years earlier William Howarth, the Runcorn agent, had complained that some of the coasters using the port were already too big to be accommodated in the docks and that

---

[1] F. Smith to G. Loch, 10 Oct., and G. Loch to F. Smith, 16 Oct. 1848, ibid. This arrangement recalled an earlier project, mooted in Captain Bradshaw's time but never carried out, for conveying brine by pipes from Northwich to Runcorn, where salt works would be erected, to save the cost of hauling salt and coal along the Weaver (C. Mitchell to G. Loch, 22 Aug. 1848, ibid.).

[2] F. Smith to A. Egerton, 17 July 1857, ibid.

[3] F. Smith to G. Loch, 19 Mar. 1855, ibid.

[4] Marsden, Mitchell, Howarth, and Macintyre to F. Smith, 2 Feb. 1852, ibid.

[5] Howarth to F. Smith, 21 May 1851, ibid.

the entrance basin from the river was inconveniently small, occasioning great delay and extra labour for the pier-head men and the crews of vessels.[1] It was avowedly the need to build up the grain trade, however, that led George Loch to issue instructions to Fereday Smith and the engineers Bateman and Illman on 11 February 1852 to prepare 'some moderate plan' for dock extension at Runcorn.[2] To this scheme was added before the year was out one for the construction of a new canal which was to run parallel to the southern shores of the Mersey estuary from the western end of the Francis dock at Runcorn to the mouth of the River Weaver navigation at Weston Point. The object of this was to provide a route, alternative to the estuary, which was difficult to negotiate at low water or in adverse weather, for that part of the salt traffic which came to Runcorn via the River Weaver. It is clear from the correspondence of the Runcorn agent and the General Manager of the Bridgewater Trust that the need to improve this particular communication had been given additional urgency by fears that the Weaver Trustees would build docks at Weston Point and that the trans-shipment of salt would then take place there instead of at Runcorn.[3]

These plans for expansion were adopted by the two Lochs without enthusiasm and mainly at the instigation of Fereday Smith and the subordinate agents. The estimates which were discussed were, therefore, for a dock which would accommodate a mere twenty additional coasters, though Howarth, the Runcorn agent, protested the need to make room for thirty.[4] Moreover, the proposals were pursued in a half-hearted manner which reflected badly upon the enterprise of the Bridgewater Trust, notably at the highest levels. Precious months were allowed to slip away whilst the Trustees' advisers wrangled about the merits of two different sitings for the new docks, and James Loch eventually came down on the side of one at the bottom of the old line of locks, despite the very cogent arguments of his General Manager in favour of a situation further to the west, which was better suited to the navigation of the

[1] F. Smith to J. Loch, 12 Aug. 1847, L.E.P.
[2] G. Loch to F. Smith, 11 Feb. 1852, ibid.
[3] Howarth to F. Smith, 7 July, 1852, ibid.
[4] F. Smith to J. Loch, 24 Mar. 1852, ibid.

estuary and could be combined with the Runcorn and Weston Canal project in such a way as to overcome the difficulty of obtaining the necessary land.[1] In 1853 the Trustees obtained an Act of Parliament authorizing them to construct the canal, but this did not remove their hesitations. During the following year Illman, the Trustees' engineer, himself a slow worker, was distracted from the important task of making his working drawings and specifications by being ordered to give evidence against the Bolton Improvement Bill.[2] George Loch afterwards endeavoured to throw the blame for the delay on him, on account of the slowness of his preparations, but the letter in which he did so revealed his own spontaneous willingness to defer all action until the price of labour and materials had begun to fall.[3] Later, when the arbitrator's award for the compulsory purchase of the land needed for the new canal was known, he thought the price too high, and aired his doubts as to the expediency of continuing with the scheme.[4] Thus, in June 1855, for all practical purposes, matters stood as they had done three years earlier. Neither upon the docks nor upon the Runcorn and Weston Canal had work been started.

The loss of time was all the more regrettable in that Runcorn was being subjected increasingly to competition from the railway ports which arose in quick succession on the coasts of north-west England in the middle of the nineteenth century. Fleetwood, vigorously developed by the Lancashire and Yorkshire Railway Company after 1847, was already abstracting the traffic in Scottish pig-iron brought by sea to England in the later 1840s.[5] By 1854 the pottery manufacturers were beginning to send earthenware to Birkenhead, where storage under cover was promised, instead of to Runcorn,[6] and in the following year Garston, on the extended St. Helens Railway, where docks were opened in 1853, was mentioned as a probable rival to Runcorn for the exportation of salt and coal, two of the commodities which the Bridgewater Trustees were

---

[1] F. Smith to G. Loch, 22 Oct., 10 Nov., and 7 Dec. 1852; J. Loch to F. Smith, 7 and 8 Dec. 1852, ibid.
[2] F. Smith to G. Loch, 6 Mar., and G. Loch to F. Smith, 7 Mar. 1854, ibid.
[3] G. Loch to F. Smith, 2 June 1854, ibid.
[4] G. Loch to F. Smith, 1 Mar. 1855, ibid.
[5] F. Smith to G. Loch, 12 and 21 Aug. 1848, ibid.
[6] F. Smith to G. Loch, 6 Mar. 1854, ibid.

especially anxious to make available at the latter place, in order to attract the foreign and Irish vessels there.[1]

But Runcorn's ability to hold her own against assailants was not wholly determined by the capacity of her docks and warehouses. It also depended upon the costs and efficiency of her shipping relative to those of vessels using other ports. In order to build up a traffic in Scottish iron through Fleetwood, the Lancashire and Yorkshire Railway Company had itself chartered vessels from Glasgow to sail there.[2] The Bridgewater Trustees were obliged, therefore, to do the same in times of scarcity of tonnage such as occurred in February 1849 and December 1853.[3] They nevertheless regarded this as a somewhat extreme measure to be employed only in the most exceptional circumstances. In June 1854 George Loch positively refused to resort to it in order to prevent the traffic in slates for Yorkshire, which had previously been conveyed by sea from North Wales to Runcorn and thence inland by canal, from being annexed by the Chester and Holyhead Railway, which had been developing branches to the quarries of Port Dinorwic and Port Penrhyn. The trade was threatened by the action of the Welsh shipmasters, 'a stubborn and rather impracticable race of men', who chose this unfortunate time to raise their sea freights from what had been as low as 3*s*. 3*d*. or 3*s*. 6*d*. per ton to 4*s*. in July 1853 and 5*s* 6*d*. in April 1854.[4] The Bridgewater Trustees had at first tried to counter the ill effects of this folly by reducing their tolls and canal freights,[5] but finding that these concessions only encouraged the shipowners to maintain their freights when such charges were generally falling, they withdrew them again in July 1854. It was in these circumstances that the suggestion to charter vessels was submitted by Fereday Smith to Loch, and refused by the latter.[6] The traffic, therefore, continued to leak away to the rails.

Another factor influencing (adversely) the power of Runcorn to compete for traffic was the pressure of the Liverpool

---

[1] F. Smith to G. Loch, 19 Mar. 1855, L.E.P.
[2] F. Smith to G. Loch, 7 Dec. 1847, ibid.
[3] G. Loch to F. Smith, 16 Feb. 1849 and 26 Dec. 1853, ibid.
[4] Marsden to F. Smith, 10 Apr. 1854, ibid.
[5] F. Smith to G. Loch, 8 and 25 May, and 1 June 1854, ibid.
[6] G. Loch to F. Smith, 29 June and 5 July 1854, ibid.

town dues upon her trade. These last were an ancient tribute levied by the Corporation of Liverpool throughout the whole of the port of Liverpool, an area which extended southwards from the mouth of the Ribble to the mouth of the Dee and comprised the whole estuary of the Mersey including Birkenhead, Ellesmere Port, Garston, and Runcorn as well as Liverpool proper.[1] The tax cannot have been overwhelmingly oppressive, for although the yield of the dues taken at Runcorn rose from £1,172 in 1836 to £3,182 in 1855, the tonnage of ships using the port increased in almost equal proportion in the intervening period.[2] It pressed heavily, however, on articles like salt, small in value in relation to their bulk, and was of decisive importance for the trade in iron with areas of the country which in other respects could equally well import that commodity from Scotland through Fleetwood, Poulton, or Preston, ports which were not subject to the dues. The unpopularity of the duty was enhanced, moreover, by the fact that its proceeds were devoted not to the improvement of the upper Mersey estuary but to general municipal purposes in Liverpool, and that the freemen of the borough were exempt from payment. Prejudice against the dues was widespread, for they taxed a wide variety of trades, and it was encouraged by the prevailing free trading sentiments of the age. The Corporation of Liverpool itself provided the opportunity for an attack on these charges by going to Parliament in 1854 for permission to mortgage the dues for purposes of dock and warehouse extension.[3] Led on by the Chamber of Commerce and Corporation of Manchester, a vast coalition of interests— the Corporations of Salford and Warrington, the authorities of Birkenhead, the South Staffordshire iron trade, the corn trade, the salt trade, and the pottery trade—formed to present a case against them before the Commissioners on Charges upon Shipping, who were then in session. The Duke of Bridgewater's Trustees gave evidence at the inquiry, stressing the adverse effect on Runcorn's iron trade,[4] but they afterwards

---

[1] *Commissioners to Inquire into Local Charges upon Shipping . . ., Report*, p. ix; 1854 [1836] xxxvii.

[2] *Select Committee on Local Charges upon Shipping*, Minutes of Evidence, p. 316; 1856 (332) xii.

[3] F. Smith to G. Loch, 22 Feb. 1854, L.E.P.

[4] F. Smith to G. Loch, 12 Apr. 1854, ibid.

declined to become associated with a Bill to abolish the dues
promoted by the dock interests of Birkenhead or with a
general agitation for that purpose.[1] Their policy was to wait
for the government to follow up the report of the Commission, which had commented adversely upon the duties,
with a public measure against them. George Loch, who was
principally responsible for the adoption of this quiescent
attitude, was mainly influenced by two considerations. The
first was that the Trustees themselves levied some question-
able duties upon traffic at Runcorn, duties which might be
challenged during a popular campaign; the second was his
desire to retain the favour of Liverpool Corporation, which
leased to the Trustees valuable dock properties in Liverpool.
The lease of one of these had but a very few years to run, and
the Trust would have to look to the Corporation, when it
expired, for facilities to conduct their trade in Liverpool.[2]

It was perhaps understandable prudence for the Trustees
to refrain from fighting on this issue. The same cannot be said,
however, of their discouragement in 1854 of Messrs. Haddock
& Parnell's application to have land from them at Runcorn
for the purpose of building chemical works upon it. A leading
explanation of their conduct was to be found in Lord Ellesmere's desire to avoid damaging the estates of Sir Richard
Brooke, the powerful and ill-disposed squire of Norton Priory,[3]
by allowing the establishment of an industry which, it was
believed, emitted fumes that killed trees by the hundred,
caused crops to wilt and sheep not to fatten, and impaired the
health of the inhabitants. It was unfortunate, however, for

---

[1] F. Smith to G. Loch, 30 Nov. 1854; G. Loch to F. Smith, 1 Dec. 1854; and
J. Loch to F. Smith, 18 Jan. 1855, L.E.P.

[2] Memorandum on the Liverpool Town Dues, 19 Jan. 1855, B.T.P. (Mertoun),
File 152. It was arguable that the freight charges on the Bridgewater Canal
exceeded the legal maximum of 6s. 0d. per ton imposed by the Duke of Bridgewater's Acts, 32 G. II, c. 2, 33 G. II, c. 2, and 2 G. III, c. 11, though the
Trustees had long maintained, probably correctly, that the maximum did not
include such items as the charge for conveyance on the Mersey estuary or on
that portion of the Canal made under the terms of the Trent and Mersey Canal
Act. A further difficulty was that the charges for the use of the line of locks at
Runcorn constructed by the Marquess of Stafford had never been confirmed
by an Act of Parliament. See correspondence arising from a hostile article
published in the *Liverpool Mail* in 1856 (B.T.P. (Mertoun), File 153).

[3] G. Loch to F. Smith, 11 and 18 May 1854; F. Smith to G. Loch, 17 July
and 24 Aug. 1854, L.E.P.

the prospects of employment in the locality that the Trustees should have adopted this attitude, for the industries of the town had become relatively stagnant between 1840 and 1860 after a rapid growth in the two preceding decades.[1] Inevitably the Trustees were blamed for the failure of Runcorn to grow industrially at the same rate as its neighbour, Widnes, on the other side of the river. The *Chester Courant* for 27 October 1858 carried a statement that Widnes was 'indebted for its existence to the course pursued by the Bridgewater Trustees in refusing to lease on reasonable terms land for the erection of factories and chemical and other works for which Runcorn is more eligibly situated'.[2] This was undoubtedly a great exaggeration, but the neglect of Runcorn interests, of which the reluctance to make land available for manufacturing purposes was one manifestation, enabled a radical opposition to the Trustees to develop within the local Improvement Commission[3] and led to overtures from the townspeople to link Runcorn with the railway system.[4]

Moreover, lethargy with regard to Runcorn was only part of a general creeping paralysis which extended to all branches of the concern in the early 1850s. Initiative among the Trustees' employees was stifled by the growth of a bureaucratic system of internal organization which proliferated more and more as the scope of the Trust's responsibilities widened. This was deliberately rendered more complex than it need have been by rules devised in the interests of economy. James Loch and his son George, who was by that time handling most of the detailed business for his father, built up an elaborate procedure of checks and balances designed to arrest expenditure on day-to-day maintenance. A memorandum issued from the Bridgewater offices on 14 October 1850 required that all demands by the agents for repairs and purchases should be first attested by the appropriate carrying committee (the Steam Towage Committee, the Staffordshire Committee, or the Northern Carrying Committee), then submitted to the General Manager for approval, then dispatched to the Cashier,

---

[1] Nickson, op. cit., pp. 167–8.
[2] Newspaper cutting enclosed in F. Smith to A. Egerton, 29 Oct. 1858, L.E.P.
[3] F. Smith to A. Egerton, 3 and 11 Dec. 1855, ibid.
[4] Howarth to F. Smith, 27 May 1854, ibid.

who would refer them to George Loch for sanction before
registering them and returning them to the agents to act upon.
Not so much as a ladder could be purchased without Loch's
assent, and even the General Manager was rebuffed when he
tried to cut through this cumbrous routine early in 1855.[1]
In 1853, moreover, ordinary expenditure was savagely cut back
in order to allow certain extraordinary outlays to be made.[2]

The chief justification for this cheese-paring policy was to be
found in the state of the finances. Never before was the over-all
profit from the Bridgewater properties so consistently low as
in the years 1850–3—between £44,000 and £47,000 per
annum as compared with a figure often above £80,000 and
sometimes well above it.[3] This was the result of an unusually
marked coincidence of adverse circumstances—the fierce
battle between the two navigations and the railways at the
beginning of the decade, the conflict between the L. & N.W.R.
and the G.W.R. over the Stour Valley line which drove down
the freight charges on iron so low that the Trustees' carrying
trade to and from South Staffordshire showed a loss of £7,560
in 1852 and £13,650 in 1853,[4] the mid-century depression in
the Worsley collieries, and the continuing drain of the interest
payments on the Old Quay purchase. There were also the
traditional obstacles to capital accumulation which led the
Trustees, in 1853, to plan to throw the cost of erecting new
warehouses in Manchester upon the builders, who were to be
reimbursed out of income over a period of ten years.[5] George
Loch reminded Lord Ellesmere about that time, 'Your Lordship is not a joint stock company' and that he had 'no convenient capital account'.[6] These difficulties, however, were less
serious than they had been, for an Estate Act passed in 1851
had empowered the Trustees to borrow up to £150,000 against
the security of their own estates and the Old Quay shares to

---

[1] Correspondence between G. Loch and C. W. Rippon relative to regulations
for the authentication of demands and enclosed memoranda, Jan. 1855;
F. Smith to G. Loch, 23 and 28 Feb. 1855; G. Loch to F. Smith, 25 Feb. 1855,
L.E.P.

[2] F. Smith to G. Loch, 23 Sept. 1853, ibid.

[3] See below, Appendix A.

[4] Abstract of Bridgewater Trust Accounts, 1851, 1852 and 1853, B.T.P.
(Mertoun).

[5] G. Loch to F. Smith, 13 Jan. 1853, L.E.P.

[6] G. Loch to the Earl of Ellesmere, 5 Sept. 1853, B.T.P. (Mertoun), File 149.

defray the cost of improving their two navigations and of
constructing or improving any line of locks or other means of
communication between them.[1] There are grounds for thinking
that James and George Loch made less use of their borrowing
powers than the circumstances warranted. Not until June
1852 did they exhaust those which were conferred upon them
by an Estate Act passed ten years earlier,[2] and they afterwards
kept large quantities of saved or borrowed capital locked up
in exchequer bills. By February 1858 a fund of £90,000, thus
invested, lay at the Trustees' disposal,[3] exactly the amount
borrowed under the terms of the Estate Acts of 1842 and 1851
between December 1847 and June 1852.[4] It is difficult to
understand why. Legal doubts as to the Trustees' power to
apply moneys raised by an Act of Parliament to purposes not
specifically mentioned in the Act may have been partly
responsible. It is more likely, however, that the Trustees'
obsessive determination to dispose of their canals by sale to a
railway company rendered them unwilling to invest in improvements from which they might never reap the financial benefit.
As interim owners they perhaps preferred the immediately
available income from the exchequer bills.

Whilst matters thus stood James Loch died, on 28 June
1855. He was succeeded as Superintendent by Lord Ellesmere's
third son, the Hon. Algernon Fulke Egerton, a young man of
twenty-nine. Educated at Harrow and Christ Church and
already a Fellow of All Souls,[5] Egerton was an able, serious-
minded, and well-intentioned man, destined for a political
career of second- rather than first-rank importance, but totally
devoid of experience of canals and coal-mines. He accepted
office on condition that he would resign whenever Lord Ellesmere or his eldest son expressed a desire to that effect, and
told his father that he wished 'to be considered virtually your
agent'.[6] His appointment, therefore, set the seal on the victory

[1] 14 and 15 Vict. (Private), c. 12.
[2] The Estate Act of 1842 authorized the borrowing of £50,000. Of this,
£14,181 was borrowed on 7 Dec. 1847 and £35,819 on 17 June 1852. See preamble of 28 and 29 Vict. (Private), c. 50.
[3] A. Egerton to F. Smith, 4 Feb. 1858. L.E.P.
[4] In addition to the sums mentioned in n. 2 above, £5,000 and £35,000
were borrowed in June 1852. See preamble of 28 and 29 Vict. (Private), c. 50.
[5] *Annual Register*, N.S., 1891, Pt. II, p. 170.
[6] A Egerton to Lord Ellesmere, 29 July 1855, B.T.P. (Mertoun), File 152.

which Lord Francis Egerton had won eighteen years earlier when he ousted the last of the completely independent Superintendents of the Trust. But the real beneficiary of the change in command was not Lord Ellesmere, who had had the final say for many years, but George Fereday Smith, the General Manager. Smith's previous career had not been without frustrations. Appointed initially as Deputy Superintendent, he had suffered the humiliation of having George Loch's authority interposed between his own and that of the Superintendent, and from 1845 onwards his official status was reduced to that of Principal Agent.[1] Moreover, in the closing years of the Loch regime, he found his position further encroached upon by the rising power of the Cashier, C. W. Rippon, whom the Lochs, growing increasingly distrustful of their General Manager, whose expansionist ideas conflicted with their own cautious approach on almost every count, seemed to be pushing forward as a check upon him. In December 1854 Smith was deprived of all power to extend or withdraw credits to the coal customers, on the grounds that this would encroach upon the Cashier's distinctive preserve—recovery of debts.[2] In the new order, however, his stock quickly rose, for the untried young Superintendent leaned heavily upon a subordinate who had helped to guide the Canal through eighteen years of unparalleled difficulty. Except on navigational matters, where he appeared to possess some expertise, as befitted a future Secretary to the Admiralty,[3] and on labour questions, where he sometimes intervened to promote greater generosity, he usually contented himself with accepting the proposals which were put up to him from below by Fereday Smith. The trend towards exalting the Cashier at the expense of the General Manager was abruptly reversed. It was accepted in October 1855 that in future no customer should be bankrupted without the Manager's written sanction,[4] and by the end of the year

[1] Salaries Book, Bridgewater Trust, 1843–50, Lancs. C.R.O.

[2] G. Loch to F. Smith, 29 Dec. 1854, and enclosure from James Loch; F. Smith to G. Loch, 30 Dec. 1854; memorandum by G. Loch, 28 Dec. 1854, L.E.P.

[3] He held this position in the second Disraeli ministry, 1874–80 (*Annual Register*, N.S., 1891, Pt. II, p. 170).

[4] A. Egerton to F. Smith, 17 Oct. 1855; F. Smith to A. Egerton, 16 Oct. 1855, L.E.P.

the latter had won back control of the drafting and exchanging of coal leases, agreements, and conveyances, which he had lost during the two or three preceding years.[1] His salary, which had been £600 per annum in 1850, rose to £1,000 by 1857 and to £1,500 in 1864.[2] Above all, the confidence which was bestowed upon him by the new Superintendent enabled him to put many of his own stored-up ideas into practice and to implement some overdue reforms.

His first step was to lay the axe to the top-heavy administrative structure of the Trust. The Lochs had encouraged the growth of bureaucracy in the hope of restraining expenditure, but the process was self-defeating, for the annual outlay on clerkage, agency, and stationery needful to maintain the system was enormous. An investigation into the manner of conducting the office and other departments instituted by Fereday Smith in September 1855 was quickly followed, therefore, by a very considerable reduction in the number of clerks, especially at the Birmingham and Wolverhampton stations, where the trade was unremunerative.[3] To reduce still further the costs of clerkage and stationery, as well as to ensure that the accounts for freight charges reached the customer more swiftly, a reform of the system of accounting used in the carrying departments was ordered to be introduced at the beginning of 1856. The issuing of duplicate letters of acknowledgement was to be discontinued, and Peacock, the Assistant Cashier, was set free from the dreary routine of examining accounts to see that they were properly attested and of comparing the Cashier's quarterly balances with the sums shown in the agents' books, to visit the stations more frequently. Before remoulding their own system, the Trustees sought the advice of the Shropshire Union Canal Company and the L. & N.W. and L. & Y. Railway Companies as to their experience.[4] Smith, an engineer by training, was the inveterate enemy of the complexities which accountants were wont to introduce into the keeping of accounts. When a double set of accounts was introduced in 1857, he protested that it was

[1] F. Smith to A. Egerton and A. Egerton to F. Smith, 28 Nov. 1855, ibid.
[2] Salaries Books, Bridgewater Trust, 1843–50 and 1857–70, Lancs. C.R.O.
[3] F. Smith to A. Egerton, 5 Sept. and 15 Oct. 1855; A. Egerton to F. Smith, 17 Sept. 1855, L.E.P.
[4] F. Smith to A. Egerton, 22 Nov. 1855 (two letters), ibid.

increasing the work of the Cashier's Department. Shortly afterwards he introduced a general ledger at both the Runcorn and Liverpool offices.[1] He also cut through the red tape entangling the authorization of repairs and purchases by arranging that the recommendations of the carrying committees should go direct to himself after they had been approved by the Superintendent, instead of first being sent to the Cashier for endorsement.[2]

Reform did not stop at office procedures; the whole position of the Trust as a trading concern was brought under review. Adjustments were mainly in a conservative direction, towards reaffirming the Trustees' traditional function as canal proprietors and toll takers and restricting their commitments to the carrying business on distant canals and railways. In November 1855 the General Manager persuaded his superior to agree to the abandonment of the agencies at Hull and Gainsborough.[3] Nine months later the Trustees withdrew from the Burton, Derby, and Nottingham agencies, disposing of the boats which they had maintained on the Trent Navigation to private carriers. They continued, however, to convey the traffic in their own boats between Preston Brook and Manchester, and retained control of the freight charges made by the carriers to Derby and Nottingham. They also remained members of the Midland Association of carriers.[4] The retreat from the Trent was followed during 1857 by a gradual withdrawal from carrying to and from South Staffordshire on the Trent and Mersey Canal, a proportion of the trade being transferred to the boats of commission agents.[5]

It was the unprofitable character of these distant trades that furnished the principal motive for reversing the trend towards extending them which had been so much in evidence during

---

[1] F. Smith to A. Egerton, 11 July and 26 Dec. 1857, L.E.P.

[2] A. Egerton to F. Smith, 25 Sept. 1855, ibid.

[3] F. Smith to A. Egerton, 7 Nov., and A. Egerton to F. Smith, 10 Nov. 1855, ibid.

[4] F. Smith to A. Egerton, 29 Aug. 1856, and Memorandum of Arrangement with Cockshott and Brown, 25 Aug. 1856, ibid.

[5] The amount of merchandise carried in the Trustees' boats between Wolverhampton and Liverpool fell by 4,082 tons from 1856 to 1857, whilst that conveyed by the commission agents rose by 4,960 tons. Nevertheless, the Trustees still carried 40,891 tons in 1857 (F. Smith to A. Egerton, 3 Dec. 1857, ibid.).

the preceding decade. The heavy losses on the South Staffordshire trade resulted not only from the rate-cutting warfare
of the L. & N.W. and G.W. Railway Companies, which was
ended by an agreement of December 1854, but from rising
costs. Within the last two or three years the Trustees had been
obliged to abandon the old practice of looking to the boatmen
to provide their own horses and to lay out a further £3,000
or £4,000 per annum on horse traction. The change was
adopted on account of the delays which resulted from the
inability of the labouring boatmen to replace worn-out horses.
The Trustees also found it difficult to impose an efficient
control upon an establishment of boats and horses scattered
all over the country.[1] In the past the Trustees' expansion into
the carrying trade on the Midland canals had been undertaken
less for its own sake than as a means of safeguarding the long-
distance traffic of the Bridgewater Canal against the defection
of the independent carriers. It was now realized that the trade
of the Trustees' navigations must be secured by other means—
a consolidation of the canal interest to achieve a viable structure of tolls. Fereday Smith wrote in December 1855:

> As regards the future, I think it would be well to endeavour to
> induce the North Staffordshire Railway Company and the the
> Staffordshire and Worcestershire Canal Company to unite with
> the Trustees (either directly or by some arrangement whereby the
> tolls on the Trent and Mersey and Staffordshire and Worcestershire
> canals shall rise and fall according to circumstances) in the future
> arrangements with Shipton and Co., Price and Co. and Fellows,
> and in regard also to any South Staffordshire traffic the Trustees
> may continue to work in their own boats, in order if possible that
> the burden of any contest shall in future be shared in by the canal
> companies who benefit by the continuance of the traffic, and in
> that case I would propose that negociations be entered into with
> all the above-named carriers to work the heavy trade in their own
> boats via Preston Brook, and thus leave the Trustees to continue
> only so much through canal heavy traffic as shall enable them to
> keep the carriers in check and continue to them (the Trustees) a
> knowledge of what is going on in South Staffordshire and an
> interest in the discussion with the railway companies, or as may be
> workable to an ascertained profit.[2]

[1] F. Smith to A. Egerton, 12 May 1856, ibid.
[2] F. Smith to A. Egerton, 6 Dec. 1855, ibid.

So grand a design was unlikely, however, to be achieved quickly, when vital links in the canal network rested under railway ownership. Smith himself recognized that the present orientation of the North Staffordshire Railway Company (which owned the Trent and Mersey Canal) towards the L. & N.W.R., a company possessing a strong interest in diverting the traffic between the Midlands and Liverpool away from Preston Brook, constituted a serious obstacle to its immediate implementation.[1]

A more practical proposal was to repair the ravages wrought by past neglect upon the fleet of steamers used by the Trustees to tow flats or carry passengers along the Mersey estuary between Runcorn and Liverpool and between Ellesmere Port and Liverpool. This came not a moment too soon, for the vessels were beginning to break down. The paddle shafts of two of them snapped in rapid succession in November 1855.[2] At the time of Loch's death the Bridgewater Trust possessed eight steamers on the Mersey estuary varying in tonnage from about 40 to 100 tons. Three of these are known to have been more than twenty years old, three were between sixteen and twenty,[3] and all were suffering from lack of maintenance or ill-usage by their crews, or from both. In May 1857 the Trustees were obliged to caution the masters of steam vessels, notably the drunken captain of the *Rival*, who was 'from some cause or other knocking the boat to pieces', to be more careful in the future.[4] Less than twelve months earlier the *Hercules* was damaged by careless mooring at Runcorn.[5] Under Fereday Smith's guidance the work of overhaul was undertaken swiftly and systematically. One inefficient vessel, the *Countess of Ellesmere*, was put up for sale,[6] two more, the *Pilot* and the

[1] F. Smith to A. Egerton, 6 Dec. 1855, L.E.P.

[2] F. Smith to A. Egerton, 3 and 5 Nov. 1855, ibid.

[3] The eight were the *Alice* (built in 1839), the *Blanche* (1842), the *Pilot* (1832), the *Tower* (1836), the *Rival* (1834), the *Hercules* (1830), the *Countess of Ellesmere*, and the *Thomas Royden* (1837). These particulars are drawn from F. Smith to A. Egerton, 15 Oct. 1859, a manuscript register of steamers kept by the Trustees' engineer, George Forrester; and a *Return of the Name and Description of All Steam Vessels Registered in the Ports of the U.K.*, 1845 (349) xlvii.

[4] Illman to F. Smith, 21 Mar., and F. Smith to A. Egerton, 6 May 1857, L.E.P.

[5] A. Egerton to F. Smith, 17 June 1856, and enclosed report of Steam Towage Committee, ibid.   [6] A. Egerton to F. Smith, 26 Oct. 1855, ibid.

Hercules, were broken up for fencing,[1] and extensive repairs and renewals were made to the rest. The *Alice* was fitted with new boilers,[2] the *Rival* with a donkey-engine.[3] Meanwhile an iron hull named the *Bridgewater* was built to house the engines of the *Pilot,*[4] and a completely new steamer, the seventy-two tonner *Earl of Ellesmere,* was constructed to replace the worn-out *Countess.*[5] Both reached completion in 1857. Altogether the Trustees must have spent between £10,000 and £15,000 on refitting their ships between 1855 and 1857.[6] When the task was completed, the General Manager could boast that 'the Trustees' steam fleet is at present in better condition than it has perhaps ever hitherto been'.[7] It was upon his promptings backed by the representations of an *ad hoc* committee of the permanent staff that the move had been made.

The improvement had been partly self-financing, the proceeds of the sale of the *Countess of Ellesmere* steamer being devoted to the renewal of other vessels, but the Trustees had also been assisted to carry it through by the sale of stock consequent upon the decrease of their establishment in South Staffordshire.[8] There was but little prospect, however, that any sustained investment in the betterment of the docks and canals would occur whilst uncertainty prevailed about the future ownership of the properties.

Doubts upon this score were never greater than in 1856–7, when the Trustees were in treaty to lease their canals to the North Staffordshire Railway Company. Such a deal was rendered possible by the defeat in May 1855 of the last of four attempts to carry through Parliament a Bill amalgamating the North Staffordshire Company with the London and North Western. The Bridgewater Trustees had themselves played an

---

[1] F. Smith to A. Egerton, 19 and 26 Dec. 1857, ibid.

[2] A. Egerton to F. Smith, 4 Sept. 1855, ibid.

[3] A. Egerton to F. Smith, 8 Nov. 1855, ibid.

[4] F. Smith to A. Egerton, 1 Jan., and A. Egerton to F. Smith, 3 Jan. 1857, ibid.

[5] A Egerton to F. Smith, 8 Nov. 1856 and 13 Aug. 1857, ibid.

[6] £8,000 was earmarked for the *Earl of Ellesmere,* the *Bridgewater,* and the repairs to the *Tower* (A. Egerton to F. Smith, 8 Nov. 1856, ibid.). To this must be added the cost of refitting the other four ships. The bill for the *Alice* alone was expected to be about £1,700 (F. Smith to A. Egerton, 22 Apr., and A. Egerton to F. Smith, 25 Apr. 1856, ibid.).

[7] F. Smith to A. Egerton, 21 Dec. 1857, ibid.

[8] A. Egerton to Earl of Ellesmere, 1 Dec. 1856, B.T.P. (Mertoun), File 153.

active part in frustrating this proposed consolidation. Indeed George Loch claimed that they 'beat it off [their] own bat' during the preceding session, though the opposition on that occasion also included the proprietors of the Macclesfield, Coventry, Staffordshire and Worcestershire, and Grand Junction canals, the ironmaster interest, and the pottery interest.[1] Vexed and dismayed by the unwillingness of the L. & N.W.R. to persevere further with the amalgamation, the North Staffordshire Company rounded on its former ally, and began to seek by all available means to form an independent connection between its own localized network and Liverpool and Manchester. Probably the main object of these manœuvres was to put diplomatic pressure on the North Western to resume negotiations. The directors promoted Bills early in 1856 for building two new lines of railway—from Sandbach to Moore near Warrington, and from Garston to Liverpool.[2] At the same time, however, they opened a negotiation with the Bridgewater Trustees 'for obtaining possession on a perpetual lease of the whole of their canals, stations, wharves, dock accommodation, and warehouses', hoping thereby to get facilities at Liverpool and elsewhere for the collection and delivery of goods.[3] As a gesture of goodwill they withdrew the Bills for the extension of their lines towards Liverpool.[4] Although the terms which they first offered seemed to Lord Ellesmere not to be unduly generous, viz. that the rental should be based upon the average net profit of the canals for the term of five, seven, or more preceding years (years when the competition of railways had drastically reduced the yield of the undertakings) His Lordship declared himself 'prepared to pay handsomely for certainty and safety'.[5] By the early part of February the transaction was being discussed by the public as if it was a *fait accompli*. Fereday Smith wrote:

The upper class of Manchester people have . . . expressed, without one exception, their approval of it, having an especial eye to Lord Ellesmere's individual position, and to the risks of the future. The

---

[1] G. Loch to Earl of Ellesmere, 17 Sept. 1854, B.T.P. (Mertoun), File 151.
[2] *J.H.C.* cxi (1856), 11, 20.
[3] C. Hadfield, *The Canals of the West Midlands*, p. 224.
[4] *J.H.C.* cxi (1856), 154.
[5] Earl of Ellesmere to G. Loch, 5 Jan. 1856, B.T.P. (Mertoun), File 153.

more thoroughly trading part of the community have generally intimated their opinion that the bargain is rather in His Lordship's favour as a commercial arrangement than otherwise, whereas the feeling amongst the senior officers of the concern rather tends in the opposite direction, believing that His Lordship's interests lie in remaining as he was. The Commission Agents were at first very much frightened, and they still seem most anxious that the policy which has hitherto directed the affairs of the Trust should continue to influence the management under the new owners.[1]

When, however, an application was made to Parliament for the necessary powers, it was defeated on Standing Orders on 4 March,[2] and the parties then began quarrelling about what to do next. J. L. Ricardo, the N.S.R.'s chairman, anxious to gain control of the navigations as soon as possible to further his own diplomacy in the railway world, now wished for the immediate conclusion of an *interim* agreement for a temporary lease, to be confirmed, if necessary, by reference to the Court of Chancery. Lord Ellesmere, however, refused to concur in this. His advisers were angling for a permanent transference of the properties to the North Staffordshire Company at a fixed price, and feared, not unreasonably, that if a lease for twenty-one years was conceded, the railway directors would then do nothing to promote a Bill for converting the temporary into a permanent lease. 'Their purpose would be very well served by an arrangement for twenty-one years, while nothing could be more fatal to the Trustees', wrote George Loch who still privately advised Lord Ellesmere.[3] Bellenden Ker, the eminent company lawyer, who was consulted by Lord Ellesmere, suggested as a compromise a method of giving the N.S.R. an immediate interest in the management of the Trustees' navigations by the appointment of an inspector, which would be conditional upon the making of an application to Parliament in the following session to approve the sale of the canals to the Railway Company. This was opposed, however, by Lord Brackley, Lord Ellesmere's eldest son, who feared that if nevertheless the permanent transfer did not take place,

---

[1] F. Smith to A. Egerton, 6 Feb. 1856, L.E.P.
[2] *J.H.C.* cxi (1856), 81.
[3] G. Loch to Earl of Ellesmere, 21 Mar. 1856, B.T.P. (Mertoun), File 153; A. Egerton to F. Smith, 2 July 1856, L.E.P.

his father would have 'submitted to an interference and insight into the working details of his private affairs on the part of a company which may for ought he knows one day become hostile'.[1] Fereday Smith, the General Manager, also threw in his influence in favour of the Trustees' retaining full control of the management until the transfer Bill was through.[2] A further difficulty was that Ricardo desired to see the accounts of the Bridgewater Trust before a binding contract was made,[3] and this was objectionable on grounds similar to those expressed by Viscount Brackley.

By the end of July both sides had given up all thought of an *interim* agreement, and were content to wait until the ensuing parliamentary session, when the attempt to procure an Act would be renewed.[4] Early in the following month the N.S.R. Company's lawyer agreed that the Bill should be drafted without mention of a twenty-one year lease and in such a way as to embody details of the price.[5] It is not clear, however, whether the company was now seriously committed to the idea of purchasing or permanently leasing the canals, or whether it was merely manœuvring for position. Certainly a Bill to 'vest' the two waterways in the North Staffordshire Railway Company was presented in February 1857, re-introduced, and passed its first and second readings in the following May. It was abandoned, however, in committee on 4 June.[6] The reasons for the breakdown may be deduced from a letter written by Fereday Smith to Algernon Egerton six weeks earlier, from which it may be concluded that the N.S.R. Company was striving to drive down the Trustees' price and to force them to abandon a number of their requirements.[7]

---

[1] Viscount Brackley to R. Du Cane, 18 Mar. 1856. See also R. Du Cane to Viscount Brackley, 19 Mar. 1856, and Report on Lord Ellesmere and the N.S.R. Company by H. Bellenden Ker, 15 Mar. 1856, B.T.P. (Mertoun), File 153.

[2] Memorandum by F. Smith to A. Egerton, 23 May 1856, ibid.

[3] F. Smith to A. Egerton, 7 June 1856, and enclosures, L.E.P.

[4] A. Egerton to F. Smith, 28 July 1856, ibid.

[5] A. Egerton to Earl of Ellesmere, 6 Aug. 1856, B.T.P. (Mertoun), File 153.

[6] *J.H.C.* cxii (1857), 22, 138, 189.

[7] Quoted below, p. 279. Among the requirements which the Bridgewater Trustees had shown anxiety to insert in the Bill was one to prevent the new masters of the Bridgewater Canal from raising to a maximum the tonnage on coal from the Worsley collieries, which they proposed to retain in their own hands (F. Smith to W. Slater, 12 Nov. 1856, L.E.P.).

A subsidiary factor, perhaps, was the opposition to the merger inside and outside the Trust which the long delay in proceeding with the scheme had allowed to develop. At Runcorn rumours were afloat that the North Staffordshire Company would refuse to tow coasting vessels to and from Liverpool.[1] There was resistance too in the Chamber of Commerce of the Staffordshire Potteries, where fears of monopoly were aroused by the prospect of the N.S.R.'s controlling in future all the main links with Merseyside.[2]

After the withdrawal of the transfer Bill, the Bridgewater Trustees and the North Staffordshire Railway Company drew sharply apart. The latter began to treat with the Birkenhead, Lancashire, and Cheshire Junction Railway Company for the facilities which it was seeking to conduct a through traffic between Liverpool and London in competition with the L. & N.W.R. The Birkenhead Company asked that in return the N.S.R. should channel a portion of the pottery trade to the rails through Birkenhead, and it was not long before the Trustees were accusing the N.S.R. Company of soliciting one of their Longton customers with the object of diverting his traffic in earthenware from the Trustees' boats to the railway route to Birkenhead. The allegation was denied, but not in a way which was calculated to reassure the Trustees that the attempt would not be made in the future. An acrimonious correspondence on the subject passed between the two concerns in November 1857.[3] It seems clear that the main object of the N.S.R. was to exert such pressure upon neighbouring railways as would bring about its own consolidation into one of the larger railroad systems. In the middle of the month the company gave public notice of its intention to apply to Parliament for power to amalgamate with 'the L. and N.W. Co., the Great Northern Co., the Midland Co., the Sheffield Co., and the South Staffordshire Co., or some or one of them'. The directors had the audacity to couple with this a second notice seeking authority to take over the Bridgewater navigations, compulsorily if necessary.[4] Probably the latter was merely

[1] Howarth to F. Smith, 31 Dec. 1856, L.E.P.

[2] Correspondence enclosed in F. Smith to A. Egerton, 13 Mar. 1857, ibid.

[3] F. Smith to A. Egerton, 20 July 1857; correspondence enclosed in F. Smith to A. Egerton, 1 Dec. 1857, ibid.

[4] F. Smith to A. Egerton, 17 Nov. 1857, ibid.

a piece of bravado designed to persuade the L. & N.W.R. directors that the N.S.R. already had the means of conducting a competing trade with Liverpool and Manchester, and thereby to bring the former to terms. The Bridgewater Trustees were in no way a party to it. By that time they had set their feet upon a more independent course, and they were not prepared to yield to compulsion what they had failed to procure by negotiation.

CHAPTER XIII

The Age of Improvement (1857–1872)

MORE than the change of command in 1855, the failure of the negotiations for a transfer of the canals to the North Staffordshire Railway Company two years later marked the beginning of a new era for the Bridgewater Trust. As the prospects of a rapid sale receded, so the voices within the Trust which had long been agitating for the adoption of a more vigorous and self-reliant policy gained in influence. On 22 April 1857 Fereday Smith addressed a long and important letter to his superior. In it he referred to the more hopeful features of the Trustees' trading position—the considerable increase in their estuarial traffic during the last few years, the probability that it would grow still more as a result of the L. & N.W.R.'s plans to work its traffic into Liverpool via Birkenhead, the 'very good spirits' of the commission agents as to the future of their trade, and the possibility of fostering and improving the commerce of Runcorn by a judicious expenditure of money on the docks. He continued as follows:

The more I reflect on the subject the less necessity do I think there is for yielding to Mr. Ricardo's demands for reduction of price and abandonment of your requirements generally, although I think, if you can be made secure of the terms you have asked, you will do well to close the bargain, but I am thoroughly convinced that almost any course is safer than a delay which may cause the Trustees' general policy, interests and opportunities to be endangered, and if any engineering works are to be undertaken this summer (and summer is the proper time for executing works cheaply), each day's delay may prove a serious loss to you, both of money and trade.[1]

Algernon Egerton was evidently impressed by his manager's faith and sense of urgency, for on the following day he

[1] F. Smith to A. Egerton, 22 Apr. 1857, L.E.P.

authorized him to confer with Slater about financial arrangements for the long-deferred works at Runcorn.[1] These proved
less intractable than the dallyings of the closing years of the
Loch era would have led one to expect. An Estate Act, which
became law on 25 August 1857, removed the principal legal
doubts as to the Trustees' power to execute the Runcorn and
Weston Canal works and to apply funds borrowed under the
provisions of the Estate Act of 1851 to this and other objectives connected with the navigations.[2] But the Trustees were
able to begin work on the new canal without the necessity
of resorting to fresh borrowings at the then inflated rate of
interest. Algernon Egerton decided that the existing fund of
£90,000 invested in exchequer bills should be drawn upon for
the purpose.[3] He also decreed that certain other much needed
improvements in Manchester and at the Stanley Dock and
elsewhere in Liverpool should be undertaken by means of
ploughing back a portion of the income.[4] A new wind was
clearly blowing in the council chambers of the Trust. When
George Loch, now an executor of the first Earl of Ellesmere,
who died on 18 February 1857, protested to Algernon Egerton
against the decision to use the £90,000 fund, which he considered to be a breach of trust, and suggested that instead
recourse should be had to the former policy of borrowing from
the Egerton–Ellesmere family, Fereday Smith brushed his
objections aside. He assured Algernon Egerton that 'the most
certain means of securing permanent good will in a family is
to avoid either lending money to or borrowing from each
other'.[5] During the next fifteen years the Bridgewater Trustees
drew more heavily than ever before upon their own resources
to provide the capital for the development of their properties.[6]
They were enabled to do so not only by the greater flexibility
conferred upon them by their Estate Acts but also by events
within the family of the life tenant. On 19 September 1862 the

[1] A. Egerton to F. Smith, 23 Apr. 1857, L.E.P.

[2] *J.H.L.* lxxxix (1857*b*), 82, 198, 434; F. Smith to A. Egerton, 22 May 1857,
L.E.P.

[3] F. Smith to A. Egerton, 5 and 25 Feb. 1858, L.E.P.

[4] Memorandum of Proposed New Works, 3 Aug. 1857, in F. Smith to
A. Egerton, 3 Aug. 1857, ibid.

[5] F. Smith to A. Egerton, 1 Mar. 1858, ibid.

[6] See below, p. 317, for the extensive reinvestment of income in the collieries
in the 1860s.

second Earl of Ellesmere died, less than six years after his father, leaving as his heir a son aged fifteen. The provisions of the Duke of Bridgewater's curiously all-providing will for the conduct of affairs during a minority now came into operation. By these, as the Superintendent interpreted them, the Superintendent of the Trust was to pay only £1,000 annually for the upkeep of the minor, and having done that, might 'spend as much as he thinks proper of the annual income of the Trust estate on such new works and repairs as he may think necessary or advantageous', investing the remainder of the surplus income for the future benefit of the *cestui que trust*. Explaining these provisions to his sister-in-law, the boy's guardian, Algernon Egerton gave some indication of how he intended to use his enormously extended power to plough back profits. 'In order', he observed, 'to increase traffic and to raise more coal it is necessary to make new works and to sink new pits, both expensive operations.'[1]

Strengthened by these improvements in the availability of capital, the Trustees were able to embark upon a phase of vigorous expansion of plant which lasted for the remainder of their tenure of the canals. It was the most sustained attempt at self-improvement that they had ever undertaken, and showed that they still possessed remarkable powers of recovery from the disasters which the railways had earlier brought upon them. Work on the construction of the Runcorn and Weston Canal, pending for so many years, was actually in progress by March 1858 and reached completion about November 1859.[2] The new dock entrance and the half-tide dock at Runcorn were finished shortly afterwards, the water being let into the basin in July 1860, when the dock was named the Alfred Dock at Lord Ellesmere's request. Despite the competition for labour from the vast new works then being undertaken at Liverpool and Birkenhead and from harvesting during the summer of 1859, the Runcorn docks were completed in record time, reflecting the greatest credit upon the new engineer George Forrester, who had replaced Illman in the middle of the operation.[3] They

---

[1] Algernon Egerton to Mary, Countess of Ellesmere, 14 July 1864, B.T.P. (Mertoun).

[2] F. Smith to A. Egerton, 13 Mar. 1858 and 10 Nov. 1859, L.E.P.

[3] F. Smith to A. Egerton, 27 Oct. 1859 and 14 July 1860; A. Egerton to F. Smith, 18 July 1860, ibid.

were equipped with Armstrong's hydraulic cranes which were mainly used for weighing and trans-shipping salt.[1] Whilst they planned and built, the Trustees also worked to ensure that the facilities which they were creating would be fully used. In order to attract shipping to Runcorn, they took up again, this time in a more determined manner, the struggle to liberate the trade of the port from the pressure of the Liverpool town dues. These dues had not been made more palatable to Runcorn by having been transferred in 1857 from the Corporation of Liverpool to the newly created Mersey Docks and Harbour Board, a body which was as firmly under the control of Lower Mersey interests as the Corporation had been, though the interests were different ones. During the following year the Board went to Parliament for permission to pay the dues, together with the dock dues, into a common fund applicable to the construction of docks at Liverpool and Birkenhead. The Bridgewater Trustees succeeded, with Board of Trade support, in amending the Bill so as to make it promise a revision of the dues under the supervision of the Board of Trade.[2] Although the revised list lowered the duty on salt and other articles of small value, the Trustees were not long content with a qualified victory. In 1860, acting with the Manchester Chamber of Commerce, they promoted a Bill to buy out that portion of the dues which fell upon the ports of the Upper Mersey.[3] They contributed £20,000, the first instalment of the purchase money, from their own Improvement Fund,[4] and Fereday Smith became the first Chairman of the body of Upper Mersey Dues Trustees to which the dues were assigned.[5] Once the loans contracted to facilitate the purchase had been repaid, the docks at Runcorn and at

[1] F. Smith to A. Egerton, 24 Dec. 1860, and A. Egerton to F. Smith, 28 Dec. 1860, L.E.P. Entry dated 28 Sept. 1861 in the Manuscript Diaries of George Forrester.

[2] F. Smith to A. Egerton, 16 and 29 Apr. 1858, L.E.P.

[3] The Trustees appear to have been the moving spirits behind this Bill. Fereday Smith talked the Manchester Chamber into petitioning in favour of it (F. Smith to A. Egerton, 20 Feb. 1860, ibid.), and afterwards persuaded other Upper Mersey interests, such as the Weaver Trustees and the Shropshire Union Railways and Canal Company, to refrain from counter-petitioning, a course which they were at first somewhat unaccountably disposed to pursue (F. Smith to A. Egerton, 12 Apr. 1860, ibid.).

[4] A. Egerton to F. Smith, 21 Apr. 1860, ibid.

[5] F. Smith to A. Egerton, 25 July 1860, ibid.

The Duke's Canal at Runcorn, showing Bridgewater House and the entrance to the docks and to the Runcorn and Weston Canal, 1955

other ports of the Upper Mersey were declared free of the impost.[1]

Strenuous exertions were also made during the years 1857–9 to recover for Runcorn the sea-borne trade in iron from Ardrossan and the other Ayrshire ports, and also that from Whitehaven, which had been slowly drawn away to Fleetwood during the preceding decade. Fleetwood had the edge upon Runcorn for several reasons—the rail communications with the hinterland, the shorter sea trip, avoidance of the delays and risk of damage in the circuitous channels of the Mersey estuary and of the difficulty of getting over the sill of the old docks at Runcorn except at high water; also finally the availability of a suitable backloading of Cumberland iron ore at Barrow for the ships which brought the iron to Fleetwood.[2] Defiant, however, of the facts of geography, the Duke of Bridgewater's Trustees set out to equalize the sea freights as between the two routes. They arranged to subsidize Bairds, the Glasgow ironmasters, to the extent of 2*d.* or 3*d.* per ton for shipping to Runcorn,[3] and to allow the Whitehaven Haematite Iron Company 9*d.* per ton on iron landed at Runcorn and carried to Manchester by their own waterways. As a result, the Whitehaven Company's agent in Manchester was able to quote the same price to buyers at Runcorn as at Fleetwood. Previously the difference had been 1*s.* per ton.[4] Furthermore, in order to ensure that an adequate quantity of shipping was available, they hired a steamer of their own, the *Deva*, experimentally for the period of a month,[5] and, though the experiment failed, they also made arrangements with Merry & Cunningham, the Scottish iron manufacturers, to share with them any losses on chartering vessels at 4*s.* 6*d.* per ton to work exclusively to Runcorn.[6] To overcome the difficulty about backloading, these were to operate a triangular trade—from the Scottish ports to Runcorn with iron, from Runcorn to Belfast with salt, and from Belfast back to Scotland.[7]

[1] Nickson, op. cit., p. 175.

[2] F. Smith to A. Egerton, 16 May 1859, L.E.P.

[3] G. Marsden to F. Smith, 8 Dec. 1858, ibid.

[4] G. Marsden to F. Smith, 17 May 1859; G. Marsden to F. Smith, undated, enclosed in F. Smith to A. Egerton, 25 June 1859, ibid.

[5] F. Smith to A. Egerton, 7 Mar. and 6 Apr. 1859, ibid.

[6] G. Marsden to F. Smith, 8 Dec. 1858, ibid.

[7] F. Smith to A. Egerton, 9 Apr. 1859, ibid.

In their bid to attract trade to Runcorn the Duke's Trustees made use of the through (canal and steamship) rate as an instrument of policy. In April 1862 they established an agency at Dublin, and arranged for a through rate to be charged by themselves, the commission agents, and the City of Dublin Steam Packet Company between the Irish capital and Manchester.[1] Six months later they issued notices to convey traffic from the Potteries and iron from South Staffordshire and Birmingham to Le Havre, Rouen, and Paris at throughout rates.[2] These were encouraging signs of a disposition to escape from the each-company-for-itself isolationism which had for so long hampered British canals in their struggle against the the railways, but they came somewhat late. The Trustees were forced into taking these steps to checkmate the English railway companies, which had anticipated them in the making of through-rate agreements both with steamship operators and with the proprietors of French railroads. By such arrangements the madder traffic from Avignon to Manchester was tied to travel by rail inland from the British ports as soon as it left Avignon. This applied whether the commodity was conveyed by Bordeaux and Liverpool or by Dunkirk and Hull.[3]

Fostered by these exertions the commerce of Runcorn boomed merrily during the 1860s. The impact was chiefly felt in the growth of a large foreign trade through the port. The conclusion of the famous Cobden–Chevalier commercial treaty between Great Britain and imperial France raised in the minds of the Trustees extensive hopes of developing a profitable interchange between Runcorn and the ports of Western Europe. In April 1862 they sent two of their agents, Mitchell and Howarth, on an extensive tour of France and Spain. These men visited Le Havre, Paris, Nantes, Bordeaux, Cette (? Sète), Montpellier, Marseilles, Barcelona, Santander, Bilbao, and Bayonne, interviewing wine and corn merchants and importers of iron, earthenware, and porter, and sending back to England detailed reports which throw an interesting light on the trading

[1] F. Smith to A. Egerton, 8 Apr. 1862; also reports of Marsden and Brydon, enclosed in F. Smith to A. Egerton, 17 Apr. 1862, L.E.P.

[2] F. Smith to A. Egerton, 30 Oct. 1862; A. Egerton to F. Smith, 31 Oct. 1862, and enclosures, ibid.

[3] Mitchell and Howarth to F. Smith, 25 Apr. 1862, ibid.

connections of Great Britain and Western Europe at the time. At most of the places which they visited the prospects of a trade with Runcorn were severely limited. Hull was a serious rival to the Mersey ports for the export of British iron and earthenware to Le Havre, especially on account of the through rates which were quoted, whilst London had an almost unshakable grip on Bordeaux wines imported into England. Nevertheless, the Bridgewater representatives were sufficiently encouraged by what they heard to establish agencies at Le Havre and Bordeaux.[1] Already in December 1860 they had appointed a Norwegian who spoke French and German as their shipping clerk at Runcorn,[2] and the restoration of the separate Customs establishment to Runcorn on 1 January 1862[3] gave further promise of an exchange with countries overseas. In 1862 the tonnage of shipping cleared from Runcorn to colonial and foreign countries was only 16,061 tons, as compared with 145,075 tons cleared coastwise. By 1868 the colonial and foreign clearance had risen to 36,303 tons.[4] The rise in the declared value of exports—from £4,178 in 1857 to £28,480 in 1869 and £44,553 in 1871[5]—was even more startling. On the import side so many vessels arrived at Runcorn with grain from Ireland and flour from France in December 1862 that the Trustees had to hire flats specially to convey the produce to Manchester.[6]

The expansion of trade compelled in its turn a further extension of the capacity for handling it. In July 1867 the Trustees laid the first stone of a new dock at Runcorn, and the work of constructing it, held up by financial difficulties in the depressed years of the later sixties, was still in progress in May 1870.[7] More important still, they made extensive alterations to the configuration of the river estuary near Runcorn in order to remove the long-standing obstacles to navigation

---

[1] See various reports by Mitchell and Howarth to Fereday Smith, Apr. and May 1862, ibid.

[2] F. Smith to A. Egerton, 28 Dec. 1860, ibid.

[3] *Commissioners of Customs, Seventh Annual Report*, p. 48 ; 1863 [3157] XXVI.

[4] *Annual Statement of Trade and Navigation, U.K., 1862*, pp. 393, 418; 1863 [3218] LXV. Statement for *1868*, p. 457 ; 1868–9 [4199] LVIII.

[5] Statement for *1859*, p. 36 ; 1860 [2752] LXIV. For *1869*, p. 37 ; 1870 [c. 220] LXIII. For *1871*, p. 27 ; 1872 [c. 664] LVI.

[6] W. Howarth to F. Smith, 17 Dec. 1862, L.E.P.

[7] Forrester Diaries, 29 July 1867 and 4 May 1870.

by flats and coasting vessels. They carried out excavations and fillings at the Castle Rock, deepened the Gut, and walled round Runcorn Island with the object of creating a new channel.[1] These works, which were effected slowly between 1865 and 1867, were combined with bringing the railway to Runcorn, a task which was accomplished at last by the London and North Western Railway Company and the Bridgewater Trustees jointly. The line was authorized by an Act of Parliament passed in 1861, which provided for a route from Aston on the old Grand Junction line between Crewe and Warrington to Ditton on the Warrington and Garston (transferred to the L. & N.W.R. by lease in 1860), crossing the River Mersey by a bridge at Runcorn Gap. In return for permission to go through Runcorn, the L. & N.W.R. Company agreed to pay half the cost, estimated *in toto* at £20,000, of making the improvements to the estuary. The pretext for this was that the pillars of the railway bridge would otherwise interfere with the course of the channel, but as Fereday Smith stated frankly to his superior, 'the object of the Island works was in reality to protect you against contingencies on the Lancashire shore irrespective altogether of the Bridge'.[2] The wily Trustees also took steps to guard against any undue abstraction of their canal traffic by the new line of railway, for they insisted on constructing themselves, and afterwards controlling, a vital section of the branch line joining the railroad to the docks.[3] Assured of this control they rather welcomed than discouraged the building of the railway, fearing that Runcorn would remain at a permanent disadvantage with Fleetwood in attracting shipping if it continued unable to convey passengers inland by rail.[4]

---

[1] Forrester Diaries, 25 Apr., 18 and 19 May, and 3 and 28 Oct. 1865.

[2] F. Smith to A. Egerton, 17 Feb. 1862, L.E.P.; see also A. Egerton to F. Smith, 22 Jan. 1862, ibid., which shows how much the strategy was Fereday Smith's and how little Algernon Egerton's honest but unsubtle mind managed to grasp it.

[3] The Trustees' engineer ordered the rails and chairs for this line from Barningham's iron works in Pendleton in March 1869 (Forrester Diaries, 18 Mar. 1869).

[4] F. Smith to G. Loch, 5 Nov. 1852, L.E.P. There was also a growing pressure from the townspeople for a line to Runcorn. In 1859 the Trustees had been attacked by the local correspondent of the *Chester Courant* for keeping the railway out of Runcorn (F. Smith to A. Egerton, 27 Oct. 1859, ibid.).

Because a large part of the export and import trade of the Bridgewater Canal and the Mersey and Irwell Navigation, especially in commodities carried across the Atlantic, had to be trans-shipped at Liverpool rather than at Runcorn, the Duke's Trustees also found it necessary to extend their facilities at the larger port. The most pressing problem arose from the expansion of the Liverpool docks northwards along the waterfront and the transference of important trades, such as the timber trade and the general export trade, to the extremity of the line, where the ocean-going vessels could not easily be reached by the canal and river flats. By 1855 the general line of the Liverpool docks had been carried more than two miles north of the little Duke's Dock frequented by the canal craft.[1] The difficulty was accentuated by the fact that the new steamships, unlike the sailing vessels which had moored in the river, loading and unloading over the side into and out of Duke's flats, habitually berthed in the large new docks which were only accessible to the canal boats at high water. To have restricted the approach to those times would have been to upset the delicate time-tabling arrangements for the passage of flats along the estuary. The Trustees were, therefore, obliged to discharge their flats at the Duke's Dock or Manchester Basin, carting the contents overland for considerable distances to the steamships in the docks, but this increased the cost of conveying goods by canal and led to an overcrowding of the two small docks.[2] In 1857, however, the Trustees leased from the Corporation of Liverpool some premises at the Stanley Dock, near the northern end of the docks, which they converted into a depot.[3] Their power to handle traffic there was further augmented two years later when the Mersey Docks and Harbour Board leased them eight cranes for working the timber trade.[4] By 1865 they were engaged in tackling the problem of overcrowding at the Duke's Dock.

[1] It stretched as far as to include the Huskisson Dock (B. D. White, *A History of the Corporation of Liverpool, 1835–1914*, p. 68).

[2] Letter to the Chairman and Members of the Mersey Docks Board in F. Smith to A. Egerton, 6 June 1859; correspondence enclosed in F. Smith to A. Egerton, 22 Mar. 1862, L.E.P.

[3] F. Smith to A. Egerton, 22 Apr. 1857, ibid.

[4] F. Smith to A. Egerton, 30 Apr. 1859; correspondence enclosed in F. Smith to A. Egerton, 7 May 1859, ibid.

A sum of £43,000 was authorized to be spent on purposes which included the erection of a new warehouse and offices and the installation of a traveller crane able to lift 30 tons.[1]

Although the Bridgewater Trustees threw most of their energy into improvements of the terminal facilities on Merseyside, which benefited their two navigations only indirectly, they also gave some attention to the canals themselves. During the years 1861–2 the electric telegraph was installed on the banks of those waterways to connect the Bridgewater offices in Hulme with the subsidiary stations at Stretford, Sale Moor, Broadheath, Burford Lane, Stockton Quay, Howley Quay, Preston Brook, Runcorn, and Weston Point, and with the Egerton Dock in Liverpool. There were two systems, one constructed by the United Kingdom Telegraph Company in an extended arc from Runcorn through Manchester to Wigan and Liverpool, and a second built by the General Electric Telegraph Company, crossing the Mersey at Runcorn Gap. Both were erected and maintained free of charge to the Trustees in return for permission to go along the Canal.[2] The installations soon proved their worth in terms of the economies which they enabled to be effected in the carrying trade. Henceforth an agent requiring additional boats for a temporary purpose would refrain from hiring them until he had telegraphed to discover whether any spare ones were available at other stations, and the cost of hiring them might thus be saved.[3] Telegraphic communications also helped to raise the standard of alertness in all the Bridgewater offices. Such an effect had been anticipated by the staff of the Bridgewater Trust, when they objected to an earlier proposal to introduce the electric telegraph on the grounds that 'it would keep everybody in a constant ferment and often lead to hasty and ill-considered communications',[4] to which James Loch, who was then Superintendent, had retorted sarcastically: 'What you call keeping everyone in

[1] Forrester Diaries, 16 May and 9 Nov. 1865, 7 and 15 May 1866.
[2] See correspondence of Algernon Egerton and Fereday Smith on this subject, and other papers, Dec. 1859–Dec. 1860, and Jan.–May 1862, L.E.P.
[3] 'As soon as our Liverpool Telegraph was completed I at once put a stop to the Harrington agent hiring boats till he should telegraph to Mr. Mitchell's office to enquire if the Trustees had any spare ones at Liverpool or Birkenhead . . .' (F. Smith to A. Egerton, 27 Mar. 1862, ibid.).
[4] F. Smith to J. Loch, 7 May 1851, ibid.

a state of ferment, I would call constant activity and attention: one main object of having such a powerful rememberer of duty.'[1] Unfortunately the Trustees were about a dozen years behind the railway companies in adopting this improvement.[2]

In the early 1860s the Bridgewater authorities turned to rescue the Mersey and Irwell Navigation from the consequences of their own previous neglect. During the sixteen years after it passed under the same control as the Duke's Canal, that waterway had been slowly silting up, with the result that by the late fifties carriers were complaining of shallows which delayed and damaged their boats. 'I regret to say', wrote C. J. Faulkner, in January 1859, 'the Old Quay Navigation remains in such condition that it is extremely difficult to get vessels along at 3 ft. 6 in. draught when it used to be navigated as easily at 5 ft. 4 in.'[3] The Trustees were disposed to put the blame for this state of affairs on the landholders, coal-owners, and industrialists on the upper reaches of the Irwell and its tributaries above Manchester, who had been persistently throwing large quantities of cinders, rubble, and other refuse into the stream to be washed downwards by the current.[4] It seems probable, however, that their own inadequate and inefficient dredging was, in large measure, responsible. Early in their tenure of the navigation, the Trustees, in an attempt to evade the cost of dredging, had erected dam boards across the sill to raise the level of the water, but this had only increased the risk of flooding,[5] which in its turn tended to promote silting by bringing down fresh deposits. Moreover, when they dredged, they laid the extracted cinders on the banks of the river to be swept back into the water by the next 'freshet'.[6] After the disastrous flood of December 1860, which left new deposits at Throstlenest, a little to the west of Manchester,[7] on which three of the New Quay Company's boats were grounded,[8] they

---

[1] J. Loch to F. Smith, 9 May 1851, ibid.

[2] By the middle of 1848 about half the railways open had their telegraphic equipment (J. H. Clapham, *The Early Railway Age, 1820–50*, p. 396).

[3] C. J. Faulkner to F. Smith, 12 Jan. 1859, L.E.P.

[4] F. Smith to A. Egerton, 12 Dec. 1860, ibid.

[5] Opposition . . . Bridgewater Navigation Co. . . . to the M.S.C. Bill . . ., 1885, Minutes of Evidence, qu. 12450.

[6] C. J. Faulkner to F. Smith, 12 Jan. 1859, L.E.P.

[7] F. Smith to A. Egerton, 12 Dec. 1860, ibid.

[8] W. Hall to F. Smith, 10 Dec. 1860, ibid.

bestirred themselves to action. Joining with other water
carriers and with the Corporations of Manchester and Stockport they promoted a Bill during the 1862 session to prohibit
under heavy penalties the fouling of the upper streams of the
Mersey and the Irwell and their various tributaries. After a
spectacular parliamentary battle, during which they were
obliged to run the gauntlet between Cheshire landowners and
the representatives of the manufacturing interest, groupings
as jealous of one another as they were of the Trustees, they
eventually carried their measure in a diluted form, with its
coercive powers reduced.[1] In order to secure an Act which was
never fully effective, they were obliged to lay out at least
£2,000 on legal and parliamentary expenses.[2] They would have
done better to spend the money on replacing some of the old
fixed stone weirs, which held up accumulations of silt, by tilt
weirs which would permit a more effective scouring action to
take place. It was left to their successors, the Bridgewater
Navigation Company, to try this with good effect.[3]

The Bridgewater Canal was in better condition than the Old
Quay Navigation. Nevertheless, a widening of certain sections
of it seems to have been undertaken just before 1860 in order
to afford better facilities for the traffic.[4] Apart from that, the
principal outlay was for social convenience rather than private
profit—the cleansing of the Canal from the noxious and
odiferous fluids poured into it at the Manchester end by the
River Medlock, a recipient for the city's sewage outfall and
bleach works refuse. During the 1850s the polluted liquid
spread slowly westwards along the Canal, eliciting protests
from first one locality and then another. In 1854 Edward
Watkin, the railway magnate, remonstrated that his house

---

[1] See correspondence between F. Smith, A. Egerton, and the Earl of Ellesmere on this subject, Feb.–Aug. 1862, L.E.P.; also details of the passing of the
Mersey, Weaver, and Irwell Protection Bill in the *J.H.C.* and *J.H.L.* for 1862
and in Hansard's *Parliamentary Debates*, 3rd ser., clxvii and clxviii.

[2] The Trustees' solicitor submitted a bill for £1,922. 11*s.* 11*d.*, which
excluded the expenses of counsel and witnesses (F. Smith to A. Egerton,
12 Dec. 1862, L.E.P.).

[3] Opposition . . . Bridgewater Navigation Co. . . . to the M.S.C. Bill . . .,
1885, Minutes of Evidence, qu. 11594–6 and 12279–81.

[4] I owe this information to Mr. Lloyd, formerly Canal Inspector of the
Bridgewater Department of the M.S.C.C., but have been able to find no
documentary evidence in support of it, except the proposal made in December
1850. See below, p. 319, text and n. 5.

at Timperley was filled with 'as "vile a compound of vilanious [*sic*] smells" as ever tried human nostrils'.[1] By 1859 complaints were being received from Moore, only a short distance from Preston Brook. For many years the Duke's Trustees, deterred by thoughts of the expense, did nothing to abate the nuisance, preferring to wait for 'some General Public Measure' to prevent the fouling of rivers.[2] In 1866, however, acting under strong pressure from Manchester Corporation, they undertook impressive engineering works in Manchester to insulate the Cheshire reaches of their canal from the outpourings of the River Medlock. The contaminated water was confined by stop lock gates to the area above the Hulme Locks, while a pure supply was carried by an underground pipe laid in the bed of the Canal from the Rochdale Canal Lock to the Canal below the locks. Under the expert direction of George Forrester these intricate operations were conducted with a stoppage lasting no more than six and a half weeks.[3]

The one outstanding omission in this extensive sequence of improvements was the failure to resort to mechanical aid to span the gap in operational efficiency between the horse-drawn canal boats and the railroad locomotives. In June 1859 the inventor Joseph Burch tried out a steam tug on the Duke's Canal at Manchester. The trial was written up as a success in the *Manchester Guardian*, but after taking a trip in the vessel, the General Manager of the Trust concluded that the old objections to this mode of traction still obtained, and advised against using the Trustees' money to finance further experimentation.[4] Some doubt is cast on this conclusion by the fact that in the following year Burch constructed for the Grand Junction Canal Company a small screw-propeller boat which could tow a narrow boat loaded with 12 tons of cargo at $3\frac{1}{2}$ miles per hour without damaging the canal banks. The Company found that it would carry at about one-third the cost of horse-power, taking a load itself and pulling another laden vessel. The Bridgewater Trustees inspected the device,

---

[1] E. Watkin to F. Smith, 6 Sept. 1854, L.E.P.

[2] F. Smith to A. Egerton, 9 Aug. 1859, ibid.

[3] Forrester Diaries, 12 Jan. and 4 June–19 July 1866.

[4] F. Smith to A. Egerton, 5 July 1859; A. Egerton to F. Smith, 30 June 1859, L.E.P. See above, pp. 111–13, for earlier attitudes to this question.

but there is no evidence of their having adopted it.[1] Their
General Manager, despite the normal progressiveness of his
outlook, seems to have developed almost a closed mind on the
subject of mechanical traction. Along certain lines he was
disinclined even to allow experiment.[2]

The new course which the Trustees had adopted in systematically developing their equipment did not save them, however, from further encroachments upon their position by
the railway companies. For a while, in fact, in the later fifties
the conflict flared with a new intensity. In 1857–8 the Trustees
found themselves locked in a desperate struggle to prevent
the Warrington and Stockport Railway, completed in 1854
from Timperley on the M.S.J. & A. to Warrington on the St.
Helens Railway, from capturing the traffic in market produce
from the rural districts of northern Cheshire into Manchester,
which the original Liverpool and Manchester line had left
untouched, because it ran so far to the north. In an effort
to compete with the railway, canal freights from Preston
Brook, Stockton Quay, Lymm, and Altrincham were slashed
to cost price, and tolls were also reduced.[3] This, however, was
but a local skirmish opening the way to warfare upon a
grander scale, into which the Trustees were plunged not by
their own activities, nor merely by jealousy of others towards
them, but by rivalries germinating in the railway world.

The principal cause of dissension was the London and North
Western Railway Company's dominant position, which was
coming increasingly under challenge. Surrounded by its satellites of the so-called Euston Confederacy—the L. & Y.R., the
East Lancashire, the Midland, the Manchester, Sheffield, and
Lincolnshire, the Eastern Counties, and the North British—
the Company stood jealously on guard over its preserves in
north-west England and the western Midlands, striving by all

---

[1] G. Anderson to F. Smith, 5 Dec. 1860; G. Forrester to F. Smith, 22 Nov.
1860, L.E.P.

[2] In 1860 he did all in his power to prevent the trial of a chain propeller
boat operating by means of a chain laid on the bed of the canal. 'I cannot
understand how on mechanical principles', he observed, 'this mode of propulsion can be economical, as the fulcrum has to be lifted, as well as the boat has
to be dragged' (F. Smith to A. Egerton, 26 Nov. 1860, ibid.).

[3] F. Smith to A. Egerton, 1 Apr. and 5 June 1858; A. Egerton to F. Smith,
5 Apr. and 8 June 1858, ibid. The toll was reduced from 2s. to 1s. 6d. per ton
between Warrington and Stockton Quay and Manchester on 8 June 1858.

available means to ward off invasion by the Great Northern on its eastern flank and the G.W.R. to the west. Both companies were to be feared, in that like the L. & N.W.R., they had the means of supplying the region, once they gained access to it, with a route to London. The personal qualities of Captain Mark Huish, the L. & N.W.R.'s General Manager, his ruthlessness, ill temper, and above all his duplicity, fanned the flames of enmity, and ensured that even the North Western's satellites would ultimately revolt. Nemesis struck in June 1857 when the M.S. & L., headed by Edward Watkin, an equally thrustful character, trained by Huish himself, broke with the Confederacy and aligned itself with the Great Northern to divert goods and passenger traffic between London and Manchester away from the L. & N.W.R. lines to their own joint easterly route through Retford.[1] Whilst this contest was in progress the old enmity between Huish's company and the Great Western flared up afresh, leading, at the beginning of 1858, to the suspension of the Northern Alliance, a system of regular meetings of the representatives of the two railway companies and other railway and canal concerns interested in the carrying trade north and south of Wolverhampton for the purpose of regulating freight charges.[2] In the parlance of the day the North Western people were rapidly becoming what the Great Northern had once been dubbed, the 'Ishmaelites',[3] or outcasts, among railways. They were attacked in the following August by the North Staffordshire Company, which handed its London traffic, previously exchanged with the L. & N.W.R. at Colwich, to the Midland and Great Northern lines. The L. & N.W.R. retaliated by placing its own agents in the pottery towns and by arranging to cart goods, which would otherwise have travelled south by the trains of the N.S.R., overland to its own main line station at Whitmore, about a dozen miles away.[4]

---

[1] A vivid account of this episode in railway history is given in Roger Lloyd, *Railwaymen's Gallery*, pp. 46–78; for further particulars see George Dow, *Great Central*, vol. i, ch. xiv.

[2] M. Huish to F. Smith, 4 Mar. 1858, L.E.P., offering to resume the meetings 'as we are now arrived at a settlement of our differences with the Great Western Company'.

[3] F. Smith to A. Egerton, 20 July 1857, ibid.

[4] F. Smith to A. Egerton, 1 Sept. 1858, ibid.

These hostilities threatened the Bridgewater interests in two main ways. In the first place they helped to bring about a widespread disturbance of the rates of carriage. They did so indirectly even when the Duke's was not itself interested in the trades for which the railway companies were contending. Thus the quarrel between the L. & N.W.R. and the M.S. & L. over the London traffic prevented the completion of a formal agreement between the Trustees and the L. & N.W.R. and L. & Y.R. Companies for raising charges between Merseyside and south-east Lancashire which had been negotiated just before the breach occurred. Captain Huish declined to ratify the compact on the grounds that the M.S. & L., which he could no longer control, was party to a section of it,[1] and the relations between the carriers in the Lancashire traffic slithered downwards to the brink of contest in the winter of 1857–8.[2] When the parties resumed negotiations for a settlement in the following June, it was assumed on all sides that a resolution of the differences between the Sheffield Company and the North Western over the north–south traffic must precede the placing of the Liverpool–Manchester down rates on a satisfactory footing.[3] This was because London and Liverpool were competitors for the export of Manchester manufactured goods to the Far East. Any attempt to raise charges between Manchester and Liverpool whilst the Manchester and London rate was depressed by the contest of the two companies might result, therefore, in a diversion of trade from Liverpool to London. Meanwhile, the demise of the Northern Alliance had unsettled the rates in many of the trades in which the Duke's Trustees were involved, notably the traffic in iron and iron ore from Cumberland to South Staffordshire conducted by them through Runcorn. It was reported early in March that the low through rates offered by the Midland Railway Company were interfering with the charges on pig-iron between Whitehaven and the Black Country.[4]

The disruption of formal rate-fixing compacts might have

---

[1] F. Smith to W. Cawkwell, 26 Oct. 1857, L.E.P.

[2] For evidence of the atmosphere of mutual suspicion between the Trustees and the L. & N.W.R. in March 1858, see M. Huish to F. Smith, 13 Mar. 1858, and F. Smith to A. Egerton, 26 Mar. 1858, ibid.

[3] F. Smith to A. Egerton, 23 and 24 July 1858, ibid.

[4] F. Smith to M. Huish, 5 Mar. 1858, ibid.

been less damaging to the carrying interest had it not occurred at a time of trade depression consequent upon the international economic crisis of the autumn of 1857. In periods of prosperity or recovery, such as occurred in 1852–4, early in 1857, and again in 1859–60, the larger railway companies were often disposed to act with the canals to stabilize charges. During a slump, however, when they had an excess of carrying capacity on their hands, they were usually obliged to compete more fiercely with their neighbours in order to fill their wagons.[1] 'The present diminished carrying trade of the country rather tends to create competition and to reduce rates', observed Fereday Smith in December 1857.[2]

Quarrels among the railway companies also embarrassed the Trustees by leading to the promotion of new lines. Having severed his connections with Euston, the indomitable Edward Watkin of the M.S. & L. gave full rein to the ambitions which he had been obliged previously to restrain—to acquire for his company an access to Merseyside independent of, and, as far as the Manchester trade was concerned, competitive with, the L. & N.W.R. In January 1858 he announced his intention to lease the Warrington and Stockport line (as yet in reality a Warrington and Altrincham line only) and extend it to Stockport, and to promote, in conjunction with the St. Helens and Great Northern Companies, the construction of a line of railway from Garston into Liverpool.[3] This would provide him, through his satellites the M.S.J. & A., the W. & S., and the St. Helens, with a continuous line from Manchester to Liverpool and with the early prospect of connecting the system east of Stockport with his own main line, in a route which altogether avoided Manchester, where facilities had to be shared with the L. & N.W.R. These proposals gave the Duke of Bridgewater's Trustees many sleepless nights, for the formation of a south line of railway between Manchester and Liverpool seemed to them likely to intensify the competition with the canal trade already maintained by the L. & N.W.R. and L. & Y.R. lines.[4] It was something which they had feared and

[1] See above, p. 255, n. 4.

[2] F. Smith to A. Egerton, 3 Dec. 1857, L.E.P.

[3] Dow, op. cit., vol. i, p. 192.

[4] They attached a paramount importance to keeping up freight charges, thinking this more desirable than the winning of new trade. Fereday Smith

schemed against for years. Later in 1858 they were assailed
by threats in a different area. In pursuit of its quarrel with
the North Staffordshire, the L. & N.W.R. began, towards the
end of October, to make a survey for a line of its own into the
Potteries from Whitmore or Madely on the old Grand Junction
line.[1] The Bridgewater Trustees could not but apprehend
that, once constructed, it would divert traffic not only from
the N.S.R.'s lines north and south of Stoke but also from the
Preston Brook canal route. For the railway route into the
Potteries through Birkenhead and Crewe would become vastly
more competitive if it was no longer obliged to depend on the
N.S.R. Company's line from Crewe to Stoke, which was laden
with monopolistic freight charges out of all proportion to its
length.[2] They shuddered when they learned that the L. &
N.W.R.'s agents were whipping up the potters to support their
proposed line with promises to lower the cost of transporting
their raw materials from Birkenhead and to carry their manufactured goods with greater dispatch and safety.[1]

The Trustees' first response to this crisis in their affairs was
to muster all their resources for a campaign in Parliament to
defeat the more objectionable railway Bills and to amend
others in the interest of the canals. For the Duke's 1858 was
almost as heavy a parliamentary year as 1846,[3] and it was also
successful. The M.S. & L.'s Garston to Liverpool extension
Bill and a similar measure promoted independently by the St.
Helens Railway Company were rejected outright;[4] so also
were the proposals for leasing and extending the Warrington
and Stockport line.[5] A more formal opposition was also pressed
against the L. & Y./E.L.R. and M.S. & L./Great Northern
railway amalgamation Bills to compel a revision of the tolls on
canals belonging to the contracting railroads.[6] The concessions

---

remarked later that they 'would have sacrificed if a reduction of only one shilling per ton had been forced upon them, upwards of twenty thousand pounds
per annum' (F. Smith to A. Egerton, 20 Jan. 1859, L.E.P.).

  [1] W. H. Boddington to F. Smith, 23 Oct. 1858, ibid.

  [2] Out of an 8*s.* freight the N.S.R. received 4*s.* 11*d.* for between a third and
a quarter of the total rail distance from Birkenhead to Stoke, ibid.

  [3] F. Smith to A. Egerton, 11 June 1858, ibid.

  [4] F. Smith to A. Egerton, 16 and 17 June 1858, ibid.

  [5] W. Cantrill to A. Egerton, 21 July 1858, ibid.

  [6] Agreement was reached with the L. & Y.R. and E.L.R. Companies that, if
their Amalgamation Bill passed the House of Lords, the tolls on the M.B. &

thus extracted were very timely, for evidence of the blocking of trade on railway-owned canals by the imposition
of heavy tolls was growing in the middle fifties. After the
Rochdale Canal passed under the control of four northern
railway companies in 1855, the tolls were gradually levered
up, until in October 1856 they stood at 2*d.* per ton per mile on
all merchandise except timber, which remained at 1*d.*[1] Cases
such as this help to explain the growing anti-railroad solidarity
of the canal proprietors which was a feature of the 1858
parliamentary campaign. There is proof of planning by a
Canal Association to present a case against railway and canal
amalgamations before a Select Committee established by
Colonel Wilson Patten.[2] The Bridgewater manager, Fereday
Smith, approached Wilson Patten for a proper representation
of the Canal interest on the committee and arranged for the
giving of evidence by the Canal agents.[3]

It was not believed, however, that force alone could stanch
the inconveniences arising from the battle of the railway
giants. Diplomacy must also be tried. Fereday Smith conceived a sort of Grand Design to mediate between the contending companies and thus promote a general pacification,
leading to a universal restoration of freight charges to a
profitable level and a withdrawal of contentious new promotions. The task, however, was Sisyphean and the means were
inadequate, sometimes, in fact, laughably so. The Trustees
first addressed themselves to healing the breach between the

B.C. should be reduced to 1*d.* per ton per mile on all timber, dyewoods, and
brimstone from Liverpool or Runcorn, and on all pig-iron passing between
Liverpool or any place on the Trustees' navigation and places on the M.B. &
B.C. See F. Smith to A. Egerton, 8 June 1858, ibid. Though the Trustees no
longer opposed it, the Bill was lost in the Lords, but when it was reintroduced
in the following session, the L. & Y.R. Company agreed with the Trustees to
maintain the reduced tolls if it was allowed to pass. See F. Smith to A. Egerton,
26 Feb. 1859, and A. Egerton to F. Smith, 28 Feb. 1859, ibid. This time it was
passed, and the canal tolls were modified (Marsden and others to F. Smith,
26 Mar. 1859, ibid.).

[1] F. Smith to A. Egerton, 16 Oct. 1856, ibid. The M.S. & L.R. Company,
also, charged 1½*d.* per ton for pig-iron on the Ashton Canal, contrary to the
spirit of the Act vesting the canal in them. The breach was justified on the
ground that the Act did not specifically mention pig-iron (F. Smith to A.
Egerton, 4 Oct. 1855, ibid.).

[2] F. Smith to A. Egerton, 13 July 1858, ibid.

[3] F. Smith to Wilson Patten, 14 June 1858 ; F. Smith to A. Egerton, 19 June
1858, ibid.

L. & N.W.R. and the St. Helens Company. On 18 June 1858 Smith met Lord Chandos, the Chairman of the L. & N.W.R., and persuaded him to have a letter of explanation sent to the St. Helens for an earlier missive which had been construed as an insult. The letter was dispatched and favourably received.[1] They then proposed to the L. & N.W.R. and L. & Y.R. boards that they should appease the M.S. & L.R. by granting it proper legal facilities for the joint traffic, which it conducted with the Great Northern from London and elsewhere, to get to Liverpool along their own lines at agreed rates. The Trustees would then join them in assisting the St. Helens and Warrington and Stockport lines to conduct their local traffic, in such a way as to avoid upsetting the through trade between Liverpool and Manchester.[2] What these proposals overlooked was that the conflict between the greater companies was not merely, or even mainly, about access to Liverpool. The L. & N.W. and L. & Y. directors gave the Trustees a hearing at a conference in London on 10 September, when the L. & Y. party and a minority of the L. & N.W.R. board seemed disposed to support the recommendations,[3] but it was not until after the L. & N.W.R., the M.S. & L.R., and the Great Northern had reached a general settlement of their differences in November that steps were taken to advance the charge for the delivery of Manchester export goods in Liverpool with effect from 1 January 1859.[4] The overthrow of Captain Huish by a revolt within the L. & N.W.R. and the gradual national recovery from economic depression probably did more than any persuasions of the Bridgewater Trustees to bring about the reconciliation. These factors also helped to restore harmony in other directions. In 1859 the L. & N.W.R. and the North Staffordshire Company reached a fresh agreement,[5] and a Bill to authorize the amalgamation of the two concerns was again introduced into Parliament.[6] By February the North Western and the Great Western, having resolved some long-standing disagreements, were striving to persuade the lesser partners

---

[1] F. Smith to A. Egerton, 19 and 21 June 1858, L.E.P.

[2] Memorandum enclosed in F. Smith to A. Egerton, 4 Aug. 1858, ibid.

[3] F. Smith to A. Egerton, 11 Sept. 1858, ibid.

[4] F. Smith to A. Egerton, 28 Dec. 1858, ibid.

[5] Hamilton Ellis, *British Railway History 1830–76*, p. 196.

[6] F. Smith to A. Egerton, 3 June 1859, L.E.P.

of the former Northern Alliance to agree to charge equal rates on the South Staffordshire trade. Advances averaging 1*s*. 6*d*. per ton were soon afterwards effected on the pig-iron and iron ore trades between the Lancashire and Cumberland ports and South Staffordshire.[1]

From this time forward the Trustees' fortunes entered a calmer phase. The elevation of the rates of carriage coincided with an increase in quantities, perceptible in the iron and earthenware trades before the end of 1858.[2] For this reason, and also because the collieries and the income from the Worsley estates were growing fast, the net profit on the Trust properties soared to almost forgotten heights. In 1860 it reached £106,535, a level higher than in any known year since 1844, and comparable with the best yields of the 1820s. It continued above the £70,000 mark in three other years of the 1860s for which evidence is available. Owing to certain ambiguities introduced into the keeping of the later accounts,[3] it is impossible to chart exactly the growth in the income from the navigations, but there can be little doubt that the Trustees' canal business, especially the carrying trade which they conducted upon their own and adjacent canals,[4] was experiencing an Indian summer round about 1860. The volume of traffic passing annually on the Duke's Canal, which had been relatively stagnant in the late forties and early fifties, rose by

[1] Minutes of meetings of former members of the Northern Alliance enclosed in F. Smith to A. Egerton, 10 Feb. and 10 Mar. 1859; F. Smith to A. Egerton, 7 May 1859, ibid. See E. T. MacDermot, *History of the Great Western Railway*, vol. i, p. 421, for details of three agreements made between the G.W.R. and the L. & N.W.R. in 1858.

[2] Leslie to F. Smith, 21 Dec. 1858; H. Shipton to F. Smith, 21 Dec. 1858, L.E.P.

[3] See below, Appendix A, for details of fluctuations in profit. The problem arises from the large deficits shown in the Profit and Loss Account under the heading 'Worsley Yard' in the post-1860 accounts. It is possible that certain running expenses on equipment and repairs, previously charged to the separate Canal and Colliery Departments, had now been transferred to the general account in this way. But the later account books provide no information as to where these deficiencies arose. On the other hand, the losses may represent capital outlay made out of income. Caution must, therefore, be exercised in interpreting the detailed analysis of departmental profit shown in the Appendix, at least for the years 1864 onwards.

[4] Despite earlier reductions the Trustees still carried iron, iron ore, grain, and other commodities on the Trent and Mersey Canal to and from South Staffordshire. Through the Anderton Company, which they owned, they also traded to Macclesfield and the Potteries.

about 400,000 tons between 1855 and 1860,[1] and the net profit of that waterway, inclusive of the carrying trade, was higher in 1860 by about 56 per cent than the average for the three years 1851–3.[2] In 1860 the Trustees also made £6,606 on carrying the Great Western Railway Company's traffic across the Mersey estuary from Birkenhead into Liverpool,[3] an interesting survival of their earlier efforts to build up a many-sided interchange of trade with that company.

Behind this façade of restored prosperity, however, lurked the spectre of uncertainty. The general pacification in the railway world after the fall of Huish did not banish the threat of the construction of new lines, nor even postpone the development for any lengthy period. In fact the high level of the canal freight charges, which rendered the Trustees so comfortable, tended to coax fresh capital into the transport industry in the early sixties in much the same way as it had done in the middle twenties, when the Liverpool and Manchester line was planned. Nowhere was this more apparent than in the vicinity of Stoke-on-Trent, where in 1862 the potters were in full cry against the 'North Staffordshire Monopoly', by which they understood principally the heavy charges levied upon their raw materials by the North Staffordshire Railway Company both as a railway proprietor and as the owner of the Grand Trunk Canal.[4] Two years earlier the Severn Navigation Commission, led by its engineer E. Leader Williams, had promoted an experiment to undercut the carriers from the Mersey by putting on steamers which would convey clay from Poole and the Cornish ports up the Severn as far as Stourport, where it would be trans-shipped into canal boats.[5] Now, in 1862, two separate schemes for building railways into the area—the Wellington and Silverdale project which was to connect with the G.W.R. at Wellington and a proposal for a line from Market Drayton—were being actively promoted.[6] At a meeting at Tunstall in March there was even talk of

---

[1] See below, Appendix B.
[2] See below, Appendix A.
[3] Bridgewater Trust General Accounts, 1860, p. 40, B.T.P. (Mertoun).
[4] G. Joynson to F. Smith, 29 Mar. 1862, L.E.P.
[5] J. Roscoe to F. Smith, 23 June 1860, ibid.
[6] F. Smith to A. Egerton, 15 Mar. 1862; J. Roscoe to F. Smith, 10 Nov. 1862, ibid.

cutting a new canal, wide and deep enough to admit flats of 130 tons burthen, from the Potteries to the River Weaver somewhere between Northwich and Winsford.[1] Alarmed especially by the railway proposals, and chivvied by the Bridgewater Trustees, the N.S.R. eventually agreed to reduce its canal tolls on potters' materials from and after 1 January 1863, and, on the strength of this assurance, the Trustees reduced the freights charged by the Anderton Company as carriers by 10*d*. per ton and lowered their own charges between Runcorn dock and Preston Brook from 2*s*. 4*d*. to 2*s*. 2*d*. per ton.[2] This concession did not prevent the construction of new rail connections with the Potteries, but the N.S.R. was itself left to make them. Under an Act passed in 1864 it extended the original Silverdale and Newcastle line to Madeley and Market Drayton, whence it would be connected with Nantwich and the London and North Western Railway.[3]

Meanwhile the pressure was on again in the area west of Manchester. When the Manchester, Sheffield, and Lincolnshire Railway Company made its peace with the North Western in November 1858, it abandoned to the latter the right to make the Garston to Liverpool extension. As the L. & N.W.R. proceeded to lease first the Warrington and Stockport and then, in 1860, the Warrington and Garston branch of the St. Helens Railway, one avenue of independent approach to Merseyside was soon locked and barred against the Sheffield Company.[4] But the ingenious Watkin, whose drive to the west was always more than a mere tactical counter-stroke against the imperialism of Captain Huish, merely turned to open another. Acting in conjunction with the Midland and Great Northern Companies, the M.S. & L. nursed into being the Cheshire Lines network. One arm of this, the Cheshire Midland and the West Cheshire, extended from the M.S.J. & A. at Altrincham through Northwich to Mouldsworth, where it turned abruptly north, as if impatient to reach the waters of the Mersey, to join the Birkenhead Railway at Helsby. It was completed to Northwich

[1] G. Joynson to F. Smith, 29 Mar. 1862, ibid.

[2] F. Smith to A. Egerton, 1 Dec. 1862, and A. Egerton to F. Smith, 6 Dec. 1862, ibid.

[3] E. Carter, *An Historical Geography of the Railways of the British Isles*, pp. 306–7.

[4] Dow, op. cit., vol. i, p. 192.

in 1863 and to Helsby in 1869. The other arm, consisting of the Stockport, Timperley, and Altrincham and Stockport and Woodley Junction lines, connected with a branch of the M.S. & L.'s main line at Woodley, thus giving the M.S. & L. an outlet into Cheshire which avoided Manchester.[1] In 1865 Watkin bought off his master-stroke, carrying through Parliament against strong opposition a Bill authorizing him to build a new trunk line from Cornbrook in Manchester to Garston, which was by that time connected to Liverpool by a Cheshire Lines link opened in 1864 as far as Brunswick Dock. The Manchester to Garston line took eight years to build, and was not completed until 1873.[2]

The morale of the Duke of Bridgewater's Trustees must have fallen sharply as they watched this web of iron rail being woven about their canal. It is not surprising that they began to think seriously again of disposing of the canals and docks by sale. Already in November 1864 they were treating for a transfer to the L. & N.W.R. and L. & Y. Companies jointly. As a preliminary they valued the properties at just over £2,000,000,[3] an optimistic figure which may explain why nothing further was heard of the deal.

To the last, however, the attitude of the Trustees to the growth of railways remained ambivalent, and the 1860s brought forth several instances of their active encouragement of railway building. The motives for this collaboration were mixed. The Trustees undertook to help the M.S. & L. Company forward the Stockport, Timperley, and Altrincham Junction Railway in October 1860, because they were promised a branch from the railway to the Duke's Canal near Broadheath which they hoped would turn that line into a feeder of the canal.[4] They virtually forced the L. & N.W.R. to carry its branch line over the Mersey estuary at Runcorn Gap,[5] because they anticipated benefits to the port of Runcorn. Later they supported the Lancashire Union Railway scheme, partly to bring

---

[1] R. P. Griffiths, *The Cheshire Lines Railway*, passim.

[2] Dow, op. cit., vol. ii, pp. 7, 8, 132.

[3] Forrester Diaries, 1 Nov. and 12 Dec. 1864.

[4] F. Smith to A. Egerton, 25 Oct. 1860, and 6 Jan. 1862 (and enclosed notice); A. Egerton to F. Smith, 26 Oct. 1860, L.E.P.

[5] By opposing the Company's earlier plan to cross at Fiddlers Ferry, further upstream (F. Smith to A. Egerton, 25 Feb. 1860).

trade to Runcorn and partly to develop their collieries.[1] This project, to link the south Lancashire coalfield with the ports of the Upper Mersey, was promoted in 1864 with the object of providing the coal-owners with compensation in the export market for the reduction of domestic demand due to the Cotton Famine. Colliery considerations were paramount in the support given to the L. & N.W.R.'s Eccles, Tyldesley, and Wigan branch which first brought the railway to Worsley. Lord Ellesmere cut the first sod for Worsley railway station in 1861.[2] His Lordship and the Trustees also supplied a more material encouragement by selling land for the construction of the line.[3] The Trustees looked to the new railway to bring the cotton industry to Worsley, a development desired less for its own sake than for incidental benefits to the coal-mines. Fereday Smith explained these to A. F. Egerton: 'The factories will probably provide occupation for the daughters of the colliers, and the increased prosperity of the district will, I hope, in the end yield us abundant labour for the pits as well as a good market for the coal and for the building land.'[4] A subsequent letter made his meaning clearer: 'Our great want is an abundance of labour, and I am more and more convinced that this can be best obtained by the establishment of cotton and other factories, where the colliers' daughters can find employment.'[5]

Varied though the interests of the Trustees were, it is unlikely that what was still mainly a canal concern would have encouraged the growth of railways unless the management was convinced that the canals could hold their own in the increased rough and tumble. For such self-confidence, both past and present experience supplied the ground. Through forty years of sharp railway competition they had enlarged their trade, and had achieved a real though fluctuating success in coming to terms with their challengers to maintain charges

---

[1] Fereday Smith gave evidence in favour of the scheme before a committee of the House of Commons. He stated that the Trustees had spent £100,000 during the preceding three or four years at Runcorn, and were contemplating another large expenditure, contingent upon better railway facilities being given (*Colliery Guardian*, 14 May 1864).

[2] F. Mullineux, *The Duke of Bridgewater's Canal*, p. 30.

[3] F. Smith to A. Egerton, 9 and 28 Jan. 1862, L.E.P.

[4] F. Smith to A. Egerton, 7 July 1860, ibid.

[5] F. Smith to A. Egerton, 5 Dec. 1860, ibid.

at a profitable level.¹ They could hope at least, therefore, for a more modest achievement in future. In fine, though the prospects of the canals may have undergone a setback in the years before those waterways were sold, they were still very far from being desperate.

¹ As late as the years 1867–75 a Canal Traffic Committee consisting of representatives of the Bridgewater Trust, the Shropshire Union Railways and Canal Co., and the N.S.R. Company (interested as a canal owner) met at irregular intervals to fix freight charges between North Staffordshire and Liverpool. This committee raised the charge on iron by 6*d.* per ton on 1 Jan. 1869, but was obliged to rescind the increase some eighteen months later, owing to competition from carriers on the Weaver Navigation. See Minute Book of Canal Traffic Committee, 1867–75, T.M.C. 1, B.T.H.R.

CHAPTER XIV

Progress and Paternalism in the Worsley Mines

———

THOUGH the one was originally constructed partly to assist the other, the two main industrial assets of the Bridgewater Trust developed out of phase during the nineteenth century. The Canal experienced its maximum expansion of traffic during the first half of the century, and the growth curve was already beginning to flatten in the later 1840s. For the collieries, however, the largest and the most significant increase in production did not begin until the middle fifties. Notable advances occurred before that time, but they were never sustained for more than a short period.

The pattern of growth in the Trustees' coal-mines was roughly as follows. A slowly rising trend from about 1812 onwards, punctuated by cyclical fluctuations, gave place in the 1830s to a truly astonishing advance, the output of coal being approximately doubled between 1829 and 1839. The forties, by contrast, were a period of stagnation, with production figures tending slightly downwards.[1] They ended in utter gloom. Prices and profits, low from 1847 onwards, slumped even more disastrously in 1850, as railways brought in distant coal at cheap rates to compete with the Trustees in their habitual markets. In August 1850 prices were in many cases so low that nothing but the royalties were being realized on the coal that was sold.[2] By 1853, however, recovery had set in. It was first noticeable in the sharp increase in the selling price of coal at the Castlefield wharf between 1851 and 1853, and

---

[1] For the statistical evidence upon which the statements about the output of coal made in this chapter are based see below, Appendix C.

[2] Fereday Smith's Coal Report, 8 Aug. 1850, L.E.P.

in the consequent rise in profits.[1] Shortly afterwards the production of coal began to increase markedly, and continued to
do so well beyond the end of the period covered by this book.
The Trustees opened up rich new mines on the northern edge
of the Worsley field in the 1850s—at Ashton's Field in the
Trencherbone about 1853 and at Linnyshaw some five years
later.[2] Further new collieries reached completion in the later
sixties and early seventies—the Ellesmere (*c.* 1866),[3] the
Mosley Common mine[4] and the Bridgewater (*c.* 1868),[5] and the
Machine pit at Farnworth (*c.* 1873).[6] In the decade 1877–87 no
fewer than twelve were opened,[7] bringing the coal output of
the Bridgewater collieries in 1886 to a level almost five times
higher than in 1855. Even after that the growth continued, and
a commentator in a public journal, writing three years before
the outbreak of the First World War, could still observe that
the mines were 'at the height of their output and prosperity',
adding, as a preview of the future, that they had the largest
unworked coalfield in Lancashire.[8]

It is instructive to compare these trends with what is
generally believed to have been happening in the coal industry
nationally during the period under review. This can be done

[1] For fluctuations in the price of coal at Castlefield see *R. C. on Coal*, vol. iii,
Appendix to Report of Committee E, p. 210; 1871 [C. 435 ii] XVIII. For
colliery profits, see below, Appendix A.

[2] Full details of the Ashton's Field pit are given in a Return for the Government Inspection of Mines, 31 October 1853, but no entry is made in the
column provided for the number of tons raised in 1852, suggesting that the pit
had only just been opened. The return is in B.T.P. (Mertoun). Mention is made
of 'the new Linnyshaw pits' in F. Smith to A. Egerton, 8 Sept. 1858, L.E.P.

[3] The engine house is dated 1866. I owe this information to Mr. Frank
Mullineux.

[4] The 'successful completion of the sinking and fixing of the last set of
pumps at the Mosley Common Colliery' was celebrated in November 1868
(*Colliery Guardian*, 7 Nov. 1868).

[5] The foundation stone for the winding-engines was laid in June 1866
(*Colliery Guardian*, 9 June 1866). The chimney bears a datestone, 1868. I
owe the second piece of information to Mr. Mullineux.

[6] It was first mentioned in the Lists of Owners and Collieries, Manchester
District, given in the Annual Reports of H.M. Inspectors of Mines, in 1873,
B.P.P.

[7] See the Lists of Owners and Collieries, Manchester District, in the Annual
Reports of H.M. Inspectors of Mines, 1867–82, and, after 1882, in the occasional
Mining and Mineral Statistics of the U.K., B.P.P.

[8] Supplement, entitled 'An Historic Colliery', to *Manchester Guardian*,
23 June 1911.

only in a very tentative fashion, for a standard history of the industry comparable to those of J. U. Nef and Ashton and Sykes for earlier epochs does not yet exist for the nineteenth century. Clapham, in his *Economic History of Modern Britain*, which is still the most useful and the most used reference book for the general history of the period, came near to denying that an industrial revolution ever occurred in that sector. There was no decade of outstanding technological break-through, at least before the 1880s, merely a steady growth in output coaxed by a rising domestic and industrial demand.[1] Recent historians, however, have been more aware of the discontinuities. Professor A. J. Taylor has singled out the twenty years 1837–56 as being 'among the most formative in the history of the British coal industry',[2] whilst Phyllis Deane and W. A. Cole argue that the fastest growth occurred between 1830 and 1865, especially in the first fifteen years of the period.[3] The experience of the Bridgewater Trust supports the thesis of jerky growth, but the decisive breakthrough both in techniques and in output came later than the last two state-ments would lead one to expect. The Trustees' mines furnished an example of arrested development—a surge forward in the 1830s giving promise of a more continuous growth not to be realized until after 1855.

In order to discover the influences under which this pattern of development was moulded, we must explore firstly the conditions of the market in which the Trustees traded, secondly the factors operating within the concern which governed its ability to supply coal, and thirdly the means of transport available for conveying the coal to its destination.

The principal outlet for the Trustees' coal was in Manchester and the surrounding cotton-manufacturing towns of south-east Lancashire. A return compiled in 1837 shows that in the preceding year, 194,288 tons of coal were brought to Man-chester by the Duke's Canal for sale at the Castlefield wharf or for distribution down the Rochdale Canal.[4] Not all this came

---

[1] *The Early Railway Age*, pp. 216, 430–1 ; *Free Trade and Steel*, pp. 99–100.
[2] 'Combination in the Mid-Nineteenth-Century Coal Industry', *T. R. Hist. S.* 5th ser. iii (1953).
[3] *British Economic Growth, 1688–1959*, pp. 217, 219.
[4] *R. C. on Coal*, vol. iii, Appendix to Report of Committee E, p. 77 ; 1871 [C. 435 ii] XVIII.

from the Bridgewater collieries in Worsley—perhaps about one-seventh was drawn from Wigan along the Leigh branch of the Canal[1]—but almost certainly the greater part of it did, and further supplies were carted into Manchester by road from the Worsley mines. The uses to which this coal was put were very varied. That much of it was for domestic purposes is evident from the seasonal character of the sales mentioned in a report by the Trustees' manager in July 1850.[2] There was also, however, a considerable industrial demand, which was itself very diverse. A list of the firms in Manchester and district whose engineers received 'Christmas boxes' from the Trustees in the winter of 1841–2, in order to induce them to sustain their orders for coal, comprised two railway companies, four gasworks, two cotton spinners, two dyers, one machine maker, one glass bottle manufacturer, and another establishment engaged in flint glass manufacture.[3] Inevitably, however, in an area such as this, much of the demand for coal stemmed directly or indirectly from the cotton industry, though, according to Wheeler, ancillary processes such as were conducted in dyeworks, bleachworks, and foundries consumed about twice as much coal as cotton factories.[4] It would be reasonable, therefore, to look for an explanation of the changing fortunes of the Bridgewater mines in the trends in the development of cotton manufacture. This approach, however, does not take us very far. The rapid growth of Lancashire's staple industry in the post-Waterloo era—it was at its maximum rate of expansion, $6\frac{1}{2}$ per cent per annum, between 1815 and 1840—helps to account for the progress of the collieries during that period.[5] Perhaps, also, the stagnation of the 1840s owed something to—it cannot be wholly explained by—the deceleration in the growth of cottons which occurred late in that decade. Certainly, in particular years such as 1842 and 1847, the Trustees' coal sales suffered from the misfortunes of the industry. William

---

[1] Approximately the proportion in 1834 (ibid.).

[2] Fereday Smith's Coal Report, 12 July 1850, L.E.P.

[3] Account enclosed in F. Smith to J. Loch, 23 Mar. 1842, L.E.P. *Pigot and Slater's Directory of Manchester and Salford*, 1843, has been used to identify those firms whose business is not stated.

[4] J. Wheeler, *Manchester, its Political, Social and Commercial History*, p. 449.

[5] For the trends in the growth of the cotton industry referred to here and below see Deane and Cole, op. cit., pp. 186–8.

Denby, their coal agent in Manchester, wrote despondingly in July 1842: 'I shall be 140 tons less in sale this week than last owing to the closing of mills and dyeworks.'[1] But the remarkably high and sustained advance after 1855 can hardly be explained by trends in cotton manufacture, for the development there, as measured by the intake of raw cotton, was slower during the second half of the nineteenth century than during the first.

One influence which brought depression to the Trustees' coal trade on occasions in the second quarter of the century, and especially round about 1850, was the rise of competition in established markets. This was due to mining developments elsewhere and to the revolutionary impact of railways on regional supply lines. The Trustees encountered one serious challenge in the Manchester market in the early 1830s, when deep sinkings at Pendleton, within two miles of the centre of the town, in 1832, together with an extension of mining capacity at Rochdale, forced down the price of engine coal by as much as four shillings a ton, bringing two years of unusually low profits to the Bridgewater mines.[2] A more serious crisis occurred in the forties when the market was subjected to the competition of distant coal brought in by rail. By the end of 1844 the coming of Yorkshire coal was being noted as a cause of the depression which had prevailed for some years past. Later the opening of the Lancashire and Yorkshire Railway Company's new line from Liverpool in 1849 greatly increased the competitiveness of Wigan coal in Manchester, and threatened to do the same in Bolton, where Worsley coals were also sold.[3] Selling prices fell early in the following year, and a new realization of the power of railways to influence the supply of coal began to dawn upon the experts. Previously it had been believed, as by Wheeler writing in 1836, that canals would enjoy a 'permanent superiority' over railroads in this branch owing to the direct access of their boats to factories sited upon their banks. In 1850, however, the Trustees' manager observed more soberly that railways had the advantage of cheapness,

[1] W. Denby, jun. to F. Smith, 4 July 1842, L.E.P.

[2] Wheeler, op. cit., p. 450; *Manchester Guardian*, 22 Sept. 1832; see also below, Appendix A.

[3] Draft of Lord F. Egerton's Address to the Colliers, Dec. 1844, E.B.C.; F. Smith to G. Loch, 17 Apr. 1850, L.E.P.

in that coal could be lowered directly from a railway wagon into a cart instead of having to be shovelled laboriously from the bottom of a boat.[1]

It was not only in the vicinity of Manchester that railways hampered the coal trade of the Bridgewater Trust. In the early 1830s the Trustees exported Worsley coal to Ireland through Runcorn in vessels which brought back cargoes of Irish corn, meal, and flour for distribution inland via the Duke's Canal. During James Sothern's superintendentship (1834–7) this traffic was discontinued, and the Irish trade through Runcorn passed into the hands of the Old Quay Company, which dealt in St. Helens coal. James Loch was disposed to ascribe the loss to the slackness of the management and the Sothern family connection with the Rushy Park colliery at St. Helens.[2] The explanation probably lies more in the opening in 1833 of the railway from St. Helens to Runcorn Gap, which, coinciding with an extension of the Sankey Canal from Fiddlers' Ferry to Widnes, prepared the way for a great expansion of coal-getting in the St. Helens district and an intrusion of St. Helens coal into the Irish market.[3] The Trustees managed to revive their Irish coal trade through Runcorn in the 1840s, partly by inducing Wigan coal along their waterway by means of a sliding scale of tolls,[4] but it was in sharp decline again at the end of the decade. Exports of coal through the Bridgewater docks at Runcorn fell from 41,724 tons in 1847 to 28,188 tons in 1849. This was partly due to the growing competition of Ayrshire, Cumberland, and Welsh coal in the Irish market, and partly to factors restricting the backloading of Irish agricultural produce. Prominent among these was, of course, the Famine, but again transport changes played a part. In consequence of railways, Irish grain and flour were being driven from the Manchester market by flour from the eastern counties of England. They found a refuge still in the remoter recesses of

[1] F. Smith's Colliery Report, 8 Aug. 1850, L.E.P.; cf. Wheeler, op. cit., p. 450.

[2] J. Loch to Lord F. Egerton, 27 Mar. 1837, and J. S. Tonge to Lord F. Egerton, 12 May 1837, E.B.C.

[3] For these developments see T. C. Barker and J. R. Harris, *A Merseyside Town in the Industrial Revolution: St. Helens, 1750–1900*, ch. xiv, xv.

[4] J. Loch to Lord F. Egerton, 10 Nov. and 9 Dec. 1837, and 9 Dec. 1840, E.B.C.

northern Lancashire, but for that reason came by Fleetwood rather than by Runcorn.[1]

For the traffic which they took away, however, railways held out a recompense in the shape of the demand of their own locomotives for coke. In July 1837 the Duke's Trustees signed a year's contract with the Grand Junction Railway Company to supply the company with a hundred tons of coke per week.[2] Two years later, in June 1839, the London and Birmingham Company ordered up Worsley coke by the Oxford and Grand Junction Canals,[3] and shortly afterwards applications for coke were received from the Birmingham and Derby, the Gloucester and Birmingham, and the Manchester and Leeds Companies.[4] Encouraged by this demand, the Trustees enlarged their coke-producing capacity. In August 1839 they started to build twelve new ovens at Worsley, intending to follow this up with a further twelve in the spring of 1840 and twelve more in the following autumn.[5] But the immediate results were disappointing. The quantity of coal sent for coking rose to a mere 34,500 tons in 1846, and fell subsequently.[6] Sales were held back, both by the deficiencies of the ovens which were admitted to be far inferior in construction to the long-burning ovens kept by Pease and Partners of County Durham and the Marley Hill Coke Company of Carlisle,[7] and by the frequent transshipments attendant upon canal transport, which resulted in the coke's being broken into small pieces. For the second of these reasons the Trustees had lost their contract with the London and North Western Railway Company by 1852.[8] In this case, therefore, it was not so much a failure of demand as an inability to meet it efficiently that impeded the development of the trade.

Improvements in the market doubtless played some part in pulling the collieries out of stagnation after 1853. The General Manager's coal report for January of that year

---

[1] Howarth to F. Smith, 5 July 1850, L.E.P.
[2] F. Smith to J. Loch, 26 July 1837, ibid.
[3] F. Smith to J. Loch, 6 June 1839, ibid.
[4] F. Smith to J. Loch, 31 July and 13 Aug. 1839, ibid.
[5] F. Smith to J. Loch, 13 Aug. and 21 Nov. 1839, ibid.
[6] Bridgewater Trust General Accounts, 1844–50.
[7] G. Loch to F. Smith, 10 Nov. 1848, L.E.P.
[8] Fereday Smith's Coal Report, 12 Apr. 1852, ibid.

testified to a revival in all markets except Bolton, and called attention, in particular, to the demand at Liverpool and that arising from 'the Trustees' arrangements with the salt makers on the Weaver'.[1] Five years earlier the Trustees had made a special agreement with Messrs. Kay & Blackwell for salt to be brought from Winsford by way of the River Weaver and the Trent and Mersey Canal to Runcorn.[2] The object of the arrangement was to build up a supply of salt to serve as a back-loading for coasting vessels at Runcorn, but an incidental effect was apparently to bring Worsley coal to Winsford as a reverse cargo for the salt boats. Fresh avenues of sale were also opened in the third quarter of the nineteenth century by the great expansion of the gas-making industry which, as Clapham demonstrated, increased its intake of coal from perhaps 600,000 tons in 1850 to 8,400,000 tons in 1885.[3] The Trustees were heavily committed to this branch of the trade. By 1857 they supplied cannel to the gas companies of six Lancashire and Cheshire towns—Bolton, Macclesfield, St. Helens, Runcorn, Farnworth, and Knutsford. They were even approached by the Duke of Bedford, who needed it to furnish gas to the village of Thorney near Peterborough.[4] Rising demand alone, however, cannot account for the rapid growth in output during the second half of the century, for there were, at the outset, obstacles to production operating from within the firm. The coal report for January 1853 stated that 'several thousands of tons of coal could latterly have been weekly disposed of, in addition to the present sales, at Northwich, and Liverpool, and elsewhere, if the mines could have yielded a larger supply'.[1] For a better understanding, therefore, of the trends in output we must turn to the factors controlling that supply.

Over-all shortage of coal was not one of these. It was observed in the *Manchester Guardian* as late as 1911 that the Bridgewater collieries had 'still the largest unworked coalfield

---

[1] Fereday Smith's Coal Report, Jan. 1853, ibid.
[2] F. Smith to G. Loch, 10 Oct. 1848, and G. Loch to F. Smith, 16 Oct. 1848, ibid.
[3] *Free Trade and Steel*, p. 105.
[4] F. Smith to A. Egerton, 24 Apr. 1857 ; A. Egerton to F. Smith, 21 Apr. 1857, L.E.P.

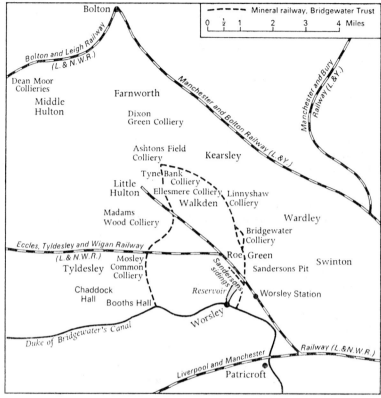

Map 5. Collieries and Canal and Rail Connections in the Worsley District, *c.* 1870

in Lancashire '.[1] Nevertheless, the state of mining technique, the availability of capital, and the level of efficiency could upon occasions, impose a brake on the continuous exploitation of these resources, producing the sort of stop–go development which we have had occasion to notice. In the late eighteenth and early nineteenth centuries the owners of the Worsley mines had resorted to relatively extensive methods in a bid to increase output. They had moved swiftly round the district, tapping the most accessible resources and saving capital by leasing rather than by purchasing additional supplies of coal. At first, they pushed northwards from Worsley along the main level of the underground canal.[2] Between 1762 and 1782 seven leases of coal in Dean and Farnworth were granted to His Grace the Duke of Bridgewater by sundry landowners. In the eighties and nineties of the eighteenth century, however, the Duke was beginning to contract his principal new leases in the Tyldesley area, on the western flank of the main Walkden field.[3] This policy was continued by the Trustees, Bradshaw helping by buying personally the Chaddock and Booths estate in 1810 and the Garrett Hall estate in 1829, and by leasing the coal measures under his properties to the Trust.[4] Some years before the middle forties mines were even leased at Pemberton and Hindley on the Wigan field.[5]

There were limits, however, to what could be achieved by these methods, and the collieries emerged from the convulsive boom of the 1830s exhausted and incapable of sustaining a further vast extension of output until a thorough overhaul of organization and methods had been undertaken. Their condition at the end of James Sothern's superintendentship was such as to involve the Trustees in 'a necessary though unfair expenditure in the years 1837, 38 and 39', the fruits of which

[1] See above, p. 306, n. 8.

[2] F. Mullineux, 'The Duke of Bridgewater's Underground Canals at Worsley', *T. R. Lancs. and Ches. Antiquarian Society*, lxxi (1961).

[3] Copies of coal leases granted to His Grace the Duke of Bridgewater before January 1803, Lancs. C.R.O.

[4] J. Lunn, *A Short History of the Township of Tyldesley*, p. 105; *Victoria County History of Lancashire*, vol. iii, pp. 442–3. In 1832 Bradshaw received from the Trustees £1,653 for royalties on four feet, Brassey, and Crumbouke coals, underlying his estates in Tyldesley and Little Hulton (Bridgewater Trust, General Abstract of Accounts, 1832).

[5] J. Loch to Lord F. Egerton, 6 Feb. 1846, E.B.C.

were almost lost again in the savage retrenchment of the 1840s.[1] Disturbed by the deteriorating situation, James Loch arranged to have the mines inspected in 1843 by Liddell, a distinguished Northumbrian surveyor, and for Fereday Smith to visit the more important collieries of Northumberland two years later under Liddell's guidance. The results of these exchanges led him to conclude that the Worsley pits were 'worked in an old-fashioned way, less productive in the result, more expensive in their output and less capable of meeting the demand than they used to be'.[2]

The faults which came to light were many. Some were merely the result of fair wear and tear not properly made good. The Edge Fold pumping engine, explained the General Manager in 1846,

is probably the oldest extant in this part of the country; and should it stop or fall down, it will involve a large outlay and cost in re-opening the mines, which will thereby be drowned out for the time. ... We have also got behind-hand with the repairs of the tub-boats in the lower levels, and with our stock of tubs and baskets.[3]

Others were more serious, reflecting a general slackness and conservatism, a failure to keep pace with advances in the methods and technique of mining. The mines were not regu-larly surveyed (or 'dialled'), a process which was vitally necessary, as Loch put it, to ensure 'that it may be known whether they are regularly and economically worked, that the whole amount got is regularly accounted for, that there is no trespass committed upon the neighbouring proprietor or that he commits none upon us'. By the increase of trade and the leasing of mines as far away as Pemberton and Hindley, the whole establishment had grown too big for a single bailiff (Ridyard, an aging man) to manage. Moreover, in Loch's view the art of sinking pits was 'imperfectly understood in Lanca-shire, especially at Worsley, so much so that the pits at Wardley have cost a great deal more money and taken a great deal more time than they ought to have done'.[4] There is evidence to suggest that several of the older pits were reaching

[1] F. Smith to J. Loch, 11 July 1846, L.E.P.
[2] J. Loch to Lord F. Egerton, 6 Feb. 1846, E.B.C.
[3] F. Smith to J. Loch, 11 July 1846, L.E.P.
[4] J. Loch to Lord F. Egerton, 6 Feb. 1846, E.B.C.

exhaustion at the middle of the century,[1] a fact which could go far towards explaining the stagnation of output in the forties, for well-used pits were generally more difficult to work. Attention to new sinkings, especially at a deeper level, was vital, therefore, to the future of the concern.

During the later 1840s the Trustees began to reform their methods and to bring them into line with those prevailing in the more progressive areas. In February 1846 Loch asked Lord Francis Egerton's permission to employ an engineer from Staffordshire to supervise the sinking of the pits, and in due course a Mr. P. E. Timmins, who supervised the making of deep sinkings in the district, was engaged.[2] At some indeterminable date between February 1847 and July 1850 the Northumbrian method of pillar and stall working was introduced at Worsley in the place of the local system, which, though differing from the long-wall technique used in Staffordshire, left less of the coal unworked than was the case in north-eastern England.[3] This was a change of uncertain value. It probably produced a larger coal, more suitable for domestic use and therefore capable of fetching a higher price. But it also entailed, according to one contemporary estimate, an additional 25 per cent loss of coal in the getting,[4] and was not so well suited, as Fereday Smith himself pointed out, to the steep angle of inclination of the Lancashire seams.[5] In other respects, however, the gains were undoubted. By April 1852 the disrepair was rectified and the mines were reported to be 'in good order'.[6] James Kent, the new coal agent or wharfinger,

---

[1] Planning to start work on the new Linnyshaw pit in 1851, Fereday Smith stated that he intended it to be ready for full work by the time some of the present pits were worked out (F. Smith to G. Loch, 22 Feb. 1851, L.E.P.). A comparison of the pits listed in the Return for the Government Inspection of Mines, 31 Oct. 1853, in B.T.P. (Mertoun), with the List of Owners and Collieries, Manchester District, given in the *Annual Report of H.M. Inspectors of Mines for 1867*, p. 35; (1867–8 [4063] XXI), shows that seven pits were closed in the intervening period.

[2] J. Loch to Lord F. Egerton, 6 Feb. 1846, E.B.C.; *Colliery Guardian*, 9 June 1866; I am grateful to Mr. F. Mullineux for information identifying Timmins as the Staffordshire engineer.

[3] The change is dated by two letters in the L.E.P., viz. F. Smith to J. Loch, 10 Feb. 1847, and F. Smith to G. Loch, 20 July 1850.

[4] Wheeler, op. cit., pp. 451–2.

[5] F. Smith to J. Loch, 10 Feb. 1847, L.E.P.

[6] Fereday Smith's Coal Report, 12 Apr. 1852, ibid.

tightened up the arrangements for screening or sieving the coal in the mid fifties, thus ensuring a more uniform product.[1] With the sixties came heavy capital outlays on replacing the antiquated coke ovens by those of a more up-to-date character[2] and on installing the huge pumps and winding-engines which made possible the spectacular achievements in deep mining. At the Mosley Common colliery operations were long held up by the large quantity of water encountered soon after sinking commenced, but with the aid of four large pumps it was at last possible to cut down through four or five valuable seams to a depth of 1,020 feet.[3] The new Linnyshaw pit completed in the late fifties was almost as impressive an achievement. It was designed to have shafts 300 yards deep and to yield not less than 8,000,000 tons of coal.[4] This was a great advance on the position at the beginning of the decade, when nearly all the Trustees' pits were less than 500 feet in depth and many were less than 300.[5] The gain was only made possible by a loosing of the purse-strings, similar to that which facilitated the improvement of the Canal after the death of James Loch. It was claimed by a representative that in all the Trustees spent £23,000 on new mining plant every year from 1861 to 1871. The money had to be found from income.[2]

Among the factors holding back development before 1853, transport was a vital consideration. A hundred years earlier the third Duke of Bridgewater had equipped his mines with what was then a first-rate and almost unique system of communications. The surface canal, which conveyed the coal to Manchester, was carried into the rock face at Worsley at a place called the Delph and continued underground to the workable coal measures lying well to the north of Worsley. Below ground the canal operated at four different levels, two below and one above the main level which communicated with the entrances, and in 1795 the main level was connected with the upper level by means of an inclined plane. Lateral cuts

---

[1] Copy of Kent's letter in G. Loch to F. Smith, 28 Apr. 1855; Fereday Smith's Coal Report, May 1855, ibid.

[2] F. Mullineux, *The Duke of Bridgewater's Canal*, p. 30.

[3] *Colliery Guardian*, 7 Nov. 1868.

[4] F. Smith to G. Loch, 2 May 1851, L.E.P.

[5] Return for the Government Inspection of Mines, 31 Oct. 1853, B.T.P. (Mertoun).

were also made where a thick enough seam was encountered, and the system was slowly extended until about 1840, by which time it covered a distance of about 46 miles, stretching north to Dixon Green in Farnworth. The coal, when hewn, had only to be carried a short distance in baskets (and later in wagons running on rails) to reach the side of one of these channels, where it could be loaded into a tub boat and carried by water to the surface. Nevertheless, this excellent system had begun to decay even before it was completed. The higher level and the inclined plane were abandoned after 1822, side arms fell derelict as the coal on them was worked out,[1] and on one estimate two-thirds of the network had become inaccessible by 1844.[2] That part which remained workable was totally inadequate to cope with the demands of an expanding coal industry. The General Manager observed in August 1846: '. . . we could sell a much larger quantity [of coals] if we had the means of getting them, but our levels are nearly choked up with boats, and, indeed, we are short of boats.'[3] Increasingly the Trustees turned to alternative methods of transporting their coal. Between 1833 and 1835 they laid down a tramway from the Tynesbank colliery to the Duke's Canal near Booths-town Bridge, and commenced another from Sanderson's Dam to the navigation at Worsley.[4] In the early forties they employed the farm tenants on the Worsley estate to cart the coal to Manchester overland.[5] The more they schemed, however, the more it was borne in on them that only the building of railways through the colliery district could ease the problem of communications and remove the bottleneck from production.

Ironical though it is that the Bridgewater Trustees, perhaps the largest canal proprietors in England, should have been obliged to seek salvation in railroads, they first fixed their hopes on the Manchester and Southport Railway Company,

---

[1] The above particulars of the underground canals are mainly drawn from F. Mullineux, 'The Duke of Bridgewater's Underground Canals at Worsley', *T. R. Lancs. and Ches. Antiquarian Society*, lxxi (1961).

[2] E. Malley, 'The Financial Administration of the Bridgewater Estate, 1780–1800' (unpublished M.A. Thesis, University of Manchester), p. 90.

[3] F. Smith to G. Loch, 28 Aug. 1846, L.E.P.

[4] Bridgewater Trust, General Abstracts of Accounts, 1833–5 (Colliery Payments).

[5] F. Smith to J. Loch, 23 Nov. 1842, LE.P.

a subsidiary of the L. & Y., authorized by an Act of 1847,[1] which promised to construct branches into the Tyldesley, Hindley, Middle Hulton, and Worsley areas.[2] How much they depended on it is shown by a letter from Fereday Smith to James Loch in December 1848:

> As soon as it is really known what will be done about the Manchester and Southport Railway and its branches, etc., I shall be in a position to lay before you a plan for very extensive mining operations, calculated to last for a very long period of years; but it would be useless in the present state of uncertainty in these matters to report thereon.[3]

In the event, however, the vital Pendleton to Hindley section of the M. & S. was not laid until the 1880s,[4] and the Trustees had to proceed with the sinkings at Ashtons Field and Linnyshaw in the fifties with no greater assurance of improvement than a prospect of widening the surface canal between Patricroft coal-yard and the Barton aqueduct,[5] and permission, granted to them during the winter of 1854–5, to use Nasmyth's private branch railway at Patricroft as a means of distributing coke to the L. & N.W.R. and their customers in Staffordshire.[6] The much greater developments from the 1860s onwards, however, were assisted by a real breakthrough in transport in the Worsley area. In 1864 the L. & N.W.R. completed its Eccles, Tyldesley, and Wigan line through Worsley. A branch to Little Hulton was opened to colliery traffic in 1870. Eight years later the L. & Y. broke into the district with its Kearsley mineral line.[7]

The utility of these connections was greatly enhanced, moreover, by the building of the Bridgewater Trustees' own mineral railways during the 1860s. The private network,

---

[1] E. F. Carter, *An Historical Geography of the Railways of the British Isles*, p. 187.

[2] F. Smith to G. Loch, 29 Nov. 1845, 19 Jan. and 2 Sept. 1847, L.E.P.

[3] F. Smith to J. Loch, 1 Dec. 1848, ibid.

[4] It was reauthorized in August 1883 and opened in sections in 1887–8 (*Bradshaw's Railway Manual, Shareholders' Guide and Directory* (1889), pp. 169–71).

[5] The proposal to widen it was made by Fereday Smith in December 1850 (F. Smith to G. Loch, 13 Dec. 1850, L.E.P.).

[6] Fereday Smith's Coal Report, May 1855, ibid.

[7] J. R. Bardsley, *The Railways of Bolton*, pp. 18, 30; *Eccles Advertiser*, 7 May 1870.

which was completed about 1870, descended in two parallel arms from a northerly point near Ashtons Field to reach the Bridgewater Canal at Worsley, and at a point further west near Boothstown, taking in most of the important pits on its way. It was linked, not only with the Canal, but also, in due course, with the newly constructed L. & N.W.R. lines and eventually with the L. & Y.R.'s Kearsley branch.[1] Unlike the older tramways which were horse-drawn, the new mineral railway used steam locomotives. The *Eccles Advertiser* for September 1870 reported the arrival of a tank engine with 12 in. cylinders made by Manning, Wardle & Co. of the Boyne Works in Leeds, to operate on the Trustees' coal lines at Worsley. It was brought by the L. & N.W. line to Sandersons' sidings and then drawn by horses to the Bridgewater colliery, where an engine shed capable of holding two engines had just been completed.[2] The procession symbolized the tribute of the old order in coal transport to the new.

Progress in the Bridgewater collieries during the nineteenth century was not solely a matter of increasing production. Great attention was also paid to bettering the condition of the working force. Undoubtedly the mainspring of the enlightened social policies, for which Worsley became famous, was the Egerton–Ellesmere family with its stern and dutiful conception of the obligations of wealth and noble birth. Lord Francis Egerton, later first Earl of Ellesmere, settled in his smoky patrimony in July 1837, determined to live among his people, after a long interval of absentee landlordism, as a benevolent squire. He was powerfully assisted in this role by his countess, almost the classical Lady Bountiful, a woman of strong Christian conviction, who won the confidence of the miners and their wives in a truly remarkable fashion by her attention to their needs. The tradition of benevolence which they established was continued by their children—George, the second Earl, who exerted himself to find work on the estates

---

[1] See Bardsley, op. cit., p. 18, for evidence of the link with the L. & Y.R. Connections were made with the L. & N.W. Tyldesley line just to the west of Worsley station, and with the Little Hulton branch to the south of the Ellesmere colliery at Walkden. I owe this information to Mr. Mullineux.

[2] *Eccles Advertiser*, 17 Sept. 1870. The other engine had arrived four months earlier (ibid. 14 May 1870).

for the distressed operatives during the Cotton Famine,[1] and Algernon, who was Superintendent of the Trust from 1855 to 1891. It displayed itself not only in private benefactions, such as the founding of schools, churches, parks, and recreation grounds, but also, in view of the firm control obtained by Lord Francis in 1837, in the policies of the Bridgewater Trust. There, indeed, it appeared in a diluted form, for it had to jostle against the calculating practicalism of the management and, until 1855, against the Whig-Malthusianism of James Loch which did not perfectly accord with his master's Tory paternalism. Loch's social thinking belonged to a type which was already becoming out of date in the 1840s. He attacked Lord Ashley's inquiry into the employment of children in mines on the ground that it was 'loosening the authority and the duty of the parent towards the child'. 'It is a sad, meddling, busybody age, everyone taking care of his neighbour's actions', was his comment on the social attitudes of early Victorian England.[2] In July 1842 he made an order forbidding the Trustees' cottage tenants at Worsley to allow their newly married sons and daughters to take up residence with them without special authorization, in order to cure 'the evils which an overcrowded population entails upon the poorer classes of society'.[3] But even he could see the need for a large employer of labour to assume responsibility for the welfare of his workpeople.

When Lord Francis took control of the Trust from James Sothern, there was much that needed reform. The Trustees' colliers were among the lowest paid in the south-east Lancashire coalfield. They were paid according to a sliding scale established in Sothern's time, by which the piecework rates rose and fell in sympathy with the selling price of coal.[4] Weekly earnings differed from pit to pit and from fortnight to fortnight, but it is clear from figures cited by Fereday Smith in September 1842 that the average weekly wage at the Bridgewater collieries during the previous six months was lower than in many of the neighbouring mines—just over 9s. 7d. per week gross as compared with 15s. at Grundy's pit in Kearsley and

[1] *The Times*, 25 Aug. 1903.

[2] J. Loch to F. Smith, 28 Dec. 1840, L.E.P.

[3] Memorandum initialled 'J. L.' and enclosed in J. Loch to F. Smith, 30 July 1842, ibid.

[4] J. Loch to F. Smith, 16 and 18 Jan. 1841, ibid.

Hulton's at Farnworth and with 10s. to 15s at seven out of ten
other local collieries which were listed.[1] The Trustees' men
also complained that they were paid monthly, whilst some of
their fellow workmen in the neighbouring pits were 'privileged with fortnightly pays'.[2] Their moral condition also left
much to be desired, especially when judged by the standards
of greater refinement which were beginning to prevail in early
Victorian England. Greville, who was Lord Francis's brother-
in-law, described it as 'the lowest state of ignorance and
degradation',[3] a blanket phrase which covered such pastimes
as 'drunkenness, profaneness, swearing, licentiousness, Sab-
bath breaking, cock-fighting, pigeon-flying bull-baiting, duck-
swimming, quarrelling, gambling and improvidence', to use
the words of an official guide.[4]

Among the first evils to be tackled by the new management
was the employment of women underground. The Trustees
began to put it down voluntarily before they were compelled
to do so by law. Fereday Smith issued instructions in July 1841,
at the direct behest of Lady Francis Egerton, not to take any
further girls into this branch of the service.[5] Eleven months
later, at a meeting of coal-owners with Lord Ashley to discuss
modifications of the Mines Bill which the latter had just
introduced into Parliament, Loch argued strongly against the
clause compulsorily excluding women who were already at
work in the pits. Nevertheless, it is clear from what he
wrote to his own general manager that his opposition was
based upon a fear that the measure would give rise to unemployment among women rather than upon economic self-
interest—'I fear that the severity of this retrospective
clause will be to make some of those who are virtuous have
recourse to a life of infamy and will render those that are
bad still more wicked.'[6] He objected not to the 'principle'
of banning women from the pits, which he described as

---

[1] F. Smith to J. Loch, 21 Sept. 1842, L.E.P.

[2] Memorial, 3 Sept. 1842, enclosed in F. Smith to J. Loch, 21 Sept. 1842;
J. L. to F. Smith, 24 Nov. 1842, confirms that the payments were monthly,
ibid.

[3] C. C. F. Greville, *A Journal of the Reign of Queen Victoria, 1837–52*,
vol. ii, p. 304.

[4] *Burrows' Official Guide to Worsley*, p. 19.

[5] F. Smith to J. Loch, 5 July 1841, L.E.P.

[6] J. Loch to F. Smith, 20 June 1842, ibid.

'admirable', but to the suddenness with which the change was to be effected.[1] The policy which the Trust management would have preferred to implement was one of gradualism—that of encouraging the building of iron and cotton factories in the Worsley district so as to find alternative employment for the women and children and at the same time to increase the Trustees' coal and canal trade. Fereday Smith had laid a proposal to this effect before the Superintendent in February 1838.[2] Moreover, once it was clear that Ashley's Bill would pass, no one was more insistent than Loch that steps should be taken by the Trust to assist the women who were displaced to discover a fresh means of livelihood. On 30 July 1842 he signed an order instructing the General Manager to arrange for the younger girls to be sent to Lady Francis Egerton's school to be trained for domestic service, whilst the older women, who were unfit for service and could not be taken into Lady Francis's charities, were provided with agricultural work on the estate. The parents of the girls sent to school were to be allowed one shilling per week for each child for a period of twelve months.[3] The Mines Act of 1842 excluded not only women but also boys under ten from the coal-pits. In one respect the Trustees endeavoured to improve on this. They tried to bar boys under twelve, but were obliged to relax their rule at the Dixon Green Colliery by pressure from the men, who said that they resented the degradation of having to do boys' work, which was consequent upon the shortage of boys.[4]

Attention was next turned to wages. In January 1843 the Trustees introduced fortnightly pays.[5] The change was a useful one, in that it simplified the problems of family budgeting and reduced the temptation to the breadwinner to dissipate his earnings in a single pay-night spree. But the gain was at first partly offset by the making of payments not strictly every fourteen days but on the 5th and 15th of the month, sometimes leaving up to eighteen working days between disbursements. This practice was not changed until October

[1] J. Loch to F. Smith, 23 June 1842, ibid.
[2] F. Smith to J. Loch, 28 Feb. 1838, ibid.
[3] Memorandum signed 'J. L.' in J. Loch to F. Smith, 30 July 1842, ibid.
[4] F. Smith to J. Loch, 18 June 1844, ibid.
[5] J. Loch to F. Smith, 16 Dec. 1842, ibid.

1855, when the Countess of Ellesmere cast her personal intervention against it, having been persuaded to do so by a deputation of colliers' wives.[1]

Efforts to raise the level of wages were made indirectly, not by increasing piecework rates, but by reducing the size of the labour force. According to Fereday Smith, the prices per ton paid to the Trustees' colliers were as good as, and in most cases better than, those at the neighbouring collieries in the early 1840s; the reason for the disparity in time wages lay in the fact that more hands were employed by the Trust than were positively required. He submitted a statement to the effect that, in 1842, 610 men, 313 girls, and 476 boys were engaged to do work which would have kept only 395 men, 86 girls, and 308 boys fully occupied.[2] We have only his word for this, but other evidence suggests the existence of a marked unbalance between the amount of work and the quantity of labour in the colliery district about that time. The census returns show that the growth of the population of the township of Worsley accelerated sharply during the 1840s, when the output of the mines was tending to stagnate.[3] As in the case of the depressed handicraft industries, the almost complete freedom of access to the trade made for an excess of supply. It was taken for granted that colliers' boys would at a certain age pass through the successive stages of promotion until they became full getters of coal.[4] There was also a commendably humane reluctance to throw men out of employment by dismissing them.[5]

One of the lessons which the Trustees learned in the middle years of the nineteenth century was to tailor their labour force according to their needs. They discharged forty colliers in November 1841. This was probably no more than an emergency measure designed to afford 'some relief to the collieries',[6] but in August 1849 they turned to a more considered policy

[1] Letter signed 'Harriet Ellesmere', 2 Sept. 1855; F. Smith to A. Egerton, 6 Oct. 1855, L.E.P.

[2] F. Smith to J. Loch, 21 Sept. 1842, ibid.

[3] *Census of . . . 1851* (Population Tables, North-Western Division), 1852–3 (1632) LXXXVI.

[4] G. Loch to F. Smith, 1 Aug. 1849, L.E.P.

[5] The General Manager observed that 'to turn them off would be . . . starvation' (F. Smith to J. Loch, Sept. 1840, ibid.).

[6] F. Smith to J. Loch, 11 Nov. 1841, ibid.

calculated not merely to arrest the present evil but to prevent its recurrence in the future. Twenty young miners were selected for dismissal, and regulations were issued to restrict both the intake of colliers' boys and the quasi-automatic progression to the cutter's status. In future boys were not to rise without special permission to count as more than three-fourths of a man in the distribution of work or wages.[1] As George Loch made clear in a letter to Fereday Smith, the underlying motive was humanitarian—to cure 'the distress amongst the insufficiently employed colliers'.[2] From that time forward a more continuous adjustment was practised. With the revival of the demand for coal in the spring of 1851, the General Manager began to complain that there were not enough colliers to meet the requirements of the trade and that full-grown men were to be seen doing the work of boys in the contracted roadways of the mines.[3] As a result of his remonstrances, a further forty-three boys were admitted to the collieries, and some of the young men were advanced to be getters. Forty-two more were taken on in February 1854 to meet the continuing shortage.[4] It is to the credit of George Loch, however, that he scouted the manager's suggestion that they should employ more than they needed in order to ensure that all worked and obeyed instructions:

I don't think [that] we need have recourse to the maxim of keeping rather too many men for the purpose of rendering them more manageable. We must hope to attain this in the Worsley estate (and, indeed, it has been attained) by other means. I recollect that it shocked Lord and Lady Ellesmere a good deal when we learnt through enquiries made by James Ridyard that this policy was pursued on the estates of Lord Bradford and Lord Crawford.[5]

Whatever its neighbours did, the Bridgewater Trust would have no truck with an industrial labour reserve.

Sixty years or so before the government intervened to promote social security, the Trustees had their own private

---

[1] G. Loch to F. Smith, 1 and 13 Aug. 1849, ibid.

[2] G. Loch to F. Smith, 3 Aug. 1852, ibid.

[3] F. Smith to J. Loch, 19 Apr. 1851, ibid.

[4] G. Loch to F. Smith, 29 Apr. 1851; F. Smith to G. Loch, 3 Mar. 1854, ibid.

[5] G. Loch to F. Smith, 26 Apr. 1851, ibid.

arrangements for guaranteeing their workpeople against mis-
fortune. About the year 1847 they introduced a non-contribu-
tory old age pension scheme designed to make up the incomes
of employees who had grown incapable of further work to five
shillings per week. Applications for benefit from the colliers
were embarrassingly heavy.[1] Even before that they undertook
to prevent unemployment by launching constructional work
upon their estates when the mines were stopped by trade
depression or by inclement weather. During the gloomy
winter of 1841–2 they instituted works at Cornbrook and the
Linnyshaw Reservoir to find jobs for out-of-work miners.[2]

In an occupation as hazardous as coal-mining the preven-
tion of accidents figured prominently among the objects of
social policy. In 1852 the Trustees framed elaborate regulations to ensure a daily inspection of winding-ropes, and of the
working places for the inflammable fire-damp.[3] Capital was
laid out in improving the means of winding. In the late thirties
and early forties miners still travelled up the shafts in baskets
of coal, and accidents occurred by their falling out of the
baskets or being hit by coal falling upon them from above.[4]
By the mid fifties there were cages in which they could ascend
in something approaching comfort and safety,[5] and the Madams
Wood colliery was the first in the country to be fitted with
Owen's patent catch for preventing accidents caused by the
breaking of the cage ropes.[6] Improvements in ventilation were
slower to penetrate. Furnace ventilation was the norm in the
middle of the century,[7] and although there was some experimentation with high-pressure steam jets about that time, these
were judged a failure and the furnaces restored.[8] Perhaps
because of their initial shallowness, however, the pits escaped

---

[1] G. Loch to F. Smith, 5 Nov. 1847, L.E.P.

[2] J. Loch to F. Smith, 14 Jan. 1841 ; F. Smith to J. Loch, 15 Jan. 1841, ibid.

[3] MS. draft of two sets of rules, for the men and for the inspectors and
officers ; also F. Smith to J. Loch, 12 Jan. 1852, ibid.

[4] F. Smith to J. Loch, 17 Dec. 1842 and 7 July 1843, ibid.

[5] Even these were not foolproof. In March 1856 a collier jumped out of a
cage to his death, in panic because it was accidentally lifted too high (F. Smith
to A. Egerton, 3 Mar. 1856, ibid.).

[6] *Colliery Guardian*, 4 May 1861.

[7] Return for the Government Inspection of Mines, 9 Sept. 1853, B.T.P.
(Mertoun).

[8] *Reports of H.M. Inspectors of Mines* (Report on the Collieries of Lancashire, Cheshire, and North Wales), p. 44 ; 1854 [1845] XIX.

the series of major catastrophes which began in South Wales, Warwickshire, and Yorkshire about 1845. The first serious explosion did not occur until February 1861, when nine of the colliers in the Rams mine perished. But the frequency of accidents of a less spectacular character, caused mainly by falling earth or coal, left little ground for satisfaction. In the twenty-one years 1853–73 nearly four people on the average lost their lives each year in the Bridgewater collieries.[1]

In its fully developed form, in the 1850s, the Trustees' concern for their workpeople extended also to their education. By 1859 they had established seven different night schools in the Worsley area. To supplement these the second Lord Ellesmere and his brother Algernon joined with some neighbouring colliery proprietors to engage a science lecturer, W. H. J. Traice, who began to deliver lectures at the Walkden school on 12 November 1858. The suggestion came from Fereday Smith whose motive was utilitarian—'to enlighten the population of Your Lordship's districts of country on the subject of pneumatics, mechanics, and other branches bearing on coal mines, so as to fit them for the duties of undertaker, fireman, etc., and to convince them of the importance of attending to serious points in all colliery operations'[2]—but the lecturer soon found himself giving a parallel course of a more general character, including readings from the British poets and from Charles Dickens's *Christmas Carol*.[3] He was still attracting an audience of sixty-nine two years after he began lecturing.[4]

There was a sterner side, however, to the paternalism which ruled at Worsley. It involved an almost Genevan discipline in matters of morals. Soon after Lord Francis Egerton went to live there, the Trustees laid down a rule that every servant of theirs who was guilty of seducing a woman should be dismissed the service.[5] As a goad to chastity this was self-defeating, for it acted as an inducement to parents to throw their daughters at the younger employees of the Trust in the hope that these

---

[1] The above information about accidents and explosions is based on the returns for the Manchester District in the *Annual Reports of H.M. Inspectors of Mines*, 1854–73, B.P.P.

[2] F. Smith to the Earl of Ellesmere, 11 Jan. 1859, L.E.P.

[3] F. Smith to A. Egerton, 4 Feb. 1859, ibid.

[4] Return of attendances in F. Smith to A. Egerton, 24 Oct. 1860, ibid.

[5] J. Loch to F. Smith, 27 Aug. 1843, ibid.

would be forced to marry them.[1] In 1842 James Loch issued
instructions that dissolute characters among the mining population should be moved out of their cottages. Happily the
administration of morality was tempered by Loch's Scottish
common sense, for he directed that a family at Ellenbrook
guilty of maintaining what was virtually a brothel should be
moved to an inferior dwelling instead of being turned out into
the streets. 'If they are deprived of all means of residence,' he
observed, 'it may force them to still more abandoned courses
as the means of support. By placing them elsewhere this will
to a certain degree be avoided and will give them the opportunity of improving and of being improved.'[2] Before settling
in Worsley, Lord Francis let it be known that he was 'much in
favour of the better observance of the Sunday by all in his
employment' and that he was 'taking steps to enforce this'.[3]
One of the first actions of the management under his direction was to stop all Sunday travelling on the Canal between
Worsley and Manchester in December 1837.[4] Three years later
he imposed a ban on selling the Trustees' land for building
beer shops.[5]

In so authoritarian a soil trade unionism was an alien plant.
Strikes were met with a blend of fatherly admonition and
chastisement, the latter being principally reserved for the
ringleaders. James Loch's reply to an address sent to him by
the Bridgewater colliers in January 1841, during a strike which
was designed to raise wages indirectly by forcing the masters
to increase prices, was typical of the attitude displayed. It
began by assuring them that his words would be 'those of
kindness, of affection and of advice', asked them how they
would like it if the agricultural labourers combined to compel
a raising of food prices, and warned them that dearer coal would
compel the manufacturer to transfer his capital and his works
'to other districts and to other nations'. It called to their
recollection 'what pains have been taken by Lady Francis
Egerton to educate your children, what labour she has undergone in helping to clothe them, how invariably her time has

[1] F. Smith to J. Loch, 15 July 1843, L.E.P.
[2] J. Loch to F. Smith, 8 and 9 July 1842, ibid.
[3] J. Loch to F. Smith, 5 July 1837, ibid.
[4] F. Smith to J. Loch, 8 Dec. 1837, ibid.
[5] J. Loch to F. Smith, 26 Mar. 1841, ibid.

been dedicated to increase your comforts and promote your spiritual welfare'.[1] Loch refused point blank, however, to negotiate with the leaders and had the more active of them dismissed and ejected from their cottages. 'They must comply with our terms or quit our service', was the unbending instruction which he issued to the General Manager.[2]

But the Duke's Trustees did not need to exert themselves overmuch against labour movements, for by and large their colliers were content to accept the subordinate position assigned to them from above. Dr. R. N. Soffer has argued recently that in the northern textile areas of Yorkshire and Lancashire the unskilled labourers, revolting against the industrial middle classes, took refuge, not in class consciousness, but in a romantic toryism 'based on nostalgic memories of a gentry fulfilling patriarchal responsibilities'.[3] The Bridgewater miners furnished an almost classical example of working-class deference towards the aristocracy. With Chartism they would have little to do. During the Plug Plot disturbances of 1842 they not only remained at work, except when the management, fearful of an attack from outside, deemed it prudent to retire them,[4] but also drew up the following address:

To our great and worthy master the Right Honourable Lord Francis Egerton; His virtuous and most gracious Lady; Mr. Fereday Smith, and all in legal authority over us.

From a consciousness of the good feeling that prevailed amongst us when Your Lordship addressed us in such an affectionate and kindly manner; we feel, as Your Lordship stated, that we are utterly incapable of expressing our gratitude and love towards you; therefore, as with the voice of one man, we declare our design that we are willing, as far as life and safety seems probable to make us, to defend your honour and all in connexion.[5]

[1] J. Loch to the Colliers Employed on the Bridgewater Trust Estates, 26 Jan. 1841, ibid.

[2] J. Loch to F. Smith, 16 Jan. 1841, ibid.

[3] R. N. Soffer, 'Attitudes and Allegiances in the Unskilled North, 1830–1850', *International Review of Social History*, x (1965).

[4] F. Smith to J. Loch, 16 and 18 Aug. 1842, L.E.P. It is fair to add that in the general excitement immediately preceding the Chartist demonstrations at Whitsuntide 1839, an indeterminable number of the Trustees' colliers equipped themselves with pikes; but, down to the beginning of May, the men were believed by the management to be 'satisfied and well affected' (F. Smith to J. Loch, 4 and 26 May 1839, and J. Loch to F. Smith, 25 May 1839, ibid.).

[5] Copy in F. Smith to J. Loch, 17 Aug. 1842, ibid.

Submission was never complete. There was a gradual spread of trade-unionism in the early 1840s, mainly under the influence of events outside the area, notably the formation of Martin Jude's Miners Association of Great Britain and Ireland in 1842. By December 1844, on the management's own admission, about two-thirds of the Trustees' colliers were members of the union.[1] Strikes occurred among them in 1841, in 1843, in 1846, in 1851, and in 1870. At first, however, unionism in Worsley lacked consistency and determination. The local leaders showed a child-like feudal loyalty in their dealings with the masters. In July 1844, before joining the union, the colliers at the Dixon Green colliery put out an inquiry as to whether it was Lord Francis Egerton's and James Loch's wish that they should do so. On receiving a discouraging reply, they approached Lady Francis to discover whether she had any objections to their joining. Her Ladyship, though courteous, was hardly less adverse. Nevertheless, those miners who had already committed themselves to the union represented her attitude to their colleagues as one of qualified approval, and made a telling use of her letter in winning support among them.[2] That they should have considered it worth their while to employ this argument shows how far was the rank and file at least of the mining community from the self-reliant class-consciousness which is often imputed to the working classes in the fifth decade of the nineteenth century. Five months later, James Loch described to Lord Francis Egerton how the General Manager of the Trust talked a deputation of three colliers out of the demands for higher wages and a limitation of output advanced in a printed circular which they had adopted, probably at the instigation of outside organizers:

Nothing could be more satisfactory. They were not aware what the printed paper contained which they sent to him and me. He read it to them. They said that was not what they thought. They said that they wanted more wages. He showed them that they could make at their present wages 17*s*. a week if they chose to work

---

[1] F. Smith to J. Loch, 14 Dec. 1844, L.E.P.

[2] F. Smith to J. Loch, 16 and 17 July 1844 ; copy of letter from Lady Francis Egerton to John Bennett and Joseph Parkinson for the colliers at Dixon Green, 11 July 1844, ibid.

daily. This made a great impression on them. It ended by their saying that they thought much of what he had said to them. One of them adding that he would never come on such an errand again.[1]

The situation was slowly changing. There was less deference and more independence in the fifties than there had been in the forties. Nevertheless, the persistence into the second quarter of the nineteenth century of attitudes more typical of a peasant society than a modern industrial order calls for some explanation. Part of this lies, perhaps, in the popularity earned by the first Earl of Ellesmere and his countess by their enlightened social policies. But the analysis cannot rest on a purely personal level. Even in Bradshaw's time the mines of the Bridgewater Trust were renowned for their quiescence, though Bradshaw was hardly a humanitarian reformer of the type of Lord and Lady Francis Egerton. He explained to James Loch how in 1818, a year of unusually sharp labour unrest, 'the colliers have all turned out except ours', adding that 'our people and this neighbourhood have only awaited my arrival here from some small feeling of attachment and respect'.[2] It is possible that the chronic surplus of labour which had been built up by the 1840s contributed to the docility of the miners. The fact that a more spirited attitude developed among them when conditions in the labour market were reversed at the end of the decade suggests that this influence cannot be entirely ignored. Nevertheless, the submissiveness of the forties does not appear to have been mainly dictated by fear.

The terms of a memorial of grievances dispatched by the Worsley colliers to Lord Francis Egerton in September 1842, which began by recalling appreciatively that 'circumstances induced Your Lordship to grace us with your presence', a reference to his having taken his seat at Worsley, make clear that here was a patriarchal relationship between lord and servant, more deeply rooted in history than loyalty to any individual. The genuiness of this document is proved by the fact that it went on, somewhat incongruously, to remind His Lordship, in language reminiscent of the Ricardian Socialists, that 'from the gift of Providence we are the first producers

---

[1] J. Loch to Lord F. Egerton, 4 Dec. 1844, E.B.C.
[2] R. H. Bradshaw to J. Loch, 29 Aug. 1818, S.E.P.

of that source of which we all partage'.[1] Perhaps, as Dr. Soffer suggests,[2] this clinging to aristocracy was in part the result of a sense of insecurity spread among the working classes by the growth of middle-class power and the disintegrating impact of *laissez-faire* ideas upon the social fabric. Such feelings, however, were less likely to arise where the employer was a nobleman, not a parvenu manufacturer, and it seems probable that at Worsley deference was a survival from the past rather than a reaction against the present. There was much in the nature of social organization in that locality to encourage it to survive. For Worsley, despite the encroachments of the factories on its perimeter, retained into the middle years of the nineteenth century the basic character of an estate—a unit which differed radically from the city or large town in that the strands of employment and property tenure were gathered together at a single focus. The focus, moreover, was dynastic rather than merely organizational— a squire ruling by hereditary right, or at least by the known testamentary dispositions of a predecessor.

Whilst they predisposed to loyalty, these conditions would not actually have produced it, unless a conscious attempt had been made by the ruling authority to maintain a personal relationship with all the working force. This there had certainly been in the third Duke of Bridgewater's time. The many amusing but affectionate stories concerning that nobleman which have been handed down to posterity bear witness to it. The goodwill thus engendered was sufficient to endure through the years of absentee landownership, 1803–37, and from the latter year onwards every effort was made to renew the personal link. A letter from Fereday Smith to James Loch about the arrangements for a dinner to celebrate the coming of age of Lord Francis Egerton's eldest son in 1844 shows something of the spirit in which the Trustees approached their workpeople:

I have spoken to Mr. Hathorn about the proposed dinner to the workmen. We think the suggestion in your letter of the 4th inst. a

---

[1] Memorial dated 3 Sept. 1842, and enclosed in F. Smith to J. Loch, 21 Sept. 1842, L.E.P. It should be noted that the claim to be 'first producers' was asserted more against 'the rest of your Lordship's hired servants' than against Lord Francis himself.   [2] See above, p. 329, n. 3.

very good one, to have the workmen's dinner on the 15th of June and the Ball on the 17th, but we are most decidedly of opinion that a dinner, and a good one of roast beef and plum pudding and so on, be given at all the stations and to all the men and boys. We think the occasion quite deserves it and that it is desirable that each person in the several concerns should welcome Mr. Egerton into his majority.

I hope you will concede the same privilege to the colliers. They deserve it. . . . If you will agree to the Colliers' dinner, I will undertake to dine with them myself.[1]

A subsidiary factor operating to maintain good labour relations at Worsley was the existence in the locality of the sliding scale of piecework rates, by which wages varied with the price of coal. This encouraged the miners to seek their advantage by pressing the mine-owners to raise prices. The turn-out of the colliers in the Manchester district in January 1841 was the principal factor inducing the masters to combine for such a purpose, the negotiations among the latter beginning within two or three days of the commencement of the strike.[2] The same thing happened in November 1851, when a turn-out in the Bridgewater mines, as well as at Oldham and elsewhere, led a majority of coal proprietors to agree to an advance of 10*d*. a ton in the Manchester and Bolton markets.[3] Masters and men both profited by a raising of the price of coal, and the recognition of this identity of interest by the miners themselves impeded the development of those feelings of class which so powerfully stimulated the growth of labour movements in other industries and areas. Explaining to his deputy why Lord Francis Egerton favoured clemency towards the leaders of the turn-out in January 1841, James Loch asserted that His Lordship was 'persuaded that the men were acting under some delusion that they were actually benefiting us as well as themselves'.[4] Whether this was really a delusion was a question of economics; what really mattered was that the opinion could be held.

[1] F. Smith to J. Loch, 8 May 1844, L.E.P.
[2] F. Smith to J. Loch, 13 and 16 Jan. 1841, ibid.
[3] F. Smith to G. Loch, 25 and 29 Nov. 1851, ibid.
[4] J. Loch to F. Smith, 6 Feb. 1841, ibid.

CHAPTER XV

The End of an Era

THE first of September 1872 marked the decisive break in the history of the Bridgewater Trust. On that day the Duke's Canal together with the Mersey and Irwell Navigation, the associated dock and warehouse installations, and the Trustees' carrying trade passed by sale into the hands of a joint stock company, Bridgewater Navigation Ltd. The purchase price was £1,115,000.[1] It is true that the deal did not involve the immediate liquidation of the Trust. That body survived for another thirty-one years to manage the landed estates in southern Lancashire and the Worsley coal-mines which flourished as never before. In the 1880s some £60,000 of the Earl of Ellesmere's income was paid from its resources[2] each year. There was also, down to about 1890, a continuity of directing personnel. The Hon. Algernon Egerton remained Superintendent until his death in 1891, being then succeeded by Walter Longley Bourke. Fereday Smith retired from the general managership in December 1887, after completing fifty years' service with the concern. His place was taken by his son Clifford who had long assisted his father in the management.[3] Bereft of the waterways, however, the Trust was a shadow of its former self. *The Times* observed two months before the end that since 1887 it had 'practically fallen into abeyance, out of which it will now be called to attend its own obsequies'.[4] When it eventually expired, on 19 October 1903, the collieries and estates passed into the absolute ownership of the third

---

[1] Agreement between the Bridgewater Trustees and Sir Edward William Watkin and William Philip Price for the sale of the Navigations, etc., dated 3 July 1872, E.B.C.

[2] *The Complete Peerage, by G. E. C.*, ed. Vicary Gibbs and Doubleday, vol. v, p. 56; Bridgewater Trust General Accounts, 1886–9 (incl.), E.B.C.

[3] Bridgewater Trust Salaries Journal, 1881–91, Lancs., C.R.O.

[4] *The Times*, 25 Aug. 1903.

Earl of Ellesmere in accordance with the dictates of the Duke of Bridgewater's will. In the demanding economic conditions of the twentieth century it was scarcely appropriate, however, that the burden of maintaining these large undertakings should be borne by a single family, and in 1923 a joint stock company known as Bridgewater Estates Limited was formed to take them over.[1] This corporation has continued into our own time, though the mines were, of course, nationalized in 1947.

For the canals the transfer in 1872 meant a curtailment of their independence. Bridgewater Navigation Ltd. was closely connected with the Midland and Manchester, Sheffield and Lincolnshire Railway Companies. The purchase was made in the names of William Philip Price and Sir Edward William Watkin, chairmen respectively of those two concerns, who then promoted the navigation company to take the property off their hands. Watkin was at pains to point out in the City column of *The Times* that he and Price had entered the transaction 'upon our individual responsibility alone',[2] and spokesmen of the company and of the Midland Railway afterwards claimed that the new undertaking was 'as free as though it had been formed without any interest of the railways whatever'.[3] These assurances, however, were not readily accepted by the public. *The Economist* observed sceptically:

> At least one of two things seems likely to happen. Either the public apprehensions will be justified by the management of the canal with some regard to the interests of the competing railways or the shareholders of these railways will be dissatisfied with chairmen who represent a company in active competition with them.[4]

The Manchester Chamber of Commerce resolved on 26 September 1872 'that the transfer of the canals between Manchester and Liverpool to certain railway directors is adverse to the commercial interests of the two towns'.[5] Nine years later the engineer of the Aire and Calder Navigation instanced

---

[1] *Burrow's Official Guide to Worsley*, p. 13. [2] *The Times*, 5 Sept. 1872.
[3] These were the words of W. H. Collier, the Company's manager. Evidence on Opposed Bills: Manchester Ship Canal Bill, 1885, qu. 12110; House of Lords Library. James Allport, the Manager of the Midland Railway, denied that the Duke's Canal was either directly or indirectly under railway control. *Select Committee on Canals*, Minutes of Evidence, qu. 1688; 1883 (252) XIII.
[4] Quoted in *The Times*, 9 Sept. 1872. [5] Ibid. 27 Sept. 1872.

the dependence of the Bridgewater Canal upon the railways as a possible obstacle to the union of canals between the east and west coasts of England.[1] Indirect influence is always difficult to prove, but Bridgewater Navigation Ltd. certainly held its first half-yearly meeting in the board room of the M.S. & L. Railway Company with Sir Edward Watkin in the chair.[2] Moreover, out of the nine directors of the canal company listed in *Bradshaw's Railway Manual* for 1878, six were on the board of either the Midland or the M.S. & L. Railway, and two more held seats on the South Eastern, of which Watkin was Chairman. The Chairman, William Fenton of Ribchester, was also Deputy Chairman of the M.S. & L. Five years later the Chairman and four other directors of Bridgewater Navigation Ltd. were at the same time directors of the Midland or the M.S. & L. The Deputy Chairman, Nathaniel Buckley, had served on the South Eastern down to 1878, and one other member of the board was a kinsman of Timothy Kenrick, the Deputy Chairman of the Midland. There were then eight directors in all, including the Chairman and his deputy.[3]

In the face of this evidence it is scarcely plausible to deny that the railway companies held the reins, but in practice they may not have chosen to exercise them very firmly. W. H. Collier, the General Manager of the Bridgewater Company, told the House of Lords during the debate on the Manchester Ship Canal Bill in 1885 that the directors had never 'to my knowledge (and I do not think it could escape my knowledge) interfered with the fixing or altering of any rates of freight, toll or carriage'. This they left to 'the action of their responsible officers'.[4]

To explain the anomaly we must take account of the reasons why the concern changed hands. These, too, were clearly enunciated by Collier:

It was originally bought by the respective chairman [sic] of the Manchester, Sheffield and Lincolnshire and Midland companies.

---

[1] *S.C. on Canals*, Minutes of Evidence, qu. 935; 1883 (252) XIII.

[2] *The Times*, 27 Jan. 1873.

[3] *Bradshaw's Railway Manual, Shareholders' Guide and Official Directory*, 1878 and 1883 edns.

[4] Opposition of the Bridgewater Navigation Co. Ltd. . . . to the Manchester Ship Canal Bill (printed archive copy, Bridgewater Navigation Company), Minutes of Evidence, qu. 12105.

They required land for bringing a railway into Manchester. They approached the Bridgewater Trustees, the then owners of the Canal and asked them to sell to them the necessary land. They were unable to come to an agreement to satisfy both parties unless the canal were also purchased in addition to the land wanted. They took the Canal but Parliament objected to its becoming a railway property; and in order to meet the wishes of Parliament and the wishes of the Bridgewater Trustees and their own interests as railway chairmen they formed a public company to repurchase from them the Canal undertaking.[1]

Evidently the case of the Bridgewater can be added to other known examples to be cited in support of the contention made in the dissenting report of the Royal Commission of 1909 that 'the canals were not, in the great majority of instances, voluntarily acquired by the railway companies'.[2]

The details, so far as they can be pieced together from somewhat scattered evidence, appear to support Collier's assertion. As we have seen, the Duke of Bridgewater's Trustees had been contemplating a sale of their navigations since 1844, and their determination must have been strengthened by the railway building of the 1860s. By 1869 the Cheshire Lines Committee, which was controlled by the Great Northern, M.S. & L., and Midland Companies, commanded a continuous stretch of line running westwards across the Cheshire plain from Woodley near Stockport to Helsby which lay a few miles to the south of Runcorn, and the M.S. & L. individually had received authority from Parliament to construct yet another railway communication between Manchester and Liverpool, by joining the Garston and Liverpool line to the Manchester, South Junction, and Altrincham at Cornbrook. It was completed in 1873.[3] Faced with this increasing competition, the Bridgewater Trustees became so determined to dispose of their waterways that in November 1871 they gave notice of their intention to ask Parliament during the ensuing session for blanket permission

[1] Evidence on Opposed Bills: Manchester Ship Canal Bill, 1885, qu. 12110; House of Lords Library.

[2] *Royal Commission on Canals and Inland Navigations of the United Kingdom, Fourth and Final Report*. Minority Report by J. C. Inglis, p. 207; 1910 [Cd. 4979] XII.

[3] For details of these projects see R. P. Griffiths, *The Cheshire Lines Railway*.

to transfer them to, or share the ownership of them with, one or more of a number of railway and canal companies, viz.

the London and North Western Railway Company, the Shropshire Union Railway and Canal Company, the Lancashire and Yorkshire, the Great Western, the Great Northern, the Manchester, Sheffield, and Lincolnshire, the North Staffordshire, and the Midland Railway Companies, and also the Cheshire Lines Committee, the undertakers of the Aire and Calder Navigation, the owners or proprietors of the Calder and Hebble Navigation, the undertakers of the Canal Navigation from Leeds to Liverpool, and the Rochdale Canal Company.[1]

Early in the following year, owing to a turn of good fortune, a sale to two of these parties became a real possibility. The Cheshire Lines Committee was about to go to Parliament for permission to construct its own terminus in Manchester, close by the present Central station, and to connect it with the South Junction by means of a short line to Cornbrook. This would involve building a viaduct across the Trustees' land at Castlefield and crossing the Manchester and Salford Junction Canal, also the property of the Trustees, near Watson Street. Moreover, the M.S. & L. and Midland Companies, which stood behind Cheshire Lines, needed from the Trustees the Egerton Dock at Liverpool. They also needed some warehouse, wharf, and canal basin property near London Road, Manchester, probably to enable them to realize their initial hope of connecting the proposed new Central station with their lines on the eastern side of the town. The M.S. & L. directors resolved upon acquiring these assets jointly with the Midland at their meeting on 31 January.[2] On 13 April an indenture of agreement was drawn up between the Trustees and the Cheshire Lines Committee, granting the latter permission to go over the lands and navigations of the former subject to the payment of proper compensation. This was confirmed by the Cheshire Lines Act of June 1872.[3] Less than three months after the indenture came the agreement for the sale of the canals to Watkin and Price, which was dated 3 July. It is

---

[1] *Joint Select Committee of the House of Lords and House of Commons on Railway Companies' Amalgamation*, Appendix, pp. 954–8; 1872 (364) XIII, Pt. II.

[2] M.S. & L.R. Company: Proceedings of the Board of Directors, no. 13, minute 2212, B.T.H.R.   [3] 35 and 36 Vict. (Local) c. 57.

significant that the first act of the new owners was to sell to their respective companies the Egerton Dock at Liverpool and the following properties in Manchester which had previously belonged to the Trustees, viz. the Union warehouse and the buildings and land adjacent, the warehouse, wharf, canal basin, and land abutting on Chorlton Street and Little David Street, a warehouse, yard, and canal in Minshull Street, a yard and canal basin in Chorlton Street and Pump Street, an ease-ment for the construction of a double line of railway of a length of 1,034 yards, and the surplus land between Robinson's timber-yard and the river. There is an agreement for the sale dated 10 August.¹ The remainder of the Canal properties then passed to Bridgewater Navigation Ltd.

This roundabout procedure cannot easily be explained except as a device for circumventing the known opposition of Parliament to railway–canal mergers. Of this antagonism there was abundant evidence. A joint select committee of the two Houses (Chichester Fortescue's committee) aired the sub-ject during the first half of the year and reached adverse con-clusions. When the Midland Railway Company applied to take over the Worcester and Birmingham Canal, the House of Commons interposed a check on 29 April.² It is little wonder that the Trustees abandoned the intention to proceed by Bill, of which they had given notice at the end of the previous year. As it was, the private negotiations with the two chairmen were watched with the utmost suspicion. Fortescue's commit-tee noted that 'the sale is believed to have been effected', and resolved 'that no such transfer of the ownership and manage-ment of so important a channel of traffic as would place it virtually under the control of a railway company ought to be made without the express sanction of Parliament'.³

The advice was ignored, but no consequences seriously prejudicial to the public interest followed. Though many canals appropriated by railways may have suffered from neglect and prohibitive tolls, the Duke's was not one of them. The change of masters was not a knock-out blow but a blood

¹ M.S. & L.R.: Proc. Board of Directors, no. 12, minute 2632.
² *J.H.C.* cxxxvii (1872), 165.
³ *Joint S.C. on Railway Companies' Amalgamation, Report*, pp. xx–xxi; 1872 (364) XIII, Pt. I.

transfusion. Aided by one of the most outstanding civil engineers of his time, Edward Leader Williams the younger, Bridgewater Navigation Ltd., embarked upon a programme of modernization far in advance of anything which the Trustees had undertaken. The locks at Runcorn were enlarged. The Canal was deepened from 4 ft. 6 in. to 6 ft., and steam traction was at last substituted for horse traction.[1] The last improvement was envisaged from the outset, being mentioned in the Company's prospectus. By January 1873 a contract had been made with Mr. Fowler of Leeds to experiment with a system of towing boats by a cable laid on the bed of the Canal. Watkin announced that this was similar to a plan used on the Seine in Paris and on the canals in Prussia, Belgium, and the U.S.A., and that it would bring down the cost of towage by one-half or two-thirds.[2] The system did not answer, however, as well as was expected, and was soon replaced by steam tugs similar in design to those on the Thames. By 1885 twenty-six or twenty-eight of these were employed in the Manchester–Runcorn trade. One of them could draw a train of boats for the 28 miles from Manchester to Runcorn in 7 hrs. 50 min., not a great advance, admittedly, on the speed of horses, but the cost of haulage was reduced by 50–60 per cent. Down to the middle eighties, however, the saving had not been passed to the public. It had been absorbed by the Company in erecting a vertical wall along one side of the Canal to save the banks from being eroded by the increased wash generated by the steamboats.[3]

Less prosperous under the new regime was the fate of the Old River. This did not share the improvement in traction, mainly because its locks, ten in number, evenly dispersed along its course would have entailed too much delay to steam-drawn trains. On the Duke's, where the locks were concentrated at the Runcorn end, it was a different matter. The several components of a train of boats could be worked simultaneously through consecutive locks. Hence, when the tugs were installed on the Bridgewater Canal, the Runcorn–Manchester traffic deserted the Mersey and Irwell Navigation

---

[1] *D.N.B.*, *Second Supplement, 1901–11*, vol. 3, p. 673.

[2] *The Times*, 27 Jan. 1873.

[3] Opposition of B.N.C. to M.S.C. Bill, Minutes of Evidence, qus. 11560, 11565, 11568; *D.N.B.*, *1901–11*, vol. 3, p. 673.

which was left to pass a local trade at the Manchester and Liverpool ends. The final humiliation for this ancient concern was that it had to fall back on the role of collector and distributor within Manchester for its old rival the Duke's. Of the 775,816 tons of traffic which it carried in 1884, 243,323 tons travelled only between the Hulme Locks, which joined it to the Bridgewater Canal, and the Bridgewater warehouses which backed on to Water Street.[1] But the river was not wholly excluded from the improving attentions of the Company. From 1878 onwards large sums were expended on reconstructing the weirs at Howley, Woolston, and Throstlenest by fitting tilt weirs in the place of the old solid erections. The work was originally undertaken in response to pressure from local authorities anxious to guard against flooding (which had been exceptionally severe in 1866) but was found to result in an improvement of the navigation by the scouring of the silt on the bed of the river.[2]

It is not immediately obvious why a canal company which was under the influence of railways should have exerted itself so strenuously to improve at least one of its navigations. In the comparatively few instances in which railway companies have been known to develop their canals, the explanation has usually been found in the role of the canal in question as a feeder to the railway. But once the Cheshire Lines network had been created, and the new Manchester–Liverpool line had been completed, the Duke's must have appeared to the Midland and M.S. & L. directors more as a competitor than as a source of traffic. It is perhaps more realistic to assume that the railway men, who sat on the board of Bridgewater Navigation Ltd., improved the Canal for its own sake and for the benefit of the shareholders rather than out of respect for the interests of the railroads. In this connection the ideas on railway–canal competition expressed by Sir Edward Watkin from the chair at the first half-yearly meeting of the Company on 24 January 1873 take on a particular significance:

The amalgamation report of the Lords and Commons Committee proposed that canals should, if possible, be a competitive element

---

[1] Opposition of B.N.C. to M.S.C. Bill, Minutes of Evidence, qus. 11565–7, 11633, 11645, and statistical table submitted by W. H. Collier, pp. 34–5.

[2] Ibid., qus. 11596, 12279–81, 12445.

against railways. Having had a good deal to do with the practical management both of canals and railways, he thought this as absurd as to expect a donkey to compete with an elephant. Narrow canals, and those with locks or a scarce supply of water, could not possibly compete with railways; but a broad and deep canal like the Bridgewater, if steam could be substituted for horse-power, might hold its own against the railways.

He proceeded to observe that 'there was no antagonism worthy of the name between the Midland, the Sheffield, and the Bridgewater Navigation Company' and that 'he could see nothing in those three undertakings which should produce anything but co-operation'.[1] It was a striking reassertion from the hub of the railway world of the doctrine of co-existence held by James Loch more than thirty years earlier.

Sir Edward's remarks were also prophetic. The two great waterways changed hands again, being sold to the Manchester Ship Canal Company in 1887, for £1,710,000.[2] Henceforth the Mersey and Irwell Navigation was badly cut about in the making of the Ship Canal, but the Duke of Bridgewater's Canal remained a flourishing concern into the twentieth century. As late as 1905 the two navigations carried between them 2,170,381 tons of merchandise and yielded a joint profit of £32,926.[3] The railways had done their worst, and it was for the tempest of road transport, which blew upon railroads and canals alike, to carry the work of demolition to far greater lengths after the First World War.[4] Even so, the Duke's survived, though in a much reduced capacity. As late as 1954 almost half a million tons of coal passed along the Worsley arm of the Canal.[5] Perhaps an age when planning has replaced the cut and thrust of competition will yet find a place for the proven veteran of so many wars.

[1] *The Times*, 27 Jan. 1873.
[2] Frank Mullineux, *The Duke of Bridgewater's Canal*, p. 31.
[3] *Royal Commission on Canals and Inland Navigations, Appendices to Fourth and Final Report*, Table 27; 1910 [Cd. 5204] XII.
[4] Figures at the Bridgewater Department, M.S.C.C., show a fall in the tonnage of the Bridgewater Canal from 1,811,447 tons in 1913 to 1,108,124 tons in 1923 and 815,391 tons in 1938. I owe these data to Mr. Charles Hadfield.
[5] Herbert Clegg, 'The Third Duke of Bridgewater's Canal Works in Manchester', *Transactions of the Lancashire and Cheshire Antiquarian Society*, lxv (1955).

CHAPTER XVI

Retrospect

———

THE history of the Bridgewater Trust does not fit neatly
into the categories into which historians usually divide their
material. That is what makes it peculiarly difficult to write,
but also what gives it interest. It overlaps not only the lines
of division between economic, social, legal, and political history, but also the various sub-divisions of economic history
itself. The roles of coal-owner and canal proprietor were,
indeed, reasonably homogeneous, whilst the Duke's Canal
remained a sufficient vent for the coal extracted from the
Bridgewater collieries, but this had ceased to be the case by
the mid 1840s at the latest, and the future of the mines had
become dependent in a curiously paradoxical fashion on the
construction of railways which would compete with the Canal.
Further contrasts emerge from the connection of the industrial
properties with landed aristocracy implicit in the creation of
the Trust by the will of an eighteenth-century duke and
sustained throughout the period by the successive roles of the
houses of Leveson-Gower and Egerton–Ellesmere as life tenants
and of their agent James Loch and their kinsman the Hon.
Algernon Egerton as Superintendents; also from the links
of the canals with the railways through the shareholdings of
the two families and the directorships of James and George
Loch. These may be considered in turn.

It is now realized that, despite the Reform Act of 1832, the
nobility and gentry continued to exercise a preponderant
political influence until well into the second half of the nineteenth century.[1] A study of the Bridgewater properties and of
the tangled negotiations in which they were involved makes
clear the extent to which men of these classes exercised also
economic power, even in the new industrial England which

[1] See G. Kitson Clark, *The Making of Victorian England*, chs. vii, viii.

was growing up in the provinces. James Loch, a land-agent in the service of two successive beneficiaries, who ended by managing the Trust estates for them, was also one of the most active figures in the railway world in the twenties, thirties, and early forties of the nineteenth century. He came forward with suggestions as to the mode of making iron rails and of draining Chat Moss,[1] and engaged in the larger strategy of ensuring that railroad development was planned in such a way as to damage as little as possible the existing Leveson-Gower interests in the Bridgewater Canal and the Liverpool and Manchester Railway. His support and that of his masters was eagerly canvassed by John Moss and other leading railroad promoters of the time. Moreover, Lord Stafford and his son Lord Francis Egerton were not the only noblemen to be concerned in transport undertakings in the north and Midlands. The canal companies, in particular, often had grandees as their patrons, and negotiations between them could be undertaken privately by these. When Loch, the agent of the Marquess of Stafford, wished to promote concerted action of the canals with regard to the proposed Birmingham and Liverpool Railway in March 1830, it was to Lord Clive acting for the Ellesmere and Chester and Birmingham and Liverpool Junction Canal Companies and to Lord Harrowby for the Grand Trunk that he appealed. Seven years later he treated with Clive to detach him from the support which the Ellesmere company was then giving to the projected canal from Middlewich to Altrincham, which the Trustees then opposed. The desire to go hand in hand with Lord Francis Egerton was acknowledged by Lord Clive to be a factor which weighed with him in the matter.

Ties with the landed nobility influenced the values by which the Trustees' business was conducted. Paternalism in Worsley village and among the workpeople in the coal-mines was to some extent a matter of private charity on the part of Lord and Lady Francis Egerton, but it required the co-operation of the Trustees in order to be fully implemented. It was a projection into industrial society of the benevolent interest which most eighteenth-century landed proprietors had taken in the welfare of their tenants by abating rents in bad

[1] J. Loch to J. Bradshaw, 12 Oct. and 11 Dec. 1826, S.E.P.

seasons, paying funeral expenses, and forgiving debts.[1] Considerations other than those of immediate profit and loss entered even into business transactions involving the Canal. The fact that opposition to railway Bills and adverse canal projects was seldom carried to extremes, especially when the schemes were strongly supported by the large mercantile communities of Manchester and Birmingham, was partly a result of Lord Francis Egerton's sense of obligation to the public; so also was the encouragement of the passenger traffic on the Canal in the later 1830s. Lord Francis was himself an altruist, but a strong element of prudence entered into these policies. Even this stemmed largely, however, from the predicament of the traditional element in government and society. To those who advised the aristocratic beneficiaries of the Bridgewater estates, if not to the beneficiaries themselves, it had become abundantly clear that inherited wealth was the object of suspicion and that political position resting upon birth could only be sustained by allying itself with public opinion. Huskisson, who talked the Marquess of Stafford into supporting the Liverpool and Manchester Railway, acted in deference to the wishes of the merchants of Liverpool, his own constituency and one which the Tory government deemed it especially desirable to nurse. As the Member for South Lancashire from 1837 to 1847, Lord Francis Egerton was hardly in a stronger position to neglect the commercial interests of that great county even when they conflicted with the claims of the Duke of Bridgewater's Canal. James Loch perceived this clearly for, as he afterwards explained to Lord Francis, he told a deputation of canal delegates hostile to the Manchester and Birmingham Junction Canal scheme in 1838 'that it was a difficult matter for a person with a public character, as you are, and in the prominent situation which you hold, to oppose yourself to any great public improvement called for by any great body of the public'.[2] Even in economic history decisions are not always taken purely on economic grounds.

It was no unmixed blessing for the industrial properties of the Bridgewater Trust to be linked so closely with landed estate. Management suffered from an importation of the

[1] G. E. Mingay, *English Landed Society in the Eighteenth Century*, p. 271.
[2] J. Loch to Lord F. Egerton, 29 Nov. 1838, E.B.C.

traditional vices of land agency—amateurism and soulless
routine. In the past stewards had been recruited less for their
expertise than for their supposed probity and their familiarity
with the landowner. Personal friends of the landlord, retired
army officers, and above all lawyers had been the favourite
choice. The methods which they had employed had been
legalistic, concerned with the relations of landlord and tenant
and with the guardianship of certain routine processes against
dishonesty and embezzlement so as to be able to hand over
an accustomed surplus to the owner for his personal expenditure. During the nineteenth century all this was rapidly
changing under the influence of the agricultural and transport
revolutions. Professionalism was gaining ground among land-
agents and estates were coming to be viewed as units of positive management, with investment and supervision of farming
practices.[1] It was the old order, however, that was inherited
by the Trust. None of the superintending Trustees appointed
during this period was by training and previous experience
primarily an industrialist. Bradshaw's origins are obscure, but
his background was metropolitan and official rather than
northern and industrial. James Loch was by training a barrister, so also was his son George to whom he committed
most of the detailed work of supervision. Algernon Egerton
was a younger son of the Egerton–Ellesmere family with an
academic education in the law. It is true that some of the
great barrister auditors of the early nineteenth century led the
way in the movement to improve aristocratic estates, and of
these auditors James Loch was the king. From his previous
experience as a land-agent he brought to the administration of
the Bridgewater properties many excellent qualities—notably
a grasp of detail, a sanguine common sense, and a wise discretion in his choice of a subordinate manager.[2] But possibly
because of a want of familiarity with industry he was disposed
to rivet on the Canal and coal-mines a regime which in certain
important respects looked backwards rather than forwards.
The reforms which he introduced at the outset, though in
accord with liberal principles as he understood them, were

[1] F. M. L. Thompson, *English Landed Society in the Nineteenth Century*,
ch. vi.
[2] D. Spring, *The English Landed Estate in the Nineteenth Century*, pp. 88–96.

focused upon administrative tidiness, economy of expenditure, and the elimination of corruption rather than upon development by capital investment. His original idea was to turn the estate into one vast milch cow yielding a steady flow of revenue and requiring little in the way of management or additional outlay. Hence, he planned to lease out the mines, throwing the expense of improvement on to the lessees, and sought to encourage the toll-paying private carriers to take over the carrying trade on the Duke's Canal from the Trustees' own carrying department. Circumstances enforced a reappraisal of these principles as time progressed, but it was usually in the face of initial resistance from Loch and from his son George, who brought to his duties more of the lawyer's caution than the businessman's capacity for risk-bearing. Thus it was that most of the enterprise and most of the enthusiasm for development displayed during the period came from the manager, George Fereday Smith, whose background, unlike that of his superiors, was thoroughly industrial and whose education had been scientific. Until 1855 Fereday Smith's ideas had been held in check to a considerable extent by the Lochs. After that date he had things more his own way, and a period of sustained investment in docks, mines, and canal works ensued.

Loch's policies of restraint can be viewed more sympathetically when account is taken of the unfavourable legal framework within which the Trustees had to operate. This too was a part of the *damnosa hereditas* from land. An express, executed private trust presented an acute anomaly when applied to a business concern faced with the problems of a changing economy. The rules governing the powers and responsibilities of trustees were first closely defined by the Court of Chancery in the years between the Restoration and the close of the eighteenth century. They were framed for the benefit of a preponderantly landed society which placed an estate under trusteeship for one of three main reasons—to rescue it from impending bankruptcy by curbing waste, to look after it during a minority, and to preserve contingent remainders under a strict settlement. In each case the object was restrictive—to check unnecessary expenditure and to hand on the property undiminished. Naturally, therefore, the law allowed to trustees little discretion beyond what was specifically conferred upon them by the will or trust deed. It forbade unauthorized sales or mortgages, confined investment by the trustees to the safest securities, viz. government stock, and barred interference by the life tenant. Assuming, moreover, that the trustee would be a landowner, or at least well versed in the management of landed property, it made no satisfactory provision for the delegation of his authority to experts. Throughout the nineteenth and early twentieth centuries these rules have been continually modified by statute (and by court decision) in the direction of greater freedom to take account of changing social conditions.[1] When our period opened, however, the transformation was not far advanced, and the Bridgewater Trust was left to face the problems of railroad competition encumbered by the provisions of an intricate devise from which the law allowed but little deviation.

Restrictions on the power of borrowing on mortgage and on investment proved a considerable embarrassment when, in order to keep pace with new developments in transport, the Trustees needed to modernize and expand, to assume not less responsibility but more. So also did the concentration of power in the hands of a single Trustee. 'You see the boundaries to which the Trustees are restricted', wrote James Loch in 1838, 'to administer well and efficiently what they have charge of, is quite enough for any one person to undertake.'[2] *The Times* perceived the true character of the dilemma in a leading article published two months before the demise of the Trust. Noting that the history of the concern 'furnishes an apt example of the mischief which may sometimes be wrought by the dead hand, even of the most pious founder', it added that 'the elasticity which it is frequently one of the chief objects of a trust to restrain may often be the only quality by which the unexpected can be so dealt with as to be turned to the advantage of those concerned'.[3]

Two solutions of the problem were suggested at the time and in turn tried. One was that the tenant for life should

---

[1] See G. W. Keeton, *Social Change in the Law of Trusts*, for a survey of the changes and the social factors which moulded them.

[2] J. Loch to F. Smith, 10 May 1838, L.E.P.

[3] *The Times*, 25 Aug. 1903.

assume personal liability for improvements. Before 1837 the separation of equitable interest from management militated against this, for beneficiary and Trust Superintendent were often at loggerheads, but the closing of the gap by the nomination of James Loch to the superintendentship in that year paved the way for such action to be taken. In the late 1830s and the early 1840s Lord Francis Egerton financed a number of important additions to the Canal property, notably the building of the Egerton Dock at Liverpool, the purchase of the Anderton Company's properties, and the initial purchase of the Mersey and Irwell Navigation. But the capital hunger of the Canal soon outstripped the capacity of the beneficiary's purse. The young nobleman's income looked better on paper than it turned out to be in practice, for out of it he had to establish a fund to provide for his wife and younger children, and his own personal expenditure upon his household and on building made further heavy demands upon it. Moreover, his income was his principal asset, for unlike most aristocrats he did not inherit a vast estate of his own.

As family resources failed the Trustees turned increasingly to the alternative, viz.—breach of trust. For this they sought the authority of Parliament. In 1842, 1845, 1851, 1857, and 1865 they obtained Estate Acts permitting them to raise money on mortgage of the Trust estates, purchase shares in other specified undertakings, lease the canals or their tolls for thirty years, grant leases of land and water rights, accept the lease of other people's mines and quarries, and in sundry other ways to exceed the powers conferred upon them by the Duke of Bridgewater's will. With each successive Act the scope of the permission widened until finally in 1865 power to sell outright any portion of the Trust properties including the canals was conferred.[1] It may be asked why this solution was not adopted earlier. The explanation lies partly in the need for concurrence of Trustees and life tenant, which could not easily be had before 1837, partly perhaps in the changing climate of opinion and partly in the deterrent effect of the formalities which attended the passage of an Estate Act until the procedure was modified round about the mid-century. Once embarked upon, however, legislation conferred progressively

---

[1] 28 and 29 Vict. (Private) c. 50, s. 22.

upon the Trustees the freedom which they needed either to develop the Canal and coal-mines in accordance with their current needs or to dispose of them to others who could do so. It was supplemented, moreover, by an increasing private discretion. Fereday Smith indicated both the steps by which this had come about and the wide extent of it at the time of writing when he explained to Algernon Egerton his objections to a recent allegation of breach of trust made by George Loch. That was in 1858 when Loch was no longer connected with the management:

I cannot . . . willingly permit Mr. Loch's letter to pass without remarking that he appears to have overlooked the fact of his father's tenure of the Bridgewater Trust, from the commencement down to the year 1851 having been one continued and necessary breach of Trust. . . . I beg to refer you in support of my meaning to the Bridgewater Estate Act, 14 & 15 Vic. Cap 12, 1851, which had become necessary in consequence among other reasons, of the long continued and repeated deviations from the letter of the Duke's will. . . .

It is an absolute impossibility that the Duke of Bridgewater could in the year 1803, foresee and provide for, the various circumstances in which his Trustees were likely to be placed during the probable and possible continuance of the Trust, and Parliament has consequently in 1851 enacted that 'and generally the said Trustees or Trustee are hereby authorised in the administration of their aforesaid Trust to do all such matters and things whatsoever, and enter into such contracts as they or he with a fair and honest discretion, may consider necessary to be done in the execution of the Trusts of the said will; and all such matters and things as shall be done in pursuance of this provision, shall be taken to have been done in all respects as if they were expressly authorised by the Trusts, Powers and Authorities of the aforesaid will'. . . . Mr. James Loch, himself, perhaps the last man likely to commit an improper breach of Trust used to say that if he had conducted the Trust affairs in strict technical conformity with the will, the concern must inevitably have been ruined. Indeed, in the present state of Railway competition, it is easy to imagine the result of conducting the Bridgewater affairs under the strict rules of a Receiver in Chancery.[1]

The contrast between the successful improvement and extension of the properties after 1855 and the stagnation which

[1] F. Smith to A. Egerton, 25 Feb. 1858, L.E.P.

beset them before the construction of the Liverpool and Manchester Railway is in some degree a product of the intervening growth in institutional flexibility.

Whilst an exploration of the connection between the Bridgewater Trust and the land gives depth to our understanding of the problems confronting canals at the onset of competition from the railroads, a study of the links with the railway world modifies our view of the nature and extent of the competition. The history of the relations between rail and water has been written hitherto as that of a battle between irreconcilables. It would be utterly misleading to deny the reality of the conflict between them, but there were also elements of mutuality which have usually escaped notice. The Trustees assisted the growth of railways by conveying the metal from which the lines were constructed, by supplying fuel for the locomotives from the Worsley coke ovens in their own boats, and by using their canal boats and their steamers on the Mersey estuary to bridge the gaps in the railway system whilst it was still immature. In return for concessions, which admittedly proved illusory, they even employed their trading connections in the Midlands to build up a traffic for the G.W.R. in that region, and their influence to suppress a trade on another canal at the behest of the Railway Company. Nor was this all. Although the Bridgewater people undoubtedly opposed railroad projects during the period, they were by no means undiscriminating in their opposition. James Loch throughout his career drew a sharp distinction between friendly railways and hostile railways, nor did this correspond, as might have been imagined, with the division between those which were feeders to the Bridgewater Canal and those which ran parallel to it. No such simple explanation will suffice to explain his preferences. It was largely a matter of trusting certain promoting groups and certain railway boards rather than others. The Liverpool party —John Moss, Henry Booth, and others, even Joseph Sandars —were looked upon as friends. Loch and his son George were plunged into their midst by being appointed directors of the Liverpool and Manchester Railway as Lord Stafford's representatives, and a real community of interest existed between that company and the Duke's Trustees after Loch had been installed as Superintendent of the Trust in 1837, despite the obvious rivalry imposed upon the Bridgewater Canal and the Liverpool and Manchester Railway by the facts of geography. The Grand Junction, London and Birmingham, and North Union lines were also regarded as part of the family during most of the 1830s. All were under Liverpool influence. On the other hand, the Birmingham promoters and the Manchester and Leeds together with its successor the Lancashire and Yorkshire were viewed with much suspicion. As late as 1849 Loch was disposed to trust the London and North Western Company far more than the Lancashire and Yorkshire.

The underlying reasons were partly social. As the spokesman of a noble family with liberal inclinations, James Loch was doubtless aware of the distinction between cultivated merchants and roughspun manufacturers, between Liverpool gentlemen and Manchester men. At least we know that he thought of the Birmingham people as 'adventurers',[1] and disliked what he described as the 'Quaker interest', in railway politics.[2] Allied to this was the belief carefully nurtured in his mind by the Liverpool promoters and not lacking in foundation that they, in contradistinction from other men, were not disposed to reduce the rates of carriage excessively. For almost the whole of the period covered by this book and not merely, as is popularly supposed, in the heyday of pre-railroad prosperity under Bradshaw, the Duke of Bridgewater's Trustees aspired to keep up freight charges in concert with other carriers. They believed in competition, but it was a competition of services within a framework of agreed rates that commanded their allegiance, and they found that they could enter into agreements for this purpose with the tiny Liverpool and Manchester Railway in the 1830s and with the L. & N.W.R. and L. & Y. in the fifties just as they had done with the Mersey and Irwell Navigation Company in the 1810s. Bridgewater Navigation Ltd. was still agreeing rates with the railroads in the 1880s, as W. H. Collier admitted to the House of Lords during the battle over the Manchester Ship Canal Bill.[3] Concern for the maintenance of charges led the Trustees eventually to prefer that the construction of new lines should be

[1] J. Loch to Viscount Clive, 4 Apr. 1830, S.E.P.
[2] J. Loch to W. W. Currie, 28 Mar. 1830, ibid.
[3] Opposition of B.N.C. to M.S.C. Bill, Minutes of Evidence, qus. 11535–7.

undertaken by any large, existing company already interested in the trade rather than by a newcomer, for the latter would have an inducement, not possessed by the former, to establish a foothold in the traffic by slashing rates.

The Trustees were encouraged to perform this delicate balancing act by the belief that if cut-throat competition in the matter of charges was avoided, their waterways could hold their own. It was unnecessary to resist all railway projects indiscriminately, for canals like the Duke of Bridgewater's could maintain themselves. This assumption was, for the most part, proved to be correct. The volume of trade carried on the Bridgewater Canal increased almost threefold in the thirty years after the opening of the Liverpool and Manchester Railway.[1] Some trades were lost during the period—long-distance traffic using a chain of canals, the passenger service (though even this survived for longer than is often supposed, being reinforced in the early 1840s as a means of fending off the construction of railroads), trade in perishable agricultural produce and in goods of the highest value. On the other hand, the Trustees' navigations were remarkably successful in retaining not only the cheap bulk consignments—coal, gravel, cinders, and salt—which most authorities have admitted to be suitable to be conveyed by canal even in an age of generalized rail transport, but also some semi-valuable commodities which paid a higher freight charge or toll. A manuscript rate-book preserved in the Bridgewater Department of the Manchester Ship Canal Company shows that in 1876 the toll traffic alone on these two waterways upwards from Liverpool consisted of 60,000 tons of raw cotton, 5,000 tons of groceries, 69,000 tons of grain, 57,000 tons of timber, and 45,000 tons of sundries, whilst the bulk of the return cargo was composed of 53,000 tons of bale goods.[2]

These facts bear testimony to the continuing strength of canals, but it would be misleading to regard the Bridgewater navigations as typical. James Loch wrote in 1845:

Their position between Manchester and Liverpool and other places is peculiar. The distance between these two places is not

[1] See Appendix B.
[2] These figures exclude quantities exported and imported through Runcorn, which included many cheaper materials.

great. A portion of the way is river navigation, requiring no outlay for repairs. The time required for the transit is little more than that occupied by railway. Where necessary the vessel that fetches the goods to Manchester can receive them directly from the vessel that brings them into port, and so, on the other hand, goods from Manchester can be put on board the vessel at Liverpool without intermediate transhipment. . . . In addition to this comes the advantageous position of your several [dock] properties in Liverpool.[1]

Other advantages which he might have mentioned were the clustering of locks on the Duke's Canal, highly favourable to the introduction of trains of boats and the extensive warehouse accommodation belonging to the Trustees in Manchester. The latter enabled the canals to enlist the aid of the cotton spinners' carts in their competition for the trade of the districts adjacent to the town.

Falling rates of tonnage and of freight coupled with the loss of some of the more lucrative trades deprived the Trustees of much of the financial benefit of their extended traffic. The net profit from the Canal and carrying trade averaged about £45,000 per annum in the years 1806–26, whilst in one year of exceptional prosperity it exceeded £80,000. In 1849–53 (incl.), even when the Mersey and Irwell Co.'s profits had been added to those of the Duke's Canal, the average was still only £53,000, from which an annual sum of rather more than £7,000 representing interest on a debt run up by the Old Quay directors should properly be deducted in order to obtain a true picture. This represented a drastic fall in the return per unit of capital, for the Trustees and the life tenant jointly must have increased their investment in the canals and ancillary works between twofold and threefold in the twenty years after 1826. From the middle fifties onwards the comparison improved. In 1860 the net profit of the two waterways was nearly £76,000[2]—6·8 % of their value when they changed hands in 1872. Moreover, the Bridgewater Navigation Company paid its shareholders a dividend of 8 per cent per annum in the years 1878–81. Even so, these are rough indications of a lower

---

[1] J. Loch to Lord F. Egerton, 19 Oct. 1845, E.B.C.
[2] See below, Appendix A.

percentage profit on the canals than the Duke's yielded in the twenty years before the railways came.[1]

The over-all impression is a sobering one. As regards their canal business the Trustees were rather in the position of a man moving up a downward escalator who has to run very hard in order to avoid slipping backwards. At least, however, they showed that they could run. The years 1825–72 were years of growth—growth and diversification. Spurred on by competition which at first came principally from rival waterways, but increasingly, as time progressed, from railways, the Trustees added to their docks and warehouses, constructed a new canal along the shore at Runcorn, bought out competitors, built up a large fleet of steamers on the Mersey estuary, and used it to draw traffic across the river for canal and railway companies alike. Intent, moreover, on retaining a long-distance traffic and on stabilizing the rates at which it was conveyed, they assumed responsibility for carrying to remote parts. They maintained boats upon the Midland canals and on the River Trent, carted for the railway companies in the Birmingham and Black Country area, and treated with the railroad directors for trans-shipment and agency agreements which would enable them to trade with places as far away from Lancashire as London, Bristol, and South Wales. Owing to the difficulties discussed earlier in this chapter, progress was slow at first and interrupted. There were bursts of improving energy in 1826–8 under Bradshaw's superintendentship, in 1837–44 under Loch, and with greater sustention in 1855–72 under Algernon Egerton, but these were intercepted by phases of stagnation, misdirected endeavour, and even decay. Despite that, however, the Duke's Trustees must be credited with having embarked upon a sustained development of their equipment almost twenty years before the public at large awoke to the possibility of reviving water transport in the 1870s, and they had made some exertions of this kind even earlier. It has been suggested that one reason for the failure of canals to compete with the railways was the apathy displayed by the management of the former—'the lack of tone and spirit in the system itself, and the failure, due partly to

[1] *Bradshaw's Railway Manual*, 1879, 1880, 1881, and 1882 edns.; cf. above, p. 7.

inability and partly to indifference, to adapt themselves to the changing circumstances of the times'.[1] The Bridgewater Trustees may have been exceptional, but this at least must be allowed them. Though they made many mistakes and pursued many false trails, they were never devoid of ideas. They had, indeed, their short-comings, but passivity was not among them.

[1] Jackman, op. cit., p. 657.

APPENDIX A

Income of the Bridgewater Trust, 1806–1871

THESE figures show the net financial return on the principal activities of the Trust. They are rendered in pounds sterling and, except where preceded by a minus sign to indicate a loss, represent profits. Estimated figures are introduced by the letter '*c.*'

Year	(a) Duke's Canal and Carrying Trade	(b) Mersey and Irwell Navigation	(c) Estuarial Carrying for Canal and Railway Companies	(d) Bridgewater Collieries	(e) Home Farms	(f) Estate	(g) Lime Burning	(h) Worsley Yard	(i) Standing Debt Charges	(j) Over-all Profit
1806	38,871			13,437	642	13,438	748			67,136
1807	40,259			11,245	528	10,866	539			63,437
1808	34,428			8,767	1,107	9,714	929			54,946
1809	45,393			7,255	1,000	8,935	1,008			63,590
1810	52,491			16,752	302	12,449	509			82,502
1811	31,757			9,694	37	10,896	535			52,920
1812	37,050			6,867	540	10,157	1,100			55,715
1813	49,456			8,650	1,120	10,274	1,313			70,813
1814	41,332			12,438	822	12,732	586			67,910
1815	45,038			9,239	405	16,554	582			71,818
1816	23,024			7,440	915	16,381	493			48,253
1817	29,611			2,252	626	16,826	1,093			50,409
1818	53,406			11,161	4,775	19,809	393			89,543
1819	38,198			9,181	1,788	19,794	727			69,687
1820	37,688			9,531	2,811	18,726	627			69,382
1821	51,626			8,675	3,520	19,172	741			83,734
1822	51,794			10,725	3,758	18,410	678			85,365
1823	63,744			14,926	2,975	18,323	775			100,743
1824	80,697			17,242	2,872	18,110	576			119,497
1825	53,284			18,652	2,354	19,700	929			94,919
1826	42,605			3,195	781	19,564	214			66,359
1827	61,441			7,079	2,801	18,646	722			90,689
1828	53,671			9,006	720	22,044	957			86,398

	(a)	(b)	(c)	(d)	(e)	(f)	(g)	(h)	(i)	(j)
1829	58,037			11,065	1,153	20,973	74			86,302
1830	47,650			14,219	861	22,519	484			85,732
1831	24,026			12,125	691	24,547	548			61,936
1832	22,377			4,326	357	21,069	413			48,541
1833	17,473			5,376	407	19,332	69			42,657
1834	36,143			14,856	1,895	18,571	477			71,941
1835	38,092			16,638	1,439	17,551	1			73,721
1836	58,738			19,944	2,015	20,963	199			101,859
1837	49,378			20,515	1,499	24,201	385			95,978
1838	60,657			13,507		17,688				c. 94,000
1839	74,904			13,899		21,039				c. 112,000
1840	61,621			10,476		17,381				c. 91,000
1841	47,380			11,342		19,981				c. 80,000
1842	39,447			6,884		19,005				c. 65,338
1843										
1844	76,410		9,029	18,096	(—) 347	19,237				122,425
1845	62,741		(—) 856	20,654	(—) 187	19,293				101,645
1846	60,352		1,800	15,412	(—) 4,063	17,167	1,070			91,937
1847	51,755		4,875	7,717	(—) 1,110	14,546	106			77,856
1848	48,197	13,223	2,676	c. 11,500	(—) 2,143	c. 6,900	270		(—) 23,753	56,845
1849	16,980	23,167	3,160	c. 11,142	(—) 1,961	279	402		(—) 24,203	28,966
1850	39,910	14,560	870	7,999	(—) 1,725	8,358	426		(—) 23,980	46,419
1851	38,943	20,466	2,154	2,908	(—) 2,794	6,044	353		(—) 23,951	44,130
1852	32,927	18,834	2,563	7,373	(—) 2,632	11,266	519		(—) 24,222	46,628
1853	41,062	18,262	(—) 868	16,158	(—) 2,154	6,040	32		(—) 33,505	45,027
1855	29,857	19,667	299	15,075	(—) 1,677	17,556	36	(—) 5,062	(—) 29,042	47,061
1860	c. 58,500	17,345	7,156	c. 29,500		c. 21,500	145	(—) 181	(—) 30,088	106,535
1864	c. 64,000	9,595		c. 31,000		c. 34,500		(—) 41,530	(—) 22,892	75,916
1865	c. 48,500	9,133		c. 35,500		c. 35,500		(—) 38,142	(—) 22,253	71,551
1868	c. 46,000	9,085		c. 45,500		c. 42,500		(—) 53,497	(—) 20,440	76,294
1871	c. 54,000	16,042		c. 34,500		c. 38,500		(—) 61,368	(—) 20,182	57,589

Note on Sources

The accounts of the Bridgewater Trust for this period are plentiful, but they are also discontinuous and scattered, and vary in the degree of detail with which they are analysed. For 1806–36 (incl.) a summary in the volume 'General State of His Grace the Duke of Bridgewater's Navigation, Colliery, Lime, and Farm Concerns in Lancashire and Cheshire from Midsummer 1759' (Northants. C.R.O., E.B.C. Bridgewater Canal Papers, vol. i) has been followed in the above table. This ends in 1836, and the data for 1837–42 (incl.) has been drawn from the yearly General Abstract of Accounts for 1837 (Lancs. C.R.O., National Coal Board Deposit, Bridgewater Collieries) and from three of eight separate statements of revenue, income, and trade for 1837–42 (incl.) in the B.T.P. (Mertoun). A consolidated Bridgewater Trust General Account Book, 1844–50 (Lancs. C.R.O., N.C.B. Deposit, Bridgewater Coll.) has been used for the period which it covers. It contains Annual Profit and Loss Accounts and detailed statements for the separate departments. For the years after 1850 the accounts are sporadic. A brief abstract for 1851–2–3 in the B.T.P. (Mertoun) and the annual account books for 1855, 1860, 1864, 1865, 1868, and 1871 in the same collection have furnished the information embodied in the table. Moreover, discontinuity is not the only problem. From 1848 onwards a more elaborate differentiation was progressively introduced into the accounts. New items appeared, and items previously included under the larger departments obtained separate recognition. In order to build up a comparable series of figures it has been necessary to consolidate some of these and even to subdivide entries in cases where data which was once distributed over several departments has been brought together in a new category. This has entailed the making of some arbitrary assumptions and the estimation of quantities which cannot be exactly ascertained. Col. (*a*) includes the income derived by the Trustees from carrying on the Midland canals (itemized in the accounts as 'Staffordshire Trade' and 'Anderton Trade'), from the steamers drawing flats along the Mersey estuary between Runcorn and Liverpool, and from the passenger traffic, as well as that given in the accounts against Canal and Carrying Departments. It omits, however, the profits of the estuarial trade conducted for the E. & C.C.C. between Ellesmere Port and Liverpool and for the Birkenhead and G.W.R. Companies between Birkenhead and Liverpool, which are rendered separately in col. (*c*). Colliery profits include the return on the coke furnaces and the royalties which were sometimes paid over to the Estate Account by the Bridgewater Collieries for coal mined under the Trustees' lands, but not the royalties on coal leased to other entrepreneurs. These are clubbed together with farm and cottage rentals under the heading of 'Estate'. Col. (*i*) is mainly interest payments on the bonded debt of the Old Quay Company and on the mortgage contracted with the Law Life Assurance Society to enable the Trustees to acquire the concern, but it also includes a number of transitory items. Canal, colliery, and estate profits from 1860 onwards have been scaled down to allow for certain overheads, such as income tax, legal expenses, management costs, and insurance, which had been charged against them previously, but were at that time made a general charge on the concern. The amounts have been estimated in accordance with the proportionate distribution of these costs among the several departments in the accounts for 1855. For the years 1806–42 (incl.) over-all profit is simply the aggregate of the separate departmental profits, a proportion being added for the missing lime and farm incomes for the last five years of that period. The figures for 1844–71 (incl.) are the balances shown on the Annual Profit and Loss Accounts. They are not, for all years, the exact totals of the amounts itemized in the preceding columns, as some small entries in the Profit and Loss Accounts have been excluded from the detailed analysis.

Note on Over-all Profit

The amounts shown as over-all profit represent the net profit on the yearly business transactions of the Trust, so far as this can be ascertained. They are not to be confused with income paid over to the life tenant. Into the calculation of the latter entered a number of additional items, such as the rise in the value of the trading stock and the surplus of good debt over that outstanding in December 1803, both of which were ordered by the Duke of Bridgewater's will to be carried to the account of profits. Increasingly, moreover, as the Trustees' discretion was enlarged deductions were made for the redemption of standing debt and for outlays on improvements, and the Superintendent's legal and parliamentary expenses may also have been subtracted. A solitary private account book kept with Drummonds (Staffordshire C.R.O. D 593/N) reveals that for the years 1834–42 (inclusive) the annual payments by the Bridgewater Trust into Lord Francis's account averaged about £68,000, i.e. about 20 per cent less than the over-all profits recorded above. The range was from £50,000 in 1840 to £114,000 in 1837. Accounts in the Bridgewater Trust and Loch–Egerton Papers at Mertoun show that the corresponding figures for 1858 and 1860 respectively were both approximately £53,000.

APPENDIX B

Quantity of Traffic Conveyed on the Bridgewater Canal, 1803–c. 1885

(to the nearest ton)

Year	Quantity	Year	Quantity
1803	334,496	1830	716,568
1804	353,263	1831	705,527
1805	347,821	1832	707,552
1806	349,496	1833	764,860
1807	349,236	1834	805,737
1808	339,283	1835	892,242
1809	384,982	1836	968,795
1810	423,707	1837	859,210
1811	372,401	1838	c. 957,000
1812	390,579	1839	990,290
1813	464,903	1840	1,015,571
1814	435,191	1841	949,728
1815	510,330	1842	952,354
1816	471,827	1843	1,055,245
1817	455,977	1844	1,280,418
1818	561,532	1845	1,391,136
1819	501,578	1846	1,469,169
1820	491,407	1847	1,444,745
1821	553,599	1848	1,360,774
1822	605,437	1849	1,536,715
1823	650,242	1850	1,460,572
1824	712,004	1851	1,399,819
1825	730,305	1852	1,479,402
1826	581,217		
1827	688,213	1855	1,573,110
1828	730,811	1860	1,978,423
1829	722,418	c. 1885	c. 2,000,000

Note of Sources

This table is based on data drawn from five main sources, viz. (1) Bridgewater Trust General Accounts, 1790–1810 and 1811–30; (2) Bridgewater Trust, General Abstracts of Accounts, 1829–37; (3) (for 1838 only) A Statement of the Trades on the Bridgewater Canal and Old Quay Navigation for the years 1838 to 1848, B.T.P. (Mertoun). An estimated quantity has been added for the coal traffic on the Duke's; (4) Statement of Gross Traffic on the Bridgewater Navigations, 1839–52.

S.C. on Railway and Canal Bills, Minutes of Evidence, p. 25; 1852–3 (246); XXXVIII, (5) Bridgewater Trust General Account Books, 1855 and 1860, B.T.P. (Mertoun). Despite the variety in the sources used, the absence of any sharp breaks in the series suggests that the figures are broadly comparable. That for *c.* 1885, however, is a pure guess, based on information given to the *Royal Commission on Canals* (Appendix to *Fourth and Final Report*, 1910, Table 25) and to the House of Lords during the Opposition to the Manchester Ship Canal Bill (Opposition of the Bridgewater Navigation Co. Ltd., etc., to the Manchester Ship Canal Bill, 1885, Minutes of Evidence, qu. 11633 and pp. 34–5).

APPENDIX C

Coal Production: Bridgewater Collieries

*Quantity of Worsley Coal sent down the Bridgewater Canal
1803–1828*

(to the nearest ton)

Year	Quantity	Year	Quantity
1803	98,279	1816	92,363
1804	100,770	1817	94,437
1805	96,647	1818	109,134
1806	90,602	1819	91,128
1807	84,660	1820	98,223
1808	81,386	1821	101,175
1809	84,745	1822	105,542
1810	95,280	1823	113,936
1811	78,133	1824	120,588
1812	87,059	1825	119,942
1813	94,111	1826	93,259
1814	96,626	1827	110,807
1815	93,494	1828	107,860

Output of Coal from the Bridgewater Collieries, 1829–c. 1860

(to the nearest ton)

Year	Quantity	Year	Quantity
1803	134,035	1845	279,212
		1846	307,649
1829	153,630	1847	270,084
1830	165,634	1848	254,030
1831	178,161	1849	281,822
1832	174,260	1850	278,713
1833	220,369	1851	..
1834	229,421	1852	274,380
1835	271,840	1853	..
1836	297,276	1854	..
1837	273,225	1855	279,140
1838	..		
1839	308,660	1860	371,408
1840	283,709	1871	c. 550,000
1841	254,117		
1842	..	1886	1,303,625
1843	..		
1844	282,678		

Note on Sources

The first of these two tables is based on figures drawn from Bridge-water Trust General Accounts, 1790–1810 and 1811–30. The second depends on six sources, viz. (1) General Accounts, 1790–1810 and 1844–50; (2) General Abstracts of Accounts, 1829–37; (3) (for 1839, 1840, and 1841) F. Smith to Loch, 9 Feb. 1842, L.E.P.; (4) (for 1852) A Return for the Government Inspection of Mines, Sept. 1853, B.T.P. (Mertoun); (5) General Account Books, 1855, 1860, and 1871, B.T.P. (Mertoun); (6) Bridgewater Collieries, Production Outputs, 1886–91, Lancs. C.R.O. The figure for 1871 is a very rough estimate based on a statement in the General Account Book for that year that the net revenue from the collieries was £250,281 and the probability (calculated on the basis of the more detailed accounts for 1860, and what is known of trends in the price of coal in the subsequent decade) that the average selling price of the Trustees' coal was about 8s. 2d. per ton at that time. The quantity is computed not from the whole net revenue but from the sum of £233,000, which appears likely from earlier accounts to have been the approximate amount derived from the sale of coal.

APPENDIX D

Officers of the Bridgewater Trust

Superintendents of the Trust

Robert Haldane Bradshaw, 1803–34
James Sothern, 1834–7
James Loch, 1837–55
Algernon Fulke Egerton, 1855–91
Walter Longley Bourke, 1891–c.1903

Deputy Superintendents

Captain James Bradshaw, R.N.,[1] c.1818–33
James Sothern, 1833–4
George Samuel Fereday Smith, 1837–44
George Loch,[1] c. 1844–55

Principal Agents and General Managers

Benjamin Sothern, Principal Agent and Inspector of the Navigation, 1803–26
James Sothern, Principal Agent, 1832–3
George Samuel Fereday Smith, Principal Agent and General Manager, 1845–87
Clifford Smith, General Manager, from 1888

[1] In practice but not, perhaps, in name.

BIBLIOGRAPHY

ARCHIVE SOURCES

Papers relating to the history of the Bridgewater Trust are both very voluminous and very scattered. Their dispersion reflects the changing ownership of the canals and coal-mines since 1872 and the varied aristocratic interests in the properties before that time. The material is listed below by its present location and in the approximate order of its importance to the historian:

MERTOUN (SEAT OF THE SIXTH DUKE OF SUTHERLAND)

The Bridgewater Trust Papers: a heterogeneous collection of deeds, letters, and accounts. Of notable importance are twenty-one files of correspondence (numbered 128–35, 139, 141–2, and 145–54) dealing with the years 1803–37 and 1847–57. These include letters to and from the principals in the concern, viz. R. H. Bradshaw, James Loch, and the first Earl of Ellesmere. There are also some account books of the Bridgewater Trust for the years 1849 to 1871.

The Loch–Egerton Papers: the detailed business correspondence of Fereday Smith, the General Manager of the Trust, with his superiors, James (and George) Loch and the Hon. A. F. Egerton. About 17,000 letters and copies cover the period 1837–62.

STAFFORDSHIRE COUNTY RECORD OFFICE

The Sutherland Estate Papers: Chief Agents' Correspondence, 1631–1900, D.593/K: contains the correspondence of James Loch as agent to the first and second Dukes of Sutherland, 1812–55. Until recently this was divided between the Shropshire and Staffordshire Record Offices, but is now mainly concentrated in the latter.

Receipt and Accounts made on the Account of Lord Francis Egerton by Messrs. Drummond, D.593/N: contains the private account of Lord Francis Egerton with his bankers.

The Diary of E. J. Littleton, first Baron Hatherton, D.260.

NORTHAMPTONSHIRE COUNTY RECORD OFFICE

The Ellesmere Brackley Collection; Canal Papers: includes deeds, letters, accounts, and other miscellaneous papers relating to the Bridgewater Trust. The most useful portions are a volume entitled 'General State of His Grace the Duke of Bridgewater's Navigation, Colliery, Lime, and Farm Concerns in Lancashire and Cheshire from Midsummer 1759' (which contains a year-by-year summary of the profits for 1806–36), some General Account Books for 1886–1903, and a collection of letters passing between James (and George) Loch and Lord Francis Egerton, 1837–46. This correspondence spans the gap in the Bridgewater Trust Papers at Mertoun.

LANCASHIRE COUNTY RECORD OFFICE

National Coal Board Deposit, Bridgewater Collieries Ltd., BW.: contains the Bridgewater Trust General Accounts, 1791–1810 and 1844–50; General Abstracts of Accounts, 1829–37; Coal Production Output Books, 1886–97; copies of coal leases granted to the third Duke of Bridgewater before January 1803; and various cash books and salaries' journals. When at the N.C.B. Offices in Walkden, these papers also included the General Accounts, 1811–30, which were consulted there by the author in 1961.

HERTFORDSHIRE RECORD OFFICE

Ashridge House Collection, AH: throws light on the arrangements for the management of the estates just before the third Duke of Bridgewater's death.

MANCHESTER SHIP CANAL COMPANY, BRIDGEWATER DEPARTMENT

Mersey and Irwell Navigation Company, Orders of the Board of Directors. The books for the years 1796–1844, etc., are relevant.

Statement on the Part of the Bridgewater Trustees Re Contests and Competition of Railways, undated [1850].

Duplicate Conveyance and Assignment of the Bridgewater Canal, the Runcorn and Weston Canal, and Divers Lands, Hereditaments, etc., dated 27 June 1874.

Opposition of the Bridgewater Navigation Co. Ltd., and of the Company of the Proprietors of the Mersey and Irwell Navigation, to the Manchester Ship Canal Bill in the House of Lords, 1885 (printed archive copy).

Manuscript Rate Book, Bridgewater Navigation Company, *c.* 1887.

Diaries of George Forrester, Canal Engineer, 1861–70, and Register of Steamers compiled by Forrester *c.* 1857. These manuscripts, which belong to the family of the late George Forrester, were seen by the author whilst on temporary deposit with the M.S.C. Company.

MANCHESTER UNIVERSITY LIBRARY

Acts Relating to the Third Duke of Bridgewater's Canal Schemes, etc. Collected by Lord Francis Egerton.

CHESHIRE COUNTY RECORD OFFICE

Trustees of the River Weaver, Minute Books and Northwich–Acton Bridge Tonnage Books.

BRITISH TRANSPORT HISTORICAL RECORDS DEPARTMENT

Ellesmere and Chester Canal Company, General Committee Orders, 1827–46; Carrying Committee Minutes, 1836–8.

Canal Traffic Committee, North Staffordshire Railway Company, Minute Book, 1867–75 (T.M.C. 1).

Liverpool and Manchester Railway Company Board Minutes, 1838–45.

London and North Western Railway Company Board Minutes.

Manchester, Sheffield, and Lincolnshire Railway Company, Proceedings of the Board of Directors, 1872–4.

Manchester, Sheffield, and Lincolnshire and Midland Railway Companies, Joint Lines Committee, 1869–81.

THE BRITISH MUSEUM

The Huskisson Papers, Add. MS. 38746.

LIVERPOOL CITY LIBRARY RECORD OFFICE

Liverpool Parliamentary Office Manuscript, 1792–1836.

HOUSE OF LORDS LIBRARY

Collections of Private Acts.

Minutes of Evidence on Private Bills.

ORIGINAL PRINTED SOURCES

(*a*) PARLIAMENTARY PAPERS

Account of the quantity of wheat and of wheat meal and wheat flour in quarters and bushels imported from Ireland into Great Britain: 1799–1806 and 1820–27, 1826–7 (123) XVI.

Return of the name and description of all steam vessels registered in the ports of the U.K., 1845 (349) XLVII.

Census of Great Britain, 1851 (Population tables, north-western division), 1852–3 (1632) LXXXVI.

Select committee on the principle of amalgamation applied to railway or railway and canal bills, third report, 1852–3 (246) XXXVIII.

Commissioners to inquire into local charges upon shipping in the ports of the U.K., report and appendix, 1854 [1836] XXXVII.

Select committee on local charges upon shipping, report, minutes of evidence, and appendix, 1856 (332) XII.

Commissioners of customs, seventh annual report, 1863 [3157] XXVI.

Annual reports of H.M. Inspectors of mines, 1854–   .

Mining and mineral statistics of the U.K., 1882–7.

Annual statements of trade and navigation, U.K.

Royal commission on coal, reports, etc., vol. iii, 1871 [C. 435 ii] XVIII.

Joint select committee of the House of Lords and House of Commons on railway companies' amalgamation, report, etc., 1872 (364) XIII.

Select committee on canals, report, etc., 1883 (252) XIII.

Royal commission on canals and inland navigations of the United Kingdom, fourth and final report, etc., 1910 [Cd. 4979] XII, and *Appendices to fourth and final report*, 1910 [Cd. 5204] XII.

Other official sources consulted include the *Journals* of the House of Commons and the House of Lords and Hansard, *Parliamentary debates*, third series.

(*b*) JOURNALS AND NEWSPAPERS

The Annual Register.
The Colliery Guardian.
The Eccles Advertiser.
The Edinburgh Review.
Herapath's Railway and Commercial Journal.
The Liverpool Mercury.
The Manchester Guardian.
The Manchester Mercury.
The Railway Times.
The Times.

(*c*) CONTEMPORARY ACCOUNTS

BOOTH, H., *An account of the Liverpool and Manchester railway* (Liverpool, 1830).

GREVILLE, C. C. F., *A journal of the reigns of King George IV and King William IV* (London, 1875).

—— *A journal of the reign of Queen Victoria from 1837 to 1852* (London, 1885).

LOCH, J., *An account of the improvements on the estates of the Marquess of Stafford* (London, 1820).

—— 'Memoir of George Granville, late Duke of Sutherland' (London, 1834), privately printed.

PRIESTLEY, J., *Historical account of the navigable rivers, canals, and railways, of Great Britain* (London, 1831).

SANDARS, J., *A letter on the subject of the projected railroad between Liverpool and Manchester . . .* , 3rd edn. (Liverpool, 1825).

SMITHERS, H., *Liverpool, its commerce, statistics and institutions* (Liverpool, 1825).

SPENCER, A. (ed.), *Memoirs of William Hickey* (London, 1948).

(*d*) DIRECTORIES

Scholes' directory of Manchester, 1794.
Scholes' directory of Manchester and Salford, 1797.
Bancks' directory of Manchester and Salford, 1800 and 1802.

Deans' & Co.'s directory of Manchester and Salford, 1804 and 1808–9.
Pigot and Slater's directory of Manchester and Salford, 1843.
Slater's directory of Manchester and Salford, 1845.
Gore's directory of Liverpool, 1805.
Bradshaw's railway manual, shareholders' guide and directory, 1879, 1880, 1881, 1882, and 1889.

(*e*) LEGAL
Will of the Duke of Bridgewater (London, 1836).

SECONDARY WORKS: BOOKS, ARTICLES, ETC.

ASHTON, T. S., and SYKES, J., *The coal industry of the eighteenth century* (Manchester, 1964).
AXON, W. E. A., *The annals of Manchester* (Manchester, 1886).
BAMFORD, F., and WELLINGTON, DUKE OF (eds.), *The journal of Mrs. Arbuthnot, 1820–32* (London, 1950).
BARDSLEY, J. R., *The railways of Bolton, 1824–1959* (Bolton, undated).
BARKER, T. C., and HARRIS, J. R., *A Merseyside town in the industrial revolution: St. Helens, 1750–1900* (London, 1959).
BRICKELL, E. (*née* Malley), 'The financial administration of the Bridgewater estate, 1780–1800' (University of Manchester unpublished M.A. thesis, 1929).
BRIGGS, A., 'Thomas Attwood and the economic background of the Birmingham political union', *Cambridge historical journal*, ix (1947–9).
BROCK, W., *Lord Liverpool and liberal toryism, 1820 to 1827* (Cambridge, 1941).
BUCKLEY, J. K., *Joseph Parkes of Birmingham* (London, 1926).
BUDDLE ATKINSON, R. H. M., and JACKSON, G. A. (arr.), *Brougham and his early friends: letters to James Loch, 1798–1809* (London, 1908), privately printed.
Burke's landed gentry, 1952 edn.
BURROW, J., *Official guide to Worsley* (London—various editions).
CARTER, E. F., *An historical geography of the railways of the British Isles* (London, 1959).
CHALONER, W. H., *The social and economic development of Crewe, 1780–1923* (Manchester, 1950).
—— 'The Canal Duke', *History Today* (October 1951).
—— 'Charles Roe of Macclesfield, 1715–81', *Transactions of the Lancashire and Cheshire Antiquarian Society*, lxii (1950–1).
CLAPHAM, J. H., *An economic history of modern Britain*: vol. i, *The early railway age, 1820–50* (Cambridge, 1950); vol. ii, *Free trade and steel, 1850–86* (Cambridge, 1932).
CLEGG, H., 'The third Duke of Bridgewater's canal works in Manchester', *Transactions of the Lancashire and Cheshire Antiquarian Society*, lxv (1955).
CLEVELAND-STEVENS, E., *English railways, their development and their relation to the state* (London, 1915).

DEANE, P., and COLE, W. A., *British economic growth, 1688–1959* (Cambridge, 1964).

Dictionary of national biography (London, 1885–1901), and *Second supplement, 1901–11* (Oxford, 1920).

DOW, G., *Great Central*, 2 vols. (London, 1959–62).

DUCKHAM, BARON F., *The Yorkshire Ouse: the history of a river navigation* (Newton Abbot, 1967).

EDWARDS, M. M., *The growth of the British cotton trade, 1780–1815* (Manchester, 1967).

ELLESMERE, FRANCIS, FIRST EARL OF, *Personal reminiscences of the Duke of Wellington, edited with a memoir of Lord Ellesmere by his daughter Alice, Countess of Strafford* (London, 1904).

ELLIS, H., *British railway history, 1830–76* (London, 1954).

FALK, B., *The Bridgewater millions* (London, 1942).

FAY, C. R., *Huskisson and his age* (London, 1951).

FEREDAY, R. P., 'The career of Richard Smith', *The Acorn* (Journal of the Round Oak Steel Works Ltd.), summer 1966–summer 1967.

FOSTER, J., *Alumni oxonienses, 1715–1886* (Oxford, 1888).

—— *Men at the Bar* (London, 1885).

GAYER, A. D., ROSTOW, W. W., and SCHWARTZ, A. J., *The growth and fluctuation of the British economy, 1790–1850* (Oxford, 1953).

GILL, C., and BRIGGS, A., *The history of Birmingham* (London, 1952).

GRIFFITHS, R. P., *The Cheshire Lines railway* (Lingfield, 1958).

HADFIELD, C., *British canals* (London, 1950).

—— *The canals of the west Midlands* (Newton Abbot, 1966).

HODGSKINS, D. J., 'The origin and independent years of the Cromford and High Peak railway', *Journal of transport history*, vi (1963–4).

JACKMAN, W. T., *The development of transportation in modern England*, 2nd edn. (London, 1962).

JEANS, J. S., *Jubilee memorial of the railway system* (London, 1875).

KEETON, G. W., *Social change in the law of trusts* (London, 1958).

KITSON CLARK, G., *The making of Victorian England* (London, 1962).

LEWIN, H. G., *Early British railways* (London, 1925).

LLOYD, R., *Railwaymen's gallery* (London, 1953).

LOCH, G., *The family of Loch* (Edinburgh, 1934), privately printed.

LUNN, J., *A short history of the township of Tyldesley* (Tyldesley, 1953).

MACDERMOT, E. T., *History of the Great Western railway*: vol. i, *1833–63* (London, 1927).

MALET, H., *The Canal Duke* (London, 1961).

Manchester historical recorder, the (Manchester, undated).

'Manifold', *The North Staffordshire railway* (Ashbourne, 1952).

MARSHALL, C. F. DENDY, *Centenary history of the Liverpool and Manchester railway* (London, 1930).

MINGAY, G. E., *English landed society in the eighteenth century* (London, 1963).

MORSE, H. B., *The chronicles of the East India Company trading to China, 1635–1834* (Oxford, 1926–9).

MULLINEUX, F., *The Duke of Bridgewater's canal* (Eccles, 1959).
—— 'The Duke of Bridgewater's underground canals at Worsley', *Transactions of the Lancashire and Cheshire Antiquarian Society*, lxxi (1961).
NAMIER, L. B., and BROOKE, J., *The House of Commons, 1754–90* (London, 1964).
NEF, J. U., *The rise of the British coal industry* (London, 1932).
NICKSON, C., *History of Runcorn* (London and Warrington, 1887).
POLLARD, S., *The Genesis of Modern Management* (Harmondsworth, 1968).
POLLINS, H., 'The finances of the Liverpool and Manchester railway', *Economic history review*, 2nd ser. v (1952–3).
PREBBLE, J., *The Highland clearances* (London, 1963).
ROBBINS, M., *The railway age* (London, 1962).
ROLT, L. T. C., *George and Robert Stephenson: the railway revolution* (London, 1960).
—— *Thomas Telford* (London, 1958).
SIMMONS, J., *The railways of Britain* (London, 1961).
SMILES, S., *The story of the life of George Stephenson* (London, 1862).
SOFFER, R. N., 'Attitudes and allegiances in the unskilled north, 1830–50', *International review of social history*, x (1965).
SPRING, D., *The English landed estate in the nineteenth century: its administration* (Baltimore, 1963).
TAYLOR, A. J., 'Combination in the mid-nineteenth-century coal industry', *Transactions of the Royal Historical Society*, 5th ser. iii (1953).
THOMPSON, F. M. L., *English landed society in the nineteenth century* (London, 1963).
TOMLINSON, V. I., 'Salford activities connected with the Bridgewater Canal', *Transactions of the Lancashire and Cheshire Antiquarian Society*, lxvi (1956).
—— 'Early warehouses on Manchester waterways', *Transactions of the Lancashire and Cheshire Antiquarian Society*, lxxi (1961).
TOOKE, T., and NEWMARCH, W., *A history of prices* (London, 1928).
VEITCH, G. S., *The struggle for the Liverpool and Manchester railway* (Liverpool, 1930).
Victoria county history of Lancashire, the (London, 1906–14).
WHEELER, J., *Manchester: its political, social, and commercial history* (London, 1836).
WHITE, B. D., *A history of the corporation of Liverpool* (Liverpool, 1951).
WILLAN, T. S., *The navigation of the river Weaver in the eighteenth century* (*Chetham Society, remains etc.*, 3rd ser., iii, Manchester, 1951).

Bibliography

INDEX

Abercromby, James, barrister and auditor, 32, 33.

Accrington, 198.

Acton, 203.

Adam, Rt. Hon. William (of Blair Adam), barrister and auditor, 30.

Adam, (probably William George, K.C., son of above), 32, 69.

Ale and porter, trade in, 125, 162.

Alice (steamboat), 108, 168, 272 n. 3, 273 and n. 6.

Allport, James, manager, Midland Railway, 335 n. 2.

Altrincham, 107, 108, 109, 110, 111 and n. 1, 112, 128, 130, 131, 132, 172, 173, 178, 232, 244, 292, 295, 301.

Anderton, 124, 125, 129, 169, 170, Appendix A—note on sources.

Anti-Corn Law League, 242.

Arbuthnot, Harriet, 39.

Ardrossan, 283.

Aristocracy, industrial activities of, xv, 343–4.

Armstrong, William, inventor, 282.

Ashley, Lord (later 7th Earl of Shaftesbury), 321, 322.

Ashton, T. S., and Sykes, J., 307.

Ashton-under-Lyne, 159, 160, 169, 197, 210, 212, 213, 217.

Ashton's Field Colliery, 306 and n. 2, 319, 320.

Aston, 153, 286.

Attwood, Thomas (of Birmingham), banker, 33 n. 1.

Australia, 241.

Autherley, 34.

Ayrshire, 310.

Baird, William & Co. (of Glasgow), ironmasters, 283.

Baltic, 13.

Banbury, 229, 231, 244.

Bancroft, Alderman James, chairman, Birkenhead Railway, 244.

Banktop (Piccadilly, Manchester), 172.

Bantock, Thomas, agent, Bridge-

water Trust, Wolverhampton, 239 n. 1.

Barbridge Junction, 126.

Baring, family of, financiers, 33.

Barningham, William (of Pendleton), ironmaster, 286 n. 3.

Barratt, James (of Warrington), attorney, 186, 187, n. 3.

Barrow-in-Furness, 283.

Barton Aqueduct, 319.

Barton Lock, 164.

Bateman, John Frederic La Trobe, civil engineer, 152 n. 1, 182, 260.

Baxendale, Joseph, head of Pickfords, carriers, 121.

Bazley, Thomas, chairman, Manchester Chamber of Commerce, 242, 244.

Beaufort, 6th Duke of, 78.

Beaumont, 8th Baron, 239 n. 4.

Bedford, 7th Duke of, 312.

Bedford manor, Lancs., 2.

Beer shops, 328.

Belfast, trade with, 283.

Belgium, 340.

Benbow, Mr., solicitor, Trustee of 1st Earl Dudley, 98.

Bentham, Jeremy, 31, 100.

Bibby, John, director, Manchester, Bolton, and Bury Canal and Railway Co., 81.

'Billy Boys', boats, 199.

Birkenhead, 181, 184, 227, 232, 250, 255 n. 1, 261, 263, 264, 277, 279, 281, 282, 288 n. 3, 296 and n. 2, 300, Appendix A—note on sources.

Birmingham, 4, 5, 27, 28, 29, 31, 32, 35, 36, 63, 65, 66, 74 and n. 3, 76, 77, 124, 127, 131, 133, 134, 136, 145, 148, 183, 191, 200, 204, 226, 227, 238, 239, 244, 245, 246, 248, 250, 253, 254, 269, 284, 345, 352, 355.

Black Country, 98, 148, 150, 227, 229, 234, 253, 294, 355 ; *see also* Staffordshire.

Blackburn, xvii, 137, 138.

Blair, Harrison, railway promoter, 232.

Blair Adam, 30.

Blanche (steamboat), 108 and n. 3, 163, 272 n. 3.

Bleach works, 290, 308.

Blore, Edward, architect, 118.

Board of Trade, 173, 184–5, 215, 282.

Boats, canal:
  building of, xi–xii.
  fly boats, 238.
  gauging of, 141, 164–5, 243.
  horsing of, 239, 271.
  swift boats, 108–11, 172, 173.
  tide boats, 108.
  tub boats, 318.
  see also Duke of Bridgewater's Canal, steam traction, experiments with.

Bollin, River, 131.

Bollington (nr. Altrincham), 131.

Bolton, 63, 81, 93, 94, 123, 137, 147, 185, 196, 309, 312, 333; Improvement Bill, 261.

Booth, Henry, secretary and treasurer, L. & M.R.; later secretary, Northern division, L. & N.W.R., 48, 49, 70, 155, 160, 161, 162, 196, 241, 351.

Boothstown, 318, 320.

Bourke, Walter Longley, superintendent, Bridgewater Trust, 334.

Brackley, xviii, 9, 83, 88.

Brackley, Viscount, *see* Ellesmere, 2nd Earl of.

Bradford, Earl of, 325.

Bradford, Yorks., xvii.

Bradshaw, Captain James, deputy superintendent, Bridgewater Trust, 10, 15, 21, 41, 42, 45 and n. 3, 46–7, 48, 49, 50, 55, 56, 57, 64, 77 n. 1, 79, 83, 84, 85–6, 104, 259 n. 1.

Bradshaw, James, supercargo, East India Company, 8.

Bradshaw, Robert Haldane, superintendent, Bridgewater Trust, 33, 39, 71, 82 n. 1, 86 n. 6, 88, 117, 192.
  background and character, 8–12, 9 nn. 2 & 3, 10 n. 3, 80, 83, 84–5, 346.
  management of the Bridgewater Canal, 12–26, 35, 36, 54–6, 57–62, 85, 91, 100, 102–3, 106, 352, 355.
  and other waterways, 12, 13–14, 16–17, 25, 106.

  and railways, 37–8, 41–2, 49, 51–4, 56–61, 64, 67–8, 72, 74–5, 78–9, 81–2, 106.
  and the collieries, 81, 314 and n. 4, 331.
  private estates, 86 and n. 6, 87, 314 and n. 4.
  retirement, 83–7.

Bradshaw, Thomas, secretary of the Treasury, 8.

Bradshaw, William Rigby (son of Robert Haldane), 86 and n. 2.

Brass, John, steward, 88.

Braunston, 203.

Brazil, 27.

Bridgewater, Francis Egerton, 3rd Duke of, xv–xviii, xix, 2, 3, 10, 17, 20, 22, 33, 117, 314, 350.
  will of, xviii–xix, 6, 10, 22–4, 86 and n. 2.

Bridgewater (steamboat) 273 and n. 6.

Bridgewater Collieries, Lancs., 96, 144, 266, 276 n. 7, 299, Chapter XIV *passim*, 334, 335, 343, 346, 347.
  efficiency, 113, 115–16, 312–17.
  growth, 305–6, Appendix C.
  labour conditions and policies, 49, 320–33, 344.
  labour movements, 10, 328–32, 333.
  markets, xvi, 3, 81, 113, 307–12.
  profits, Appendix A (d).
  railway communication, 188–9, 303, 318–20, 343.
  size, 1–2.
  tramway and mineral railway, 318, 319–20, 320 n. 1 and 2.
  underground canal, 317–18.
  see also Bridgewater Trust, organization and efficiency.

Bridgewater Colliery, The, Wardley, 306 and n. 5.

Bridgewater Estates Ltd., 335.

Bridgewater House, London, 118, 119.

Bridgewater Navigation Company Ltd., 106, 290, 334–6, 339–42, 352.

Bridgewater Trust:
  organization and efficiency, 100–2, 269–70, 334–5, 343–56.
  profits of, 7, 83, 90, 266, 299 and n. 3, 300, Appendix A.
  see also Bridgewater Collieries; Duke of Bridgewater's Canal;

Financial Problems; Landed Estates; Bradshaw, R. H., Egerton, A. F., Loch, J., and Sothern, James, superintendents; Smith, G. S. F., general manager.

Brimstone, trade in, 296 n. 7.

Brindley, James, engineer, xvi, 8, 54.

Bristol, 5th Earl of, 78.

Bristol, 247, 249, 355.

Bristol Channel, 124.

Broadheath, 22, 102, 108, 254, 288, 302.

Bromilow, David, land agent, Bridgewater Trust, 91.

Brooke, Sir Richard, 6th Bart., 183, 231, 264.

Brougham, Henry, 1st Baron Brougham and Vaux, 31.

Brougham, William, barrister, 32.

Brydon, R., employee, Bridgewater Trust, 220.

Buckley, ? Edward, director, Old Quay Company, 158.

Buckley, Nathaniel, deputy chairman, Bridgewater Navigation Co., 336.

Building, sale or lease of land for, 215, 303, 328.

Building materials, trade in, 126; *see also* Slates; Timber.

Burch, Joseph, inventor, 112, 291.

Burford Lane, 102, 288.

Burk, William, inventor, 36.

Burnage, 172.

Burton on Trent, 125, 270.

Bury, 195, 196, 197, 198.

Canada, 113.

Nova Scotia, 98.

Canals and River Navigations (general):

amalgamation with railways, *see* Railways, ownership of canals.

carriers, carrying by rail, 217–21, 224–5, 237, 239, 245, 246, 247, 248, 249, 250, 251, 253, 254, 270, 351.

carrying trade on, 149–50; *see also* Duke of Bridgewater's Canal.

competition between, 121, 122, 132, 300, 355; *see also* particular canals and railways.

competition with railways, 121–2, 132–3, 141, 174, 194, 226, 300,

345, 351, 355–6; connection with trade cycle, 255 and n. 4, 294–5; *see also* particular canals and railways.

freezing of, 232.

Canals and River Navigations (particular):

Aire and Calder Navigation, 335, 338.

Arun River, xv.

Ashton-under-Lyne Canal, 52, 125, 139, 145, 169, 180, 187, 297 n. 1.

Birmingham and Liverpool Junction Canal, 33–4, 35–6, 66, 68–9, 71–2, 76, 113, 126, 127, 128, 136, 149, 150, 179, 344.

Birmingham Canal Navigations, 33, 34, 68, 229.

Bollington Canal (proposed), 131.

Bridgewater Canal, *see* separate entry, Duke of Bridgewater's Canal.

Calder and Hebble Navigation, 338.

Chester Canal, *see* Ellesmere and Chester Canal.

Coventry Canal, 140, 274.

Cromford Canal, 139, 140.

Dee, River, 263.

Ellesmere and Chester Canal, 34, 35, 66, 68–9, 71, 76, 124, 125, 126, 127, 128, 130, 138, 144, 145, 149, 150, 167, 168, 169, 179, 344, Appendix A—note on sources; *see also* Middlewich branch.

Erewash Canal, 140.

Grand Junction Canal, 140, 202, 203–4, 248, 254 and n. 1, 274, 291, 311.

Grand Trunk (Trent and Mersey) Canal, xvii, 3, 6, 17, 33, 34, 35–6, 59, 68, 72, 76, 77, 124, 125, 126, 127–8, 129, 130, 131, 132, 136, 138, 139, 140, 141, 145, 147, 149, 150, 169, 180, 183, 188, 191, 201, 202, 203, 232, 234, 235, 236, 237, 238, 240, 245, 252, 253, 265 n. 2, 270, 271, 272, 299 n. 4, 300, 312, 344.

Grand Union Canal, 140.

Huddersfield Canal, 180, 187, 205, 206.

Irwell, River, xvi, 37, 38, 50, 51, 52, 53, 93, 94, 289–90.

Canals and River Navigations (particular) (*cont.*):

Lancaster Canal, xvii, 137, 138.

Leeds and Liverpool Canal, xvii, 25, 137, 138, 149, 338.

Llangollen branch, Ellesmere Canal, 149.

Llanymynech branch, Ellesmere Canal, 149

Macclesfield Canal, 59, 124, 125, 132, 145, 180, 188, 203, 274.

Manchester and Birmingham Junction Canal (proposed), 128 and n. 2, 131 and n. 3, 132, 344, 345.

Manchester and Salford Junction Canal, 93–4, 122–3, 123 n. 2, 338.

Manchester, Bolton, and Bury Canal, and Railway, 9 n. 3, 25, 80–1, 93–4, 137, 142, 177, 178, 180, 196, 197, 206, 213, 296 n. 7.

Manchester Ship Canal, 106, 336, 342, 352, 353; precursors, 153, 174, 228.

Mersey, River, 290.

Mersey and Irwell Navigation: independent career, xvi, 4, 12, 13, 14, 15, 16, 17, 41, 51, 58, 59, 76, 88, 92–4, 95, 96, 103–4, 105, 115, 119, 122–3, 134, 141, 144, 152–6, 157, 158, 160–3, 310, 352; purchase by Lord Francis Egerton and the Bridgewater Trust, 162, 163–7, 187, 193, 349; under Bridgewater control, 168, 171, 174, 190, 198, 199, 209, 216, 228, 231, 241, 242, 243, 255, 257, 266, 287, 289–90, 342, 354, Appendix A (b); under Bridgewater Navigation Ltd., 334, 340–1, 342.

Middlewich branch, Ellesmere and Chester Canal, 34, 35, 36, 69, 126, 127, 128, 130, 149, 150

Ouse (Yorks), River, 21.

Oxford Canal, 127, 138, 140, 203, 229, 311.

Peak Forest Canal, 125, 139, 145, 180, 188.

Portsmouth and Arundel Canal, xv.

Ribble, River, 263.

Rochdale Canal, 3, 52, 93–4, 122, 123, 131, 179, 180, 187, 188, 291, 297, 307, 338.

Runcorn and Weston Canal, 260–1, 280, 281.

St. Helens Canal and Railway, 177, 261, 292, 295, 296, 298, 301. Sankey Brook Navigation, 153, 177, 310; *see also* St. Helens Canal and Railway.

Severn, River, 300.

Sheffield Canal, 16.

Shropshire Union Railways and Canal, 179 and n. 3, 180, 188, 191, 203, 208, 234, 240 and n. 1, 269, 282 n. 3, 304 n. 1, 338; *see also* Ellesmere and Chester Canal, and Birmingham and Liverpool Junction Canal.

Sir John Ramsden's Canal, 206.

Staffordshire and Worcestershire Canal, 33, 34, 126, 150, 202, 234, 235, 271, 274.

Thames, River, 21, 340.

Trent, River, 138, 139, 270, 355.

Trent and Mersey Canal, *see* Grand Trunk.

Warwick and Birmingham Canal, 229.

Warwick and Napton Canal, 229.

Weaver, River, xvii, 4, 16, 59, 76, 124, 125, 126, 129, 130, 138, 169, 170, 203, 259, 260, 282 n. 3, 301, 312.

Wey and Arun Junction Canal, xv.

Worcester and Birmingham Canal, 339.

Canal Association, 200–1, 297.

Canal Traffic Committee (North Staffordshire trade), 304 n. 1.

Cannel, 312.

Canton (China), 8.

Cardwell's Committee (Select Committee on the Principle of Amalgamation Applied to Railway or Railway and Canal Bills 1852–3), 243.

Carlisle, Earls of, estates, 30, 34, 48.

Carlisle, 7th Earl of, *see* Morpeth, Lord.

Carriers (particular):

Anderton Carrying Co., 124–5, 129, 130, 132, 144, 145, 146, 149, 169, 299 n. 4, 301, 349.

Barnby, Faulkner & Co., 198, 219, 220; *see also* Faulkner, C. J.

Barrow, Richard, 139.
Carver, William & Co., 198, 213, 217, 219.
Cogswell, J., 15.
Fellows, Joshua, 271.
Garstang, Almond & Co., 160.
Hargreaves, John, 137, 141.
Harrington Timber Carrying Co., 199 ; agent, 288 n. 3.
Henshall, Hugh & Co., 129, 132, 144, 149, 150.
Jackson, Thomas, 145.
Jackson, William, & Sons, 219.
Kenworthy & Co., 146, 199, 206, 219.
Mackay(s), *see* Thompson, Mackay & Co.
Manchester Grocers' Co., 15, 58, 199, 216.
Marsdens, Hartley & Co., 15.
Merchants' Co., 219, 220.
Nall, Joseph, 198, 200.
New Quay Co., 51, 199, 216, 241, 242, 243, 255 n. 4, 289.
Patchett & McKay, 160.
Pickford & Co., 121, 144, 146, 191, 245.
Price & Co., 271.
Reid, Alexander & Co., *see* Anderton Carrying Co.
Shipton & Co. (of Wolverhampton), 202, 204, 231, 245, 248 and n. 1, 271.
Skey, George (of Wolverhampton), 234.
Soresby & Flack, later J. W. Soresby & Co., 139.
Sutton & Co., 139, 146.
Thompson, E. and I., 15.
Thompson, Mackay & Co., 213, 217, 219.
Union Co., 116.
Veevers, J. and J., 158, 199, 219.
Worthington & Co., 136.
Carting by road as an adjunct to canals, 210, 211, 212, 218–19, 223, 238, 254, 318, 354.
Castlefield (Castle Quay), Manchester, xvii, xviii n. 1, 3, 5, 15, 16, 23, 50, 51, 52, 53, 78–9, 93, 123, 137, 142, 152, 172, 210, 305, 306 n. 1, 307, 338.
Cawdor, 1st Earl, 78.

Chaddock and Booths estate, Tyldesley, Lancs., 86 n. 6, 314.
Chadwick, Edwin, 100.
Chancellor, The Lord, 119.
Chancery, Court of, 88, 89–90, 92, 96, 347, 350.
Chandos, Marquess of (later 3rd Duke of Buckingham), 255, 298.
Charges upon Shipping, Commissioners on (1854), 263–4.
Charterhouse, 99.
Chartism, 329 and n. 4.
Chat Moss, xvii, 2, 44, 48, 344.
Chemical industry, 257, 264–5.
Cheshire, 4, 5, 170, 178, 184, 292.
Chester, 34, 109, 126, 167, 168, 172, 178, 181, 227.
Chester Courant, 265.
Chesterfield, 6th Earl of, 78.
Chichester Fortescue's Committee (Joint Select Committee on Railway Companies' Amalgamation 1872), 339.
China, trade with, 222.
Cholera, epidemic of, 207.
Chorlton, Cheshire, 76.
'Christmas Boxes', given to ensure custom, 308.
Churches, foundation of, 321.
Cinders, 353.
Clanricarde, 1st Marquess of, 78.
Clanwilliam, 3rd Earl of, 78.
Clapham, J. H., 121, 122, 307, 312.
Clarendon, 3rd Earl of, 78.
Clive, Viscount (later 2nd Earl of Powis), chairman, Ellesmere and Chester and Birmingham and Liverpool Junction Canal Companies, 32, 66, 69, 71–2, 76, 128, 130, 344.
Clive (steamboat), 168.
Coal industry, xv, 6–7, 135, 306–7, 309.
  miners:
  children as, 321, 323.
  education of, 327.
  labour, conditions of, 326–7.
  labour movements of, 328–32.
  moral condition of, 322, 327–8.
  payment, frequency of, 322 and n. 2, 323–4.
  supply and recruitment of, 324–5.
  wages of, 321–2, 324, 333.
  women as, 322–3.

Coal industry (*cont.*):
 mines:
 accidents in, 326–7.
 draining of, 317.
 sinkings, deep, 316, 317, 319.
 ventilation of, 326–7.
 winding, 317, 326 and n. 5.
 working, systems of, 316.
 trade in, 125, 147, 206, 258, 259
  n. 1, 261, 268, 281, 303, 307–12,
  353.
 see also Bridgewater Collieries;
  cannel; cinders; coke.
Coasting trade, 4, 92, 114, 129, 132,
 153, 190, 195, 199, 259, 260, 262,
 263, 283, 285, 294, 300.
Cobden–Chevalier commercial treaty
 with France (1860), 284.
Coke, production of and trade in, 113,
 133–4, 144, 311, 317, 351.
Cole, W. A., 307.
Collier, W. H., assistant manager,
 Bridgewater Navigation Co., 106,
 207, 335 n. 1, 337, 352.
Colwich, 293.
Combermere, 1st Viscount, 78.
Congleton, 144, 169.
Cork, 27.
Cornbrook, Manchester, 302, 326,
 337–8.
Cornwall, 4, 300.
Cotton, raw, consumption of, 5 n. 2,
 309.
Cotton, trade in, 4–5, 5 n. 1, 27,
 136, 139, 140, 154, 157, 159–60,
 162, 197–8, 205, 210, 211, 217,
 218–19, 221, 222, 223, 241, 243,
 353.
 industry, 303, 308–9, 321, 323.
Countess of Ellesmere (steamboat),
 272 and n. 3, 273.
Coventry, 5.
Cranes, 282, 287, 288.
Crawford and Balcarres, 24th and 7th
 Earl of, 325.
Crewe, 296.
Cubitt, William, engineer, 115, 152
 n. 1.
Cuerdley Marsh, 181.
Cumberland, 48, 234, 283, 294, 299,
 310.
Currie, W. W., director, L. & M.R.,
 45, 47, 64, 68, 79, 80, 87.

Dalhousie, 10th Earl of, president,
 Railway Department, Board of
 Trade, 184–5.
Dam boards, 289.
Dart (swift boat), 109.
Davies, Mr., inventor, 113.
Dean, Lancs., 314.
Deane, Phyllis, 307.
Decoy, The, 20.
Delaroche, Paul, artist, 118.
Delph, The, 317.
Denby, William, coal agent, Bridge-
 water Trust, 308–9.
Derby, 270.
Derby, 12th Earl of, 32, 37–8.
Derby, 13th Earl of, 177.
Derbyshire, 5, 122, 178, 234.
Deva (steamboat), 283.
Devon, 4.
Devon, 10th Earl of, Bridgewater
 Trustee, 94, 97.
Devonshire, 6th Duke of, 32.
Dialling of mines, 315.
Dickens, Charles, 96, 327.
Didsbury, 172.
Discrimination in rates of carriage,
 130, 201, 215.
Ditton, 286.
Dixon Green, 318, 330.
Donnington, 30.
Dorset, 4.
Dover, 1st Baron, 78.
Dowling, M. M. G., Commissioner and
 Head Constable of Liverpool Police,
 198.
Droitwich, 254.
Drummonds & Co., bankers, 22, 86,
 117, 192.
Drylaw, 30.
Dublin, 27, 284.
Dublin, City of, Steam Packet Co.,
 284.
Dudley, 29.
Dudley, Trustees of the 1st Earl, 30,
 98.
Duke of Bridgewater's Canal:
 and other waterways, 92–4, 106,
  122–32, 144–6, 149–51, 152–6,
  157, 158–70, 189–90, 191, 200–3,
  208, 240 and n. 1, 304 n. 1, 344.
 and railways, 106, 132–44, 146–9,
  152, 170–3, 180–9, 189–90, 191–
  2, 194, Chap. X *passim*, Chap.

XI *passim*, 261–2, 286, 292–9, 300–4, 309–11, 335–9, 344, 351–6.

building, xvi–xvii, xvii n. 1, 7 and n. 5

carrying trade, carriers, xviii, 1, 14–16, 89 and n. 4, 96, 103–5, 145–6, 159–60, 161, 162, 166–7, 195–6, 198, 199–200, 201–3, 204, 216, 217–19, 241, 242, 248 and n. 5, 258, 262, 266, 270–1, 270 n. 5, 283, 288, 299 and n. 4, 342 and n. 4, 347, 353, 355; by rail, 212–13, 214, 215, 216 n. 1, 217–21, 224–5, 235, 237, 239, 245, 246, 247, 248, 249, 250, 251, 252, 253, 254, 355; *see also* under particular carriers.

condition, 17–22, 23–4, 54–5, 61, 85, 95, 244, 290–1, 319 n. 5, 353–4, 355.

passenger service, 60, 61, 106–11, 172, 173, 183, 207, 267, 272–3, 328, 345, 353.

plans to sell, lease, or convert to railway, 66–8, 174–5, 228, 232–3, 235–6, 240, 245, 255, 273–7, 277–8, 302, 335–9.

profits, 7 and n. 5, 15–16, 60–2, 85, 104, 170, 189, 210 and n. 1, 215, 342, 354–5, Appendix A.

rates of carriage, 12–14, 43, 57–9, 89, 95–6, 105–6, 138, 152, 153–63, 165, 166, 168, 195, 196, 197–8, 204, 205, 211–12, 214, 217–19, 221, 223–5, 241 and n. 2, 259, 262, 264 n. 2, 283, 284, 292 and n. 3, 295 n. 4, 301, 352.

steam traction, experiments with, 111–13, 291, 292 and n. 2, 340

traffic, xvi–xvii, 3–5, 34, 35–6, 52, 60, 81, 170, 189–92, 209, 214, 220, 224, 245–6, 270 n. 5, 299–300, 353 and n. 2, Appendix B, Appendix C.

transfer to Bridgewater Navigation Ltd., Chap. XV, *passim*.

transfer to Manchester Ship Canal Co., 342.

value, 7 and n. 5, 174, 302, 334, 342.

see also Bradshaw, R. H., Egerton, A. F., Loch, J., and Sothern, James, superintendents; Smith, G. S. F., general manager; Bridgewater Trust.

Durham, 109.

Dutton, 59.

Dyewoods, trade in, 159, 296 n. 7.

Dyeworks, 308–9.

Earl of Ellesmere (steamboat), 273 and n. 6.

Earl Powis (steamboat), 168.

Earle, Hardman, director, L. & M.R., 56, 155.

Earlestown, 182.

East India Company, 8, 31.

Eaton, James, agent, Bridgewater Trust, 91.

Eaton, William, corn receiver, Bridgewater Trust, 90.

Eaton family, connection with Bridgewater Trust, 90, 91.

Edge Fold, 315.

Edinburgh, 31.

Edinburgh, University of, 31.

Edinburgh Review, 31.

Educational facilities, provision of, 321, 327.

Egerton, Lady Francis, *see* Ellesmere, Harriet, Countess of.

Egerton, Lord Francis, *see* Ellesmere, 1st Earl of.

Egerton, the Hon. Algernon Fulke, superintendent, Bridgewater Trust, 267, 276, 279, 280–1, 286, 303, 321, 327, 334, 343, 344, 346, 350, 355.

death of, 334.

Egerton of Tatton, Wilbraham, 172.

Egremont, 3rd Earl of, xv.

Electric Telegraph, 288, 289.

Ellenborough, 2nd Baron, 78.

Ellesmere, Francis Charles Granville, 3rd Earl of, 281, 335.

Ellesmere, Francis Egerton (formerly Leveson-Gower), 1st Earl of, 1, 25, 82 and n. 1, 99, 155, 170, 184, 215, 264, 316, 344, 345, 349.

and the Bridgewater Canal, 42, 55–6, 94–5, 100, 107, 116–17, 174, 193, 349.

and other canals, 131–2, 131 n. 3, 132 n. 1, 164, 165, 169, 345.

and railways, 32, 37, 39, 55, 66–7, 68, 74–5, 134, 135–6, 172, 173, 181, 182, 183, 187, 239 and n. 4, 255, 274–5, 276, 345.

Ellesmere, Francis Egerton (*cont.*)
as squire at Worsley, 320–33, 344
death of, 280.
private estates, 86–7, 86 n. 6,
118.
private expenditure, 84, 117–18,
192–3.
succession to Bridgewater estates,
xviii, 82, 84–90, 94–7, 267–8.
Ellesmere, George Granville Francis,
2nd Earl of, 169, 267, 275–6, 281,
320–1, 327, 332–3.
Ellesmere, Harriet, Countess of, 37,
114, 320, 322, 323, 324, 328, 329,
330, 331, 344.
Ellesmere, Mary, Countess of, 281.
Ellesmere Colliery, Walkden, 306 and
n. 3, 320 n. 1.
Ellesmere Port, 34, 69, 115, 126, 127,
130, 147, 149, 150, 168, 191, 203,
208, 240 and n. 1, 263, 272, Appendix A—note on sources.
Estate Acts, 118–20, 266, 267 and n. 2,
280, 349–50.
Etruria, North Staffordshire, 129, 150.
Euston Confederacy, 292.
Ewood Bridge, 212.
Exeter, Henry Philpotts, Bishop of,
98.

Famine, Irish potato, 259, 310.
Farms, Bridgewater, 96.
Farnworth, 23, 306 and n. 6, 312, 314,
318, 322.
Faulkner, C. J., of Barnby, Faulkner
& Co., carriers, 199, 289.
Fenny Compton, 226.
Fenton, William (of Ribchester),
Chairman of Bridgewater Naviga-
tion Co., 336.
Fereday, Samuel, ironmaster, 98.
Fiddlers Ferry, 134–5, 302 n. 5, 310.
Financial problems, Bridgewater
Trust, 22–4, 38, 55–6, 83, 84, 104,
116–20, 164, 187, 192–4, 266–7,
280–1, 347–51, Appendix A (i).
Fleetwood, 195, 261, 262, 283, 286,
311.
Foodstuffs, trade in, 5, 27–8, 34, 126,
130, 138–9, 140, 146, 152, 153, 154,
155, 157, 158, 159, 162, 197, 259,
263, 284, 285, 299 n. 4, 310, 353.
Fowler, Mr. (of Leeds), inventor, 340.

France:
Paris, 9, 40, trade with, 284
system of towing boats on the
Seine, 340
trade with Avignon, Bayonne,
Cette (? Sète), Dunkirk, Mont-
pellier, Nantes, Rouen, 284;
Bordeaux, 284, 285; Le Havre,
284, 285; Marseilles, 247, 284.
Froghall, 234.
Forrester, George, engineer, Bridge-
water Trust, 281, 291.
Foster, Mr., inventor, 199.
Fourdrinier, G. H., inventor, 111, 112.

Gainsborough, 249, 270.
Garrett Hall estate, 314.
Garston, 153, 177, 228, 261, 263, 274,
295, 296, 301, 302, 337.
Gas industry, 308, 312.
Gatty, Edward, solicitor, 90.
General Electric Telegraph Co., 288.
General Mining Association, 98.
Geological, Statistical, and Zoolo-
gical Society, 31.
Germany, 99.
Ghorall, Mr., agent, G.J.R., 135.
Gilbert, John, agent, xvi, 8.
Giles, Francis, engineer, 77.
Gladstone, Robert, railway pro-
moter, 40.
Gladstone, William Ewart, 100.
Glasgow, 262.
Glass manufacture, 308.
Gold strikes, California and Australia,
241.
Gosford, 2nd Earl of, 78.
Gower, George Granville Leveson-
Gower, Earl (later 2nd Duke of
Sutherland), 32, 35, 39, 66, 68, 84,
86, 95, 135, 155, 156, 158, 179, 185.
Grafton, 3rd Duke of, 8.
Granville, 1st Viscount, 76.
Gravel, trade in, 353.
Gravesend, 4.
Greville, C. C. F., diarist, 30, 322.
Grosvenor, 2nd Earl, 78.
Grundy's pit, Kearsley, 321.
Guano, trade in, 217.

Haddington, 9th Earl of, 78.
Haddock and Parnell, manufacturers
of chemicals, 264.

Hadfield, Mr. Charles, 229.
Harcourt, family of, 119; *see also* Vernon-Harcourt.
Hardware, trade in, 136, 137.
Harecastle, 178.
Harrow School, 8.
Harrowby, 1st Earl of, 32, 72, 78, 344.
Harter (probably James Collier, of Manchester, merchant), 242.
Haslingden, 212.
Hatchford, 118.
Hatherton, 1st Baron, Trustee of the 1st Earl Dudley, 98.
Hathorn, John, cashier, Bridgewater Trust, 332.
Hayes, William, salt manufacturer, 259.
Haywood Junction, 126, 127, 191, 237.
Helsby, 301, 302, 337.
Hercules (steamboat), 168, 272 and n. 3, 273.
Herrick, Mr., inventor, 112.
Hertfordshire, xviii.
Hetton, 28, 34.
Heywood, 196, 212, 213.
Hindley, 314, 315, 319.
Hollinshead, Alderman J. B. (of Liverpool), 43.
Hooton, 178.
Hornby, Joseph, director, L. & M.R., 155.
Horner, Francis, barrister, 31.
Horwich End, 54.
Hosiers Rocks, 20.
Howard de Walden, 6th Baron, 78.
Howarth, William, agent, Bridgewater Trust, Runcorn, 259, 260, 284.
Howley Quay, 288.
weir, 341.
Huddersfield, 206.
Huish, Captain Mark, general manager, G.J.R. and L. & N.W.R., 148, 171, 233, 235, 237, 293, 294,, 298 300, 301.
Hull, 202, 270, 284, 285.
Hulme (Manchester), 288.
Hulme Locks (Manchester), 94, 123, 291, 341.
Hulton's pits (Farnworth), 322.
Humber, 21, 139.
Huskisson, William, 40–1, 65, 72, 345.
Huyton, 66.

Illman, Thomas, engineer, Bridgewater Trust, 260, 261, 281.
Ince, 153.
India, trade with, 222.
Ipswich, 73.
Ireland, trade with, 114, 259, 262, 285, 310–11; *see also* Belfast, Cork, Dublin, Waterford.
Iron, trade in, 4, 126, 130, 132, 146, 147, 148, 150, 195, 202, 208, 229–31, 234, 238, 239 and n. 1, 245, 252 n. 2, 255 and nn. 1 and 3, 258, 261, 262, 263, 266, 283, 284, 285, 294, 296 n. 7, 297 n. 1, 299 and n. 4, 351.
industry, 157, 308, 323.
ironmaster interest, 274.

Jack Sharp (steamboat), 153.
Jackman, W. T., 12, 58, 70, 121.
James, William, engineer, 29.
Jardine, James, engineer, 69.
Jeffrey, Francis, editor, 31.
Jersey, 5th Earl of, 78.
Jessop, Josias, engineer, 47, 52.
Jude, Martin, miners' leader, 330.

Kay and Blackwell (of Winsford), salt manufacturers, 258–9, 312.
Kearsley, 319, 320, 321.
Keith, 1st Viscount, 30.
Kelp, production of, 24–5.
Kenrick, Timothy, deputy chairman, Midland Railway Co., 336.
Kent, James, coal agent, Bridgewater Trust, 316.
Ker, Bellenden, company lawyer, 275.
Killingworth, 28, 34.
Knott Mill (Manchester), 172.
Knox, George, secretary, Shrewsbury and Birmingham Railway Co., 232.
Knutsford, 128, 312.

Land agency, 345–6.
Landed estates, Bridgewater Trust, xviii, xx, 2–3, 299, 318, 323, 334, Appendix A (e and f).
Landseer, Sir Edwin, artist, 118.
Langton, Joseph, director, L. and M.R., 156.
Lansdale, Robert, cashier, Bridgewater Trust, 89 and n. 1.
Lardner, Dionysius, 56.

Law Life Assurance Society, 164, 193, Appendix A—note on sources.

Lawrence, Charles, chairman, L. & M.R. and G.J.R., 40, 44, 155, 184, 205.

Laws, Captain J. M., general manager, M. & L.R., 142, 144, 147, 199, 211, 212, 214, 216, 217.

Lawton, Mr. (of Manchester), railway promoter, 172.

Leicester, 5.

Leicestershire, 5.

Leigh, xvii, 138, 153, 308.

Levenshulme, 110, 172.

Leveson-Gower, Lord Francis, *see* Ellesmere, 1st Earl of.

Lichfield, 5.

Liddell, Mr. (possibly manager of Gosforth Colliery, Northumberland), 315.

Lilleshall, 30.

Lime burning, limestone, lime trade, xv, xvii–xviii, xviii n. 1, 52, 139, Appendix A (g).

Lincolnshire, 138, 203.

Lingard, Thomas, Principal Agent, M. & I.N.C., 14.

Lingard, Thomas Ogden, Principal Agent, M. & I.N.C., 94, 153, 155, 158, 160, 161, 162–3.

Linnyshaw:
colliery, 306 and n. 2, 316 n. 1, 317, 319
reservoir, 326.

Little Hulton, 86, 314 n. 4, 319.

Littleborough, 212.

Liverpool, xvi, xviii, 7, 12, 13, 14, 15, 17, 25, 36, 37, 42, 44, 49, 52, 67, 72, 73, 76, 80, 81, 90, 100, 101, 124, 125, 126, 129, 130, 132, 133, 134, 135, 136, 137, 142, 144, 145, 147, 148, 149, 150, 152, 153, 159, 160, 162, 168, 169, 170, 171, 172, 177, 178, 181, 182, 183, 185, 189, 190, 191, 192, 195, 196, 197, 198, 199, 200, 202, 203, 204, 205, 206, 207, 208, 209, 210, 211, 212, 213, 214, 217, 219, 220, 221, 222, 223, 224, 227, 228, 232, 233, 236, 238, 240, 241, 242, 244, 245, 246, 248, 251, 255 n. 1 and 3, 257, 258, 263, 264, 270, 272, 274, 277, 278, 279, 282, 284, 288 and n. 3, 294, 295, 296 and n. 7, 298, 300, 301, 302, 304 n. 1, 312, 335, 337, 338, 339, 341, 353, 354, Appendix A—note on sources.

Corporation, 43, 55, 186, 263–4, 282, 287.

docks, xvii, 21–2, 23, 24, 52, 55–6, 83, 85, 113–14, 115, 116, 119 and n. 2, 159, 193, 198, 264, 280, 287–8, 338, 339, 349, 354.

merchants, activities of, 12, 29, 31–3, 36–8, 39, 40–1, 44, 65–6, 70–1, 74–7, 345, 351–2.

trade of, 3–4, 5, 27–8, 91, 221, 239.

Lloyd, E. J., director, M. & I.N.C., 163.

Loch, George (son of James), deputy superintendent, Bridgewater Trust, 110, 157, 205, 211, 237, 242, 325, 346, 350, 351.

and Bridgewater Canal, 174, 185, 228, 247, 260, 261, 262, 264, 265, 266, 267, 280, 347.

and other canals, 201, 254.

and railways, 155–6, 171, 172, 173, 181, 186, 187 and n. 3, 197, 205, 207, 208, 218, 219, 225, 235, 238, 239–40, 239 n. 4, 243, 245, 247, 248–9, 252, 343, 351.

position in Bridgewater Trust, 185, 268.

Loch, James, superintendent, Bridgewater Trust, 15, 21, 22, 23, 36, 38, 39, 40, 42, 54, 61, 82, 88, 170, 176, 206, 267, 353, illus. frontispiece.

and the Bridgewater Canal, 55–6, 59, 83, 84, 96, 98–9, 102–5, 115, 145–6, 159, 166, 174, 193–4, 228, 247, 257, 260, 343, 346–7, 348, 349, 350, 355.

and other waterways, 25, 33–4, 35–6, 68–9, 71–2, 76, 95–6, 105–6, 129–30, 161, 162–3, 169, 170, 200–1, 215, 247, 344, 345.

and railways, 31–3, 34–5, 37, 40, 45, 46–53, 64, 65–77, 79–81, 87, 95–6, 103, 105–6, 142–4, 156, 158, 172, 181, 185, 186, 187, 194, 201, 215, 245, 247, 249, 250, 342, 344, 351–2.

and the collieries, 96, 98–9, 115, 315–17, 319, 321, 322, 328, 329, 330, 331, 332, 333, 346–7, 350.

and the organization of the Bridgewater Trust, 100–2, 265–6, 268–
9, 346–7.
death of, 267.
early life, character and opinions,
11, 30–2, 68, 71–2, 80, 98, 100,
101, 102–3, 168, 173, 346.
financial administration, 192–3,
228, 265–7
Loch, William Adam (son of James),
barrister, 185, 186.
Locke, Joseph, engineer, 134.
London, 4, 5, 9 and n. 3, 25, 63, 67, 73,
111, 124, 136, 140, 145, 171, 202,
203, 204, 221, 222, 238, 244, 245,
246, 248, 249, 251, 253, 254, 277,
285, 293, 294, 298, 355.
Longford Bridge, xvi.
Lords, House of, 83, 120, 179 n. 3.
Lowndes, Loftus, Chancery barrister,
90, 91, 96.
Lymm, 108, 116, 292.

Macclesfield, 16, 122, 125, 144, 145,
146, 169, 195, 245, 299 n. 4, 312.
McCulloch, J. R., economist, 31.
Macdonald, Sir Archibald, Bridgewater Trustee, 6, 41.
Machine pit (Farnworth), 306 and
n. 6.
Madams Wood Colliery, 326.
Madder, trade in, 154, 159.
Madely, 296, 301.
Manchester, xvi, xvii, xviii, 1, 2, 3, 4,
5, 7, 12, 13, 14, 15, 16, 17, 22, 27, 29,
34, 35, 36, 37, 38, 44, 50–4, 54–5, 59,
60, 65, 67, 69, 76, 78, 80, 81, 85, 88,
90, 91, 93–4, 95, 96, 100, 101, 102,
103, 105, 106, 107, 108, 109, 110,
111, 114, 115, 116, 122–3, 123 n. 2,
124, 125, 126, 128, 131, 132, 133,
135, 136, 137, 138, 139, 140, 141,
142, 144, 145, 146, 147, 152, 153,
154, 157, 159, 160, 162, 167, 169,
171, 172, 173, 177, 178, 181, 188,
189, 190, 195, 196, 197, 198, 199,
200, 202, 203, 204, 205, 206, 207,
208, 209, 210, 211, 212, 213, 214,
216, 217, 219, 220, 221, 222, 223,
224, 227, 228, 231, 232, 233, 238,
240, 241, 242, 244, 245, 246, 248,
250, 251, 254, 257, 258, 263, 266,
270, 274, 278, 280, 282 and n. 3,

283, 284, 285, 288, 290, 291, 292 and
n. 3, 293, 294, 295, 298, 302, 307–10,
317, 318, 333, 335, 337, 338–9, 340,
341, 345, 352, 353, 354; *see also*
Banktop, Castlefield, Cornbrook.
Manchester Times, 107.
Manning, Wardle & Co., locomotive
manufacturers, 320.
Manvers, 2nd Earl, 78.
Market Drayton, 300, 301.
Marley Hill Coke Co. (of Carlisle), 311.
Marsden, George, agent, Bridgewater
Trust, Manchester, 218, 219.
Marsh Gate, 171.
Master of the Rolls, 90.
Matlock, 140.
Maxwells, Alexander, merchants, 85.
Meacock, Samuel, agent, Bridge-
water Trust, Runcorn, 20.
Medlock, River, 290, 291.
Medstone Rock, 20.
Mere, 131.
Merry and Cunningham (of Ayr-
shire), ironmasters, 283.
Mersey Docks and Harbour Board,
282, 287.
Mersey estuary, carrying trade on,
167–8, 192, 231–2, 236, 238,
251, 254, 255 n. 1.
navigation of, 17–20, 92–3, 134.
passenger traffic on, 183.
steamers on, *see* steamships, steam
tugs.
Middle Hulton, Lancs., 2, 319.
Middleton, 213.
Middlewich, 34, 36, 126.
Junction, 127, 128, 130, 132, 234.
Midland Association (of carriers), 270.
Mill, James, 31.
Miners' Association of Great Britain
and Ireland, 330.
Mines Act of 1842, 323.
Mitchell, Charles, agent, Bridge-
water Trust, Preston Brook, 284.
Moore, 5, 110, 274, 291.
Morpeth, 34, 109.
Morpeth, Viscount (later 7th Earl of
Carlisle), 192.
Morrison, James, M.P., 73.
Mosley Common Colliery, 306 and n.
4, 317.
Moss, John, chairman, G.J.R., 10, 40,
44, 45, 50, 51, 52, 53, 57, 58, 64,

Moss, John (*cont.*):
65, 67, 69, 75, 87, 134, 135, 155, 158,
183, 344, 351.
Mossley, 217.
Mouldsworth, 301.

Nantwich, 29, 34, 66, 128, 301.
Napoleon, Emperor of the French, 99.
Nasmyth, James, engineer, 33 n. 1,
319.
Nef, J. U., 307.
Newall, John (of Manchester),
attorney and railway promoter,
181.
Newcastle upon Tyne, 109.
Newhaven, 4.
Newton le Willows, 29, 76, 134.
Normanton, 139.
Northamptonshire, xviii, 5.
Northern Alliance (of carriers), 293
and n. 2, 299.
Northumberland, 34.
Northumberland, 3rd Duke of, 78.
Northwich, 131, 169, 259 n. 1, 301,
312.
Norton, 231, 232, 238, 240, 245, 246,
250.
Nottingham, 111, 139, 140, 270.
Nottinghamshire, 5, 138.

Old Quay Company, *see* Canals—
Mersey and Irwell Navigation.
Oldham, 159, 197, 198, 210, 212, 213,
217, 219, 333.
Omnibuses, services in connection
with canals and railways, 109, 110.
Ormskirk, 198.
Owen, John, agent, Bridgewater
Trust, Liverpool, 25.
Owen's patent catch, 326.

Packet and passenger boats, 153, 222;
see also Duke of Bridgewater's
Canal—passenger traffic.
Parkes, Joseph (of Birmingham),
attorney, 31.
Parks, provision of, 321.
Parliament, proceedings on railway
bills, 177, 183, 185–8, 237, 296 and
n. 7, 297, 339; *see also* Wharncliffe
Order.
Patricroft, 319.
Patten, Col. John Wilson, M.P., 297.

Patterson, J. H., inventor, 111.
Peacock, ? William, assistant cashier,
269.
Peak Forest, xviii.
Pease and Partners (of Co. Durham),
coke burners, 311.
Peel, Sir Robert, the younger, 72,
73–4.
Pemberton, 314, 315.
Pendleton, 286 n. 3, 309, 319.
Pensions, for Bridgewater Trust
employees, 326.
Philipps, Shakespeare, director, Old
Quay Co., 158.
Pilot (steamboat), 168, 272 and n. 3,
273.
Pitt, William, the younger, 99.
'Planet', the, (locomotive), 57.
Plug Plot disturbances, 329.
Poole, Braithwaite, agent and general
goods manager, L. & N.W.R., 205,
217, 219, 221, 255 n. 4.
Poole (Dorset), 300.
Port Dinorwic, 262.
Port Penrhyn, 262.
Portsmouth, 115.
Portugal, Figara, 98.
Potteries, the, 3, 4, 29, 103, 124–5,
129, 132, 145, 146, 149, 169, 170,
171, 183, 244, 245, 247 n. 1, 249,
277, 284, 296, 299 n. 4, 301; *see also*
Staffordshire.
Pottery materials and earthenware
trade, 4, 125, 129, 132, 144, 169–70,
171, 178, 203, 249, 258, 261, 263,
274, 277, 284, 285, 296 and n. 2, 301.
Poulton, 263.
Powis (steamboat), 113.
Praeds & Co. (of Fleet St.), bankers,
25.
Preferential rates, *see* Discrimination.
Prentice, Archibald, editor, 107.
Preston, 137, 198, 263.
Preston Brook, 3, 4, 5, 16, 22, 23, 29,
59, 60, 66, 76, 77 and n. 1, 91, 101,
102, 108, 109, 123, 124, 125, 126,
127, 128, 129, 130, 131, 132, 133,
134, 135, 136, 138, 139, 140, 145,
146, 147 and n. 3, 148, 149, 150,
153, 167, 168, 170, 181, 182, 191,
202, 203, 208, 234, 237, 238, 249,
255, 259, 270, 271, 272, 288, 291,
292, 296, 301.

Price, William Philip, chairman, Midland Railway Co., 334 n. 1, 335, 338.

Priestfield Junction, 227, 253 n. 1.

Pritt, G., solicitor, 69, 70.

Provis, W. A., engineer, 128, 130, 131.

Prudhoe, 1st Baron, 78.

Prussia, 340.

'Quaker interest' (in railways), 352.

Queen's College, The, Oxford, 99.

Railway Mania, the, 176–8.

Railways (general), xix, 56–7.
  accidents, 205.
  amalgamations, 178–9, 183–4, 273–4, 277–8, 296, 298, 301–2.
  effect on coal industry, 309–11.
  exchange of traffic with canals, 229–33, 238, 239, 245, 246, 248, 250, 253, 254, 255 and n. 1, 300.
  gauges, 227.
  impact on supply lines, 221–2, 262, 309–11.
  locomotives, 28–9, 34, 44, 48–9, 63, 320.
  ownership of canals, 179–80, 205–6, 236–7, 238, 240, 243, 245, 252, 296 n. 7, 297 and n. 1, 300, Chap. XV *passim*, 335–9.
  passenger traffic, 48–9.
  state control of, 72–4, 184–5, 215.
  stationary engines, 44, 49.
  traffic control, 49.
  see also under particular railways.

Railways (particular):
  Altrincham–Levenshulme (proposed), 110, 111, 172.
  Birkenhead, Lancashire, and Cheshire Junction, 177, 178, 181, 182, 184, 192, 203, 215, 227, 231, 238, 244, 250, 251, 255 n. 1, 277, 301, Appendix A—note on sources.
  Birmingham and Derby Junction, 137, 311.
  Birmingham and Gloucester, 99, 311.
  Birmingham and Oxford Junction, 226, 227, 229
  Birmingham, Wolverhampton, and Dudley, 227, 229, 253 and n. 1.

Bolton and Leigh, 63, 103, 123, 141, 188.

Cheshire Lines Committee Railways, 301, 302, 337–8, 341.

Cheshire Midland, 301.

Chester and Birkenhead, 178, 192, 227.

Chester and Holyhead, 262.

Chester and Manchester Direct (proposed), 178, 188.

Chester, Stockport, and Manchester (proposed), *see* Newall's Line.

Cromford and High Peak, 52, 53–4, 137, 138, 139, 140, 141.

Drayton Junction (North Staffordshire Railway), 301.

East Lancashire, 195, 198, 212, 292, 296 and n. 7.

Eastern Counties, 292.

Eccles, Tyldesley and Wigan (L. & N.W.R.), 303, 319, 320.

Grand Junction (Birmingham and Liverpool), 29, 36, 37, 65–77, 133–7, 141, 147, 148, 150, 155, 171, 173, 174, 178, 181, 182, 183, 185, 188, 190, 226, 227, 259, 286, 296, 311, 344, 352.

Great Northern, 222, 277, 293, 295, 296, 298, 301, 337, 338.

Great Western, 121, 215, Chap. XI *passim*, 257, 266, 271, 293, 298, 300, 338, 351, Appendix A—note on sources.

Kenyon and Leigh Junction, 63, 188.

Lancashire and Yorkshire, 177, 178, 180, 188, 195, 196–9, 204, 205, 206, 207, 208, 210, 211, 212, 213, 214, 216, 217, 220, 221, 223, 224, 225, 240, 241, 261, 262, 269, 292, 294, 295, 296 and n. 7, 298, 302, 309, 319, 320 and n. 1, 338, 352; *see also* Manchester and Leeds Railway; Manchester, Bolton and Bury Canal and Railway; Liverpool and Bury Railway.

Lancashire Union, 302, 303 and n. 1.

Liverpool and Bury (L. & Y.R.), 177, 178, 187, 188, 196, 197.

Liverpool and Manchester, 13–4, Chap. II *passim*, 44–54, 56–9, 60, 63, 66, 68–9, 75–6, 80–1, 84, 95, 105, 110 n. 2, 131, 134, 141, 142, 147, 148, 152, 154–9, 161–2, 163,

Railways (particular) (*cont.*):
  Liverpool and Manchester (*cont.*):
    165–6, 169, 170, 171, 172, 173,
    177, 178, 179, 181, 182, 183, 184,
    185, 189, 190, 242, 292, 300, 344,
    345, 351–3
  Liverpool, Warrington, Manchester,
    and Stockport Direct ('Spinners'
    Line'), (proposed), 177 and n. 2,
    186, 187.
  London and Birmingham, 178, 226,
    311, 352.
  London and North-Western, 169,
    173, 178, 179, 180, 187, Chap. X
    passim, 226, 227, 228, 229, 232,
    233, 236, 237, 238, 239, 240, 241,
    243, 244, 245, 250, 252, 253, 254,
    255, 266, 269, 271, 272, 273, 274,
    277, 278, 279, 286, 292, 293, 294,
    295, 296, 298, 301, 302, 303, 311,
    319, 320 and n. 1, 338, 352.
  Manchester and Birmingham, 5,
    110, 135, 136, 142, 155, 171, 172,
    173, 178, 184.
  Manchester and Leeds, 137, 139, 141,
    142, 147, 171, 173, 174, 178, 179,
    183, 185, 187, 188, 196, 311, 352.
  Manchester and Southport (L. &
    Y.R.), 188–9, 318, 319 and n. 4.
  Manchester, Bolton, and Bury
    Canal and Railway, *see under*
    Canals.
  Manchester, Sheffield, and Lincoln-
    shire, 178, 187, 203, 209, 222, 277,
    292, 293, 294, 295, 296, 297 n. 1,
    298, 301, 302, 335, 336, 337, 338,
    339, 341, 342.
  Manchester, South Junction, and
    Altrincham, 172, 173, 174, 181,
    292, 295, 301, 337, 338.
  Midland, 178, 277, 292, 293, 294, 301,
    335, 336, 337, 338, 339, 341, 342.
  Nasmyth's Private Branch (Patri-
    croft), 319.
  Newall's Line (proposed Chester,
    Stockport, and Manchester Rail-
    way), 181.
  North British, 292.
  North Staffordshire, 169, 178, 180,
    191, 201, 202, 203, 231, 234, 235,
    236, 238, 243, 249, 252, 271, 272,
    273, 274, 275, 276, 277, 278, 279,
    293, 296 and n. 2, 298, 300, 301,

    304 n. 1, 338; *see also* Drayton
    Junction Railway.
  North Union, 137, 141, 188, 352.
  Oxford, Worcester, and Wolver-
    hampton, 227, 229, 253 and n. 1,
    254.
  Runcorn and Preston Brook (pro-
    posed), 182–3, 184.
  St. Helens Canal and Railway, *see
    under* Canals; also Warrington
    and Garston, Widnes and Gar-
    ston, and Widnes and Warrington
    lines.
  Sheffield and Manchester (pro-
    posed), 78–9.
  Sheffield, Ashton-under-Lyne, and
    Manchester, 142, 171–3, 179.
  Shrewsbury and Birmingham, 215,
    227, 228–9, 231–9, 244, 245, 248–
    9, 250, 251, 252, 253 and n. 1, 257.
  Shrewsbury and Chester, 185, 215,
    227, 228–9, 231–9, 240, 244, 245,
    248–9, 250, 251, 252, 253, 257.
  Shropshire Union Railways and
    Canal, *see under* Canals.
  Silverdale and Newcastle, 301.
  South Eastern, 336.
  South Staffordshire, 277.
  Stockport and Woodley Junction,
    302.
  Stockport Junction (proposed),
    53–4, 63.
  Stockport, Timperley, and Altrin-
    cham Junction, 302.
  Stockton and Darlington, 48, 49.
  Stone and Rugby Extension (pro-
    posed), 135.
  Stour Valley (L. & N.W.R.), 229,
    239, 266.
  Warrington and Garston Line (St.
    Helens Canal and Railway), 286,
    301.
  Warrington and Newton Branch,
    63, 64 and n. 5, 76.
  Warrington and Stockport, 253–4,
    292, 295, 296, 298, 301.
  Wellington and Silverdale (pro-
    posed), 300.
  West Cheshire, 301.
  Widnes and Garston Line (St.
    Helens Canal and Railway), 188.
  Widnes and Warrington Line (St.
    Helens Canal and Railway), 188.

Rainhill locomotive trials, 49, 63, 65.

Rams Mine, 327.

Rates of carriage, agreements for fixing, 12–14, 16, 58, 59–60, 95–6, 105–6, 129, 132, 150, 153–63, 165, 168, 197, 198, 208, 209, 211 and n. 1, 214, 223, 224, 241, 255, 270, 271, 284, 285, 293, 294–5, 297, 298–9, 301, 304 n. 1, 352–3.

Ravensworth, 1st Baron, 78.

Rawtenstall, 212.

Reay, 7th Baron, 22, 38.

Receipts from traffic, agreements for pooling of, 208, 224.

Recreation grounds, provision of, 321.

Red Bull, 125.

Redesdale, 2nd Baron, 120.

Reform Act of 1832, 343.

Rennie, George, engineer, 47, 48.

Rennie, John, engineer, 47, 48.

Retford, 293.

Ricardo, David, 31.

Ricardo, John Lewis, chairman, N.S.R., 275, 276, 279.

Ridyard, James, surveyor of collieries, Bridgewater Trust, 325.

Ridyard, John, surveyor of collieries, Bridgewater Trust, 315.

Ringspiggot, 213.

Rippon, C. W., cashier, Bridgewater Trust, 268.

Rival (steamboat), 168, 272 and n. 3, 273.

Robinson's timber yard (Manchester), 339.

Rochdale, 196, 197, 212, 213, 309.

Rockingham, 2nd Marquess of, xv.

Rossendale, 212.

Rosslyn, 2nd Earl of, 78.

Rothschild, family of, financiers, 98.

Rotheram, William, director, L. & M.R., 155.

Rowsley, xv.

Roy, Robert, secretary, Shrewsbury and Chester Railway Co., 235–6.

Rugby, 155.

Runcorn, xvi, xvii, 3, 16, 21, 45 and n. 3, 61, 66, 70, 91, 96, 100, 101, 102, 103, 105, 108, 109, 110, 114, 122, 125, 130, 132, 137, 149, 152, 153, 160, 162, 167, 172, 207, 257–65, 270, 272, 277, 279–88, 294, 296
  n. 7, 301, 302, 303 and n. 1, 310, 311, 312, 340, 355.
  channel at, 17, 20.
  docks, xvii, 54, 92–3, 114, 115, 116, 119, 129, 259–61, 279–80, 281–2, 283, 285, 286.
  industries, 257–8, 264–5.
  Island and the Gut, 20, 92–3, 152 and n. 1, 182, 286.
  locks, 20, 21, 23, 54, 152, 264 n. 2, 340.
  mansion at, 6, 87, illus. facing p. 282.
  railway at, 74–5, 180–1, 182–3, 286, 310.

Runcorn Gap, 20, 153, 288.
  trade, 129, 152, 190, 195, 234, 257–64, 283–5, 310, 311, 312.

Ruscoe, Ralph, agent of Grand Trunk Canal Co., 141.

Rushy Park colliery, 91, 310.

Rutland, 3rd Duke of, xv.

St. George's Hill, 118.

St. Helens, 91, 310, 312.

Sale Moor, 288.

Salford, xvi, 16, 37, 38, 44, 50, 52, 78, 142, 213, 263.

Salisbury, 2nd Marquess of, 78, 177.

Salt trade, 4, 125, 249, 258, 259 and n. 1, 260, 263, 282, 283, 312, 353.

Salt works, 135, 147, 174, 259 and n. 1.

Saltney Wharf, 234.

Sandars, Joseph, director, L. & M.R., 7, 12, 27, 31, 33, 44, 85, 87, 155, 351.

Sandbach, 64, 274.

Sanderson's dam, 318.
  sidings, 320.

Saunders, Charles Alexander, secretary, G.W.R., 227, 233, 245, 251, 252.

Say, Jean Baptiste, economist, 31.

Scotland, trade with, 262, 263, 283.

Seaford, 1st Baron, 78.

Sefton, 2nd Earl of, 32, 37, 38.

Selby, 139.

Sergeant, William (of Manchester), attorney, 9 n. 3.

Shaftesbury, 6th Earl of, 83.

Shaftesbury, 7th Earl of, *see* Ashley, Lord.

Shardlow, 5, 138, 139, 140.

Sheffield, 78, 209, 211, 222.

Shipyards, 258.

Shropshire, xviii, 7, 29, 30, 34, 35, 234.

Skey, Samuel, superintendent, Birmingham and Liverpool Junction Canal, 150.
Slater, William, solicitor, Bridgewater Trust, 280.
Slates, trade in, 262.
Smiles, Samuel, 63.
Smith, Adam, 31, 100.
Smith, Clifford, general manager, Bridgewater Trust, 334.
Smith, Edmund, engineer, Bridgewater Trust, 101, 112.
Smith, George Samuel Fereday, deputy superintendent, principal agent and general manager, Bridgewater Trust, 156, 161, 162, 177 n. 2, 194, 205, 218, 219, 220, 221, 255 n. 4.
and Bridgewater Canal, 174, 176, 260, 268, 269, 270, 271, 272, 273, 280, 282 and n. 3, 291, 292 and n. 2, 295 n. 4, 350.
and other canals, 129–30, 162–3, 168, 169, 201, 202, 203–4, 297.
and the collieries, 206, 303, 311, 315, 316 and n. 1, 318, 319, 321, 322, 323, 324, 325, 327, 329, 330, 331, 332, 333.
and the railways, 162, 185, 186, 187 and n. 3, 201, 203, 205, 206, 207, 224–5, 231–2, 233, 235, 236–7, 238, 239 and n. 4, 240, 245, 246, 247, 248, 249, 251, 252, 253, 271, 272, 273, 274, 275, 276, 277, 286, 297–8, 303 and n. 1.
career, 99–100, 268–9, 334, 347.
Smith, Richard, mining engineer and mineral agent, 90, 98, 99.
Soap, trade in, 146.
manufacture, 257.
Society for the Diffusion of Useful Knowledge, 31.
Soffer, Dr. R. N., 329, 332.
Sothern, Benjamin, principal agent, Bridgewater Trust, 10, 86, 91.
Sothern, James, superintendent, Bridgewater Trust, 6.
and the railways, 42, 45.
management of Bridgewater Trust, 86, 90–2, 93, 94, 96, 97, 100, 101, 115, 310, 314, 321.
quarrel with Lord Francis Egerton, 87–90, 93, 94–7.

Sothern, John, colliery proprietor, 91, 108.
Sothern, family of, 90, 91, 101, 310.
South of England, trade with Liverpool and Manchester, 245–6, 300.
Spain, trade with (Barcelona, Bilbao, Santander), 284.
Speculative Society, the, 31.
Spooner, Richard (of Birmingham), banker, 32, 33 n. 1.
Stafford, George Granville Leveson Gower, 2nd Marquess of (later 1st Duke of Sutherland), xviii, 6, 10, 22, 30, 32, 33, 35, 36, 37, 38, 39, 40, 41, 42, 43, 44, 45, 46, 47, 48, 49, 54, 55, 57, 60–1, 64 and n. 5, 65, 66, 67, 68, 69, 70, 74, 75, 76, 77, 79, 80, 82 and n. 2, 83, 84, 155, 264 n. 2, 344, 345, 351, 355.
Stafford, Marquess of (later 3rd Duke of Sutherland), 179.
Stafford Rd. Junction, 253.
Staffordshire, xviii, 4, 5, 29, 98, 99, 178, 237, 238, 251, 252, 319, Appendix A—note on sources.
South Staffordshire, 126, 127, 202, 203, 231, 234, 235, 238, 239, 244, 245, 254, 255 and n. 3, 266, 270, 271, 273, 284, 294, 299 and n. 4, 304 n. 1.
see also the Potteries; Black Country.
Stalybridge, 159, 197, 210, 212, 213, 217.
Stanton, Thomas, manager of E. and C.C.C., 128, 130.
Steam tugs, 21, 61, 83, 108, 126, 167, 168, 169, 199, 291–2, 340; see also Steamships; Duke of Bridgewater's Canal, steam traction, experiments with.
Steamships, xix, 108, 153, 168, 169, 207, 272–3, 272 n. 3, 273 n. 6, 283, 355, see also Steam tugs.
Stephenson, George, engineer, 29, 48, 54, 63, 64 n. 5.
Stephenson, Robert, engineer, 48, 63, 64 n. 5.
Stockport, 16, 122, 135, 169, 210 and n. 1, 212, 217, 290, 295.
Stockton Quay, 102, 108, 288, 292 and n. 3.
Stoke-on-Trent, 178, 296 and n. 2, 300.

Stourbridge, 29.
Stourport, 5, 300.
Stretford, xvi, 288.
Stuart de Rothesay, 1st Baron, 78.
Sunday, observance of, 328.
Sutherland, 1st Duke of, *see* Stafford, 2nd Marquess of.
Sutherland, 2nd Duke of, *see* Gower, Earl.
Sutherland estates, 24–5, 30, 84.
Sutherlandshire, xviii, 22, 30, 38.
Sutton limestone, xvii, xviii.
Sykes, J., *see* Ashton, T. S.

Talbot, 2nd Earl, 78.
Tallow, trade in, 159.
Tatton, Thomas William (of Wythenshawe), 172.
Taylor, Professor A. J., 307.
Telford, Thomas, engineer, 34, 35, 71, 128.
Tennant, Dr. W., chaplain and author, 31.
Thomas Royden (steamboat), 169, 272 n. 3.
Thompson, James, inventor, 112.
Thompson, Mr., land agent, 48.
Thorney (near Peterborough), 312.
Throstlenest, 289, 341.
Timber, trade in, 130, 132, 197, 223, 287, 296 n. 7, 297, 353.
Timmins, P. E., engineer, 316.
Timperley, 254, 291, 292.
Tindall and Varey, solicitors, 88, 89, 90.
Tipton, 229, 254.
Todmorden, 212.
Tomkinson, Henry, solicitor, 9 n. 2.
Tonge, James, agent, Bridgewater Trust, Runcorn, 100, 101.
Torrens, Robert, economist, 31.
Tower (steamboat), 168, 272 n. 3, 273 n. 6.
Trade Unionism, 328–31, 333.
Traffic, agreements for partition of, 161, 189–90, 196, 197, 199, 204–5, 209, 213–14, 216, 224, 251.
Trafford, Sir Thomas Joseph de, 1st Bart., 172.
Traice, W. H. J., lecturer, 327.
Trencherbone, the (coal), 306.
Trent and Mersey Guarantee, 236, 237.

Trentham, 30.
Trubshaw, Mr., of Grand Trunk Canal Co., 141.
Tunstall, 300.
Turgot, A.-R.-J., economist, 31.
Tyldesley, 86, 314 and n. 4, 319.
Tynesbank Colliery, 318.
Tyneside, 2.

United Kingdom Telegraph Co., 288.
United States of America, 27, 113, 222, 241, 340.
University College, London, 99.
Upper Mersey Dues Trustees, 282 and n. 3.

Varey, Joseph, solicitor, 88, 89, 93, 102 ; *see also* Tindall and Varey.
Vernon-Harcourt, Edward Venables, Bishop of Carlisle (later Archbishop of York), Bridgewater Trustee, 6, 40, 41, 94, 97.

Wages, *see* coalminers.
Wages, relationship to prices, 321, 328, 333.
Wages, sliding scale of, 321, 333.
Wagstaff and Barratt (of Warrington), attorneys, 186.
Wales, 1, 35, 67, 98, 128, 234, 249, 262, 310, 327, 355.
Walkden coal field, 314.
Walker, Joseph, chairman, Shrewsbury and Birmingham Railway Co., 232.
Walton, 227, 231, 232, 240, 245, 246, 249.
Wardle Green, 34, 131.
Warrington, 76, 110, 134, 135, 153, 177, 178, 181, 227, 228, 231, 232, 254, 263, 274, 292 and n. 3.
Warwick, 5.
Warwickshire, 5, 327.
Waterford, 27.
Water Witch (swift boat), 108–9.
Watkin, Edward William, general manager, later chairman, Manchester, Sheffield, and Lincolnshire Railway Co., 290–1, 293, 295, 301, 302, 334 n. 1, 335–6, 338, 340–2.
Watkins, W. B., merchant and mayor of Manchester, 242.
Weirs, 290.

Wellington, 1st Duke of, 78.
West Indies, 4.
Weston Point, 20, 125, 129, 259, 260, 288.
Wharncliffe Order (Standing Order of the House of Lords), 237, 239.
Wharton (Cheshire), 147.
Wheeler, James, writer, 2, 308, 309.
Wheeler, Mr. (of Manchester), railway promoter, 172.
White, R., inventor, 112.
Whitehaven, 283, 294.
Whitehaven Haematite Iron Co., 283.
Whitmore, 293, 296.
Widnes, 177, 265, 310.
Wigan, xvii, 63, 81, 137, 185, 188, 197, 288, 308, 309, 310, 314.
Wilkinson, John, ironmaster, 98.
Williams, Edward Leader, engineer, Severn Navigation Commission, 300.
Williams, Edward Leader (the younger), engineer, Bridgewater Navigation Co., 340.
Wilson's Biographical Index to the Present House of Commons, 1808, 8.
Wilton, 2nd Earl of, 78.
Wimbledon, 40.
Wines and spirits, trade in, 146, 155, 284, 285.
Winsford, 147, 190, 301, 312.

Winter, Gilbert, director, L. & M.R., 46, 53, 57, 79, 81, 84, 85, 86.
Wolverhampton, 29, 36, 66, 124, 191, 201–2, 208, 227, 229, 238, 239, 253, 254, 269, 270 n. 1, 293.
Wolverton, 208.
Wood, G. W., director, Old Quay Co., 158, 163 and n. 1.
Woodley, 302, 337.
Woolston, 341.
Worcestershire, 5.
Worsley, xvi, xvii, 2, 8, 9, 10, 25, 81, 90, 91, 100, 101, 102, 113, 123, 188, Chap. XIV *passim*, 344.
  boat-building yard, xviii, 1 and n. 3, 102, 167, 299 n. 3, Appendix A (h).
  collieries, *see* Bridgewater Collieries
  mansions at, 6, 87, 88, 96–7, 118, illus. facing p. 118.
  population, 324.
  railway at, 303, 318–19.
Wrottesley, Henry, barrister, M.P. for Brackley, 10.

Yarnton, 254.
York, 222.
Yorkshire, 16, 53, 93, 122, 124, 139, 142, 144, 147, 149, 157, 177, 196, 198, 217, 231, 262, 309, 327, 329.
Young, Arthur, xvii.

Zinc, trade in, 217.

DATE DUE			